T0323419

Understanding Economic Change

Although the economy has always been changing, ever more innovations now seem to accelerate the transformation process. Are there any laws governing the incessant global change? Does it accord with our intentions and desires and make us happier? Do our institutions and our democracies cope with the challenges? How does economic theory explain what is going on? In this volume, experts in the field discuss the advances that evolutionary economics has made in exploring questions like these. The broad range of topics include a review of the development of the field: its conceptual and methodological characteristics are outlined; problems posed by macroeconomic evolution and the institutional challenges are highlighted; and, last but not least, the implications of the evolution of the economy for wellbeing and sustainability are addressed. Taken together, the contributions demonstrate the potential of an evolutionary paradigm for making sense of economic change and for assessing its consequences.

ULRICH WITT is Past Director of the Evolutionary Economics Group at the Max Planck Institute of Economics in Jena, Germany. He has published a vast number of articles and books on evolutionary economics and is Editor-in-chief of the *Journal of Bioeconomics*.

ANDREAS CHAI is an applied economist and Head of Economics and Business Statistics Discipline at the Griffith Business School, Griffith University, Australia. Andreas has published in various economic journals, including the *Journal of Economic Perspectives* and the *Cambridge Journal of Economics*.

Understanding Economic Change

Advances in Evolutionary Economics

Edited by

ULRICH WITT
Max Planck Institute and Griffith University

ANDREAS CHAI
Griffith University

CAMBRIDGE
UNIVERSITY PRESS

CAMBRIDGE
UNIVERSITY PRESS

University Printing House, Cambridge CB2 8BS, United Kingdom

One Liberty Plaza, 20th Floor, New York, NY 10006, USA

477 Williamstown Road, Port Melbourne, VIC 3207, Australia

314–321, 3rd Floor, Plot 3, Splendor Forum, Jasola District Centre, New Delhi – 110025, India

79 Anson Road, #06-04/06, Singapore 079906

Cambridge University Press is part of the University of Cambridge.

It furthers the University's mission by disseminating knowledge in the pursuit of education, learning, and research at the highest international levels of excellence.

www.cambridge.org
Information on this title: www.cambridge.org/9781107136205
DOI: 10.1017/9781316477168

First published 2019

Printed and bound in Great Britain by Clays Ltd, Elcograf S.p.A.

A catalogue record for this publication is available from the British Library.

ISBN 978-1-107-13620-5 Hardback

Contents

Figures

Figures

Tables

Tables

Contributors

Martin Binder
Bard College, Berlin, Germany

Andreas Chai
Griffith Business School, Griffith University, Australia

Roger D. Congleton
College of Business and Economics, University of West Virginia, USA

Richard H. Day
Economics Department, University of Southern California, Los Angeles, USA

Reinoud Joosten
Department of Industrial Engineering & Business Information Systems, School of Behavioural, Management and Social Sciences, Twente University, The Netherlands

Brian J. Loasby
Economics Department, Stirling University, Scotland

André Lorentz
Bureau d'Economie Théoritique et Appliquée & Economics Department, Université de Strasbourg, Université de Lorraine, CNRS, BETA, Strasbourg, France

Joel Mokyr
Economics Department, Northwestern University, Evanston, USA

Dennis C. Mueller
Economics Department, University of Vienna, Austria

Christian Schubert
Economics Department, German University of Cairo, Egypt

Jack Vromen
Erasmus School of Philosophy and Erasmus School of Economics, Erasmus University, Rotterdam, The Netherlands

Ulrich Witt
Max Planck Institute for the Science of Human History, Jena, Germany & Department of Accounting, Finance and Economics, Griffith University, Australia

PART I

Introduction

1 Evolutionary Economics
Taking Stock of Its Progress and Emerging Challenges

ULRICH WITT AND ANDREAS CHAI

Introduction

Economic analysis is no less evolving than the economy itself. In a previous era, economics was considered to be the "queen" of the social sciences that possessed a relatively autonomous and somewhat elitist character. Now a brief review of the current literature in various subfields of economics reveals emerging synergies and increasingly blurred demarcation lines between the economic literature and neighboring disciplines. Some notable examples include the increasing prevalence of psychological approaches to account for seemingly irrational behavior in behavioral economics; the rise of neuro-economics that builds a bridge between neuroscience and traditional models of decision making; growing evidence that social networks and peer behavior can play a key role in individual preferences, and the growing links between the international trade literature and economic geography. Words once foreign to economists, such as "dopamine", "control group", and "network effects", have become familiar terms in the debate. Taken together, this trend seems to be irreversible and points to a future where cutting-edge research in economics is more integrated with scientific developments in neighboring fields.

This renaissance begs us to consider how the deeper methodological paradigms and principles found in other scientific fields compare to those found in canonical economics. For much of the history of economics, great scholars such as Alfred Marshall, Thorstein Veblen, and Friedrich A. Hayek have wondered to what extent economists can learn from biology and its Darwinian theory of evolution – without having much impact on their ideas. Human beings who run the economy are, after all, a biologically evolved species. It seems that almost every day new evidence is reported in the popular media that differences between humans and other animals are not as clear as once thought: crows are found to use tools; monkeys can talk. On the flipside, some people certainly do act like animals.

3

In that sense, why not consider an extension of the naturalistic perspective to economic behavior and the human economy? By such an extension, evolution would immediately become relevant to explaining what capacities, attitudes, and preferences are part of the human inheritance and how these endowments set the frame for the unfolding of the economy. Obviously, a perspective like this is not common in economics. In fact, it is not even a commonly shared perspective in evolutionary economics (unlike in evolutionary psychology or evolutionary anthropology). Since the term "evolutionary economics" was introduced to a broader audience by Veblen (1898), different conceptions and interpretations have been, and still are, associated with it (see Witt 2008a). In addition, the different interpretations have focused rather selectively on different economic topics.

For example, the main topic in neo-Schumpeterian research initiated by Nelson and Winter (1982) is the dynamics of firm organizations and industries. These dynamics are explained by means of a loose analogy to natural selection models and models of biological population dynamics. Accordingly, the authors of these contributions regard them as "evolutionary" qua the analogy to, and particular modeling tools borrowed from, evolutionary biology. In contrast, Veblen's (1899, 1914) topic was the evolution of economic and social institutions. He considered his contribution to be "evolutionary" because he tried to deal with his subject from the point of view of an extended version of Darwin's theory of descent. Other scholars focus on still other topics and may have still other notions of an "evolutionary" economics in mind.

In view of the diversity of interpretations associated with, and topics explored under, the label evolutionary economics, advances in the field depend not least on whether and how convergence to a coherent understanding of a common core can be achieved. (To that end, just enumerating a few shared theoretical features such as dynamics, bounded rationality, disequilibrium analysis, etc. – important as they are – is not sufficient.) Furthermore, it will be necessary to deal inclusively with all the topics of the different approaches. The scope of the evolutionary approach needs to be extended to the entire domain of economics from individual economic behavior to its aggregated consequences at the macroeconomic level, including normative aspects of welfare and policy making.

The chapters in this volume present advances in both respects. Some of the chapters – written by authors holding different views of evolutionary economics – extend the corresponding theorizing to topics that either have not been explored yet or not in any depth. These chapters offer new insights. They thus exemplify how their take on evolutionary economics helps to foster the understanding of economic problems and phenomena that goes beyond the grasp of canonical economics.[1] Other chapters address the conceptual problems related to the different interpretations of an evolutionary approach in economics and discuss possibilities for their integration.

In the present introductory chapter we offer a broad orientation regarding the particularities of evolutionary theorizing in the economic context. We examine the ontological and methodological challenges that an evolutionary approach faces and outline the different responses that have been given to these challenges over the history of evolutionary economics. In the second section we will claim that it is an empirical fact that the economy evolves and that its evolution therefore requires an explanation. We discuss why canonical economics has difficulties recognizing this fact and coping with it. We then turn to the problem that the unfolding of the economy is a historical process. Evolutionary theorizing presupposes that there are recurrent patterns in this process and a mechanism or mechanisms that cause them. As will be shown in the third section, the questions of what these patterns are and what causal mechanisms generate them have been answered quite differently in the more than a hundred years of evolutionary theorizing in economics. This theorizing has appeared in three distinct waves. Each one had a distinct *leitmotiv* and took rather little notice of earlier waves. Building on the preceding reflections, we give a short preview in the fourth section of the eleven chapters following in this volume and explain how they contribute to advancing evolutionary economics. The last section presents the conclusions.

On the Difficulties of Recognizing and Explaining Economic Evolution

Imagine the following hypothetical situation. An economist studying consumer behavior has an exchange with a biologist studying animal foraging behavior. What hypotheses could the two mutually agree

---

[1] By canonical economics, we mean the standard textbook versions sometimes – misleadingly – labeled "neoclassical".

on? For the biologist it may stand to reason that price and income constraints are likely to influence human behavior. It is equivalent to the fact that an animal's choice of food depends on the physical effort required to obtain it and the animal's time constraint. However, the economist and the biologist are less likely to agree on the assumption that the observed behavior is a result of optimization. The biologist would likely wonder why the economist is so focused on proving the optimality of observed behavior. As a biologist she would rather be interested in explaining the motivational mechanism that stimulates the animal to act, such as hunger, thirst, or curiosity. The economist, in turn, is unlikely to pay heed to the motivations underlying consumption behavior. He would be content with invoking a utility function in which it is left open what the variable utility represents. Considering why certain things like food may in certain quantities be part of the utility function, and how these quantities may be influenced by biological factors is perceived by economists as unnecessary.

The difference in interpretations is deeply rooted in how economists conceive of their own discipline. Many of them subscribe to what Robbins (1932, 15) postulated: "Economics is the science which studies human behavior as a relationship between ends and the scarce means which have alternative uses." This postulate is usually interpreted to emphasize that human agents "economize" and choose actions in recognition of the opportunity costs, i.e. the foregone outcome of actions not chosen. The postulate can be given different interpretations. It can mean that economics is a kind of engineering science figuring out what economic agents ought to do in order to find the most efficient way of using their means for their ends. Alternatively, the postulate can be understood to call for an explicative science of human behavior based on the hypothesis that the agents actually make efficient choices. It is a widespread conviction, if not a dogma, that the constrained maximization calculus is constitutive for both interpretations and, hence, the defining property of economics.

The scarcity of means available for pursuing alternative ends is, of course, a situation not only faced by humans. It is a universal condition of life on earth. But this fact is far from implying universal efficiency (see Dupré 1987). On the one hand, it is true that, under natural selection pressure, organisms tend to develop traits efficiently adapted to what their environment requires for survival and reproduction (Ghiselin 1974). On the other hand, nature is rather wasteful in building up selection pressure by using ample resources to generate a larger number of living beings than can be supported by the existing resources.[2] (Partial) efficiency is therefore only one aspect among many in biological research devoted to explaining the organism's actual functioning and its determinants. More important than that is the explanation of the evolution of the function under natural selection.

The functioning of organisms can be explained by physiological, molecular, and other conditions. This is called a *proximate* explanation in biology. Since the particular functioning is assumed to be a result of descent (with variation), one also needs to explain *why* this functioning has emerged. Usually this kind of explanation – called the *ultimate* explanation – focuses on an adaptive advantage that the functioning has endowed its carriers with in natural selection during the phylogeny of the species.[3] An illustrative example is the case of the evolution of flight. A proximate explanation for this functioning refers to the shape and movement of wings and tails, bodyweight–to–wing size ratio, buoyancy force, etc. The ultimate explanation for the evolution of flight draws on the hypothesis that flight endows organisms with an advantage in terms of escaping predators, accessing food (e.g., by capturing small prey, see Gauthier and Padian 1989), or other instances proven to enhance reproductive success.

---

[2] Moreover, natural selection improves adaptation by favoring heritable traits in a population that are only relatively a better fit for reproduction. When only competitors with weak traits are present in the population, this means that the selected traits may not be very efficient. (Heritable traits that are not relevant for reproductive competition may not even be subject to any gradual improvement.) This may also be true when an ecosystem implies conflicting selection tendencies so that natural selection tends to strike a compromise between them. As a result functional adaptation may be suboptimal in some traits as, for example, in the case of sexual selection; see Wilson (2000, 318–327).

[3] Proximate and ultimate explanations are part of the elaborate scheme of explanatory strategies developed in biology (see Tinbergen 1963). The criterion for an adaptive advantage is roughly to do better than competitors within the species in terms of the number of offspring carrying on the heritable trait to the next generation. On the definitional issues see Lloyd and Gould (2017). The hypothesis of an adaptive advantage can be tested by examining the fossil record of the species in view of what is known about the selection conditions faced by the species in their ancestral environment.

The difference in how economics and biology portray the consequences of scarcity is also salient when the economist's analysis of consumption is compared with the biologist's inquiry into foraging behavior. The latter observes that animals instinctively respond to (or "function" in) an environment with heavy fluctuations in the availability of food by massively expanding their food intake when food becomes available (e.g., Staddon 2009, Chap. 9). The instinctive response is brought about by an innate regulatory mechanism of the animals' metabolism (proximate explanation). The reason for why this instinctive response evolved can be explained by the advantage that such an adaptation of the regulatory mechanism has had for bridging frequent phases of starvation and thus for survival and reproduction chances (ultimate explanation).

In contrast, an economist analyzing strong fluctuations in the availability of food (and corresponding variations of food prices) would typically assume that consumers respond to these variations in a way that maximizes their utility function. Whatever the arguments of their utility functions (apart from food) may be, the usually assumed shape of the function implies the following: by the joint outcome of the income and substitution effect, a smaller quantity of food relative to the quantity of other budget items will be consumed, if the price of food goes up and vice versa (neglecting the possibility of a Giffen case).

The comparison raises a couple of interesting questions. First, what is the methodological status of the economist's analysis? Is it a rationalization (rather than an explanation) of the observed behavior in terms of an ad hoc specified utility function? Or should the analysis be seen as the equivalent of a proximate explanation, in this case, of how rational consumers "function"? Or is there even a basis for ultimate explanations, if canonical economics is interested in such explanations at all? We will come back to this issue in a minute. A second question that the comparison raises concerns the power of the utility maximization hypothesis if it is indeed used for explanatory purposes. All that can be derived from the hypothesis is the direction in which the optimal quantity of food consumption changes: it increases for lower food prices and vice versa. A different question is whether and when an increase in food consumption caused by decreasing food prices results in overeating. This cannot be answered without making a connection to physical variables and mechanisms in the first place.

However the connection is made, let us assume that consumers face a long-run trend of decreasing (relative) food prices and time costs of food consumption and/or rising income. Under such conditions, consumers have been observed to develop an obesity disease (Cutler et al. 2003). From the perspective of behavioral economics, the effect points to tensions between what Kahneman (2013) has called the fast, automatic system 1 and the slow, deliberate system 2. The former triggers the impulse to eat; the latter controls and reflects on the consequences of food intake. The distinction between the two systems obviously amounts to a major revision of rational choice theory. However, evolutionary economics suggests going even a step further, namely to explain why the impulse to overeat exists in the first place and for what reasons it has emerged. The answer is likely to be that consumers – as human animals – inherit the same evolved instinct to overeat as the biologist observes it in other animals. Yet food being constantly available in a First World environment, the still-present ancestral instinct expressed through system 1 results in what evolutionary biology calls a "mismatch" (Burnham 2016), if consumers are not sufficiently able to control their instinctive impulse through system 2.

This point highlights the difference an evolutionary approach to economics makes. It extends the focus beyond proximate explanations of the "functioning" of the economy and its agents – important as they are. Analogously to ultimate explanations, attention is directed in addition to the explanation of the historical change. This can be observed everywhere in economic behavior, technology, economic mechanisms and institutions, and even in macroeconomic regularities. At least in this respect the various approaches to evolutionary economics seem to agree despite their differing views of how to accomplish the task. However, explanations of the historical change can take quite different forms, which do not all amount to ultimate explanations. It is therefore useful to clarify what the ambition of an evolutionary approach shall be in this respect.

There are (1) historical explanations attributing observed changes to singular, historically unique, and therefore always different, causes. This form of explanation can frequently be found in historiographic research. Since it is an application of "situational logic" (Popper 1960, Chap. 31), i.e. based on ad hoc hypotheses rather than a more general theory, it will be left aside here. Another form is (2) historical explanations attributing a special class of observed changes to a special pattern of causation. Hence, different recurrent aspects of economic change are explained by different hypotheses. An example is the set of hypotheses proposed by Nelson and Winter (1982) for explaining industrial transformation processes (see the next section). The pattern of causation that these hypotheses suggest is special in the sense that an extension to other classes of economic changes (in the case of Nelson and Winter, e.g., those occurring on the demand side) is not possible and not intended.[4]

Finally, there is a form (3) of historical explanations that attributes *all* observed evolutionary change to the *same* pattern of causation. This is the form of ultimate explanations. It requires a theory of a general, causal "mechanism" of evolution that manifests itself in all instances of the ongoing evolution. In biology, the Darwinian theory satisfies this requirement. The causal mechanism is constituted by the interaction of several processes. One of them is natural selection winnowing out less well-reproducing traits. Another one is allelic variation due to mutation, gene flow, and random drift in intergenerationally transmitted traits, as well as developmental and epigenetic variation (Gilbert and Epel 2009). A third process is that of geographic isolation allowing the branching off of different lines of descent. Further, there is a process of ecology and niche building that feeds back on variation and natural selection (Odling-Smee et al. 2003). Can the evolution of the economy be expected to be governed by a similarly general, economic, causal mechanism? Are all instances of the ongoing evolution of the economy a manifestation of such a mechanism so that ultimate explanations are possible at all?

An answer in the affirmative has been suggested by the proponents of Generalized Darwinism (see Hodgson 2002; Aldrich et al. 2008; Hodgson & Knudsen 2010). As the label indicates, it is claimed that the general causal mechanism postulated by the Darwinian theory for the natural sphere is valid for all domains in which evolutionary processes occur. An abstract reduction of the mechanism

---

[4] Another, earlier example is the "causal-genetic method" of explaining the emergence and change of economic institutions proposed by Menger (1985) [1883] and applied by him to the evolution of money. The Austrian school of economics, which Menger founded, did not adopt his method, missing the early chance to put forth a genuinely evolutionary approach; see Witt and Beck (2015).

is represented by Campbell's (1965) principles of variation, selection, and replication.[5] To put flesh on the bare bones of the principles, one can focus on the variation and selective replication of knowledge constructs and technological practices in economic evolution, as Mokyr (1990, 2002) has done (see later). Like in meme theory (Roy 2017), the differential replication of impersonal knowledge constructs and practices can be argued to depend on the extent to which they entail an adaptive advantage for their "carriers".

In the case of economic agents as carriers, this interpretation begs the question of what constitutes the adaptive advantage. Is the criterion for the advantage an objective one, such as reproductive success? Or is the advantage determined by the various agents' subjective preference satisfaction criteria? Since the relevance of reproductive success as an advantage measure is not obvious in modern economies, the straightforward measure seems to be subjective preference satisfaction. This would sit well with the idea of a Robbinsian decision maker. But ultimate explanations require hypotheses about a *general* mechanism. How can they be formulated on such a basis?

Abstaining from the selection and replication rhetoric, one could think of utility maximization (together with the usual assumptions about the properties of the utility function, see, e.g., in Mas-Colell et al. 1995) as implying the general causal mechanism. However, this canonical option lacks the substance necessary for deriving nontrivial ultimate explanations. In an individualistic framework the substance required for meaningful ultimate explanations would have to come from specific hypotheses about the content of the agents' preferences.[6] Moreover, hypotheses about interindividually shared content would be needed to avoid being drawn into the situational logic of historical singular-case explanations of the form (1).

From an evolutionary point of view, the preferences and utility functions of individuals living in a community quite likely share

[5] Campbell's principles are not a complete representation of the mechanism. In fact, doubts can be raised as to whether they are an accurate representation of "Darwinism". Some variants of Darwinism do not accept all the principles; see Levit et al. (2011).

[6] Whether optimization or some form of bounded rationality adequately represents decision-making behavior in a particular choice situation would be a different, and often less momentous, issue. Bounded rationality is significant, however, in the context of innovative behavior, which is the main source of variation in economic evolution.

common elements. Humans are social animals, after all. For that reason, the diversity and subjective nature of individual preferences notwithstanding, social competition for survival and reproductive success over thousands of generations are likely to have left their traces in the human genome. Indeed, humans inherit motivational dispositions which they share with their likes (and in part also with many other species) with the usual genetic variance. These innate dispositions, finding an expression in their revealed preferences, can be conjectured to have been conducive to survival and reproductive success in the ancestral past, hence resulting in a selection advantage.[7]

Heritable motivational dispositions are, of course, not the only determinants of commonly shared preferences. Noncognitive (i.e., conditioning) learning enables humans to individually adapt their preferences and, hence, behavior (Leslie 1996). And so do their cognitive capabilities, allowing for cognitive goal setting and goal striving, which can create a motivation (i.e., a preference for acting) of its own (Bargh et al. 2010). As a result of cognitive and noncognitive learning, economic agents change their preferences and form new ones. This plasticity is subject to influences of the social groups and the culture to which the economic agents belong.

All these universally shared features in the preferences of human decision makers can be expected to leave their traces in the average choice behavior in suitably defined large populations of economic agents. (The observable variance in choice behavior is explained by the diversity of individual genetic endowments, conditioning histories, and cognitive goal-setting processes.) In the longer run, the average choice behavior determines which technological path tends to be pursued, which innovations tend to be adopted, and how institutions change (ignoring for the moment the complications due to unintended collective outcomes of individual choices). Specific hypotheses about the interpersonally shared motivational features should therefore provide the key for understanding what in the economic context the adaptive advantage is (see Witt

---

[7] Because genetic adaptation is very slow in terms of human time scales and selection pressure has decreased in recent times, they are still present without presumably having changed very much. Evidence for this hypothesis has been gathered in evolutionary psychology, see, e.g., Buss (2003). One of these motivational dispositions, arising from the need for cognitive and sensory stimulation, explains the just-mentioned human inclination to explore, search, and tinker.

2017). Reflected in the preferences revealed by the economic agents, these motivational features can be made the basis for ultimate explanations in evolutionary economics. The result would be an approach that, unlike Generalized Darwinism, refrains from a selectionist rhetoric and maintains the ambitions of a microeconomic foundation.

Three Waves of Thinking about Economic Evolution: A Brief Outline

The history of economic thought has seen many turns and changes for better or worse. The history of evolutionary thought in economics is no exception. A brief reconstruction helps in understanding what advances could be made and what further advances seem possible and desirable in the light of the discussion in the preceding section. In a rough outline, attempts to infuse evolutionary thought into economics have come in three waves. Each of the waves followed its own interpretation of evolutionary economics and took little notice of earlier interpretations. Despite the differences between them, there is, however, some common ground that the interpretations share.

The first wave of contributions has been triggered by Veblen (1898), the founder of the American institutionalist school. He was inspired by the Darwinian revolution ongoing at his time in the sciences. His endeavor – for which he coined the term "evolutionary economics" – was to extend the Darwinian theory of descent with variation to human behavior and human culture, including the economy. His interpretation of evolutionary economics can thus be inferred to rest on both a monistic ontology[8] and the assumption that, by recourse to Darwinian theory, ultimate explanations can, in principle, be accomplished. In the pursuit of his project, Veblen developed a narrative of the origins and the unfolding of the social organization of modern economies, particularly American capitalism. In this narrative he attributed a central role to innate instincts and learned habits. Thus, Veblen referred already to motivational forces driving the evolutionary process. Yet he failed to make explicit in what way he imagined them to constitute a general causal mechanism governing economic evolution. This is obvious in his major works

---

[8] For an excellent discussion of the ontology problem in economics, see Dopfer (2005).

(Veblen 1899, 1914) in which careful descriptions of the conditions of the capitalist society of his time are presented but no formal theory of how and why they have come about.

After Veblen the American institutionalist school that he had founded became increasingly vague with respect to its evolutionary legacy[9] and was eventually marginalized in the discipline. A new wave of evolutionary thinking emerged some seventy years after Veblen. It was launched in the form of a "neo-Schumpeterian" interpretation of evolutionary economics (Nelson and Winter 1974, 1975, 1977, 1978, 1980, 1982, 2002). In that interpretation, the label "evolutionary" is no longer referring to a monistic ontology as in Veblen. It instead stands for an analogy to biology, leaving aside the ontological relationships between economics and biology. A theory of industrial selection processes is constructed in loose analogy to the theory of natural selection.[10] On this basis, Nelson and Winter outline a historical explanation of the form (2) of how firms and industries evolve as follows.

The entirety of organizational routines and techniques applied by the firms in an industry are considered the analogue to the gene pool of a natural species. Routines and techniques are assumed to be subject to inertia (an assumption closely related to the theory of organizational ecology, Hannan and Freeman 1977). Therefore, changes over time in an industry are not brought about by the firms' efforts to mend poorly performing routines or techniques. Change is rather caused by market competition which, analogously to natural selection, is assumed to

---

[9] Veblen's successors kept the label "evolutionary economics". Yet they successively abandoned the Darwinian connotations, retaining only Veblen's historicizing style of analysis and his critical attitude toward contemporary capitalism (see Hodgson 2004).

[10] For a recent assessment see Winter (2014). Unlike Nelson and Winter, Andersen (2009) tries to interpret Schumpeter himself as sticking to a "selectionist" evolutionary approach despite Schumpeter's (2002[1912]) explicit rejection of biological analogies. Indeed, Schumpeter's theory of how capitalism is driven by the emergence and diffusion of innovations seems to be anchored in a quite different strand of thought. This is the nineteenth-century diffusionism school (Kobayashi 2014). It was founded in social and cultural anthropology by the German geographer Friedrich Ratzel and was given prominent expression in the "Kulturkreis" doctrine of the ethnologists Frobenius and Graebner, whom Schumpeter knew; see Schumpeter (1955, Part IV, Chap. 3, Sec. 2b). As has been argued elsewhere (Witt 2008b), Schumpeter can therefore only be considered an evolutionary economist if the notion of evolution is defined in such a way that it includes nonselectionist diffusionism as well as selectionist interpretations.

winnow out firms with routines that perform poorly. As a consequence, the composition of the industry's pool of routines and techniques is changing over time. Hence, the industry's adaptation dynamics is fueled by the heterogeneity of firms and their routines, resulting in profitability differentials.[11]

Firm heterogeneity can be captured by frequency distributions over their various properties and, in particular, their profitability. Price and cost competition within an industry that results in a selection process should then come down to systematic changes of the frequency distributions, particularly the unit cost and profit distributions. This can be modeled by means of a replicator dynamics that describes how both the composition of firms/routines and the price level in the industry converge simultaneously to an equilibrium state in which only the most efficient firms survive (see Metcalfe 1994; Holm et al. 2017).

Nelson and Winter's synthesis has more recently been blended with traditional research on the industry life cycle going back to Abernathy and Utterback (1978). The result has been fruitful explanations of the form (2) of the history of, for instance, the American automobile industry (Klepper 2002), the world synthetic dye industry (Murmann 2003), and the American tire industry (Buenstorf and Klepper 2009). All are characterized similarly by the "shake-out" phenomenon (Klepper and Simons 2005). Another important branch in the present writings associated with this brand of evolutionary economics continues Schumpeter's original research interest in innovations and their impact on the economy outside the framework of the natural selection analogy. In this branch, historical explanations of form (2) have been developed for the economic competitiveness and growth of entire nations (Rosenberg and Birdzell 1986; Amendola and Gaffard 2006; Metcalfe et al. 2006), the regional and international division of labor (Brenner 2004; Los and Verspagen 2006; Fagerberg et al. 2007), and the role of the institutional framework of national innovation systems (Lundvall 1992), to give a few examples.

In any case, with the exception of Joel Mokyr's works, historical explanations of the form (3) – ultimate explanations of the observed economic changes as manifestations of one and the same general

---

[11] To capture the heterogeneity of firms, the construct of a "representative" firm often found in economic textbooks has to be replaced by population thinking. The latter is a prerequisite for understanding selection processes which always operate on the heterogeneous composition of populations; see Metcalfe (2008).

causal mechanism – are neither attempted nor intended. If they were, it would make sense to choose an individualistic approach also in the strongly supply-side-centered Schumpeterian and neo-Schumpeterian context. Resource saving, technical progress, cost and price cutting, product innovations, etc., are driven, after all, by motivations that are expressed by the agents' preferences. They warrant an analysis that, moreover, would have brought the neo-Schumpeterian approach closer to Veblen's focus on the motivations driving the economy. Yet from the outset the neo-Schumpeterian program had little interest in the motivational side – unlike Schumpeter himself.[12]

When Nelson and Winter (1982, Chaps. 2 and 3) reflect on (organizational) behavior, they focus on and challenge the optimization hypothesis. Setting the trend for most neo-Schumpeterians after them, they substitute it with the notion of bounded rationality. The latter goes back to Simon (1955) and March and Simon (1958) who deal with the procedural aspects of *how* decisions are made. Like in the canonical approach the motivational aspects (i.e., the specific reasons for *why* decisions are made) is left open. Decision makers are assumed to have limited cognitive (and managerial) abilities. They therefore handle repetitive choice situations by resorting to behavioral routines that proved to have satisfactory results in the past rather than mulling over in each and every case what the optimal choice might be.[13] This is assumed to be true even more so for the concerted decision making in firm organizations – hence, the inference that firm behavior is largely guided by organizational routines (Cyert and March 1963; Simon 1979).

More recently, the bounded rationality premise has also been a constituent for applying simulation tools, particularly agent-based modeling, in evolutionary economics. The topics investigated in these new extensions revolve around the Schumpeterian themes of firm growth; industrial, innovative dynamics and their aggregate effects (e.g., Saviotti and Pyka 2008); or go in the direction of complexity

---

[12] To give reasons for why the elitist entrepreneurs Schumpeter (1934[1912]) had in mind pursue their path-breaking, incalculable, innovative undertakings, he reflected in detail about their nonpecuniary motivations.

[13] Starbuck (1963). Limited cognitive capacity is also a central hypothesis in the more recent brand of behavioral economics. However, the consequences emphasized in that approach are different ones, namely various systematic biases in decision making and the need to resort to standardized decision heuristics, see, e.g., Kahneman (2003).

economics (Elsner et al. 2014). Other research efforts in the neo-Schumpeterian camp are now directed at intensifying innovation studies and empirical work on industrial dynamics. In contrast, the original, evolutionary inspiration seems to have lost momentum.[14]

Evolutionary theorizing in economics is now pushed in a new, and once more different, wave of contributions. It emerged in the aftermath of the game-theoretic revolution in microeconomics and the subsequent rise of experimental economics. The new wave is disjoined from, and does not take notice of, the previous ones.[15] In several respects the contributions to this new wave interact with contemporary efforts in the sciences to gain a better understanding of human sociality. Where they do, they follow a monistic ontology and acknowledge that the consequences of human sociality for economics need to be seen within the wider framework of the evolution of the species (see, e.g. Gintis 2007). Yet it is also recognized that the broader frame leaves room for specific influences of human culture.

In the human sciences, a debate beginning in the 1970s on the relevance of sociobiology raised questions about social behavior that appeared to be "altruistic" and difficult to align with the prevailing notion of "selfish" genes (Dawkins 1976). In order to help resolve the puzzle, evolutionary game theory was developed as a new analytical tool.[16] The debate triggered a series of comparative works that

---

[14] See, for example, the handbook of neo-Schumpeterian economics edited by Hanusch and Pyka (2007) in which reflections relating to evolutionary content cover not even 50 out of 1,170 pages.

[15] While the terms "evolutionary", "evolution", etc., are frequent in these contributions, particularly in relation to evolutionary game theory, the term "evolutionary economics" is hardly ever used, perhaps because it is perceived as being associated with the concurrent neo-Schumpeterian school. Bibliometric search of the economic literature discloses that the terms "evolution" and "evolutionary" are now more closely associated with the new wave than with neo-Schumpeterian evolutionary economics; see Silva and Teixeira (2009) and Hodgson et al. (2014).

[16] Unlike rational game theory, evolutionary game theory assumes that strategies are not subject to deliberate choice. The relative frequencies with which the strategies are played are rather seen as an expression of the behavioral repertoire encoded in the gene pool of a species and as being subject to natural selection. Accordingly, the payoffs reflect the heritable strategies' contribution to reproductive success (Maynard Smith 1982). Under these assumptions "altruistic" behavior has been explained alternatively as a phenomenon of reciprocity (Trivers 1971), of inclusive fitness (Hamilton 1964), or of group selection (Wilson and Sober 1994).

confirmed genetic influences on human social behavior. At the same time, however, the comparisons revealed important differences between human social behavior and the behavior of other social animals. Most importantly, humans are capable of social cognitive learning by which they can go beyond their inherited behavior repertoire. They can establish cooperative modes of behavior in social interactions and transmit them between generations in a process of cultural inheritance.[17]

Laboratory experiments in economics also revealed that participants often engage in other-regarding and cooperative behavior in strategic interactions instead of a "self-interested" utility maximization (e.g., Güth et al. 1982; Andreoni 1995; Hoffman et al. 1996). Likewise, field studies pointed to a high prevalence across different cultures of other-regarding or "altruistic" behavior (Henrich et al. 2004). Thus, some way had to be found in economics to theoretically account for these findings. For a while evolutionary game theory was considered a potential candidate rivaling with rational game theory in resolving the puzzle.[18] However, perhaps because of the cognitive bias of economic decision theory, at the end of the day rational game theory prevailed – albeit with some adjustments.[19]

In the terms of the preceding section, the explanations given for other-regarding and cooperative behavior and its consequences are proximate explanations (if not simply rationalizations as Smith 2015 argues). The question that remains is that of the ultimate explanation:

---

[17] Animals are to a certain extent also capable of adapting their social behavior through reinforcement and conditioning learning, yet an intergenerational transmission of these acquired forms is rare and, at best, rudimentary (see Brown and Richerson 2014). The unique human condition of inheriting genes *and* culture led to the "dual inheritance theory" (Cavalli-Sforza and Feldman 1981; Lumsden and Wilson 1981; Boyd and Richerson 1985), which extends the basic model of sociobiology.

[18] In the discussion it was suggested to interpret the convergence to an equilibrium described by evolutionary games as a learning rather than genetic process, more precisely as an interactive reinforcement learning; see Börgers and Sarin (1997), and Brenner (1998).

[19] See, e.g., Binmore (2006), Gintis (2007), and Bowles and Gintis (2011). In rational game theory the puzzle of other-regarding individual behavior can be resolved by a simple modification of the assumption about the players' preferences. Other-regarding behavior results when the players choose the strategy that maximizes the utility derived not from their own payoff but from the somehow weighted sum of their own payoff and the payoff accruing to the other player(s).

What is the reason for why such behavior could evolve? Economists here borrow the answer given in evolutionary anthropology: in an environment such as the one faced by the early humans living in small groups in ancestral times, other-regarding behavior can have a reproductive advantage (Richerson and Boyd 2005). A genetic disposition accounting not only for one's own payoff but also for the payoff of other group members, can therefore be assumed to have been favored by natural selection in ancestral times. If so, it can be argued that such a social preference is still genetically represented in human behavior today and is therefore likely to influence the utility maximizing strategy choices to a certain extent.

However, other-regarding preferences are not the only social dispositions humans inherit. There is also a tendency to free-ride, to aggressively strive to dominate, and to selfishly manipulate and deceive others.[20] In a cooperative social environment, such behavior would have a selection advantage over other-regarding behavior and, if not kept in check, would drive other-regarding behavior to extinction. The challenge for explaining why a cooperative mode of social behavior could evolve is therefore to find reasons for a balance between these two opposing dispositions.

The reason may be conjectured to be that over thousands of generations of reproduction within the small ancestral human groups, a genetic disposition for developing emotional bonds to the own group may have been selected for. (Such emotional bonds support a high degree of internal cooperation, as it was necessary in ancestral times for child rearing, successful hunting and gathering, the defense against predators, and being able to compete with rivaling species for food sources.) As a consequence, the ambivalence in human social behavior has different effects in in-group vs. out-group interactions. Identification with an "own" group fosters group loyalty (particularly in the confrontation with other groups; see Bowles 2008) and other-regarding preferences in interactions with members of their own group. By the same token, it diminishes aggression, dominance striving, free-riding, and other selfish tendencies. Where such behavior nonetheless occurs within the group, it can be suppressed (if not too

---

[20] These inclinations can be conjectured to be an inheritance of our primate ancestors (Eibl-Eibesfeldt 2004, 525–560) and can still be observed as common attitudes in competition for resources and mating opportunities in many primate species.

frequent) by ostracism that is mediated by a spontaneous formation of corresponding coalitions (see Boehm 2001). Hence, a pro-social maximization of utility derived from own payoff and the payoff of others seems to be contingent on whether or not interactions are framed as an in-group activity.

The third wave of evolutionary theorizing now under way in economics has been fruitful in advancing the understanding of pro-social behavior and its evolutionary background. It has replaced the narrow self-interest interpretation often associated with Robbins's definition of economics by an interpretation allowing for the complex contingencies under which social behavior can range from altruism and cooperation to pure self-interest and opportunism. It is worth noting that social preferences are ultimately explained as inherited motivational dispositions in a way comparable to the ultimate explanation suggested in the preceding section for preferences in the context of nonstrategic economic behavior. However, not least because of the dominant analytical role of game theory, the explanation is limited to preferences relevant for economic behavior in social interactions. Such a limitation may be acceptable for an individualistic version of sociology (as claimed by Gintis and Helbing 2015). But the innate motivations and preferences relevant for other important parts of economic behavior such as consumption can evidently not be fully covered by this approach. There is, thus, still some way to go for the individualistic theorizing in evolutionary economics until the many additional aspects that matter are integrated (see Burnham et al. 2016 for a list of them).

Advancing Evolutionary Economics: Methodology, Theory, and Normative Judgement

This volume presents important extensions of the methodological, theoretical, and normative underpinnings of an evolutionary approach to economics. Some of the chapters take a bird's-eye view of the evolutionary process in the economy. Other chapters elaborate on special problems that need to be solved in order to make progress in evolutionary economics. Brian J. Loasby's Chapter 2 marks the beginning of a section on conceptual and methodological issues. With the outline of a counterfactual history of economic thought in the twentieth century he offers a broad orientation on theoretical developments that could have taken place but did not, in contrast to those that did. In this way he characterizes a kind of mental ecology of economic ideas in which the three just-discussed waves of evolutionary contributions tried to gain a foothold in economics.

Loasby explains that a significant point of controversy was the notion of market equilibrium and the concepts for the equilibrating process by which it was supposed to be attained. Since Walras, canonical economic theorizing worked on, and eventually succeeded in, proving in a thought experiment that a unique *general* economic equilibrium is logically possible under properly chosen assumptions about the price mechanism and the behavior of the market participants. The further question of how that equilibrium might be reached simultaneously in all markets was more difficult. Walras imagined an equilibrating process run by an auctioneer linking the change of price to the sign of the excess demand function in each market. However, this construction forced Walras to resort to a fiction. He had to assume that no production and exchange take place before the auctioneer's adjustment of price quotes has reached the equilibrium price (see also Fisher 1983).

As Loasby points out, the main opponent to the general equilibrium approach was Marshall. Focusing only on equilibrating market processes in single industries, he was less ambitious. On the other hand, his partial analysis did not force him to invoke Walras's no-false-trading and no-production fiction. While Marshall was lacking an analytical apparatus to present his dissenting views, the neo-Schumpeterian analogy to natural selection processes can provide one. The models by Nelson and Winter and Metcalfe that were mentioned in the preceding section discuss equilibrating processes in single industries while not excluding that production and trade take place already at nonequilibrium prices. Metcalfe (2002) even proves rigorously that the competitive price adjustment driving a shake-out process in the industry eventually results in an equilibrium constellation.

This may not be surprising as, from a formal point of view, the replicator dynamics and the optimization-based auctioneer's rule are not much different (see Joosten (2006). Regarding the explanation of the equilibrating process, the neo-Schumpeterian selection models still fit a rather conventional format.[21] The major difference between the

---

[21] In the same vein Mirowski (1983) criticizes a lack of new insights offered by the market process simulations in Nelson and Winter (1982).

canonical and the neo-Schumpeterian interpretation is that the latter looks beyond the market equilibrium and the equilibrating process. The canonical interpretation treats disruptions of the equilibrium as "exogenous shocks" that require no explanation. In contrast, following Schumpeter (1934[1912]), the neo-Schumpeterians see a substantial part of the disruptions as being caused "from within" the economy, as Schumpeter already put it. The key hypothesis for explaining this part of the market process is entrepreneurial innovativeness resulting in a "creative destruction" of the preexisting market conditions. The details of what enables a seemingly incessant stream of innovations to countervail the equilibrating processes in the markets are not yet well understood.[22] Loasby rightly insists in his thoughtful piece that to make progress, inquiry into the role of knowledge creation in the economy (enabling entrepreneurs to carry out "new combinations") will be of central importance.

Crucial contributions to that inquiry have been made by Joel Mokyr (e.g., 1990, 2002) who reviews many of his insights in his rich Chapter 3. His topic is the evolution of useful knowledge, which he considers the major driver of economic evolution and growth. Taking the perspective of evolutionary epistemology, Mokyr conceives of the evolution of human knowledge as being governed by the principles of blind variation, selection, and retention suggested by Campbell (1965).[23] The principle of variation refers in Mokyr's interpretation to how the huge variety and variability of useful knowledge has historically emerged from past innovations. In its enormous variety, useful knowledge must be constantly reproduced from generation to generation (with possible additional variation) – the equivalent of the principle of inheritance. And since the generation of useful knowledge is "super-fecund" in producing variability, not all variants can be preserved. Selection takes place by the fact that some knowledge (e.g., a particular technique) is chosen over other variants to be maintained and handed down.

---

[22] As pointed out elsewhere (Witt 2009), part of the problem is that answering these questions faces serious epistemological constraints that are difficult to overcome.

[23] As mentioned in the previous section, the proponents of Generalized Darwinism claim that these principles govern the evolution of all complex population systems from the species in living nature to human languages or the economy; see Hodgson and Knudsen (2010).

The claims of proponents of Generalized Darwinism, like Mokyr, regarding the explanatory power of the three abstract principles of variation, selection, and retention are under debate in evolutionary economics. For Mokyr there is a general, causal mechanism that shapes the evolution of the economy through the creation and selective replication of propositional and prescriptive knowledge. It can serve as a basis for ultimate explanations. For the opponents of Generalized Darwinism, in contrast, these principles are only a device that may guide the attempt to detect a common abstract mechanism underlying many seemingly diverse processes in different disciplinary domains. In Chapter 4, inspired by the philosophy of science, Jack Vromen outlines reasons that speak for that position.

Vromen argues that by invoking the three abstract principles "top down" for identifying the same features in evolutionary processes in different disciplinary domains, an attempt is made to unite the different domain-specific phenomena under the working of one and the same mechanism. Following philosopher Philip Kitcher, Vromen points out that, if successful, such a unification is an explanation of an own kind. Yet "unification-as-explanation" is different from causal explanations. To arrive at the latter, additional causal hypotheses are required, which are specific to the disciplinary domain – in this case, the economy and its evolution. Hence, whether or not one wishes to find inspiration by the abstract principles of Generalized Darwinism in looking for such causal hypotheses, the principles themselves cannot serve as such hypotheses.[24]

Proponents of Generalized Darwinism in evolutionary economics rarely formulate necessary "auxiliary", domain-specific, causal hypotheses (for an exception see Mokyr's chapter in this volume). They rather construct an abstract analogy between genotypes and phenotypes on the one side and "replicators" and "interactors" on the other. The universal patterns of causation in economic evolution are expected to follow from the interplay of replicators and interactors in the same way as descent with variation of the species is causally explicable by what happens in the interplay of genotypes and

---

[24] Indeed, Aldrich et al. (2008) admit that the principles of variation, selection, and inheritance only offer "an overarching theoretical framework in which theorists can develop auxiliary, domain-specific explanations".

phenotypes under natural selection pressure. By this construction, Vromen objects, Generalized Darwinism runs into a dilemma. On the one hand, the aim is to have three principles that are universally applicable, because all domain-specific remnants from evolutionary biology are claimed to have been stripped off. On the other hand, the principles do not suffice for the causal explanations of evolutionary processes, and the domain-specific remnants from evolutionary biology enter through the backdoor as the necessary "auxiliary" hypotheses in the disguise of the replicator–interactor construct.

Chapter 5 by Richard H. Day marks the beginning of a section on macroeconomic topics with contributions written from different evolutionary perspectives. Day presents a perspective on how the human economy has progressed in the very long run. This perspective blends ideas that he had developed in an earlier work, such as those on adaptive economic change (Day and Cigno 1978) and chaotic dynamics (Day 1982), with specific hypotheses about the historical unfolding of the economy. Economic development is portrayed as a sequence of distinct stages. It moves from hunting and gathering to quasi-settled agriculture and herding, settled agriculture, complex societies and city states, trading empires, industrial economies, and the nation-state and has now arrived at the present global information economy. Each one of these stages is characterized by a distinct interplay of production technologies, trading institutions, governance structures, and population dynamics. The result is a typical pattern of growth, maturation, and decline in the macroeconomic performance over time. The decline triggers a chaotic transition phase paving the way for the next stage.

With respect to the general causal mechanism underlying the transformation of the economy in each stage and the transitions between them, Day argues that a more detailed analysis would be desirable. However, to accomplish this, macroeconomic theory needs to be augmented with a number of features. Among his theoretical desiderata are a birth-welfare threshold that represents a standard of living below which societies perish; diseconomies related not only to inputs but also to coordination and complexity; the social infrastructure of societies and its administrative technology; and the possibility of switching between multiple technological regimes. Enhanced in this way, the theory would suggest a specific historical explanation of the earlier-discussed form (2).[25] Day's framework promises advances particularly for understanding the factors and nonlinear dynamics that are critical for triggering transition phases. Day discusses exemplarily what lesson the case of the disintegration of the Soviet Union in the 1990s carries in this respect. Furthermore, he reflects on the conditions that would point in the light of his theory of economic evolution to the possibility of a future decline of the United States. Day concludes the chapter by pondering what implications this framework has for understanding the limits to growth.

The topic in André Lorentz's Chapter 6 is the Kaldor-Verdoorn law, highlighting a special macroeconomic phenomenon. The law claims that productivity growth in a sector of an economy (e.g., an export sector) is positively related to the growth of output of that sector. The law has been applied to explaining *inter alia* the emergence of efficiency-based international specialization patterns. The law is originally a generalization inspired by the empirical observations Verdoorn had made. As such, it is not entirely clear what the causal mechanism underlying the proposed law is. In his chapter, Lorentz sets out to offer a theoretical explication of the law by means of a micro-founded macro model of an economy using agent-based modeling for that purpose. For the economy as a whole, the relationship stated by Verdoorn's law implies increasing returns when output expands. Lorentz's model derives these increasing returns at the macro level as an emergent property of the processes of innovative technical change at the micro level.

His analysis is an excellent example of recent neo-Schumpeterian theorizing aiming at explanations of the form (2), in his case of the historically observed increasing returns in the process of economic growth. The "evolutionary" part of the explanation is the analogy to natural selection. Accordingly, Lorentz starts from differences between firms in improving their technology by investments. Over time, these differences change the cost structure in the economy, which, in turn, gives rise to a competitive selection process among the

---

[25] As in the case of all stage theories, an empirical test of the theory is difficult; see Popper (1960). The idea that societies progress to ever higher stages of development is a characteristic of many economic stage theories from, e.g., Spencer to Marx and Rostow. For the difficulties of testing such theories and contradictory empirical evidence see Currie et al. (2010).

firms. This process is modeled by means of a replicator dynamics analogously to Fisher's fundamental principle of natural selection.[26] The
process is fueled by innovations – the analogue to genetic mutations –
which in Lorentz's model are generated in a random fashion contingent on technological opportunities arising with a growing capital
stock. The more capital and innovations there are, the greater the
rate of innovativeness and of the growth of labor productivity.
Knowledge spillovers taking place in the industries allow imitating
firms to improve their production technology as well, with the result
of overall increasing returns. The Kaldor-Verdoorn law follows by
implication. Lorentz's neo-Schumpeterian micro-foundation of the
law does not have to assume the existence of static increasing returns
as traditionally considered elsewhere. Where increasing returns are
caused according to Lorentz's model, they are intrinsically dynamic.

The section devoted to advances in theorizing about institutional
evolution begins with Dennis C. Mueller's Chapter 7. He takes a
wide-ranging, critical tour through institutional economics, public
choice, and political science inquiring especially into the role of the
rational actor model in these disciplines and its limitations. The
rational actor is but a variant of a fully informed Robbinsian decision
maker, a theoretical fiction already discussed earlier. Mueller's criticism of the fiction is not only based on the objections against the
rational actor model raised in the growing field of behavioral economics (see Camerer and Loewenstein 2004). He is also concerned
with the fact that the focus on rationality has impeded the understanding of ethical influences that are especially relevant in the context of political choices. The limitations of the rational actor model
turn already up in the well-known voting paradox, implying that
rational voters would never vote given the negligible influence on
the turnout that an individual vote has. For Mueller the fact that the
opposite can be observed indicates that ethical considerations induce
behavior that cannot be satisfactorily explained by the rational actor
model alone.

---

[26] The principle states that the relative frequency of individuals with fitness
higher (lower) than the average fitness in a population increases (decreases).
The pace of adaptation of the average fitness to the level of the individuals
with the highest fitness is proportional to the fitness variance in the population;
see Hofbauer and Sigmund (1988, Chap. 4).

Mueller's criticism is framed by broader reflections on the evolution of both rationality and ethics in humans, but also of superstitious and mythical thinking. These reflections – drawing on the recent discussion in evolutionary psychology – tie in to what has been labeled earlier the third wave of evolutionary theorizing in economics. In the light of these reflections Mueller goes on discussing the evolution of political institutions, particularly democratic institutions. Special attention is paid to the role of religion for the political organization of societies. While the role of religion in this context is often seen in supporting, if not enabling, the emergence of cooperativeness, Mueller develops a further, more skeptical argument. He explains that the functioning of a democracy requires both the capability and the willingness to make rational, ethically committed collective decisions. In his view, some forms of religious belief are not supportive of these requirements.

Formal organizations, i.e. the class of designed and deliberately implemented institutions, are the topic of Chapter 8 by Roger D. Congleton. He takes an evolutionary approach to these institutions in which two issues are of particular interest. One of the issues is the explanation of typical features of the institutions' historical unfolding from their creation to the subsequent adaptations. The other issue is the explanation of how they "function", i.e. of the way in which their governance structure works, as a result of the historical adaptation process and its necessities and limitations. Congleton's chapter deals with both issues concurrently.[27]

He starts from the observation that many private and nonprivate organizations such as business corporations, political bodies, and religious bodies have an organizational governance structure that follows the "king-and-council" template, as he calls it. This template is made up of a special set of organizational rules dividing the decision-making authority between two bodies. On the one side there are "formeteurs" (an individual or a small group) corresponding to the role of the king. They have created the formal organization with the purpose of generating surplus by team work synergies. In order to

---

[27] Yet another comparative approach that has recently been proposed is that of deriving inspiration from social biomimicry. This approach analyzes similarities and differences between the working of deliberately designed institutions in the human sphere and organizational features that have evolved under natural selection in social insects; see Fewell (2015).

accomplish their goals, they define the rules, recruit the team members of the organization, and determine the distribution of the rewards that can be reaped by forming the organization. On the other side there is a subgroup of senior team members forming the council. The council members have at least an advising function in the formateurs' decision-making process, but often also a partial decision-making power as well.

The question is why and how organizational change is very often attracted to the king-and-council structure. Congleton suggests that a special causal mechanism is at work, thus offering an explanation of the form (2) for this evolutionary regularity. In a nutshell, his explanation goes as follows. With a growing size of the organization, the intensity of control through the formeteurs decreases and requires delegation of decision-making authority (and responsibility) to senior team members. This requires corresponding adaptations of the organizational decision-making procedures. If such an adaptation fails or the opportunity for undertaking it is missed, the organization runs the risk of efficiency losses. Since, as a consequence of resource scarcity and competition with rivals, organizations are under selection pressure, severe efficiency losses tend to threaten the survival of the organization. Congleton argues that the king-and-council template therefore has a high probability of spreading among organizations that grow large, either because it is selected for or because it is deliberately adopted by imitation by the formeteurs who recognize its superior performance in other organizations.

In Chapter 9 Reinoud Joosten elaborates on informal institutions or, more specifically, on whether and when they do, or do not, fail to emerge spontaneously. Joosten explores a situation in which a self-imposed obligation to keep to a rule would constitute an informal institution if everybody were to obey to it. Under what conditions is abiding by the rules to be expected from rational players when following the rules is costly? The particular case serving the exemplary discussion is individual negligence in taking care of a freely accessible commons. Such behavior often results in small-scale pollution. If everybody acts in the same manner, the cumulative effect eventually adds up to a major degradation of the environment.

To capture the unfolding nature of the environmental degradation process, Joosten makes use of an advanced class of game-theoretic models (indicating that his work relates to the earlier mentioned third wave of evolutionary theorizing in economics). These are "frequency-dependent games", i.e. games in which the players' payoffs vary over time with the frequency of the previously chosen strategies. The payoffs represent the utility that the players obtain from the current state of the environment. The payoffs are also contingent on whether the players choose the strategy of conforming to the costly non-negligence rule. The latter always results in a lower payoff than the negligence strategy. Hence, from a rational choice perspective, a variant of the commons dilemma – a social trap (Cross and Guyer 1980) – is implied here in which the immediate utility gain from negligence conflicts with the cumulatively arising disastrous long-term consequences.

To ease the investigation of the intricate, time-distributed unfolding of the external effect potentially implied by the frequency-dependent game, it is assumed that the players are fully informed about the strategies and short- and long-term payoffs.[28] On this basis, Joosten is able to derive a solution that mimics the standard framework of repeated games. This means, *inter alia*, that the players are assumed to be involved in a rather direct strategic interaction, allowing a certain level of social control. Under that condition the players can threaten with the disastrous consequences of a permanent own negligence in order to discipline fellow players and to induce them to play by the rule. Indeed, Joosten derives a set of subgame-perfect equilibria of the game in which the degradation of the commons is prevented: for all players the best choice is to avoid entering the social trap, provided they are sufficiently patient. If, as often in reality, the assumed level of social control cannot be exerted or the time horizon of the players is rather short-lived, the fate of the common environment is, of course, likely to be a different one.

Chapter 10 by Christian Schubert turns to a special subset of institutional problems. These are the problems of regulating land-use conflicts by law and/or by court decisions, including the problem of compensating for governmental takings (i.e., expropriation of private property in land). These problems form a core research topic of the law and economics (L&E) literature. Schubert's reflections can

---

[28] The evolutionary process from which an institution like this emerges is not addressed. An explanation of such a historical adaptation process would presuppose incompletely informed players and an inquiry into their learning and imitation behavior.

therefore also be seen as a critique and suggested revision of the L&E approach to land-use issues from an evolutionary point of view. As he points out, the relevant tenets of L&E are informed by a thought experiment introduced by Coase (1960). Coase portrayed a bilateral conflict in the use of agricultural acreage and tried to derive conditions (summarized in what has afterwards been called the Coase theorem) under which it can be solved if the sole criterion is the efficient use of the land.

Schubert argues that this framework fails to do justice to the actual complexity of the evolving, competitive process of land uses, which in the majority of cases takes place in urbanized agglomerations. Neighborhood externalities and spillovers should therefore be expected to regularly generate repercussions that involve competing, if not conflicting, land-use intentions of a multitude of land owners/ users. This fact is not sufficiently done justice to, Schubert claims, by lumping together the consequences of the involvement of many agents in an inflated transaction cost variable. Moreover, the static efficiency concept implicit in the solution of the bargaining games usually applied in L&E for modeling land-use conflicts does not suit the actual dynamics of urban agglomerations. They are subject to continuous transformation processes resulting from changing utilization patterns, which reflect, in turn, changes in technology and adaptations to changing traffic, cost, and revenue structures. A regulation of land use that only accounts for efficiency under the momentarily prevailing constraints may therefore be at odds with dynamic efficiency. The latter may, for instance, be obstructed by regulations that are efficient only under present conditions but invoke barriers that drive up the costs of future conversion needs.

Finally, the framework invoked by Coase's thought experiment ignores that any regulation proposed for the emerging conflicts can be contested by questioning its legitimacy. Schubert holds that any practically relevant regulation needs to also take the normative legitimation problem into account. Legitimacy is contingent on the extent to which regulations respect informal institutions that have evolved in a society, particularly the social norms of distributive and procedural fairness. By referring to these additional criteria, Schubert connects to a topic that is central to much of the research in the previously mentioned third wave of evolutionary theorizing in economics. If taken seriously, a corresponding extension of L&E needs to solve two problems on which Schubert elaborates in more detail. One of them is to construct concrete measures for distributive and procedural fairness. The other problem is to properly weigh those measures against the efficiency criterion wherever tensions between the two criteria are implied.

If the results of the evolution of the economy are subjected to a normative assessment, this is not without problems, as the chapters by Dennis C. Mueller and Christian Schubert show. Further facets of such a normative assessment are discussed in the two chapters forming the last section of the present volume. An important facet is the question of what role welfare theory can play in an evolutionary approach (i.e., the assessment of the welfare effects of economic evolution). Do the intertemporal transformations of the economy also transform the very welfare measure(s)? If so, in what way can welfare theory be modified to account for these transformations? These questions are center stage in Chapter 11 by Martin Binder and Ulrich Witt. Their point of departure is the role that innovations and innovativeness play in the course of economic evolution, an issue that figures prominently in the neo-Schumpeterian approach to evolutionary economics.

Innovations help to tap new resources and to raise resource efficiency by pushing technical and organizational change. Innovations give birth to a plethora of new goods and services, many of which trigger a new demand, contributing to a growing consumption. There is no doubt, thus, that innovativeness contributes to economic growth, to improving labor productivity and working conditions, and to rising the standard of living. For these reasons, innovations and innovativeness are usually considered highly welcome not only among the neo-Schumpeterians but also among policy makers and in the public. However, in terms of a welfare-theoretic assessment it is less clear whether the role of innovations can indeed be given that much credit.

As Binder and Witt point out, there are two main reasons for that. The first one is simply that, by a kind of innovation optimism, it is often ignored that innovations can cause negative externalities. These externalities are frequently notoriously difficult to anticipate and therefore unknown when innovations are introduced. Before such innovations are stopped, they can thus develop consequences rated disastrous by any welfare measure. The second reason is that, at least as far as consumption goods and services are concerned, innovations create a demand that did not exist before. This fact points to an innovation-induced change of preference of the consumers. However, when innovations can influence the measuring rod by which their welfare effects are supposed to be assessed, an unambiguous judgment on the welfare effects is difficult, if not impossible. Can the problem be resolved by replacing preference satisfaction as the measuring rod by some other measure? Exploring in more detail how the problem might be solved, Binder and Witt review different approaches to welfare theory that use different measuring rods. As their discussion shows, however, a fundamental ambiguity in the normative foundation of the welfare judgment regarding the role of consumer innovations remains.

Consumer behavior in modern, innovative economies and, in particular, its sustainability is also the central aspect of economic evolution that Andreas Chai addresses in his Chapter 12. Many commentators have by now launched the ecological argument that current consumption trends are unsustainable. With his discussion of recent developments in evolutionary consumer theory, Chai is able to shed new light on the problem. He argues that a lack of sustainability is at least in part due to consumer preferences being determined by factors that are beyond the control of the individual, such as technological paradigms, social factors, and institutions. The consequence is that consumer preferences tend to be subject to "lock-in" effects to the extent to which these factors are themselves subject to lock-in effects.

Drawing on insights from evolutionary consumer theory, Chai seeks to clarify the precise conditions and learning regimes under which observed preferences are less likely to be cognitively reflected upon by consumers. This leads him to redefine from an evolutionary perspective the concept of consumer sovereignty, the basic condition upon which the theory of consumer welfare is founded. Chai argues that beyond considering the extent to which preferences are satisfied at one given point in time, from a dynamic perspective it is also essential to consider whether agents possess an opportunity to learn and revisit their preferences over time. This distinction can then be used to discriminate between, on the one hand, instances in which consumer preferences are satisfied but "locked-in" and, on the other hand, situations in which preferences may not be satisfied, but the agents have the ability and opportunity to learn and reflect on their preferences.

Conclusion

We have outlined how an evolutionary approach to economics affects the definition of, and perspective on, economic problems, despite the fact that, unlike in biology, psychology, or anthropology, the core of an evolutionary approach is still subject to debate in economics. To understand the present situation we have suggested taking a diachronic perspective on the contributions to evolutionary economics in the literature. In such a perspective three different waves of evolutionary theorizing can be identified. In each single wave the core is implicitly or explicitly defined differently, and evolutionary reasoning and modeling (where modeling is relevant) focus on different topics. We have argued therefore that advances in evolutionary economics can be made in two ways.

One of them is by research that develops new insights and contributes to an improved understanding of each of the topics. The basis is here the reasoning and/or modeling specific to the corresponding wave of evolutionary theorizing. The other way of making progress is to move the evolutionary approach to economics closer to a common understanding of its core. This requires more conceptual and methodological work to be done in the future. In our short preview of the subsequent chapters we have argued that both ways are represented in this volume. Some of the chapters contribute to advancing specific topics, while other chapters make progress with the debate on the core of evolutionary economics. With our introductory chapter we have tried to set the frame for both, not least by reflecting on why canonical economics has difficulties recognizing and coping with the evolutionary nature of the economy.

To advance the debate on the core we have suggested recognizing a methodological particularity of evolutionary theorizing. On the one hand, it sticks to the general presumption that evolution is a historical process in which recurrent patterns exist. On the other hand, evolutionary theorizing assumes that the current features and conditions of the economy are a result, and are hence explicable in terms of, the causal mechanism that produces the recurrent patterns. We therefore expect hypotheses about the causal mechanism and its many facets to make up the core of an evolutionary approach to economics. Future work may show to what extent the theories worked out in the three discussed waves of evolutionary economics can be integrated on this basis in an encompassing theory of a causal mechanism governing economic evolution.

References

Abernathy, W. J. and Utterback, J. M. (1978). Patterns of Industrial Innovation. *Technology Review*, 80, 40–47.

Aldrich, H. E., Hodgson, G. M., Hull, D. L., Knudsen, T., Mokyr, J., and Vanberg, V. J. (2008). In Defense of Generalized Darwinism. *Journal of Evolutionary Economics*, 18, 577–596.

Amendola, A. and Gaffard, J.-L. (2006). *The Market Way to Riches: Behind the Myth*. Cheltenham: Edward Elgar.

Andersen, E. S. (2009). *Schumpeter's Evolutionary Economics*. London: Anthem.

Andreoni, J. (1995). Cooperation in Public Good Experiments: Kindness or Confusion. *American Economic Review*, 85, 891–904.

Bargh, J. A., Gollwitzer, P. M., and Oettingen, G. (2010). Motivation, In: Fiske, S. T., Gilbert, D. T., and Lindzey, G. (eds.) *Handbook of Social Psychology*. New York, NY: Wiley, 268–316.

Binmore, K. (2006). The Origins of Fair Play. Papers on Economics and Evolution, #0614, Max Planck Institute of Economics Jena.

Boehm, C. (2001). *Hierarchy in the Forest: The Evolution of Egalitarian Behavior*. Cambridge, MA: Harvard University Press.

Börgers, T. and Sarin, R. (1997). Learning through Reinforcement and Replicator Dynamics. *Journal of Economic Theory*, 77, 1–14.

Bowles, S. (2008). Conflict: Altruism's Midwife. *Nature*, 456, 326–327.

Bowles, S. and Gintis, H. (2011). *A Cooperative Species: Human Reciprocity and Its Evolution*. Princeton: Princeton University Press.

Boyd, R. and Richerson, P. J. (1985). *Culture and the Evolutionary Process*. Chicago: University of Chicago Press.

Brenner, T. (1998). Can Evolutionary Algorithms Describe Learning Processes? *Journal of Evolutionary Economics*, 8, 271–283.

(2004). *Local Industrial Clusters – Existence, Emergence and Evolution*. London: Routledge.

Brown, G. R. and Richerson, P. J. (2014). Applying Evolutionary Theory to Human Behavior: Past Differences and Current Debates. *Journal of Bioeconomics*, 16, 105–128.

Buenstorf, G. and Klepper S. (2009). Heritage and Agglomeration: The Acron Tire Cluster Revisited. *Economic Journal*, 119, 705–733.

Burnham, T. C. (2016). Economics and Evolutionary Mismatch: Humans in Novel Settings Do Not Maximize. *Journal of Bioeconomics*, 18, 195–209.

Burnham, T. C., Lea, S. E. G., Bell, A., Gintis, H., Glimcher, P. W., Kurzban, R., Lades, L., McCabe, K., Panchanathan, K., Teschl, M., and Witt, U. (2016). Evolutionary Behavioral Economics. In: Wilson,

D. S. and Kirman, A. (eds.) *Complexity and Evolution – A New Synthesis for Economics*. Cambridge, MA: MIT Press, 113–144.

Buss, D. M. (2003). *Evolutionary Psychology: The New Science of the Mind*. Boston, MA: Allyn and Bacon.

Camerer, C. F. and Loewenstein, G. (2004). Behavioral Economics: Past, Presence, Future. In: Camerer, C. F., Loewenstein, G., and Rabin, M. (eds.) *Advances in Behavioral Economics*. Princeton: Princeton University Press, 3–51.

Campbell, D. T. (1965). Variation and Selective Retention in Socio-cultural Evolution. In: Barringer, H. R., Blankenstein, G. I., and Mack, R. W. (eds.) *Social Change in Developing Areas: A Reinterpretation of Evolutionary Theory*. Cambridge, MA: Schenkman, 19–49.

Cavalli-Sforza, L. and Feldman, M. (1981). *Cultural Transmission and Evolution: A Quantitative Approach*. Princeton: Princeton University Press.

Coase, R. H. (1960). The Problem of Social Cost. *Journal of Law & Economics*, 3, 1–44.

Cross, J. G. and Guyer, M. J. (1980). *Social Traps*. Ann Arbor, MI: University of Michigan Press.

Currie, T. E., Greenhill, S. J., Gray, R. D., Hasegawa, T., and Mace, R. (2010). Rise and Fall of Political Complexity in Island South-East Asia and the Pacific. *Nature*, 467, 801–804.

Cutler, D. M., Glaeser E. L., and Shapiro J. M. (2003). Why Have Americans Become More Obese? *Journal of Economic Perspectives*, 17, 93–118.

Cyert, R. M. and March, J. G. (1963). *A Behavioral Theory of the Firm*. Englewood Cliffs, NJ: Prentice Hall.

Dawkins, R. (1976). *The Selfish Gene*. Oxford: Oxford University Press.

Day, R. H. (1982). Irregular Growth Cycles. *American Economic Review*, 72, 406–414.

Day, R. H. and Cigno, A. (1978). *Modelling Economic Change – The Recursive Programming Approach*. Amsterdam: North-Holland.

Dopfer, K. (2005). Evolutionary Economics: A Theoretical Framework. In Dopfer, K. (ed.) *The Evolutionary Foundations of Economics*. Cambridge: Cambridge University Press, 3–55.

Dupré, J., ed. (1987). *The Latest on the Best: Essays on Evolution and Optimality*. Cambridge, MA: MIT Press.

Eibl-Eibesfeldt, I. (2004). *Die Biologie des menschlichen Verhaltens*. 5th edn. Vierkirchen: Buchvertrieb Blank.

Elsner, W., Heinrich, T., and Schwardt, H. (2014). *The Microeconomics of Complex Economies*. New York, NY: Elsevier.

Fagerberg, J., Srholec, M., and Knell, M. (2007). The Competitiveness of Nations: Why Some Countries Prosper While Others Fall Behind. *World Development*, 35, 1595–1620.

Fewell, J. H. (2015). Social Biomimicry: What Do Ants and Bees Tell Us About Organization in the Natural World? *Journal of Bioeconomics*, 17, 207–216.

Fisher, F. M. (1983). *Disequilibrium Foundations of Equilibrium Economics*. Cambridge: Cambridge University Press.

Gauthier, J. A. and Padian, K. (1989). The Origin of Birds and the Evolution of Flight. *Short Courses in Paleontology*, 2, 121–133.

Ghiselin, M. T. (1974). *The Economy of Nature and the Evolution of Sex*. Berkeley, CA: University of California Press.

Gilbert, S. F. and Epel, D. (2009). *Ecological Developmental Biology*. Sunderland, MA: Sinauer Associates.

Gintis, H. (2007). A Framework for the Unification of the Behavioral Sciences. *Behavioral and Brain Sciences*, 30, 1–61.

Gintis, H. and Helbing, D. (2015). Homo Socialis: An Analytical Core for Sociological Theory. *Review of Behavioral Economics*, 2, 1–59.

Güth, W., Schmittberger, R., and Schwarze, B. (1982). An Experimental Analysis of Ultimatum Bargaining. *Journal of Economic Behavior and Organization*, 3, 367–388.

Hamilton, W. D. (1964). The Evolution of Altruistic Behavior. *American Naturalist*, 97, 354–356.

Hannan, M. T. and Freeman, J. (1977). The Population Ecology of Organizations. *American Journal of Sociology*, 82, 929–964.

Hanusch, H. and Pyka, A. (2007). *Elgar Companion to Neo-Schumpeterian Economics*. Cheltenham: Edward Elgar.

Henrich, J. P., Boyd, R., Bowles, S., Camerer, C., Fehr, E., and Gintis, H. (eds.) (2004). *Foundations of Human Sociality: Economic Experiments and Ethnographic Evidence from Fifteen Small-scale Societies*. Oxford: Oxford University Press.

Hodgson, G. M. (2002). Darwinism in Economics: From Analogy to Ontology. *Journal of Evolutionary Economics*, 12, 259–281.

(2004). *The Evolution of Institutional Economics*. London: Routledge.

Hodgson, G. M. and Knudsen, T. (2010). *Darwin's Conjecture – The Search for General Principles of Social and Economic Evolution*. Chicago: University of Chicago Press.

Hodgson, G. M., Järvinen, J., and Lamberg, J.-A. (2014). The Structure and Evolution of Evolutionary Research: A Bibliometric Analysis of the "Evolutionary" Literature in Management, Economics, and Sociology. Paper presented at the Annual Meeting of the European Association for Evolutionary Political Economy, Paris, 2014.

Hofbauer, J. and Sigmund, K. (1988). *The Theory of Evolution and Dynamical Systems*. Cambridge: Cambridge University Press.

Hoffman, E., McCabe, K., and Smith, V. L. (1996). Social Distance and Other-regarding Behavior in Dictator Games. *American Economic Review*, 86, 653–660.

Holm, J. R., Andersen, E. S., and Metcalfe, J. S. (2017). Confounded, Augmented and Constrained Replicator Dynamics: Complex Selection Models and Their Measurement. *Journal of Evolutionary Economics*, 26, 803–822.

Joosten, R. (2006). Walras and Darwin: An Odd Couple? *Journal of Evolutionary Economics*, 16, 561–573.

Kahneman, D. (2003). Maps of Bounded Rationality: Psychology for Behavioral Economics. *American Economic Review*, 93(5), 1449–1475.

(2013). *Thinking, Fast and Slow*. New York, NY: Farrar, Straus and Giroux.

Klepper, S. (2002). The Capabilities of New Firms and Evolution of the US Automobile Industry. *Industrial and Corporate Change*, 11, 645–666.

Klepper, S. and Simons, K. L. (2005). Industry Shakeouts and Technological Change. *International Journal of Industrial Organization*, 23, 23–43.

Kobayashi, D. (2014). Effects of Anthropology and Archaeology Upon Early Innovation Studies. Paper presented at the International Schumpeter Society Conference, Jena, 2014.

Leslie, J. C. (1996). *Principles of Behavioral Analysis*. Amsterdam: Harwood Academic Publishers.

Levit, G. S., Hossfeld, U., and Witt, U. (2011). Can Darwinism Be "Generalized" and of What Use Would This Be? *Journal of Evolutionary Economics*, 21, 545–562.

Lloyd, E. A. and Gould, S. J. (2017). Exaptation Revisited: Changes Imposed by Evolutionary Psychologists and Behavioral Biologists. *Biological Theory*, 12, 50–65.

Los, B. and Verspagen, B. (2006). The Evolution of Productivity Gaps and Specialization Patterns. *Metroeconomica*, 57, 464–493.

Lumsden, C. J. and Wilson, E. O. (1981). *Genes, Mind and Culture: The Coevolutionary Process*. Cambridge, MA: Harvard University Press.

Lundvall, B.-Å. (ed.) (1992) *National Systems of Innovation. Towards a Theory of Innovation and Interactive Learning*. London: Pinter Publishers.

March, J. G. and Simon, H. A. (1958). *Organizations*. New York, NY: Wiley.

Mas-Colell, A., Whinston, M. D., and Green, J. R. (1995). *Microeconomic Theory*. Oxford: Oxford University Press.

Maynard Smith, J. (1982). *Evolution and the Theory of Games*. Cambridge: Cambridge University Press.

Menger, C. (1985)[1883]. Investigations into the Method of the Social Sciences with Special Reference to Economics (Untersuchungen ueber die Methode der Socialwissenschaften, first published 1883), English translation by F. J. Nock, New York University Press.

Metcalfe, J. S. (1994). Competition, Fisher's Principle and Increasing Returns in the Selection Process. *Journal of Evolutionary Economics*, 4, 327–346.

(2002). On the Optimality of the Competitive Process: Kimura's Theorem and Market Dynamics. *Journal of Bioeconomics*, 4, 109–133.

(2008). Accounting for Economic Evolution: Fitness and the Population Method. *Journal of Bioeconomics*, 10, 23–50.

Metcalfe, J. S., Foster, J., and Ramlogan, R. (2006). Adaptive Economic Growth. *Cambridge Journal of Economics*, 30, 7–32.

Mirowski, P. (1983). An Evolutionary Theory of Economics Change: A Review Article. *Journal of Economic Issues*, 17, 757–768.

Mokyr, J. (1990). *The Lever of Riches – Technological Creativity and Economic Progress*. Oxford: Oxford University Press.

(2002). *The Gifts of Athena – Historical Origins of the Knowledge Economy*. Princeton: Princeton University Press.

Murmann, J. P. (2003). *Knowledge and Competitive Advantage – The Coevolution of Firms, Technology, and National Institutions*. Cambridge: Cambridge University Press.

Nelson, R. R. and Winter, S. G. (1974). Neoclassical vs. Evolutionary Theories of Economic Growth: Critique and Prospectus. *Economic Journal*, 84, 886–905.

(1975). Factor Price Changes and Factor Substitution in an Evolutionary Model. *Bell Journal of Economics*, 6, 466–486.

(1977). Simulation of Schumpeterian Competition. *American Economic Review*, 67 (Papers and Proceedings), 271–276.

(1978). Forces Generating and Limiting Concentration under Schumpeterian Competition. *Bell Journal of Economics*, 9, 524–548.

(1980). Firm and Industry Response to Changed Market Conditions: An Evolutionary Approach. *Economic Inquiry*, 28, 179–202.

(1982). *An Evolutionary Theory of Economic Change*. Cambridge, MA: Harvard University Press.

(2002). Evolutionary Theorizing in Economics. *Journal of Economic Perspectives*, 16, 23–46.

Odling-Smee, F. J., Laland, K. N., and Feldman, M. W. (2003). *Niche Construction – The Neglected Process in Evolution*. Princeton: Princeton University Press.

Popper, K. R. (1960). *The Poverty of Historicism*, 2nd edn. London: Routledge & Kegan Paul.

Richerson, P. J. and Boyd, R. (2005). *Not by the Genes Alone: How Culture Transformed Human Evolution*. Chicago: University of Chicago Press.

Robbins, L. (1932). *An Essay on the Nature and Significance of Economic Science*. London: MacMillan.

Rosenberg, N., Birdzell, L. E. Jr. (1986). *How the West Grew Rich – The Economic Transformation of the Industrial World*. New York, NY: Basic Books.

Roy, D. (2017). Myths about Memes, *Journal of Bioeconomics*, 19, 281–305.

Saviotti, P. P. and Pyka, A. (2008). Micro and Macro Dynamics: Industry Life Cycles, Inter-sector Coordination and Aggregate Growth. *Journal of Evolutionary Economics*, 18, 167–182.

Schumpeter, J. A. (1934)[1912]. *Theory of Economic Development* (Theorie der wirtschaftlichen Entwicklung, first published 1912), Cambridge, MA: Harvard University Press.

(1955). *History of Economics Analysis*. London: Allen & Unwin.

(2002). The Economy as a Whole (seventh chapter of *Theorie der wirtschaftlichen Entwicklung*, 1912). *Industry and Innovation*. 9, 93–145.

Silva, S. T. and Teixeira, A. C. (2009). On the Divergence of Evolutionary Research Paths in the Past 50 Years: A Comprehensive Bibliometric Account. *Journal of Evolutionary Economics*, 19, 605–642.

Simon, H. A. (1955). A Behavioral Model of Rational Choice. *Quarterly Journal of Economics*, 69, 99–118.

(1979). Rational Decision Making in Business Organizations. *American Economic Review*, 69, 493–513.

Smith, V. L. (2015). Adam Smith: Homo Socialis, Yes; Social Preferences, No; Reciprocity Was to Be Explained. *Review of Behavior Economics*, 2, 183–193.

Staddon, J. E. R. (2009). *Adaptive Behavior and Learning*. Cambridge: Cambridge University Press.

Starbuck, W. H. (1963). Level of Aspiration Theory and Economic Behavior. *Behavioral Science*, 8, 128–136.

Tinbergen, N. (1963). On Aims and Methods in Ethology. *Zeitschrift fuer Tierpsychologie*, 20, 410–433.

Trivers, R. L. (1971). The Evolution of Reciprocal Altruism. *Quarterly Review of Biology*, 46, 35–57.

Veblen, T. (1898). Why Is Economics Not an Evolutionary Science? *Quarterly Journal of Economics*, 12, 373–397.

Veblen, T. B. (1899). *The Theory of the Leisure Class – An Economic Study of Institutions*. New York, NY: MacMillan.

(1914). *The Instinct of Workmanship, and the State of the Industrial Arts*. New York, NY: MacMillan.

Wilson, E. O. (2000). *Sociobiology. The New Synthesis*. 25th edn. Cambridge, MA: Belknap Press.

Wilson, D. S. and Sober, E. (1994). Reintroducing Group Selection to the Human Behavioral Sciences. *Behavioral and Brain Sciences*, 17, 585–654.

Winter, S. G. (2014). The Future of Evolutionary Economics: From Early Intuitions to a New Paradigm? *Journal of Institutional Economics*, 10, 613–644.

Witt, U. (2008a). What Is Specific about Evolutionary Economics? *Journal of Evolutionary Economics*, 18, 547–575.

(2008b). Evolutionary Economics. In: Durlauf, S. N. and Blume, L. E. (eds.) *The New Palgrave Dictionary of Economics*, 2nd edn., Vol. 3. New York, NY: Palgrave MacMillan, 67–73.

(2009). Propositions about Novelty. *Journal of Economic Behavior and Organization*, 70, 311–320.

(2017). The Evolution of Consumption and Its Welfare Effects. *Journal of Evolutionary Economics*, 27, 273–293.

Witt, U. and Beck, N. (2015). Austrian Economics and the Evolutionary Paradigm. In: Boettke, P. J. and Coyne C. (eds.), *Oxford Handbook of Austrian Economics*. Oxford: Oxford University Press, 576–593.

Conceptual and Methodological Problems

2 Missed Connections and Opportunities Forgone
A Counterfactual History of Twentieth-Century Economics

BRIAN J. LOASBY

Introduction

The core of orthodox economics is the theory of choice. Now choice cannot be very important unless the available options have significantly different consequences; hence a central concept in economics – certainly in microeconomics – is that of opportunity cost. Yet relatively few contemporary economists pay much attention to the opportunity cost of theory choices – what might have been achieved on the path not taken. Either they believe this cost to be small (for example, the cost of ignoring psychology) or, perhaps more often, they do not ask the question. The objective of this chapter is to encourage economists to ask the question by presenting a sketch of one way in which economics might have developed if theoretical choices had been different. (There is no claim that the alternative presented is the only credible possibility.) The choices to be considered are those of both content and method.

The Creation of Knowledge

We begin with the broadest of contexts for our inquiry. The Renaissance, as its name suggests, signified the recovery of much of the knowledge which had been produced in the Classical period and subsequently lost to Europe but substantially preserved in the Arab world, where it had been further developed. This stimulated the emergence of novel ideas and practices in art, architecture and technology (epitomised by Leonardo da Vinci), from which we can trace the combination of ideas, investigation and experiment which we now sometimes take for granted. The idea of a wide-ranging scientific enterprise may be associated with Francis Bacon, and the notion that such an enterprise could be encouraged by formal organization led to the creation of the Royal Society in 1660.

The apparent success of this expanding programme for the growth of knowledge attracted the attention of one of the greatest philosophers, David Hume, who identified two fundamental problems in understanding this process. 'No kind of reasoning can ever give rise to a new idea' (Hume 1896[1739–40]: 164); and 'even after the observation of the frequent conjunction of objects, we have no reason to draw any inference concerning any object beyond those of which we have had experience' (Hume 1896[1739–40]: 77). In other words, although it is possible to demonstrate (or falsify) the internal coherence and implications of a particular theoretical system, it is not possible to prove that this system embodies an ultimate truth; nor is it possible to construct a new system purely by deduction. Thus established knowledge, in any field, is forever subject to falsification, and new knowledge cannot be attained by logical operations but requires a new combination.

These two propositions apply not only to economic theory, which claims to develop usable knowledge within its own particular field, and may therefore differ in both method and content from other disciplines, such as psychology and sociology, but also to economic systems, which not only rely on knowledge but also allocate substantial resources to the generation of knowledge, the extent and content of which are substantially dependent on the organization of those systems.

What purports to be knowledge is itself a set of elements which are connected in particular ways, with many elements and connections implicitly, and some explicitly, omitted; and each set relies on some principle of organization which seems appropriate to its subject matter. Thus the growth of knowledge is framed by the emergence of fields of knowledge, each with particular ideas of scope and method; and these ideas may change over time. What is distinctive about economics as a discipline is that its proper subject matter is the creation and application of knowledge within economic systems, most of which is scientific, technical, psychological or operational, so we might expect economic theory to be particularly – even primarily – concerned with the influence of organizational arrangements both within and between firms on both the generation and application of knowledge. We should also recognize that neither the creation nor the application of knowledge within economic systems can be adequately treated as a logical operation – either by economists or by practitioners. The bidirectional connections between organization and knowledge provide the theme of this chapter.

Knowledge and Organization

It is not surprising, although certainly not inevitable, that Hume's friend Adam Smith attempted to develop a theory of the growth of knowledge which respected Hume's principles. (The relationship between Smith's and Hume's ideas about human knowledge is discussed by Raphael and Skinner (1980: 15–21) in their General Introduction to Smith's *Essays on Philosophical Subjects*.) The standard title which is applied to Smith's response, 'The History of Astronomy', conceals the fact (embodied in his full title) that he explicitly uses that history as an illustration of a universal theory of the growth of knowledge, which he presents as motivated by attempts to 'lay open the concealed connections that unite the various appearances of nature' (Smith 1980[1795]: 51). In accordance with Hume's constraints, new knowledge is not revealed; it is created by the imagination of new connecting principles. The search for such principles is motivated by the psychological discomfort (or worse) which is provoked by confrontation with the apparently inexplicable, matched by the delight which is produced in particular individuals and groups by their apparent success in imposing order. Later events may destroy that order and prompt a search for a replacement. It is Smith's universal theory which is the foundation of this counterfactual history.

Smith's account shows that, although some kinds of discomfort may be widely shared, it is typically those who are particularly concerned with the effects of a particular phenomenon who are most powerfully motivated to contrive a new kind of order: differentiated foci of attention are crucial. In an important sense, every kind of order within human knowledge is a partial equilibrium, limited in both time and scope – although these limits are not known until they are violated. Not surprisingly, therefore, what seems highly satisfactory for one generation may not satisfy some of their successors, who find an existing scheme of order inadequate in new circumstances or perceive new kinds of disorder, especially when rising standards of living allow some people to encounter new phenomena or to examine existing phenomena more closely. Smith is very careful to avoid any claim that the growth of human knowledge may arrive at the final truth, despite apparently conclusive confirmation, observing that he had been 'drawn in' to present Newton's 'connecting principles ... as if they were the real chains which Nature makes use of to bind together her several operations', rather than an extraordinarily powerful invention of Newton's imagination (Smith 1980[1795]: 105). To enquire how Newton had succeeded in discovering the truth was to ask the wrong question.

The apparently recent theme of the growth of knowledge through conjecture and exposure to refutation, which for older readers may be particularly associated with Karl Popper (e.g., Popper 1963), was therefore created by Smith. The liberating effect of this conception in promising an unending supply of unsolved problems was celebrated by Medawar (1982), Nobel Prize winner for Medicine. There is no closed set of contingencies which might support a general equilibrium of knowledge in any field of science.

Although Smith was critical of the 'man of system' who sought closure, because this would impede the continuing creation of knowledge, he was a natural system builder. Therefore it is not surprising that his *Inquiry into the Nature and Causes of the Wealth of Nations* gives due attention to the effects of organization; but he emphasizes that what has to be organized is a process, in which a great variety of foci does not simply lead to the efficient application of familiar techniques to known resources, but encourages the perception of new problems and inspires new ideas. This combination of efficiency and creativity (which, in Ryle's (1949) terminology, includes both 'knowledge that' and 'knowledge how') is the basis of Smith's theory of economic development through the division of labour; and we should not forget that its effectiveness depended on Smith's principle that '[t]he very different genius which appears to distinguish men of different occupations, when grown up to maturity, is not upon many occasions so much the cause, as the effect of the division of labour' (Smith 1976[1776]: 28). It is this power to create, and not merely to exploit, differences between people in both their skills and their perceptions which makes the organization of the division of labour so crucial in shaping economic performance (and, of course, in many other contexts). Smith's economic theory is founded on his theory of the growth of knowledge.

Because economists' analysis of formal organization has so often been based on the assumption of 'opportunism, defined as self-interest seeking with guile' (Williamson 1996: 6), it is necessary to add that Smith's account of economic development also depends on the argument in his *Theory of Moral Sentiments* that we typically have 'an original desire to please, and an original aversion to offend' others, together with 'not only a desire to be approved of, but a desire of being what ought to be approved of' (Smith 1976[1759]: 116–17); and that we 'sometimes seem ... to be eager to promote the happiness of our fellow-creatures, rather from a view to perfect and improve a certain beautiful system, than from any immediate sense or feeling of what they either suffer or enjoy' (Smith 1976[1759]: 185). Smith is clearly aware that these sentiments must not be overstrained; but they are certainly powerful enough, often enough to reject any simple invocation of the premise that defection always pays – for example, in explaining the boundaries or internal organization of firms. Barnard's (1938) analysis of the functioning of organizations, which was based substantially on his own experience, is consistent with Smith's view. Barnard insisted that successful organizations were necessarily co-operative systems; 'the decision as to whether an order has authority or not lies with the persons to whom it is addressed' (Barnard 1938: 163).

For Smith, therefore, the nature and causes of the wealth of nations were to be found primarily in the organization of their economic systems as means for the generation and application of new productive knowledge. There are, of course, substantial allocation problems here, but the most important of these is the allocation of the potential to generate many kinds of new knowledge. If we accept Smith's vision, then economics may certainly be classed as a science which aims to improve our understanding within a particular field of knowledge, but it is unique in being concerned precisely with the creation and application of knowledge (broadly defined, as we shall see later) within economic systems.

Equilibrium and Equilibration

The divergence between actual and counterfactual history may be identified in Jevons's (1871: 255) definition of the central problem of economics as that of optimal allocation: 'Given, a certain population, with various needs and powers of production, in possession of certain lands and other sources of material: required, the mode of employing their labour so as to maximise the utility of the produce.' Jevons' specification introduces the combination of extreme optimism and extreme pessimism which characterizes general equilibrium theory: the allocation problem is soluble (at least conceptually), but improvements in productive skills and the set of goods beyond those which can be presently envisaged are impossible. Walras was more ambitious and wished to analyse both coherence and change in market systems. He conceived a three-stage research programme. It seemed logical to begin by establishing the possibility of coherence, which was achieved by constructing an existence proof for a competitive general equilibrium which encompassed all the knowledge, which was currently dispersed within an economy. He then intended to demonstrate how that equilibrium configuration could in practice be attained; and he hoped finally to develop a theory of economic growth, in the form of continuous adjustment to changing data. Both the second and third stages relied on tatonnement – a systematic process of trial and error, which Walras conceived as a real-time and real-world process – indeed the only available real-world process.

Having demonstrated existence, he began the second stage with the simplest case: the achievement of equilibrium in highly organized markets for the exchange of well-defined commodities, the total stock of which is fixed – as exemplified by the Paris Bourse, where prices were called by participants and adjusted until the quantities on offer matched the quantities sought. However, since he failed to see the crucial relevance of Menger's concern for transaction costs, which normally (even in the Bourse) caused the seller to receive somewhat less than the buyer paid, he did not ask how highly organized markets came into existence. It is therefore not surprising that he gave no thought to unorganized markets, in which there is no recognized location in which all potential trading partners can be found and no agreed product specification, in which indeed there is no well-defined search space.

Instead Walras turned directly to the equilibration process in production; and he began auspiciously. He recognized that most goods were produced in advance of any specific order, and he offered an explicit theory of entrepreneurship, which had one advantage over the basic model subsequently produced by Kirzner (1973); for his entrepreneurs did not perceive an opportunity which had already emerged, but made conjectures, and even committed themselves to production on the basis of these conjectures. They then quoted a price at which they hoped to dispose of their output. If they could not, they reduced that price; if, on the other hand, they could not supply all their customers, the price would rise. Any divergence between the expected and realized price influenced the next set of production decisions, and if demand and supply curves were well behaved, the economy moved towards equilibrium.

However, because this process of equilibrium depended on trading at disequilibrium prices, which necessarily redistributed income, there was no reason – even ignoring the costs of trading – why the equilibrium which was eventually reached should be the equilibrium that was calculated from the original data. As the process took much longer, it might also be diverted by further acts of entrepreneurship. But if this was so, what was the point of starting with a calculation, or even a proof of existence, of an equilibrium which was unlikely to come about? Walras avoided this problem until 1899; then he resolved it by removing the problem of path dependency from his model, but at the cost of removing his model from the world. In place of a real-world process of trial and error, in which producers' incomes depended on the success of their conjectures, Walras introduced an exchange of pledges between producers and prospective purchasers which was acceptable to all and assumed that trading was completed before production began in order to ensure that the quantity produced would never diverge from that required to clear the market (Walker 1987). Time-dependent production was thus assimilated to highly organized anticipatory exchange.

The expedient of settling everything by contracts before the world is allowed to start turning, without enquiry into the feasibility, or even the costs, of doing so, has become a core convention of general equilibrium theory. This has served for many years to preserve the internal coherence of the theoretical structure and allowed the continued invocation of Pareto optimality as if it were a credible point of reference; but Walras seems to have recognized that it meant the abandonment of his ambition to explain change, which required a response to real-time disequilibrium, and therefore of his hopes for a real-world economics.

This theoretical choice by Walras might be seen as the single defining act of twentieth-century economics. That is not to claim that, had Walras made the opposite choice, economics would have developed along very different lines; on the contrary, I believe that the reasons that led to his decision would in any event have caused most theorists to reveal their preference for formal consistency over more representational theory. (For some the obvious conclusion was that optimality could be achieved only by central planning.) But there was an alternative, and it may help to assess the significance of the choice which is so clearly symbolized by Walras's recourse to his pledges model by considering where that alternative might have led. In doing so we shall note ideas and theories which were conceived but generally ignored or even unnoticed.

Marshall

The leader of the opposition was Alfred Marshall, who in the literal, though not the modern, sense was the most neoclassical of all economists: he shared Adam Smith's view of the central problem of economics as the organization of the growth of human knowledge, recognizing both the limitations and the potential of human thought. He did not prove to be a very effective leader, partly because of his temperament, partly because of his concern for the professionalization of economics, and partly because of the absence of a well-developed theoretical apparatus; yet it does not take much imagination to interpret his *Principles of Economics* as (among other things) an opposition manifesto. I am not suggesting that he ever thought of it as such; but it does appear that he had a good sense of the issues at stake.

As with Walras, his eventual objective was the analysis of change; but Marshall's view of change was much broader. It included, to take two striking examples, changes in individual preferences for the existing set of goods, which he believed were essential to many of the improvements in the quality of life that he wished to see, and 'what Roscher calls a characteristic task of the modern manufacturer, that of creating new wants by showing people something which they had never thought of having before' (Marshall 1961: 280) – a notion which is more readily associated with Schumpeter's conception of disruptive entrepreneurship, whereas a complete general equilibrium system, as modelled by Arrow and Debreu, requires a closed possibility set, to which all agents have already responded optimally.

Marshall believed that it was impossible to deal adequately with change while handling the myriad interactions of a complex economy; and he therefore broke up the problem into manageable parts – which, as we shall see, is how any human system necessarily works.

He therefore took the industry as the primary unit of analysis – but an industry in which ideas were continually being developed, adopted and modified; he selected different time periods to focus on different kinds of change and sought to handle inter-industry effects by giving considerable emphasis to externalities. His long-period analysis did not seek to deduce an equilibrium which was implicit in the original data but described a never-ending process of changing the data through improvements in methods and organization which created new knowledge, leading to lower costs and new products, all of which were both unpredictable and irreversible.

In Shackle's (1965: 36) view,

Marshall's peculiar triumph is his creation of a unity out of the conceptions of equilibrium and of evolution ... Equilibrium is a state of adjustment to circumstances, but it is a fiction, Marshall's own and declared fiction, for it is an adjustment that *would* be attained if the endeavour to reach it did not reveal fresh possibilities, give fresh command of resources, and prepare the way for inevitable, natural, organic further change.

Marshall's (1961: 318) conception of increasing return was a discovery process in real time, relying not on scale but on human ingenuity. This perspective provides a sharp contrast to Samuelson's (1967: 39) judgement: 'Increasing returns is the enemy of perfect competition. And therefore it is the enemy of the optimality conditions that perfect competition can ensure'. We may respond by citing Richardson's (1998[1975]: 353) Gladstonian verdict that 'perfect competition might reasonably be regarded as a denial of Smith's central principle erected into a system of political economy', because its optimality conditions are simply not good enough.

There is indeed a fundamental methodological issue here which is often overlooked. Walras consciously adopted the Cartesian programme and the axiomatic method. Now Marshall had been thoroughly trained in Euclidean geometry at a time when it was commonly believed that Euclidean geometry had succeeded in proving the necessary truth of crucial empirical propositions by axiomatic reasoning. But through his friendship with the mathematician Clifford, when both were Fellows of St John's College between 1868 and 1871, he had learnt of the development of non-Euclidean geometry, which was equally axiomatic, equally coherent, but with very different conclusions, and had recognized its significance for the theory of human knowledge. He had also discovered Cournot's analytical system and tried to adopt it, only to find that Cournot's logic 'led inevitably to things which do not exist and have no near relation to reality' (Marshall 1961, II: 521); and so he had a double reason to be wary of axiomatic reasoning. (There was also a religious dimension which I will not discuss.) Marshall was never prepared to follow his models boldly, because any closed models were necessarily incomplete representations of the world, and therefore were liable to mislead if they were not continually checked. Unlike many subsequent theorists, Marshall was not prepared to assume that if the world was not like the model, then it must be the world which was wrong – a perspective shared by industrial scientists who know that success in the laboratory is very often misleading.

As is now well known, Marshall was much impressed with the ideas of Darwinian evolution. What needs to be emphasized here is that Darwin explained how each species evolved in a particular situation: his theme was the origin of species, not their destination. Neither the emergence nor the perpetuation of any species was predictable. Equilibrium as the terminating point of an equilibrating sequence was a teleological concept more congenial to Darwin's opponents; it was not likely to satisfy Marshall. General equilibrium was particularly unhelpful: as Raffaelli (2008: 37) has pointed out, Georges Cuvier claimed that his 'principle of the correlation of parts', that every element in a living organism is necessarily in a precise relationship with every other part, explained the fossil record of extinct species by their incompatibility with a changed environment and also proved that biological evolution was impossible – just as an Arrow-Debreu equilibrium includes a complete set of contracts for all contingencies and therefore excludes the emergence of any event or innovation hitherto unthought of. Yet there was no comprehensive evolutionary theory available on which Marshall might base his economic analysis. So he attempted to make the best of the closed-system models which he had, while attempting to avoid being locked in to what he declared would eventually prove to be an inferior analytical technology. When confronted with alternatives similar to those faced by Walras in 1899, Marshall consistently took the option that Walras rejected, refusing to close his formal models by depriving them of real-world reference. It was, of course, precisely this policy for which he has been so consistently criticized.

My own criticism would be quite different. Without assuming that Marshall could have invented ideas or techniques of analysis which emerged later, it is possible to argue that he could have extended Adam Smith's theory of economic development through domain-specific motivation to create both theoretical and practical knowledge, by a systematic exploration of his own double proposition that '[k]nowledge is our most powerful engine of production' and that 'organization aids knowledge' (Marshall 1961: 138). This he expressed in his 'general rule' (adopted from Herbert Spencer) of development through a combination of 'increasing subdivision of functions' and 'a more intimate connection between them' (Marshall 1961: 241).

Thanks primarily to the work of Tiziano Raffaelli (summarized in Loasby 2006; Raffaelli 2003, 2006), we now know that Marshall had developed the cognitive basis for his twin principles of economic organization in the late 1860s before he had chosen a specialism but was engaged in discussions of philosophical problems as a member of the Grote Club in the University of Cambridge. In a remarkably austere paper he sought to examine how far the working of the human mind could be explained by pure mechanism. Drawing on ideas from Alexander Bain and Herbert Spencer, but above all from Charles Babbage, he produced a conceptual specification for a 'machine' composed of a 'body', which receives 'impressions' from its environment, and a 'brain', which uses these impressions to generate ideas for actions to be performed by the 'body'. The impressions generated by the perceived result of those actions then either reinforce the connection, if favourable, or stimulate a search for an alternative; successful responses are automatically repeated in apparently similar situations. If nothing works, the problem can be referred to a higher level for what we might call 'trials of concept': these are typically much more expensive in time and energy, and successful performance over time – perhaps even survival – therefore requires a preponderance of routine responses. A world population of identical machines which were located in different environments might then be expected to develop locally appropriate patterns of behaviour, and even in identical environments they might develop different routines if there were several viable options, thus supporting Marshall's (1961: 355) generalization, based on his own observations, that 'even in the same place and the same trade no two persons pursuing the same aims will pursue exactly the same routes', and that this 'tendency to variation is a chief cause of progress'.

Once aware of this early work, it is not difficult to see its compatibility with Marshall's views on industrial organization – in particular, his preference for partial equilibrium and the tendency to variation. What Marshall could not have been expected to know when working out his Babbage-inspired concept was that Prony's success in organizing the production of mathematical tables in France, on which Babbage had drawn, was itself based on Smith's argument that the division of labour was capable of generating substantial differences between people who were inherently very similar. However we may surmise that his own model may have made him more receptive to Smith's central principle of economic development by creating differences when he encountered it later – though there seems to be no evidence that Marshall knew of its ultimate foundation in Smith's fundamental ideas about human knowledge which underpin his 'History of Astronomy'.

Much of the criticism of Marshall is essentially a complaint about his failure to focus on the logic of efficient allocation; but Marshall, like Smith, knew that a focus on efficient allocation was itself a dangerous misallocation of human potential. I have examined elsewhere (Loasby 1990) Marshall's failure to reorganize his five chapters 8–12 on industrial organization (in Book IV) to provide a systematic exposition of his themes of development; what I prefer to emphasize here is their relevance to Book V – his apparently unsatisfactory theory of value.

Samuelson's (1998: 458–9) condemnation of Marshall for adopting 'the gratuitously fuzzy paradigms of *partial* equilibrium analysis: a distinct (and unnecessary) step down from the *general* equilibrium analysis that had been implicit in Cantillon, Smith, and J. S. Mill', reveals a total failure to recognize either the inability of general equilibrium theory to explain innovation or the significance of Adam Smith's conception of the transformative effect of decomposing the economic system into manageable segments for the generation and testing of ideas.

If we appraise this theory as Marshall's equivalent of the first stage of Walras's programme, then it is indeed unsatisfactory; but if one thinks of it as an analysis of equilibrating processes, the outcomes of which are created rather than discovered, then it looks rather impressive – especially now that the attempt to explain how an economy can attain the ideal equilibrium which is supposedly inherent (although inaccessible) in the data has effectively been abandoned. As Hayek (1937: 48) pointed out, 'how much knowledge and what sort of knowledge the different individuals must possess in order that we may be able to speak of equilibrium' is a key issue; indeed 'the "Division of Knowledge" ... seems ... to be the really central problem of economics as a social science' (Hayek 1937: 49). Unfortunately Hayek's paper makes no reference to Marshall's exploration of the creation of knowledge through appropriate organization, which is at the heart of his theory. Since, by Marshall's general rule, the coordination of subdivided functions requires intimate connections, we should not expect to find the anonymity that is a condition of perfect competition; what we find instead is a good deal of personal contact between firms, developed over time, which not only reduces transaction costs but also influences the content of transactions. (Richardson's [1960] exploration of the significance of these relationships, and the consequent inadequacy of a simple juxtaposition of firm and market, was ignored for many years.) Marshall's market structures, as well as his market outcomes, are time-dependent. That they are also rule-dependent is implicit in his treatment, but the importance of rules in economic life has only begun to be appreciated relatively recently, notably in the later work of Hayek.

Marshall begins with an explanation of equilibration in exchange; and, like Walras, he introduces us to a highly organized market. The corn market in a country town is not as highly regulated as the Paris Bourse, but it is not lacking in either rules and conventions or regular traders; and these provide the informational and reputational basis on which the search for an equilibrium price takes place, thus reducing transaction costs. More fundamentally, Marshall never attempts to solve the problem which was posed by Jevons, Walras and modern textbooks, and which Hayek was exploring in his 1937 paper, of producing an equilibrium allocation which is derived from the basic data of the economy, which is presumed to be given; his focus is on the problem of responding to what is perceived by the participants, and to changes in these perceptions. Moreover these responses may be creative – for what attracted Marshall to economics was the prospect of improving the condition of the people, which depended on innovation of many kinds and on many scales – notably including the development of better preferences. (The importance of economists' preferences will receive attention in a later section.) His analysis is forward-looking but historically based, and therefore much closer to the practicalities of management than are optimal planning models.

When we move away from exchange to short-period and long-period analyses of production, the markets inevitably become more diffuse; but they are not totally unorganized. The most distinctive feature of Marshall's treatment – and also the most neglected – is that the organization is undertaken by the participants, in particular by businessmen because they are usually the volume traders. A natural consequence is that goods markets are normally organized by suppliers and labour markets by customers. Unfortunately this observation appeared only in *Industry and Trade* (Marshall 1919) and seemed to have no theoretical relevance – although it might have enhanced Coase's (1937) original analysis of transaction costs. It does sit comfortably within Austin Robinson's (1931) analysis of the working of competitive industry (and Robinson was familiar with *Industry and Trade*), but the idea of producer-organized product markets was incompatible with perfect competition, as Joan Robinson and Chamberlin both realized, drawing similar diagrams but different conclusions from this realization.

Every business requires both an internal and an external organization – a network of trade connections to provide not only a basis for trade but also channels of communication on which to base judgements of how much to produce, how to produce it and what modest changes in product or method might be worth trying. These two forms of organization make up a substantial part of the firm's capital (Marshall 1961: 377), though they do not fit easily into the standard conception of a production function. The transaction costs to which Coase (1937) drew attention are the costs of continuing adjustment to changing perceptions; they are therefore necessarily absent from theories which endow agents with rational expectations. New businesses are most likely to be founded by people with some experience in the trade; but the creation of reliable connections must take time; reputations have to be built, not bought. Thus the market structures within which people act are being continuously modified by the activities themselves. Indeed Marshall combines the second and third stages of Walras's programme into an analysis of an adjustment process which continually changes the data to which it is adjusting – a process which embodies 'development ... from within' at a more fundamental level than Schumpeter (1934: 63) later offered;

for Schumpeter's entrepreneurial new combinations are based on technical change which he thought needed no explanation, whereas Marshall's three forms of business organization – within each firm, between firms undertaking similar activities and between firms whose activities are complementary – served to originate, foster and disseminate technical as well as other kinds of change.

A Counterfactual Theory of the Firm

Now it is just such a pattern of internal organization and external connections within the economics profession which generates the path-dependent evolution of economics as a subject and allows such defining acts as Walras's abandonment of disequilibrium production as a focus of attention to have such momentous consequences. We can now try to imagine how economics might have developed had Walras not abandoned his research programme in 1899 and had Marshall not been prepared to make the best use that he could of partial equilibrium models while awaiting the emergence of evolutionary theory and (perhaps more important) had not continued to produce further editions of the *Principles* instead of publishing much of the material which eventually appeared in *Industry and Trade*.

We could then have avoided the dominance of structure–conduct–performance models and their inadequately founded and often misleading diagnoses of market failure and recognized Chamberlin's (1933) very different concerns: a world of diverse preferences, which firms try to discover by trial and error in markets which they have to organize for themselves, and necessarily incur costs – which we may call transaction costs – in doing so. If Joan Robinson, as she later acknowledged (Robinson 1969: vi), offered 'comparisons of equilibrium positions dressed up to appear to represent a process going on through time', what Chamberlin offered might now be perceived as a theory of processes dressed up to look like a theory of equilibrium; in this counterfactual history he might not have felt impelled to dress it up, but could have faced directly the problems of disequilibrium production and repeated conjectures from which Walras had turned away. Indeed we might have seen Chamberlin's analysis as a Marshallian development of Walras's theory of the entrepreneur, perhaps with an admixture of Schumpeterian innovation. Denis O'Brien (1983: 39–40) noted that Chamberlin was interested in Philip

Andrews's consciously Marshallian analysis but reported that his attempts to make contact seemed to have had little effect. However, Lowell Jacobsen (personal communication) reports that Andrews' papers, deposited at the London School of Economics (LSE), provide evidence of a continuing relationship, impeded by Chamberlin's failing health.

That possibility may seem more plausible if we suppose that Allyn Young, who was Chamberlin's thesis supervisor and had been selected to guide the development of economics at LSE, had not succumbed to a London winter but had survived to pursue his interest in increasing returns into the creation of a theory of economic diversity and the continuing emergence of new markets and to provide continuing guidance to Chamberlin in the lengthy process of developing his thesis into a book. '[C]hange … is qualitative as well as quantitative. No analysis of the forces making for economic equilibrium will serve to illumine this field, for movements away from equilibrium, departures from present trends, are characteristic of it' (Young 1928: 528); and 'the progressive division of labour and specialisation of industries is an essential part of the process by which increasing returns are realised' (Young 1928: 537). Romney Robinson's (1971) appraisal of Chamberlin's work emphasizes the difficulties of corralling economic development, which entails the imagination of new possibilities, within any fully specified model. We would not then have needed Schumpeter (1943: 83) to remind us that an economy 'that at *every* given time fully utilises its possibilities to the best advantage may yet in the long run be inferior to a system that does so at *no* given point of time', because we would have recognized that effectiveness is more important than efficiency, and that optimization is not good enough as a key concept for economic analysis or business management, precisely because it requires all possibilities to be known in advance.

We would have realized that effectiveness in generating and using new knowledge required investment in both internal and external organization in order to focus on particular domains of activity and enquiry. Economists might then not have needed Coase (1937) to draw their attention to the costs of using the price mechanism, which those who read German could have found in Menger's (1981[1871]: Chapter 5) insistence that in organized exchanges the price received by sellers must always be less than the price paid by buyers.

Transaction costs are crucial in all evolving markets because they are costs of acquiring knowledge – as Coase clearly stated but as Williamson's emphasis on opportunism has obscured. Such knowledge costs are precisely what Chamberlin's firms encounter in their attempts to discover and meet some segments of consumer demand; they are what cause the demand curves facing some of Marshall's experimenting firms to be 'very steep' (Marshall 1961: 458) – in a footnote to a paragraph in which 'a great part' of supplementary cost is attributed to investment in external organization. They legitimize the incorporation of marketing in economic theory, not as an obstacle to competition but as an instrument of competition and discovery.

But Allyn Young died, and Lionel Robbins returned to the LSE to provide a powerful impetus towards the modern conception of economics as the logic of choice, to the exclusion of any attention to the institutions or processes of production, which, as exemplified in Book IV of Marshall's *Principles*, yielded only 'insufferable dreariness and mediocrity' (Robbins 1932: 69–70, quoted by Coase 1991: 53). It was perhaps because Robbins feared that Coase's article might become a signpost to dreariness and mediocrity that he never spoke to Coase about it, although they were on good personal terms (Coase 1991: 53). However, we can now see that Coase was implicitly raising Shackle's (1972: preface) objection to Robbins' programme. 'The economic analyst ... assumes that men pursue their interest by applying reason to their circumstances. And he does not ask *how they know* what their circumstances are.' Shackle was fascinated by the workings of business and its fundamental paradox in 'the conflict between our assumption that we know enough for our logic to bite on, and our *essential*, prime dependence on achieving *novelty*, the novelty which by its nature and meaning in some degree discredits what had passed for knowledge' (Shackle 1970: 155). Coase and Shackle were at the LSE between 1935 and 1939 but failed to make a methodological connection: In our counterfactual history, what might they have accomplished?

Transaction cost economics had the potential to become one of the more useful developments in the subject; but that usefulness has been limited precisely because 'discussion of "production" is an integral part of the theory of equilibrium', as Robbins (1932: 70) desired, rather than an exploration of ways of organizing a process, formal and informal, which both embodies and encourages change within particular domains – on which Marshall had focussed his attention. This necessarily requires the continuing management of transactions both within and between firms. However, the conceptual basis of much contemporary transaction cost economics is the extension, with important modifications, of rational choice theory to the most efficient choice of governance structures. In our counterfactual history we would not have found it so easy to assume, as transaction cost theorists almost always do, that production costs, unlike transaction costs, do not differ between transaction modes, because such an assumption is not appropriate in a microtheory which is focussed on the process of competitive cost reduction and product improvement. We might then have had more to contribute to the contemporary discussion in business strategy of distinctive competences, which are not natural givens but the consequences, not always intended, of human choices, including choices of organizational arrangements.

We would also have recognized, as Casson (1982) notably and exceptionally did, that it is often possible to reduce the direct cost of particular transactions by appropriate investment in transaction technology, and that this may be done not only by the creation of a firm but also (and in Casson's analysis, especially) by making a new market. This is all thoroughly Marshallian. This is not to say that what Casson has done is all in Marshall; on the contrary, Casson's analysis of market-making is distinctive and important.

The importance of investment, in management and marketing as well as in production, has been emphasized by Chandler (1990), whose theme is the creation of capabilities; and the creation of capabilities, in both individuals and working groups, including inter-company relationships as emphasized by Richardson (1972), is an investment that can justify additional costs if owners and managers are prepared to take a long view. This theme clearly has at its core the generation of increasing return through improved organization, which (unlike perfect competition) is not a denial but an adaptation of Smith's central principle. Smith wished to explain increasing productivity and argued that the system of natural liberty – a combination of freedom and competition – operating through an ever-expanding division of labour possessed a greater capacity for delivering such increases than any other system that was available.

A slight formalization of Marshall's own treatment of the firm's physical and – especially – intellectual capital would have provided a link to the interest of Menger and his successors in complexity and complementarity in capital structures and to Menger's interest, which was neglected by his successors, in the factors influencing the marketability of commodities. (How many economists know of Rogers's (1962) theoretical and empirical work on the diffusion of innovations, in which he sought to analyse the factors which influence customers' decisions?) This link would improve our understanding of organizational capabilities and their significance for organizational success and failure in ways that are beyond the reach of theories which invoke unitary firms, capital aggregates and well-defined contingency sets. But the concept of the firm as a complex organization – indeed as any kind of organization – faded into the shadows, and even Coase's (1937) explanation of the reason why such organizations emerged did not lead to any curiosity among economists about how they worked. Indeed, analyses of what organizations do, as distinct from how they are chosen, are not a prominent feature of transaction cost economics, as Coase (1991: 65) complained.

It was therefore left for Penrose (1959) to examine the process by which a firm developed its distinctive and ever-changing capabilities within an administrative framework, which is itself subject to change through the actions of its managers and their interpretation of the consequences. This is a path-dependent theory of the interaction between the creation of knowledge through reason and experiment and the changing division of labour which owes nothing to optimization models but which can be seen as a natural development of the sequence from Smith to Marshall – although, because of the exclusion of Marshall's ideas about the organization of knowledge from the teaching of economics, that is not how it came into existence. By her own account, Penrose accepted the task of applying standard theory to the results of an empirical study of growing firms, only to find that theory inadequate, and produced a new theory which worked, thus providing a remarkable example of the unintended consequences of supposedly rational choice as a driver of innovation. She was happy to acknowledge the relevance of Marshall's work, both in conversation and in her preface to the 1995 edition (Penrose 1995), but less happy that her own education had given her no hint of this relevance.

'It is not the *degree* of abstraction involved in the "theory of the firm" that makes it inappropriate as a starting point for an analysis of the growth of the firm, but rather the *kind* of abstraction' (Penrose

1959: 15). Though every firm may be described as a collection of assets, which requires an appropriate system of governance, '[i]t is the heterogeneity, and not the homogeneity, of the productive services available or potentially available from its resources that gives each firm its unique character' (Penrose 1959: 75). The range of potential services obtainable from any resource is not transparent or describable by a probability distribution, but is subject to fallible conjecture. (Schumpeter's entrepreneur makes large-scale conjectures about the bundle of services which may be obtained from a particular combination of resources.) Moreover each firm's character changes, in ways that can never be fully anticipated, as a consequence of the particular processes of operation and expansion which are chosen. In such an environment the 'threat of competition from new products, new techniques, new channels of distribution, new ways of influencing consumer demand, is in many ways a more important influence on the conduct of existing producers than any other kind of competition' (Penrose 1959: 113); and in a world of Knightian uncertainty, where there is no credible basis for assigning probabilities to a closed set of possibilities, 'the primary problem or function is deciding what to do and how to do it' (Knight 1921: 268). However, the effective management of productive opportunities which are generated as a consequence of each firm's particular processes of operation and expansion does not figure prominently in most economic analyses of corporate governance.

In our counterfactual history the equivalent of Penrose's theory might have been produced twenty, or even thirty, years earlier, building on the analyses of Allyn Young and his students Frank Knight and Chamberlin. It might then have provided a secure basis for Philip Andrews's investigations into the competitive behaviour of firms; and he would not have felt it necessary to concentrate on attempting to demonstrate the inadequacies of a theory of the firm in which the firm as an organization did not exist. Unfortunately his criticism of equilibrium modelling was published fifteen years after his own theory of real-world competition, instead of preparing the ground for it (Andrews 1949, 1964).

Andrews followed Marshall in believing that one could discover something of relevance to understanding the working of economic systems by visiting firms and talking to managers. I can provide two examples of such discoveries from my own experience. Between 1958 and 1961 I was investigating the government policy of moving both firms and people from Birmingham to 'overspill areas' in small towns. For this the standard theory of the firm seemed irrelevant – a view shared by a Cambridge economics graduate who had abandoned his postgraduate studies after a year for a job in industry. So I decided to visit the firms directly affected by this policy. Those managers whose transfer was complete or well advanced were keen to point out that, although their motivation was invariably the need for more space, the prime benefit was the increased efficiency which had been generated by rethinking their ways of operating. For some, these gains made the move formally unnecessary; but as they pointed out, efficiency was not the problem which had dominated their attention. Cognition is itself a scarce resource – as the peculiar history of economic theorizing shows. Some years later W. H. Smith deliberately chose the relocation of their supply centre as the instrument for a complete reconfiguration of their distribution system – to which the location of the supply centre was formally irrelevant; and when their first choice as supply manager, very familiar with their ways, retired due to ill health, they deliberately chose as his successor someone who had no experience of their particular activities – with excellent results (Loasby 1973). In business, in economics and in any field of study, the first requirement is to define the problem (and to switch to other problems at the right time); and the fundamental objection to rational choice theory is its assumption that the correct definition is already known by the economic agents who populate their models – and, most dangerously, by the economists who use them.

In the alternative scenario of this counterfactual history, it is hardly conceivable that Downie's (1958) explicitly Marshallian account of an evolutionary process of development from within, in which competition both transfers resources to the more efficient and stimulates improvements in efficiency, could have been so completely neglected, or that Andrews, Downie and Richardson should have had so little contact while they were all in Oxford – even allowing for the well-known peculiarities of Oxford. Richardson was advised by John Hicks, who was otherwise supportive, that contact with Andrews would not help his career.

Penrose's analysis provides an appropriate theoretical basis for Chandler's historical and comparative studies (Chandler 1962), as Chandler has acknowledged, because it addresses the central issue which was posed by Smith and Marshall: the organization of the growth of knowledge. This theme is not directly addressed either by transaction cost theory in its present form or by the agency theory of the firm, because neither can admit the growth of knowledge, except by Bayesian updating of probabilities – which is not, one can safely say, what makes economic development possible.

However, development does not depend entirely on what happens within firms, or even on what is managed by each firm in its environment, as Lazonick (1992) claimed; and so a theory of the growth of the capabilities of the firm needs to be balanced by a theory of the growth of capabilities within a set of market relationships. Within our counterfactual history such a theory finds its natural place. The organization of the firms in one industry provides for variety and the organization of firms in different industries permits complementarities and varying degrees of co-operation – in which high transaction costs may sometimes be justified by the discoveries that result from developing connections with people who have different ideas and organize them differently. The extension of Penrose's theory of capabilities to the development of capabilities within networks of firms was achieved by Richardson (1972) – in what is an exemplar of the creation of interpersonal capabilities within academic communities. (Their mutual recognition of the complementarities between their analyses is one of the happier episodes in the history of economics.) How the relative advantages of firms and markets evolve with the evolution of knowledge, from diffuse search across an industry through the management of innovation within a single enterprise, to continuous improvement within a modular (or decomposable) system has been explored by Langlois (1988, 1992); in our counterfactual history he would be one among many economists explaining how our economies actually work. They would be accompanied by credible explanations of how interactions between economists have shaped their capabilities and therefore their products.

Institutions and Knowledge

Coase (1988: 3) summarized a major consequence of the actual process of the development of capabilities within our profession in his complaint that economists' devotion to rational choice equilibria has given us 'firms without organization, and even exchange without markets'. In conventional models individuals deal directly with the problems that they face, in all their complexity, and have no need for any structure to help them to cope – quite unlike professional economists, whose expertise is highly dependent on their shared conventions. But in our counterfactual history of economics, analysis is founded on the proposition that boundedly rational human beings (including economists) face an unknowable future – and indeed a less-than-completely-knowable present and past; like professional economists, they therefore need some limits within which they might be rational. Such limits are supplied by a host of institutions, which vary enormously in their prescriptiveness and power – for example, from the decision premises which are provided by a corporate plan or the criteria of professional performance to the regulations of an organized exchange or the customary practices of a drinking party. But it is worth remembering that even the general social rules which Hayek came to see as the framework of civilization are the product of countless decisions, while the most carefully crafted procedure is liable to have unintended consequences. The distinction between pragmatic and unintended institutions is convenient for organizing our own knowledge, but it is not sufficient to support a complete theory of governance structures. Natura non facit saltum.

The counterfactual economics presented here is a study of processes, and all orderly processes require institutions; these institutions need not – indeed should not – be static, but in order to be effective they must change more slowly than the processes which they support. Institutions are not exempt from the effects of bounded rationality and imperfect knowledge; if we knew enough to compute the expected value of an institution, we could manage very well without it. As Coase (1937) explained, it is because we do not know what we shall want done that we hire people as employees rather than entering into specific contingent contracts; it is because we don't know how to find an Arrow-Debreu equilibrium that we need continuous markets. Both are 'means by which choice can be deferred until a later and better-informed time' (Shackle 1972: 160), like the means which Shackle had in mind and which we shall consider shortly. But the reasons for developing both sets of institutions imply that we cannot know that they are optimal in the conventional sense.

Since economists in our counterfactual world analyse both firms and markets as structures which help us to cope with the imperfections of our knowledge and provide a framework for improving it, they would naturally draw on theories of the growth of knowledge and of the development of knowledge communities, as Smith and Marshall did. The institutions by which knowledge is mobilized and within which it is developed help to explain both the extent of co-ordination and the kind of knowledge which is produced. In a firm or a market, as in an academic discipline, the assumptions and conventions which imprecisely define a research programme or a paradigm, a business strategy or a corporate culture, a set of trading practices and market relationships, both deepen and limit the potential for improving knowledge by the particular kinds of interactions which they facilitate. Institutional structures matter.

They matter not only because of their effects, but because the more important institutions can rarely be quickly or easily changed. Market networks provide a clear example. The creation of a market is a capital investment; that presumably is why many organized markets were originally established by kings, lords or local magistrates, who saw the prospect of recovering their investment in dues and taxes. Such is the origin of many corn markets in country towns. Marshall did not pause to explain this, although as noted earlier he indicated in *Industry and Trade* how less formally organized markets can develop as a result of investment by a series of traders or manufacturers, all seeking to integrate their own knowledge with that of potential trading partners, but creating between them a network of external economies. Marshall (1961: 318) defined his law of increasing return in these words: 'An increase of labour and capital leads generally to improved organization, which increases the efficiency of the work of labour and capital'. This is a core Smithian proposition. There seems to be no reason why that law should not apply to a firm's external organization, nor to the sum of the investments in a particular market by many firms. One firm's external organization necessarily contributes to the external organization of other firms: regular customers, for example, must have regular suppliers. The role of industry standards has received some attention; but the externalities of market-making are far more extensive. We must also remember that this process takes time: well-founded relationships require experience and the gradual emergence of a network of social rules, many of which are not the product of 'rational choice' nor even explicit. Perfect competition is not at all what is wanted; a network of reliable trading partners is.

That different institutions produce different systems, and that it is not easy to extract oneself from a well-travelled path which now seems mistaken, are propositions which are also applicable to business organizations. They explain the eventual disappearance of the great majority – a phenomenon which prompted Chester Barnard's institutionalist study of management; this study is appropriately accompanied by an appendix on the crucial role of nonlogical processes in human affairs, and not least in running a business (Barnard 1938: 301–22). The study of institutions is closely linked with the study of capabilities – which may indeed be regarded as particular kinds of institutions. Neither have any place in a universe of closed-system models in which all actions are calculated and all contingencies foreseen. But if we look around, we can see that a great amount of economic activity is devoted to the creation and maintenance of capabilities. Anything beyond the most narrowly vocational kind of education, and the majority of investments, for example, are intended to create capacities for future actions, and for future learning, few of which are adequately represented by formal models of rational choice.

This is true at all levels, from the economy to each individual. Indeed one advantage of this counterfactual economics is that it provides a direct link between the study of the economy and the study of inequality, as that has been defined by Sen (1992). The degree to which each person is capable of choosing, responding or initiating – whether by using resources which are already available or through access to resources elsewhere – is more relevant, Sen argues, than the possession of some supposedly optimal consumption bundle. A similar concept might be applied to monopoly policy: Do the actions of a supposed monopolist significantly reduce the capabilities of other firms, or of consumers, when judged in the context of imperfect knowledge, bounded rationality and the capacity to innovate in thought and deed?

A Counterfactual Macroeconomics

The potential for the integration of theory can be extended to macroeconomics by drawing on one of the most important missed connections in twentieth-century economics: that between Coase's article in *Economica* and another published in the same journal earlier in the same year by an already-distinguished member of the LSE on the theme of 'Economics and Knowledge', having been presented to the London Economic Club in the previous November. In our counterfactual sequence, Hayek's (1937) insistence that co-ordination depends on the use of dispersed and incomplete knowledge provides a link between Marshall's theme of the need to organize knowledge and Coase's reminder of the costs involved in such organization – which Marshall, as we have seen, did not ignore. Since real-world equilibration processes must be organized, they may fail because the costs of organizing them are too high. Neither Coase nor Hayek gave attention to this possibility, but in our counterfactual environment we might reasonably expect them to do so. That would bring them into direct contact with Keynes's (1936) theory, in which involuntary unemployment is linked to the absence of that knowledge which is a prerequisite of microequilibrium theory and also of new classical macroeconomics.

Coase's explanation of the firm is neoclassical in Marshall's, not the modern, sense since it relies on entrepreneurs' imperfect knowledge of how they would wish to use resources in the future. This is implicit, but unrecognized, in Austin Robinson's (1931) explanation of the working of competitive industry, which is presented in a sequence of chapters as a continuing search for subsystem optima which are continually changing and then for the reconciliation of these suboptima. But if knowledge is insufficient, it must be supplemented by confidence in those elements of the future which are particularly relevant to each specific project; and if businessmen have insufficient confidence in any commitment that they can think of, resources may simply be left unused. This explanation of depression has a long history but fell out of favour with macroeconomists who were fascinated by the mathematical potential of rationality: those who appeared to be unemployed were actually maximizing their utility by choosing leisure while wages were low and employment when wages rose in the future. The crucial role of confidence in investment decisions and the implications for employment – including the likelihood of cumulative effects – is clearly identified, although not analysed, in the last chapter of Marshall's *Principles* (Marshall 1961: 710–11), in a passage which, as Marshall notes, is reproduced from *The Economics of Industry* (Marshall and Marshall 1879).

It is not possible to provide a sound analytical basis for any practical macroeconomic theory which excludes uncertainty. It cannot be a monetary theory, for without uncertainty there is no role for money, as Hicks (1982: 7) discovered eighty years ago. If, however, co-ordination requires knowledge, then it should be no surprise that the absence of knowledge, or even the costs of acquiring it, could be the source of co-ordination failure, even on a very large scale – as in Russia after the collapse of the Soviet Union or in the USA and much of Europe in 2008. Nor should it be a surprise that failure to co-ordinate the real economy should be associated, as both cause and consequence, with monetary disorder. Theories which recognize the imperfections of knowledge can neither exclude money nor confine their departures from conventional theory to monetary institutions.

But Hayek was not yet prepared to abandon general equilibrium as an organizing principle. Despite his assertion that 'hypotheses or assumptions that people do learn from experience, and about how they acquire knowledge ... constitute the empirical content of our propositions about what happens in the real world' (Hayek 1937: 45), he turned away from the examination of such hypotheses to the apparently easier problem of 'how much knowledge and what sort of knowledge the different individuals must possess in order that we may be able to speak of equilibrium' (Hayek 1937: 48). He still placed too much faith in prices as sufficient statistics. Though he made what is probably the first reference by any economist to Karl Popper's (1963 [1934]) *Logic of Scientific Discovery*, it was only in connection with the testing of economic theories – not the testing of the informal and sometimes implicit theories on which we rely all the time.

Had he taken what now seems the obvious step of applying the Popperian combination of conjecture and exposure to refutation to the formulation and testing of plans in the economy, he would have had a basis for analysing co-ordination processes which could accommodate the ideas of Marshall, Chamberlin and Coase, and also of those Swedish economists, notably Lindahl, Myrdal and Ohlin, who had developed a sequence analysis in which plans were based on expectations that were known to be fallible and then revised in the light of perceived outcomes. In such an analysis, instead of attempting to show how disequilibrium production could lead to a predetermined equilibrium – the strategy which Walras had tried and abandoned – the focus would have been on a sequence of disequilibrium production plans which are continually adjusted in response both to the refutations of elements of past conjectures and to the apparent implications of novel conjectures – some of which might induce a refusal to make any substantial commitments, as Keynes argued.

At the centre of such analysis we might find Shackle's (1949, 1969) theory of choice, which was designed for a world in which decision makers cannot know what their circumstances are. We should not rely on the intuition of Schumpeterian entrepreneurs because, contrary to Schumpeter's implicit assumption, 'the capacity of seeing things in a way which afterwards proves to be true' (Schumpeter 1934: 85) is in practice inextricably entangled with the capacity for seeing things in ways which afterwards prove to be false – notably in the creation of financial instruments based on theories which assume the possibility of ensuring protection against all eventualities, which have a long history of failure.

We might venture to explore the sources of imagination; we certainly ought to explore the institutional constraints on imagination and the distribution of these constraints within and between markets and firms. This Darwinian idea is embedded in Marshall's analysis, even in the apparently technical 'principle of substitution', which entails the generation and testing of alternatives, as in Marshall's early model of 'Ye machine' (Raffaelli 2006). Within this mode of analysis, co-ordination, both micro and macro, would necessarily be problematic; some degree of 'failure' would hardly be avoidable, and indeed would be a major stimulus to progress, as it is in Popperian accounts of the growth of knowledge, and in Smith's theory. Ideas which prove unsatisfactory may be shaped towards success, often by others, who make new connections.

There would be no need to distinguish between microeconomics and macroeconomics. There would, however, be a great deal of attention paid to the ways in which forms of organization aid or impede the growth and use of knowledge, and the ways in which these forms of organization themselves evolve, change and decay. (Exchange rate regimes come readily to mind.) The natural focus of this attention would be on firms and markets, but there is no reason why it should not also include voluntary organizations and governments.

Human Knowledge and the Human Mind

The opening section of the 2000 Report of the Max Planck Institute for Research in Economic Systems contained a review of the work of the Institutional Economics Unit, which closed in that year because of the retirement through illness of its founder, Manfred Streit. In a retrospective article Streit (2000: 4) insists that 'the basic function of institutions is ... to channel the activities of actors who have a constitutional lack of knowledge [and] to allow a co-ordination of economic activities and their control by competitive actions'. Appropriate and effective institutions within any organization and in any field of study lower the costs of transactions; but institutions cannot be created by individual choice. In the following article Stefan Voigt (2000: 9) notes that Streit's (1992, 1993) obituaries of Hayek 'interpret Hayek's *Sensory Order* as the centrepiece of his work from which all else could be understood more easily'.

Before briefly examining the content of this understanding, we may note that the analysis developed in *The Sensory Order* is an unintended consequence of Hayek's desire to understand the variety of behaviour among the units of the Austrian army which he had witnessed after the Armistice in 1918. This prompted him to study psychology and – crucially – its physiological basis, leading to his identification of 'the transmission of impulses from neuron to neuron ... as the apparatus of classification' within the brain (Hayek 1952: 52). But although he felt he 'had found the answer to an important problem', he 'could not explain precisely what the problem was' (Hayek 1952: v), and so put aside his work for a few years – which turned out to be much longer. The question he subsequently identified was why 'events which to our senses appear to be of the same kind may have to be treated as different in the physical order, while events which physically may be of the same or at least a similar kind may appear as altogether different to our senses' (Hayek 1952: 4).

For this chapter the central points of Hayek's analysis may be summarized in his own words. First, '[a]ny apparatus of classification must possess a structure of a higher degree of complexity than is possessed by the objects that it classifies and that, therefore, the capacity of any explaining agent must be limited to objects with a structure possessing a degree of complexity lower than its own' (Hayek 1952: 185). Thus no human brain can fully explain its own operations, let alone the operations of a group of humans, and certainly not the working of an economic system, even if this is not changing. Second, 'what we perceive can never be unique properties of individual objects but always only properties which the objects have in common with other objects' (Hayek 1952: 142); our interpretation depends on the classification systems which we employ, and many such systems are conceivable. Therefore the key decision is what objects should be grouped together for what purposes – a decision which may be crucial for a firm or a field of study. Third, 'all we know about the world is of the nature of theories, and all "experience" can do is to change those theories' (Hayek 1952: 143); and, as Hayek well knew, 'experience' provides the motive for seeking such change, but not the replacement theory. (This may be regarded as a drastic summation of Smith's view of 'The Principles Which Lead and Direct Philosophical Enquiries'.) Fourth, we may need to apply formally incompatible theories to a set of objects for different purposes, as indeed 'the physical sciences have been forced to define the objects of which this world exists increasingly in terms of the observed relationships between these objects, and at the same time to disregard the way in which these objects appear to us' (Hayek 1952: 2–3) – these appearances being 'a set of relationships by which our nervous system classifies them' (Hayek 1952: 143). Fifth, 'all we can ever learn from experience are generalizations about certain kinds of events, and since no number of particular instances can ever prove such a generalization, knowledge based entirely on experience may yet be entirely false' (Hayek 1952: 168).

Hayek was apparently unaware that this final principle had been established by David Hume and had helped to stimulate Adam Smith's (1980[1795]: 105) conception of 'all philosophical systems as mere inventions of the imagination'. As we have seen, Smith applied this conception even to Newton's cosmology, which was so successful in linking phenomena into a comprehensive system that, as Smith observes, he had been 'insensibly drawn in to make use of language expressing [its] connecting principles as if they were the real chains which Nature makes use of to bind together her several operations'. In Smith's lectures on rhetoric, delivered a few years later than the apparent date of his 'History of Astronomy', he illustrated the special appeal of a unifying principle as 'ingenious and for that reason more engaging' by citing not only Newton's system but also the Cartesian system which 'does not perhaps contain a word of truth' (Smith 1983: 146). Schemes for economizing the scarce resource of individual human cognition can be extraordinarily effective – and extraordinarily dangerous. The assumption of closed possibility sets, each with its closed set of consequences, in order to facilitate the calculation of optima and equilibria may induce disastrous actions.

If we now make the counterfactual assumption that Hayek had drawn the conclusions which appeared in *The Sensory Order* before writing his paper on 'Economics and Knowledge', to which we have already referred, then his argument that 'the *Division of Knowledge* ... seems to be the really central problem of economics as a social science' (Hayek 1937: 49) might have inspired two major comments. The first is a warning that this divided knowledge, which is typically expressed in different classification systems, can easily lead different people to impose incompatible interpretations on significant reports or data sets, and consequently to make incompatible decisions. This possibility is obviously relevant to analyses of the economic situation in the 1930s (and more recently); it may also cause problems in the management of any substantial business. However, it is this division of knowledge, as a response to the limitations and potential of human cognition, which drives economic progress. It also drives progress in the natural sciences, and is manifest in the division between sciences and within each science, and in the universal use of artificial closure, achieved by experimental design, to identify partial equilibria as a route to wider knowledge, as argued extensively by Ziman (2000). It may do so in economics.

The implications of the great disparity between the powers of the individual human brain and the complexity of the human environment also attracted the attention of the psychologist George Kelly, whose work deserves attention here for three reasons. The first is that, like Hayek in 1918, Kelly was looking for a better psychological understanding, although what he perceived as the prime obstacle to this understanding was the commitment of the leaders of the profession to deal only with observables, as so many economists seem committed to equilibria, such as the Arrow-Debreu system, which are unobservable. This methodological imperative for professional psychologists is the primary reason why, on returning to his early work, Hayek found that the problem which he had been exploring had received very little attention from psychologists (Hayek 1952: vi); so the internal history of psychology is part of the Hayek story. The second reason is that he was advocating a system which shares major features with Hayek's, although his major work, published in 1955, gives no indication that he knew anything about *The Sensory Order*. The third reason is that Kelly's work was identified by a successful innovator and manager of innovation as both a stimulus and a guide to alternative ways of thinking.

The first three chapters were republished in 1963. Instead of the notion of 'science' as a distinctive category, Kelly begins with the idea of 'man-as-scientist', trying to make sense of at least parts of the universe by 'transparent patterns or templets which he creates and then attempts to fit over the realities of which the world is composed. The fit is not always very good. ... Even a poor fit is more helpful to him than no fit at all' (Kelly 1963: 8–9). In Hayekian terms Kelly asserts that '[e]xperience is made up of the successive construing of events. It is not constituted merely by the succession of events themselves' (Kelly 1963: 73). Moreover, although 'there are always some alternative constructions available to choose among in dealing with the world', the search for improvement 'is repeatedly halted by the damage to the system that will apparently result from the alteration of a subordinate construct' (Kelly 1963: 15, 9). These interactions between problems and possibilities are pervasive both in the functioning of economic systems and in the attempt to understand such systems – or in any other complex field of enquiry.

The importance of recognizing the implications of the extreme disparity between the complexity of the universe and the capacity of the individual human brain was also a persistent theme in the work of Herbert Simon, whose conception of human powers and limitations, and the consequent significance of the division of labour and organizational arrangements, and also of the crucial importance of different perspectives, were far closer to Hayek's ideas about the necessary limitations of human cognition than either of them realized – the chief difference being Simon's much greater focus on what happens in formal organizations. '[W]hen perception and cognition intervene between the decision-maker and his objective environment ... the perceived world is fantastically different from the "real" world. The differences involve both omissions and distortions, and arise in both perception and inference' (Simon 1982[1959]: [272] 306).

Simon's (1969) argument that the evolution of complex systems in the presence of external shocks and internal variation was made possible by a hierarchical structure which allowed a substantial scope for variation within each unit while protecting other units from resulting problems (illustrated by the advantages of producing watches by a sequence of sub-assemblies) has the direct implication that change requires decomposability – and the capacity and incentive to exploit it. Indeed our capacity to understand our environment, from working group to the universe, depends on decomposability: we can explain, and sometimes control, a major system by making simple assumptions about its components, and we can explain, and sometimes control, small systems by making simple assumptions about the influence of their particular environment. This is a pervasive theme in John Ziman's (2000) explanation of the workings of science, including the broad division into the recognized sciences, with their distinctive fields of interest and distinctive ideas about appropriate research methods, appropriate questions and appropriate answers. Intersubjective pattern recognition is of crucial importance in each science (as indeed it is in economics); but what kinds of patterns are acceptable differs between sciences – and this may be occasionally subject to a drastic revision which may be labelled a change of paradigm.

A remarkable example of a research programme in economics which attempted to incorporate the recognition of both human limitations and human potential into a theory which was based on agents searches for better equilibria has been provided by Frank Hahn, who is perhaps better known as an exponent and advocate of general equilibrium theory. In his Cambridge inaugural lecture in 1974 Hahn followed such an exposition and advocacy by arguing for another concept of economy-wide equilibrium, which would be 'sequential in an *essential* way' and incorporate expectations and uncertainty (Hahn 1984[1974]: 53). In the kinds of model which he was advocating, agents would rely on theories which are 'simple enough to be intellectually and computationally feasible', and would periodically replace them when they were 'sufficiently and systematically falsified' (Hahn 1984[1974]: 58, 59). (This seems remarkably like Simon's idea of economic progress, especially if we assume that the agent's in Hahn's system all relied on locally appropriate theories, and also remarkably like Kelly's (1963: 8) idea of developing and amending construction systems to interpret events and choose actions.)

Whether he consciously intended his proposal to apply to the behaviour of economic theorists as well as economic agents, we do not know; what we can observe from later writings is that he became increasingly conscious that economics would 'return to its Marshallian affinities to biology', adopt historical modes of analysis, become far more concerned with the complexities of particular problems (Hahn 1991: 48, 49, 50) and recognize uninsurable uncertainties and the need for a managerial theory of the firm (Hahn 1993: 209, 215).

In all these respects we can perceive the relevance of Hayek's (and Kelly's) perspective on human behaviour, and of Streit's emphasis on the importance of domain-relevant institutions as a prime means of economizing the scarce resource of individual human cognition.

We therefore seem to be back to the evolution of knowledge through the division of labour, which Smith and Marshall emphasized, and which seems best analysed by theories of partial equilibria – within which we may include the hierarchy of partial equilibria (including the overall summary perspective) which constitute a decomposable system. That all these equilibria are partial provides scope for multilevel searches for better equilibria. Most fundamentally, we have an approach to theory building which is concerned not only with the growth of knowledge within the community of economists but also the growth of knowledge within real economic systems. This is the true tradition of Adam Smith.

Conclusion

In this counterfactual history we would sacrifice some of the formal elegance of the economics that we have had – although we seem to be sacrificing much of that anyway as models multiply and axiomatization is subverted by instrumentalism. In its place we would have the unifying principles suggested by Marshall and Menger: differentiation and integration, structures of human and physical capital of increasing complexity and therefore of increasing power but also of increasing vulnerability, and an emphasis on institutions as ways of providing the capabilities which allow people to cope, in varying degrees, with an unknowable future. These institutions guide evolution; but they also emerge from an evolutionary process. We would not have needed to wait for the development of biological theories, which are of greater help in raising questions for economists than in suggesting the most appropriate ways of dealing with them. Had the remarkable efforts that have been devoted to producing the actual history of twentieth-century economics been committed instead to this counterfactual history, is it not possible that we would now be enjoying an economics that was more unified, more highly developed in many respects and more useful, being able to offer real help with major real-world problems, instead of an economics that produces advice which has sometimes done, and is still doing, great damage?

References

Andrews, P. W. S. 1949. *Manufacturing Business*. London: Macmillan.

1964. *On Competition in Economic Theory*. London: Macmillan.

Barnard, C. I. 1938. *The Functions of the Executive*. Cambridge, MA: Harvard University Press.

Casson, M. 1982. *The Entrepreneur: An Economic Theory*. Totowa, NJ: Barnes and Noble Books.

Chamberlin, E. 1933. *The Theory of Monopolistic Competition: A Reorientation of the Theory of Value*. Cambridge, MA: Harvard University Press.

Chandler, A. D. 1962. *Strategy and Structure: Chapters in the History of the Industrial Enterprise*. Cambridge, MA: MIT Press.

1990. *Scale and Scope: The Dynamics of Industrial Capitalism*. Cambridge, MA: Belknap Press.

Coase, R. H. 1937. The Nature of the Firm. *Economica*, N. S. 4, 386–405.

1988. *The Firm, the Market, and the Law*. Chicago: University of Chicago Press.

1991. The Nature of the Firm: Meaning. In: Williamson, O. E. and Winter, S. G. (eds.) *The Nature of the Firm: Origins, Evolution and Development*. Oxford, UK: Oxford University Press.

Downie, J. 1958. *The Competitive Process*. London: Duckworth.

Hahn, F. 1984[1974]. On the Notion of Equilibrium in Economics. *Equilibrium and Macroeconomics*. Oxford, UK: Basil Blackwell.

1991. The Next Hundred Years. *The Economic Journal*, 101, 47–50.

Hahn, F. H. 1993. *Incomplete Market Economies. Keynes Lecture in Economics*. Oxford, UK: Oxford University Press.

Hayek, F. A. 1937. Economics and Knowledge. *Economica*, N. S. 4, 33–54.

1952. *The Sensory Order*. Chicago: Chicago University Press.

Hicks, J. R. 1982. *Money, Interest and Wages: Collected Essays on Economic Theory Volume II*. Oxford, UK: Basil Blackwell.

Hume, D. 1896[1739–40]. *A Treatise of Human Nature*. Oxford, NY: Clarendon Press.

Jevons, W. S. 1871. *The Theory of Political Economy*. London and New York: Macmillan.

Kelly, G. A. 1963. *A Theory of Personality: The Psychology of Personal Constructs*. New York: W. W. Norton.

Keynes, J. M. 1936. *The General Theory of Employment, Interest, and Money*. New York; London: Macmillan.

Kirzner, I. M. 1973. *Competition and Entrepreneurship*. Chicago: University of Chicago Press.

Knight, F. H. 1921. *Risk, Uncertainity and Profit*. Boston: Houghton Mifflin.

Langlois, R. N. 1988. Economic Change and the Boundaries of the Firm. *Journal of Institutional and Theoretical Economics (JITE)/Zeitschrift für die gesamte Staatswissenschaft*, 144, 635–57.

— 1992. Transaction-cost Economics in Real Time. *Industrial and Corporate Change*, 1, 99–127.

Lazonick, W. 1992. Strategy, Structure, and Managment Development in the Britain. In: Kobayashi, K. and Morikawa, H. (eds.) *Organisation and Technology in Capitalist Development*. Cheltenham, UK: Edward Elgar.

Loasby, B. J. 1973. *The Swindon Project*. London: Pitman.

— 1990. Firms, Markets and the Principles of Continuity. In: Whitaker, J. K. (ed.) *Centenary Essays on Alfred Marshall*. Cambridge, UK: Cambridge University Press.

— 2006. The Early Philosophical Papers. In: Raffaelli, T., Becattini, G., and Dardi, M. (eds.) *The Elgar Companion to Alfred Marshall*. Cheltenham, UK and Northampton, MA, USA: Edward Elgar.

Marshall, A. 1919. *Industry and Trade*. London: Macmillan.

— 1961. *Principles of Economics*. London: Macmillan.

Marshall, A. and Marshall, M. 1879. *The Economics of Industry*. London: Macmillan.

Medawar, P. 1982. *Pluto's Republic*. Oxford, UK: Oxford University Press.

Menger, K. 1981[1871]. *Principles of Economics*. New York and London: New York University Press. (First published in German, 1871).

O'Brien, D. P. 1983. Research Programmes in Competitive Structure. *Journal of Economic Studies*, 10, 29.

Penrose, E. T. 1959. *The Theory of the Growth of the Firm*. Oxford, UK: Basil Blackwell.

— 1995. *The Theory of the Growth of the Firm*. Oxford, UK: Oxford University Press.

Popper, K. R. 1963. *The Logic of Scientific Discovery*. London: Hutchinson. (First published in German, 1934).

Raffaelli, T. 2003. *Marshall's Evolutionary Economics*. London: Routledge.

— 2006. Ye Machine. In: Raffaelli, T., Becattini, G., and Dardi, M. (eds.) *The Elgar Companion to Alfred Marshall*. Cheltenham, UK, and Northampton, MA, USA: Edward Elgar.

— 2008. The General Pattern of Marshallian Evolution. In: Shionoya, Y. and Nishizawa, T. (eds.) *Marshall and Schumpeter on Evolution: Economic Sociology of Capitalist Development*. Cheltenham, UK, and Northampton MA, USA: Edward Elgar.

Raphael, D. D. and Skinner, A. S. 1980. General Introduction. In: Wightman, W. P. D. and Bryce, J. C. (eds.) *Vol. 3 of the Glasgow Edition of the Works and Correspondence of Adam Smith: Essays on Philosophical Subjects*. Oxford, UK: Clarendon Press.

Richardson, G. B. 1960. *Information and Investment*. Oxford, UK: Oxford University Press.

1972. The Organisation of Industry. *Economic Journal*, 82, 883–96.

1998[1975]. Adam Smith on Competition and Increasing Returns. In: Skinner, A. S. and Wilson, T. S. (eds.) *Essays on Adam Smith*. Oxford, UK: Clarendon Press.

Robbins, L. 1932. *The Nature and Significance of Economic Science*. London: Macmillan.

Robinson, E. A. G. 1931. *The Structure of Competitive Industry*. London, Nisbet and Cambridge: Cambridge University Press.

Robinson, J. V. 1969. *The Economics of Imperfect Competition*. London: Macmillan.

Robinson, R. 1971. *Edward H Chamberlin*. New York and London: Columbia University Press.

Rogers, E. M. 1962. *Diffusion of Innovations*. New York: Free Press.

Ryle, G. 1949. *The Concept of Mind*. London: Penguin.

Samuelson, P. A. 1967. The Monopolistic Competition Revolution. In: Kuenne, R. E. (ed.) *Monopolistic Competition Theory: Studies in Impact*. New York: John Wiley.

1998. Report Card on Sraffa at 100. *The European Journal of the History of Economic Thought*, 5, 458–67.

Schumpeter, J. A. 1934. *The Theory of Economic Development: An Inquiry into Profits, Capital, Credit, Interest, and the Business Cycle*. Cambridge, MA: Harvard University Press.

1943. *Capitalism, Socialism and Democracy*. London: Allen and Unwin.

Sen, A. 1992. *Inequality Reexamined*. Oxford, UK: Clarendon.

Shackle, G. L. S. 1949. *Expectation in Economics*. Cambridge, UK: Cambridge University Press.

1965. *A Scheme of Economic Theory*. Cambridge, UK: Cambridge University Press.

1969. *Decision, Order and Time in Economic Affairs*. Cambridge, UK: Cambridge University Press.

1970. *Expectation, Enterprise and Profit*. London: George Allen and Unwin.

1972. *Epistemics and Economics*. Cambridge, UK: Cambridge University Press.

Simon, H. A. 1969. The Architecture of Complexity. In: *The Sciences of the Artificial*. Cambridge, MA and London: MIT Press.

1982[1959]. Theories of Decision-Making in Economics and Behavioral Science. *American Economic Review*, 49, 253–83.

Smith, A. 1976[1759]. *The Theory of Moral Sentiments*. Oxford: Oxford University Press.

1976[1776]. *An Inquiry into the Nature and Causes of the Wealth of Nations*. Oxford: Oxford University Press.

1980[1795]. The Principles Which Lead and Direct Philosophical Enquiries: Illustrated by the History of Astronomy. In: Wightman, W. P. D. (ed.) *Essays on Philosophical Subject*. Oxford: Oxford University Press.

1983. *Lectures on Rhetoric and Belles Lettres*. Oxford: Oxford University Press.

Streit, M. E. 1992. Wissen, Wettbewerb und Wirtschaftsordnung – Zum Gedenken an Friedrich August von Hayek. *ORDO*, 43, 1–30.

1993. Cognition, Competition and Catallaxy – In Memory of Friedrich August von Hayek. *Constitutional Political Economy*, 4, 223–62.

2000. The Institutional Economics Unit 1993–2000. *Max Planck Institute for Research into Economic Systems: Annual Report 2000*. Munich: Max Planck Institute.

Voigt, S. 2000. The Foundations Had Been Laid – Describing and Evaluating the Development of the First Unit. *Max Planck Institute for Research into Economic Systems: Annual Report 2000*. Munich: Max Planck Institute.

Walker, D. A. 1987. Walras's Theories of Tatonnement. *Journal of Political Economy*, 95, 758–74.

Williamson, O. E. 1996. *The Mechanisms of Governance*. New York: Oxford University Press.

Young, A. A. 1928. Increasing Returns and Economic Progress. *The Economic Journal*, 38, 527–42.

Ziman, J. 2000. *Real Science*. Cambridge, UK: Cambridge University Press.

3 Science, Technology, and Knowledge
What Economic Historians Can Learn from an Evolutionary Approach

JOEL MOKYR

Introduction

How are we to think of the *fundamental* causes of technological change? Although economists in the past decade have made major advances in trying to account for the appearance of modern economic growth in the West and its subsequent diffusion to other parts of the world, their work has not yet been found to be uniformly satisfactory among other social scientists or even their own colleagues.[1] Instead of criticizing standard analysis again, I propose to explore an alternative. Sustained economic growth depends crucially on the growth in human knowledge, both in terms of *what* is known and *who* does the knowing (Mokyr 2002). What is needed, then, is an historically informed framework to analyze useful knowledge. What follows is an attempt to create a framework for an evolutionary approach to the economic history of technological change. The idea that knowledge can be analyzed using an evolutionary epistemology based on blind variation and selective retention was proposed first by Donald Campbell and has since been restated by a number of scholars in a wide variety of disciplines.[2]

A reasonable criticism of such arguments has been that whereas models of blind variation with selective retention may be an instructive way to look at innovations, they add little direct insight that cannot be gained from standard models. Many insights about innovation come more naturally from evolutionary models, although most such results can also be teased from standard models, properly specified.

[1] The most ambitious of these attempts is clearly Galor (2011), but see also for example Clark (2007). An excellent summary of much of the recent literature is Helpman (2004). For critical reviews see Vries (2013) and McCloskey (2010).
[2] The original statement was made in Campbell (1987). Among the most powerful elaborations are Hull (1988) and Richards (1987). For a cogent statement defending the use of this framework in the analysis of technology see especially Vincenti (1990) and more recently Aldrich et al. (2008).

For instance, economics' knee-jerk response is to regard technological diversity as a source of inefficiency: if an identical product under very similar circumstances is made in very different ways, our first suspicion as economists is that at least one of the producers is doing something wrong. An evolutionary perspective, on the other hand, tends to regard variability as a possible source of innovation and long-run successful performance.[3] Moreover, by some standards we could define the biological processes as "wasteful" without much evidence that mechanisms that make use of scarce resources more efficiently will eventually eliminate the inefficiencies (Wesson 1991: 94).

Part of the confusion in the use of Darwinian models in the economics of knowledge and technology comes from imprecision regarding the unit of analysis. Arguably the unit is a matter of judgment, with the choices ranging from the gene to the group, including the individual, the nation, the group, and so on. The unit I am interested in here is not a living being, but an epistemological one, the *technique*. The technique is a "cultural element," something that is *known* and is shared by a subset of the population and is learned, not genetically transmitted. As such, it can be analyzed with the tools that cultural evolution has suggested to us in the seminal work by Cavalli-Sforza and Feldman (1981) and Boyd and Richerson (1985, 2005).[4] It is part of *prescriptive* knowledge (knowledge "how") as opposed to propositional knowledge (knowledge "what") – a distinction I shall come back to later.[5]

In its bare essentials the technique is nothing but a recipe or a set of instructions, a set of do-loops and if-then statements (often nested) that describe how to manipulate and harness nature for our benefit, that is to say, for production widely defined. Focusing on a *technique*

---

[3] Alfred Marshall, who always had a weakness for evolutionary models, noted that "the tendency to variation is a chief cause of progress" (Marshall 1920 [1890]: 355). Cf. Raffaelli (2003). For a similar argument, see Allen (1988: 107–108).

[4] More recent work in this tradition includes Richerson and Boyd (2005); Jablonka and Lamb (2005); McElreath and Henrich (2007); Henrich (2009); Mesoudi (2011).

[5] The papers collected in Richerson and Christiansen (2013), especially Mesoudi et al. (2013); Boyd, Richerson and Henrich (2013); and Shennan (2013), provide excellent surveys of the state of the art in the area of the application of models of cultural evolution to the growth and dissemination of useful knowledge.

underlines the main interest of students of the history of technology. Much of economics (and of Darwinian biology) is written as a story of the struggle for survival and reproduction between competing members of a single species or the emergence of cooperation between them (Bowles 2004; Bowles & Gintis 2011). But the interesting action in technology is not only people competing against each other but also struggling to better control their natural environment. Techniques are thus tools to play *a game against nature* and to produce a "material culture" from an unyielding and often niggardly environment. As such, the techniques themselves can be seen as it were to compete against each other to be used by people who choose among them. Below, I will first lay out the groundwork for an evolutionary analysis of technological knowledge and briefly examine how such knowledge changes (or does not) over time.

A Few Definitions

To start off, we need a definition of what essential elements constitute a Darwinian model. It will surely come as no surprise that there is little consensus on the matter among biologists or evolutionary theorists on the matter. Darwinian models encompass a larger set than just the evolution of living beings and population dynamics whence it first originated (Aldrich et al. 2008). Darwin himself recognized the applicability of random variation with selective retention to changes in language.[6] The biological reproduction of living things in this scheme of things turns out to be a rather special case of a broad set of such dynamic models. The main idea of a Darwinian model is a system of self-reproducing units that changes over time. A Darwinian model must contain three fundamental elements, which were already fully realized by Darwin; some of the other elements of modern genetics such as the Weismannian barrier and the randomness of mutations do not carry over (Aldrich et al. 2008; Hodgson & Knudsen 2010: 35–36; Mesoudi 2011). How, then, should we think about a Darwinian cultural model that can help us understand technological change?

---

[6] Douglass North (1990) has suggested a similar approach to the development of economic institutions, Richard Dawkins (1976) to the realm of ideas ("memes"), Cavalli-Sforza and Feldman (1981) and Boyd and Richerson (1985) to culture, Donald Elliott (1985) to the analysis of law, and Daniel Dennett (1995) to practically everything.

First, any Darwinian model must be a dynamic system of change over time, a stochastic process of some definable characteristics that are transmitted over time. The way this happens in biology is through reproduction, and the cultural equivalent of the process is socialization: beliefs, preferences, and values are transmitted from parents (and others involved in socialization) to children. Economists have begun to explore various aspects of this process and examined its implications for the evolution of culture (Bisin & Verdier 2011). In this kind of a model techniques "reproduce" from period to period and thus "carry" the knowledge embodied in them over time. A technique, in this view, uses human agents to reproduce itself to make another technique much like, as in Samuel Butler's famous quip, a chicken is the way an egg produces another egg. Through most of history, the replication process took place in the context of the master–apprentice relationship, which has recently been the subject of much research and debate in economic history. The horizontal replication of techniques (and other cultural variants) involves *imitation* or *persuasion.*[7]

Beyond just absorbing the knowledge and beliefs of others, however, people have new ideas, and thus innovation enters the system (Witt 2009). Innovations need not be random: as Nelson (1995) has stressed, these models are in a class that is more or less halfway between deterministic and purely random dynamic systems, what he calls "somewhat random variation." These innovations create internal variation that defines the options for the system to move to.

Again, the evolutionary dynamics differ in important ways between living beings and any kind of knowledge. In living beings, persistent change occurs only through gene mutation (essentially random change), and direction occurs through selection on the living beings that carry them. In knowledge systems two stochastic processes are at work. First, propositional knowledge reproduces itself over time through learning with possible "mutations" (discoveries about natural phenomena and regularities). Second, the techniques that form part of prescriptive knowledge also reproduce themselves, and there, too, there can be change, say, through experience and learning by

---

[7] Aldrich et al. (2008: 587) argue that the concept of "replicator" differs from "diffusion," as replication involves adding "developmental dispositions and capacities" that add complexity. For my present purposes, however, the distinction is unnecessary.

doing. The two stochastic processes are clearly related, with feedback going in both directions. Such feedbacks do *not* occur in living beings, where Lamarckian feedback mechanisms from phenotype to genotype are ruled out.

A second characteristic is that cultures, much like species, contain a great variation of traits. Variability is key to the selection process, by definition.[8] Cultural variability is the result of past innovations. Over time, a vast number of cultural traits have accumulated, and many of these traits are shared among certain groups of individuals and distinguish them from those belonging to other groups. Yet the lines are often blurry, as they are between species, and overlaps are common. Jews and Muslims share a belief in a single God and a taboo on the eating of pork, yet they are quite distinct groups in a way not dissimilar from two species that share the vast bulk of their genes yet are phenotypically quite distinct. The set of techniques known to society – a subset of the set of all cultural variants – falls directly under the definition of the sum of all past innovations. But other variants are equally interesting to the economic historian, such as attitudes and beliefs that affect the accumulation of human capital, the willingness to defer gratification ("patience capital" in the terminology of Doepke & Zilibotti 2008), or attitudes to work vs. leisure. The period 1500–1700 marks a time of feverish innovation in these cultural variants, even if it was not quite as prolific in terms of inventions as the subsequent centuries.

Third, there is a property of superfecundity in the system, that is, there are more entities than can be accommodated, so there must be some selection. In biology, what drives evolution is superfecundity: species have the capability to reproduce at a rate much faster than is needed for replacement, and this means that not all those who *can* be born will be, or that all those born will actually survive and reproduce. This is the Darwinian "struggle for existence." Natural selection is driven by a process in which those with the most fit features have a better chance to survive and reproduce. Cultural features are "superfecund" (perhaps "superabundant" would be a better term), in

---

[8] As argued in Aldrich et al. (2008: 582) all complex population systems can be analyzed in terms of general Darwinian principles. The systems considered here involve populations of entities. Populations are defined by members of a type that are similar in key respects, but within each type there is some degree of variation, due to past innovation and historical contingency.

that there are far too many of them produced for an individual to absorb, so that selection must take place among sometimes enormous menus. There are 10,000 distinct religions in the world and 6,800 different languages. No individual can believe in all religions and speak all languages. One has to choose. This selection process is what provides the entire system with its historical direction by determining the likelihood that a certain technique will be actually used. The nature of superfecundity in epistemological systems is somewhat different than in Darwinian biology, where entities reproduce at a rate that is faster than can be accommodated by available resources. More often than not, superfecundity means that one has to choose: no person can believe simultaneously in the Copernican and the Ptolemaic cosmological systems any more than one can be an adherent of Milton Friedman and Mao at the same time. In many other cases, however, new information is piled on top of old information, and by accepting it as valid one does not have to make a choice. In this regard the superfecundity feature of the evolutionary model is a constraint that is not invariably binding.

In the world of technology superfecundity essentially means that there are far more conceivable ways to skin a cat than there are cats and more ways to drive from i to j than can be accommodated. Selection at the level of technique in use is thus essential. However, this is far more relevant to process innovation than to product innovation: if a new and better way of making steel or curing malaria is discovered, the old technique would (in most cases) be phased out and replaced by the new one. New products, however, could take their place beside existing ones. All the same, superfecundity means selection. There are many scores of breakfast cereals on the store shelves, but households choose just a few.

As Nelson has pointed out (1995: 55), the theory's power depends on its ability to specify what precisely these selection criteria are. The – somewhat unsatisfactory – answer must be that they are historically contingent. How, for instance, does an economy pick the right technique from an array of options? Some societies such as nineteenth-century (and to some extent modern) America emphasized price and efficiency above all; others (such as France) selected against mass production and preferred individually manufactured custom-made products wherever possible. Some nations chose to generate electricity with nuclear reactors, whereas others stayed with fossil fuels. Unlike Darwinian models, however, selection is not a metaphor for an invisible-hand kind of mechanism that operates in a decentralized and unconscious manner of mindless replicators with differential reproduction: there are actually conscious units, firms, households, and authorities that do the selecting.[9] Rather than the unit of selection, then, in this kind of model economic agents are the *selectors* themselves.

The importance of selection is critical to Darwinian models because, as noted, selection lends direction to the historical purpose of change. Selection and innovation are indispensable parts of the historical process. Without innovation, selection occurs on existing entities only, and whatever variation exists at any time will eventually crystallize or disappear altogether.

Darwinian models of technology need therefore to specify the exact mode of selection that is operating on the choice set. But because innovation consists of more or less local variation on *existing* states of the world, past selections govern the range of variability on which selection can occur, yielding the path-dependent or persistence property of these models.[10] A multiplicity of conceivable outcomes, with the actual result often determined by historical contingency, is thus part and parcel of the process. Yet it is not quite the same as the standard problems that occur in economics with multiple equilibria and the need to refine them. As Witt (1997a) points out, the process of evolutionary change is *unending*, that is, unforeseeable mutations always can and do occur to destabilize an existing state of the world. Such mutations occur either in a given technique itself or in other techniques that are complementary or rivalrous, thus changing the environment faced by this mutation. Such a description seems to fit the world of knowledge as well as any.

[9] It should be noted that the combination of selection and the particular dynamic structure defined before imply that selection is "myopic" even when it is perfectly rational, conditional on what is known at the time. That is, a particular choice may seem rational, but that choice places the system on a trajectory that eventually leads to less desirable outcomes. For more details, see Mokyr (1992).

[10] By the standard definition of path dependence, this means that the final outcome depends both on the special characteristics of each technique and the historical path, which partially is contingent (David 1997).

Evolutionary Models and the Economic History of Technology

What does an evolutionary approach bring to the study of culture in general and technology in particular? For the economic historian, the great advantage of evolutionary thinking is that it tries to explain why the present is the way it is and not some other way from history. It encourages us to look on how the past shaped the present using Darwinian concepts, above all the concepts of choice and selection, and how such choices are made from past choices and innovations. Evolutionary thinking does not provide us with a clean and ready-to-use methodology like standard economics, which depends on simple rules such as profit maximization, but for historical analysis of innovation, it has considerable merits. Above all, it stresses the importance of history: the set of techniques at each point in time is what was passed on from the past, plus whatever they add or modify: a classic example of descent with modification. Some techniques are radically changed from what the past had, but even today many are not (Edgerton 2007). Next I list some of the main advantages of an evolutionary approach to the history of culture, of which technological knowledge is a subset.[11]

First, evolutionary systems are characterized by a fundamental *duality* between information and action, between what in biology is thought of as genotype and phenotype and in a more generalized version as replicator and interactor (Hodgson & Knudsen 2010: 24). Distinctions between genotype and phenotype are hazardous to extend to cultural history, but all the same, it seems, something can be learned. Culture is about matters of the mind – beliefs and preferences; behavior and actions are the observable outcomes of preferences and knowledge. But there is no easy mapping from genes to phenotypes, and the mapping from beliefs to behavior is not simpler; at best there are loose statistical associations masking the interaction of many variables.[12] One reason is that beliefs, much like other

[11] Some of the following is adapted from Mokyr (2016).

[12] A good example can once again be found in the history of technology in the relation between propositional and prescriptive knowledge. There is no easy mapping between the two (Mokyr 2002) and two-way feedback creates for complex dynamics. There are times when techniques are used with virtually no understanding of why and how they work. At other times, the necessary underlying knowledge may well be there, but the techniques fail to emerge – such as the absence of eyeglasses in the Greek and Roman world.

genotypical processes, affect "adjacent" beliefs. We can indeed speak of technological *pleiotropy*, much like in evolutionary processes. Pleiotropy means that a certain genotypic change leads to more than one phenotypical effect because of the spillover effects on genes in the proximity of the mutation, in a sort of genetic packaging. In some extreme cases, certain techniques spill over to a large number of uses, which is now known as General Purpose Technologies. A parallel phenomenon is *epistasis* in which more than one piece of information is required to jointly bring about a certain trait or behavior: To get a working bicycle, what is needed is not just a working transmission chain but also pneumatic tires.

Second, evolution is about the interaction between a preexisting environment (in which an innovation is introduced) and the innovation itself. Innovation remains a stochastic variable, even if it is in some sense directed and not purely random (as mutations are supposed to be in a pure Weismannian world). We do not know precisely why a certain idea occurs to an individual at a particular time and why in some societies certain ideas simply never occurred at all. The likelihood of an idea occurring to anyone is affected by the environment and perceived needs.[13] But even if the flow of innovations were wholly predictable, we would not be able to predict with any certainty their success unless we could measure with some precision their "fitness" relative to the environment in which they take place, which determines whether they will "catch on." What makes matters even more complicated, of course, is that even if it were possible somehow to predict the likelihood of an innovation succeeding in a given environment, that success is likely to produce complicated feedback effects because it is likely to change the environment itself.

Third, as noted earlier, evolutionary systems are based on the dynamics produced by superfecundity and selection. The system throws up more variants than it can possibly accommodate, and so some form of winnowing must take place. Like species, some ideas may go "extinct" in the face of a powerful new competitor (e.g., geocentric astronomy or miasma theories of disease), although extinction may still mean that the *knowledge* of a technique survives, just its use

---

[13] An example of such directed searches is the alleged search for labor-saving innovations in high-wage economies, which supposedly explains the occurrence of the Industrial Revolution in eighteenth-century Britain (Allen 2009). For a critique, see Kelly, Mokyr and Ó Gráda (2014).

has ceased. We could still make water clocks and sundials, but their role in time measurement is nonexistent. It is possible for knowledge to go completely extinct (that is, completely forgotten and lost), but the conditions for that are rather stringent and unlikely to be met today. "Extinction" might then be thought of as an absorbing barrier. However, as long as the underlying knowledge (or some crucial component of it) has not been lost, the technique can be regenerated, much like the imagined preservation of dinosaur DNA in a drop of amber in *Jurassic Park*. In other cases new techniques may coexist with the old ones in some kind of mixed equilibrium in which the competitive environment is insufficiently stringent to bring about a complete domination of the innovation, or in which the two techniques occupy slightly different niches. As I shall argue later, this can happen when knowledge is *untight*, that is, the knowledge is not very certain and not easily verifiable by the rhetorical criteria of the time – as was, for instance, the case with the germ theory of disease before Pasteur.

Fourth, evolutionary models are rich in that they allow change to occur on different levels. In principle, of course, there is no reason to presume that evolutionary models should be confined to finitely lived beings endowed with a genotype derived from one or two parents, subject to differential reproduction. In other words, thinking in evolutionary terms boils down to what Mayr (1982: 46–47) sees as the main power of evolutionary models, which is what he called "population thinking." As already noted, it stresses the importance of individual variation *within* populations and their ability to bring about changes in the many starting from the few. If we are interested in economic change at the macro level, such "population thinking" is critical.

There is a long debate whether this occurs in biological systems and what the appropriate "unit of selection" is. Some leading evolutionary biologists, such as George Williams and Richard Dawkins, feel that all selection happens at the level of the gene and nowhere else, but others strongly argue for selection at the level of the cell, the organism or the species, and even populations. Whatever the outcome of this literature, it seems beyond question that in cultural evolution selection can happen at many levels. To see this, consider a novel cultural trait offered to an individual in a particular society. If the individual chooses the variant and not another, this is one level of selection at which choice-based cultural evolution occurs. Now assume, however, that this variant increases the fitness of this individual and thus extends his life expectancy and/or the number of surviving children who resemble him. This increases the chances that the trait will be passed on, either vertically through the socialization of offspring or horizontally through "infecting" his immediate neighbors. Furthermore, suppose that this society has now adopted the trait and that it increases the fitness of this group (e.g., through more cooperation or adopting a superior technique); this may mean a higher population growth rate in a society that has adopted this trait, and thus is likely to increase its relative frequency in the global population. Evolution here is not a single process but a complex and intertwined system of conscious choices and "natural selection" at different levels (Jablonka & Lamb 2005).

Fifth, like all evolutionary systems, culture is resistant to change. In the technical language of evolutionary dynamics, prevalent cultural variants are evolutionary stable strategies with respect to most conceivable innovations ("mutants"). Built-in mechanisms maintain a certain stability and provide an advantage to incumbent cultural variants against innovations, but the effectiveness of these mechanisms is itself a function of the content of the system. Ernst Mayr (1989: 35) suggests that genes "perform as teams" and that "epistatic interactions form a powerful constraint on the response of the genotype to selection." Cultural elements, too, form a coherent system, which may resist change because of the interdependence of its components. Moreover, in cultural systems (with no obvious parallel in biology) culture is tied up with investments that people have made in the current beliefs and practices, and that would decline in value if the current beliefs were to be modified or overthrown. Physicists resisted quantum mechanics, physicians the germ theory, and chemists the atomic theory for precisely such reasons. No matter what kind of cultural system we are looking at, there will be some resistance to change, and many seemingly "fit" innovations will fail in a hostile environment biased toward conservatism.[14] In other cases "cultural

---

[14] Recently, economists (Benabou, Ticchi, & Vindigni 2013) have developed models to formalize the problem, pointing out that certain kinds of innovations reduced the value of existing ideas by being "belief-eroding" even if that was not their original intent. This creates an obvious conflict between those whose beliefs are being threatened and society at large, which stands to benefit from such ideas because they increase economic performance.

species" can coexist for very long periods indeed. The "new science" that emerged in the sixteenth and seventeenth centuries did not replace the Aristotelian orthodoxy in a few years or decades, but shared the same environment, at times as substitutes but often in some kind of uneasy harmony or compromises that may seem implausible to us now.[15]

Sixth, any evolutionary framework implies that any easy generalizations or predictions about the speed and direction of cultural change are doomed. Most of the time culture changes at a tectonic pace, surviving dramatic institutional and political shocks. But there are instances when culture changes quickly as a result of weakened resistance, perhaps, or some powerful exogenous shock that deeply challenges existing cultural beliefs (Jones 2006). Much like evolutionary science, the strength of the methodology is in helping us to make sense of the past rather than predict the future. Precisely because the unit of analysis continuously interacts strongly with its environment and because there are few time-invariant relations, it becomes unpredictable (Saviotti 1996: 31). Moreover, as John Ziman (2000: 50) has pointed out, selectionist models stress that what matters in history often is not statistical averages over large numbers of very similar states or agents, but rare events that get amplified and ultimately determine outcomes.[16] The challenge to historians then becomes to try to understand which rare events take on that function and under what circumstances they get "selected."

Finally, an evolutionary approach gives us a more reasonable way of thinking about how and why historical trajectories were followed. It places the analysis firmly somewhere in the middle between a materialist approach that sees outcomes as inexorable and fore-ordained and a nihilist approach that sees randomness everywhere. The Great Divergence and the Industrial Revolution that caused it were neither fluke nor necessity, to paraphrase Jacques Monod's famous title

---

[15] An example is the rather quaint model of the solar system proposed by Tycho Brahe, the late sixteenth-century Danish astronomer, who proposed a compromise between the Copernican model and the Ptolemaic one, in which the sun rotated around the earth but the other planets rotated around the sun.

[16] This has long been realized by evolutionary biologists, who have postulated that major evolutionary advances come from unusual and exceptional genotypes with opportunities to dominate their own small populations and radiate into marginal habitats. See Stebbins (1969: 142).

(1971). Neither were the Scientific Revolution or the Enlightenment.[17] They arose because historical circumstances were conducive to the sprouting of seeds that were already present in the soil. Evolutionary innovation occurs because a mutation takes place that happens in an environment that is favorable to it. But such a mutation is a minute subset of all the favorable mutations that might have happened, as well as of all the mutations that actually did happen but that did not turn out to be viable.

Evolutionary theory reminds the historian that not everything that happened had to happen, and that many things that could have happened did not. One of the most important implications of the small but fascinating literature in counterfactual history (e.g., Tetlock, Lebow, & Parker 2006) is to drive home the insight that history could have played itself out quite differently. It also reminds us that similar circumstances do not always lead to the same outcomes and that similar outcomes do not always have identical causes. The language of evolution suggests the distinction between homologies (similar outcomes due to similar origins) as opposed to analogies or homoplasies (similar outcomes with different origins). The work by economists on the interaction between culture and institutions reinforces this interpretation by recognizing that these models have multiple equilibria and that societies may start from very similar circumstances and yet end up in very different situations "depending on historical idiosyncrasies" (Alesina & Giuliano 2016). In both approaches, a guiding principle is that there was nothing inevitable about the actual historical outcomes we observe.

Evolution and Historical Issues

Many issues in economic and technological history can be re-explored using evolutionary ideas and terminology.

1. Does history make leaps? Does technological change occur in a gradual manner as Leibniz, Alfred Marshall, and the neo-Darwinian

[17] For a powerful statement in the same vein about the Scientific Revolution, see Cohen (2012: 204). He argues that the emergence of a "realist-mathematical" (i.e., modern) science was always a possibility, but its realization was not foreordained – we might still be living in a world in which Archimedes and Ptolemy still represented the summit of scientific achievement and the astrolabe and mechanical clock the supreme examples of toolmaking, with "death within a year of birth as the likeliest human fate by far."

phylogenetic gradualist orthodoxy in evolutionary biology hold, or can it move in bounds and leaps as Eldredge and Gould and their followers in the "punctuated equilibrium" literature insist (Mokyr 1990b)?[18] The debate parallels those in economic history between scholars who believe in the Industrial Revolution and the great discontinuity it constituted and those who would deny this and see continuity everywhere.[19] The distinction between macroinventions (pathbreaking innovations that open new horizons) and microinventions (that fill fairly small gaps) proposed in Mokyr (1990a) is helpful here: every once in a while a new major technological leap forward opens a new technological chapter in history. The famous Dudley Castle atmospheric engine installed by Thomas Newcomen in 1712 may qualify as a "hopeful monster" in the Goldsmith tradition even if no biological examples for them are known to exist.

2. Are Darwinian models of natural selection sufficient to explain the course of history as the ultra-Darwinians such as Dennett and Dawkins claim, or do we need additional inputs from chaos theory, self-organization theory, or something yet unsuspected? Clearly these debates mirror those between the scholars who insist on multiple equilibria and hence path dependence, such as Brian Arthur (1994) and Paul David (1997), and their opponents such as Liebowitz and Margolis (1995), who feel that the rational market – if only left alone – will get it right every time and hence there is no need to worry about path dependence.

3. What exactly is the relation between the institutional environment, innovation, and technological selection, and can we distinguish meaningfully between adaptation and innovation? What kind of environment facilitates innovation? What is the nature of historical resistance to innovation, and how is it overcome if it is? An

---

[18] In a classic but controversial work, the geneticist Richard Goldschmidt (1940) proposed a distinction between micro- and macromutations. The former accounted for changes within a species and were more or less continuous and cumulative. The latter accounted for great leaps in biological evolution that created new species. Goldschmidt believed that evolution moved at times in leaps and jerks through those macromutations. He argued, probably too rigidly, that new species arose only by way of macromutations and not by the continuous accumulation of micromutations. Following the emergence of a new species, it follows the standard evolutionary adaptive process of micromutation.

[19] For an extreme example of this position, see Clark (1985: 64–93).

example of the intersection of intellectual history and evolutionary models is the analysis of the "battle between the ancients and the moderns" that raged in the seventeenth century, in which European intellectuals overcame one of the most powerful forces of conservatism, namely the infatuation of learned people with the writings of earlier generations and the blind veneration of ancient learning, be it Aristotle, the Talmud, or Confucius (e.g., LeCoq 2001).

4. Are traits invariably explicable in terms of their functions, as fundamentalist adaptationists claim? Is there room in the history and analysis of technology for the notion of exaptation, for instance, which refers to cases in which an entity was selected for one trait but eventually ended up carrying out a related but different function?[20] Concepts like "niches," "recombination," and "extinction" come naturally to the historian of technology, although they may not mean precisely the same thing they do in biology.

5. Finally, we may ask in what sense can we think of "progress"? Biologists have long argued the point (with the late Stephen Jay Gould taking the strongest position against the notion of progress).[21] There seems to be no obvious way in which progress can be defined in the evolution of living beings. Is the same true in the history of knowledge? There are interesting questions around the "Panglossian" point that "whatever was, was good." Is it possible to rank outcomes using some kind of criterion and assess to what extent historical outcomes were "desirable"? Economists find it natural to write of "technological progress" but normally discuss "institutional change" – an indication perhaps that knowledge is normally *cumulative* and therefore progressive, whereas in the change of institutions we can expect regress as often as progress (by some well-defined criterion).

---

[20] The term was first suggested by Gould and Vrba (1982). Historians of technology have, of course, long pointed to the phonograph and the digital computer as examples of such instances in economic history. Dyson (1997: 81–82) draws the parallel explicitly: "feathers must have had some other purpose before they were used to fly ... the same thing happened to ENIAC: a mechanism developed for ballistics was expropriated for something else."

[21] For an informed contrary point of view, see Vermeij (1995: 143–145; 2004: 246–291).

Knowledge and Technique

In what follows, I shall briefly return to a framework described in Mokyr (2002) to highlight the advantages of an evolutionary approach in the economic history of technology. An evolutionary approach can help us clarify our thinking about useful knowledge, although analogies with biology and genetics can be misleading in many instances. Yet some parallels can be enlightening. Much like DNA, useful knowledge does not exist by itself; it has to be "carried" by people or in storage devices. Unlike DNA, however, carriers can acquire and shed knowledge so that the selection process is quite different. This difference raises the question of how it is transmitted over time and whether it can actually shrink as well as expand. All carriers have finite lives and thus need to reproduce themselves in some fashion. The existence of nonliving carriers such as books and models does expedite this transmission, but some crucial components cannot be codified or stored in devices that require codification. This "tacit" knowledge therefore dies with its live carrier unless it is passed on to the next generation. In this regard, evolutionary thinking points to the importance of apprenticeship in history as the main mechanism by which knowledge was transmitted intergenerationally (Doepke, de la Croix, & Mokyr 2016). The apprenticeship system is a classic case of Darwinian descent with variation: a craftsman absorbs from his master a set of skills but adds his own variation, which he subsequently passes on to his own apprentices. It might be added that knowledge received and knowledge transmitted are never quite identical, which is another source of innovation (Sperber 1996: 101–106).

It is useful to define the concept of the set of *useful knowledge,* an eighteenth-century term that roughly corresponds to our knowledge of science and technology. As already noted, we can segment this set into knowledge "what," or propositional knowledge (that is to say, beliefs) about natural phenomena and regularities, and prescriptive knowledge "how," which we may call techniques. In what follows, I refer to propositional knowledge as Ω-knowledge and to prescriptive knowledge as λ-knowledge. If Ω is *episteme,* λ is *techne.*

The distinction between Ω and λ parallels the distinction made famous by Gilbert Ryle (1949; see also Loasby 1996), who distinguished between knowledge "how" and knowledge "what." Ryle rejected the notion that one can meaningfully distinguish *within a single individual* between knowledge of a set of parameters about a problem and an environment from a set of instructions derived from this knowledge that directs an individual to take a certain action.

Is the distinction between propositional Ω-knowledge and prescriptive λ-knowledge meaningful? Both reflect some form of useful knowledge and thus are subject to the same kinds of difficulties that the economics of knowledge and technology encounters. An addition to Ω is a *discovery*, the unearthing of a fact or natural law that existed all along but that was unknown to anyone in society. An addition to λ is an *invention*, the creation of a set of instructions that, if executed, makes it possible to do something hitherto impossible. Michael Polanyi points out that the difference boils down to observing that Ω can be "right or wrong," whereas "action can only be successful or unsuccessful" (1962: 175).[22] Purists will object that "right" and "wrong" are judged only by socially constructed criteria and that "successful" needs to be defined in a context, depending on the objective function that is being maximized.

Rather than develop this framework in detail and show its historical applicability, which was the subject of Mokyr (2002), I want to stress here a few properties of the concept of knowledge that matter most to its role in technological development and economic growth. Perhaps the central one is the idea of an *epistemic base*. The epistemic base of any technique in use is basically the understanding of the natural processes that make it work. Yet what may not be true for an individual is true for society as a whole: for a technique to exist, it has to have an epistemic base in Ω. Some techniques can be made to work without any understanding of how and why they work: ancient

---

[22] Polanyi fails to recognize the important historical implications of the two kinds of knowledge and maintains that "up to [1846] natural science had made no major contribution to technology. The Industrial Revolution had been achieved without scientific aid" (p. 182). This bald statement surely will not be accepted by any economic historian. The implicit definition he uses for Ω implies a much larger entity than formal science and includes much informal and folk knowledge. In addition to "pure science," he includes an intermediate set of inquiries that are "systematic technology" and "technically justified science." Moreover, his set of propositional knowledge must include even less formal elements when he points out that "technology always involves the application of some empirical knowledge ... our contriving always makes use of some anterior observing"(Polanyi 1962: 174). If so, the role of propositional knowledge of some kind in the development of technology must have been important long before modern science came into its own.

humanity used fire for innumerable generations before the principles
of combustion were understood; farmers hauled manure to their field
before anybody understood soil chemistry.[23] Techniques were known
to work; that was all that was needed.

Except that it was not. For one thing, *some* techniques cannot
really be made to work unless something about the physics or biology
underlying them is understood. This was even true about the first
steam engine prototypes built by Denis Papin in the 1690s: without
the realization that a vacuum was possible and that the earth is surrounded by an atmosphere, the atmospheric engine would not have
emerged. The fuller epistemic base would have included thermody-
namics, which was developed *as a result of* the steam engine. In that
regard, the old adage that the steam engine did more for science than
science did for the steam engine holds true – but with the proviso that
absent a minimum epistemic base extant in 1700, there would have
been no engine. With the Industrial Revolution, many new techniques
emerged that grew symbiotically with their epistemic base, including
electricity, organic chemistry and the industries based on it, and, of
course, communications based on electromagnetic waves and phar-
maceutical industries based on the germ theory of disease.

For many of those industries, propositional knowledge and prescriptive knowledge *co-evolved*. Some minimum knowledge base is
required to get the industry set up, but after that the flows of knowledge went in both directions. The epistemic base of technology
widened both because pure science made relevant discoveries and
because of the feedback from practitioners in the industry itself. No
industry illustrates this better than steel: an ancient technique with a
minimal epistemic base, growing insights as the role of trace amounts
of carbon led to the development of cheap steel in the mid-nineteenth
century through the famous inventions of Bessemer and Siemens-
Martin. Yet much experience and many serendipitous improvements
made the product better and cheaper. After all, a major source of
scientific insights comes from the regularities and experiences learned
in the production process itself.

---

[23] The epistemic base in the limit can be infinitesimally small. If no knowledge
whatsoever exists of why a technique works, then the epistemic base is trivially
equal to the propositional statement that "the technique works."

In short, the relationship between Ω and λ is that each element in λ – that is, each technique – rests on a known set of natural phenomena and regularities that support it. It is not necessary for many people to have "access" to the epistemic base, but the people writing the instructions for the "new recipe" that constitutes an invention must be among them. They do not necessarily have to possess the propositional knowledge themselves, but they must be able to access it, for instance, by consulting state-of-the-art scientists. The historical significance of the idea of an epistemic base is not just that there is a minimum base without which some techniques could not be conceived. It is above all that the wider and deeper the epistemic base on which a technique rests, the more likely it is that a technique can be extended and find new applications; product and service quality improved; the production process streamlined, economized, and adapted to changing external circumstances; and the techniques combined with others to form new ones.[24] When an existing technique needs to be extended or adapted to different circumstances, the content and extent of the epistemic base become important, and the practitioners return to the "theorists." Trial and error and try-every-bottle-on-the-shelf might work, of course, but it is more uncertain, slower, and far more expensive. If someone, somewhere, knows the regularities and natural laws that make the technique work, that knowledge can be invoked or that expert can be consulted. In a word, the rate and scope of technological progress depends on inventors and technicians to understand what they are doing and why it works. Of course, this insight itself could be gained even without any recourse to Darwinian models. But the notion of a dual structure that parallels that of a co-evolving genotype and phenotype is helpful here (Blackmore 1999: 93–107; Jablonka & Lamb 2005).

To pursue the commonality just a bit further: not every gene ends up coding for a protein, but for any phenotype to emerge, *some* basis for it has to exist in the genome. However, much like parts of the

---

[24] This argument was well formulated by William Rankine, the great Scottish engineer, in 1859, when he noted that normal progress consists of "amendments in detail of previously existing examples." However, when the laws on which machines operate have been reduced to a science, practical rules are deduced, "showing not only how to bring the machine to the condition of greatest efficiency ... but also how to adapt it to any combination of circumstances" (Rankine 1873[1859]: xx).

DNA that do not code for any protein, some exogenous change in the environment may bring about the activation of hitherto "dormant" useful knowledge. Similarly, techniques exist that are known but currently not used, but which could be brought back with the right kind of stimulus. Economists familiar with isoquants will find that conclusion familiar. More complex, environmental changes may trigger interactions between existing genes, leading to epistatic effects.

As noted, it is not necessary that the person actually carrying out the technique possess the supporting knowledge. One can bake a bread from a recipe without understanding the microbial actions of yeasts. I typed these lines on a computer even though I have only rudimentary knowledge of the physical and mathematical rules and principles that make my computer work. It is likely that the workers who put together my laptop did not possess this knowledge either. To distinguish the knowledge needed to invent and design a new technique from that needed to execute it, I shall refer to the latter as *competence*. Competence is defined as the ability of agents to carry out the instructions in λ. The codified knowledge in the instructions still needs to be decoded, and in part competence consists of the ability to do the decoding, or if a codebook is supplied, to decode the codebook. Tacit knowledge is, therefore, an essential part of competence. It is needed for obtaining inexpensive and reliable access to the codified instructions. Moreover, no set of instructions in λ can ever be complete. It would be too expensive to write a complete set of instructions for every technique. Judgment, dexterity, experience, and other forms of tacit knowledge inevitably come into play when a technique is executed. Another element of competence is the solution of unanticipated problems that are beyond the capability of the agent: knowing whom (or what) to consult and which questions to ask is indispensable for all but the most rudimentary production processes.[25]

The epistemic base of a technique does not have to be invoked consciously each time the technique is carried out. Much of it is frontloaded in the instructions specified and the artifacts and equipment deployed, and the instructions themselves rarely need to explain why the recommendations work. Nor does every user have to possess the

---

[25] Teece et al. (1994) correctly point out that the firm's "competence" includes some skills complementary to purely technical capacities such as knowledge of markets, sources of supply, finance, and labor management.

entire competence involved in operating the technique. Hence the assumption, often made by economists, that the stock of technical knowledge is accessible to all economies seems reasonable. It seems plausible that competence – the capability to deploy a technique – is usually easier to acquire than the epistemic base. Thus even in countries where only a few people understand the finer points of electronics and microbiology, smartphones and antibiotics can be produced and used. Yet how effectively techniques are deployed may differ a great deal from society to society even if the artifacts are identical, because competence depends on tacit knowledge and cultural traits that may differ systematically.

The set of propositional knowledge Ω thus maps into the set of techniques (prescriptive knowledge) λ through the epistemic base, and thus imposes a constraint on it much as the genotype maps into the phenotype and constrains it without uniquely determining it. The rather obvious notion that economies are limited in what they can do by their useful knowledge bears some emphasizing simply because so many scholars believe that if incentives and demand are right, somehow technology will follow automatically. Even a scholar as sophisticated as Eric Jones believes that "technology seems to offer 'free lunches' but its spectacular gains are really secondary; they are attainable by any society that invests in institutions to encourage invention and enterprise" (2002: 20, ch. 3).

Yet throughout history things that were knowable but not known were the chief reason why societies were limited in their ability to provide material comforts. Certain societies, including our own, did not have access to some feasible techniques that would have benefited them a great deal because they lacked a base in Ω. Medieval Europe could not design a technique describing the ocean route to Australia or produce antibiotics against the Black Death. The Age of Enlightenment could not produce electrical light or chemical fertilizers. Our own societies have been unable to tame nuclear fusion and make effective antiviral agents because we do not know enough about high-energy physics and virology. Nonetheless, we cannot be sure that such knowledge will never exist; all that matters is that we do not have it. In that sense, again, a certain similarity with evolutionary biology emerges. It is likely that certain species of high fitness *could have* evolved if the right mutations had emerged, but these mutations simply did not occur.

In the history of useful knowledge, we can be a bit more specific than that. While in nature mutations occur because of random errors in the transmission of genetic material, scientific advances, though they have a stochastic element, can be understood. The main reasons scientific breakthroughs occurred are related to the tools that scientists have at their disposal and the agenda that institutions and culture dictate. The Scientific Revolution of the seventeenth century was in large part driven by a number of new instruments that came online: the telescope, the microscope, the barometer, the thermometer, the vacuum pump. The second Industrial Revolution of the late nineteenth century, similarly, was driven by a set of new tools and instruments that drove research. In that fashion, technology pulled itself up by its bootstraps: new research tools created new science, and the new science then created new technology across a wide spectrum.[26]

How and when does Ω provide the epistemic bases for technology? For people to willfully create a new technique, they have to believe that some underlying propositional knowledge is likely to be correct. The mapping of the route around the globe was based on the belief that the earth was spherical, much as aseptic methods are based on the belief that bacteria cause infectious diseases. One of the more important characteristics of propositional knowledge and its role in supporting technology is not only the width of the epistemic bases of technology but also the *tightness* of knowledge. Tightness has two dimensions: confidence and consensus. The tighter a piece of knowledge is, the more certain the people who accept it are of their beliefs, and the less likely it is that many people hold views inconsistent with it. Flat Earth Society members and those who believe that AIDS can be transmitted by mosquito bites may be few in number, but many Americans still do not believe in the Darwinian theory of evolution and still believe in the possibility of predicting human affairs from looking at the stars.

Tightness depends on the effectiveness of verification, that is, the extent to which rhetorical conventions accepted in a society persuade people that something is "true," "demonstrated," or at least "tested." It defines the confidence that people have in their knowledge and –

---

[26] A fascinating example is the development of x-ray crystallography around 1915 by a father and son team named Bragg; the technique was applied to a plethora of scientific projects, none more pathbreaking than the work of Rosalind Franklin, the co-discoverer of DNA.

thus what counts most for the purposes of technological change – their willingness to act upon it and to employ the techniques that are based on it. This is particularly relevant when the outcome of a technique itself cannot be assessed immediately.[27] Techniques may be "selected" because they are implied by a set of knowledge that is gaining acceptance rather than by any direct measurement of their effectiveness.[28] It is important to stress that tightness is in no way an objective ordering of knowledge: it is purely a social construction. The Ptolemaic universe and Galenian medicine were forms of tight knowledge in medieval Europe, in the sense that practically everyone who mattered believed in them and did so with a high degree of confidence on the basis of their trust in ancient authorities. As the rhetorical conventions changed after 1500, doubts crept in and the knowledge became looser.

Finally, where social science departs from evolutionary biology is in the social dimensions of knowledge. In the end, what each individual knows is less important than what society *as a whole* knows and can do. Even if very few individuals in a society know quantum mechanics, the practical fruits of the insights of this knowledge to technology may still be available just as if everyone had been taught advanced physics. For the economic historian, what counts is *collective* knowledge. The knowledge available to society as a whole is the *union* of all sets of knowledge residing in individuals, reflecting the inevitable division of knowledge in advanced societies. But collective knowledge as a concept raises serious aggregation issues: How do we go from individual knowledge to collective knowledge beyond the mechanical definitions employed earlier? Making it available to those who need it depends on access. Progress in exploiting the existing stock of knowledge will

---

[27] Many techniques can be selected by individuals on the basis of readily measured characteristics: laser printers are preferred to dot matrix printers for the same reasons air conditioning is preferred to room fans. But in many other cases the judgment is difficult: Does broccoli consumption reduce the risk of cancer? Do nuclear power plants harm the environment more than fossil fuel-burning generators? In those cases, people might choose the technique that is based on the tighter Ω. More people choose antibiotics over homeopathic medicine or Christian Science when they suffer from a disease whose etiology is well understood.

[28] Techniques implied by rather untight knowledge can be shown to be effective. Knowledge in Ω will become tighter and more difficult to resist if it maps into techniques that actually can be shown to work. To put it crudely, the way we are persuaded that science is true is that its recommendations work visibly (Cohen and Stewart 1994: 54).

hence depend first and foremost on the efficiency of distribution and the *cost of access* to knowledge possessed by others. What makes knowledge a cultural entity, then, is that it is distributed to, shared with, and acquired from others; if that acquisition is too costly, important Ω knowledge will not be accessible to those who do not have it but are seeking to apply it. As the amount of knowledge expands, the fraction of it contained in the mind of an individual will decline and the importance of access technology increases.

Between the two extreme cases of a world of "episodic knowledge" as it is said to exist among animals and a world in which all knowledge is free and accessible to all at no cost, there is a reality in which some knowledge is shared but access to it requires the person acquiring it to expend real resources. Access costs depend on the technology of access, the trustworthiness of the sources, and the cultural norms of "sharing knowledge."[29] It also depends, of course, on the total size of Ω; the larger Ω, the more specialization and division of knowledge is required. Experts and special sources dispensing useful information will emerge, providing access. Information technology (IT) is exactly about that. The inventions of writing, paper, and printing not only greatly reduced access costs but also materially affected human cognition, including the way people thought about their environment.[30] But external memory came at a cost in that it codified and in some cases crystallized useful knowledge and gave it an aura of unassailability and sanctity that sometimes hampered its continuous revision and perfection. All the same, the insight that the invention of external storage of information is much like networking a computer that previously was a standalone has some merit.[31]

---

[29] The emergence of "open science" in early modern Europe, in which new useful knowledge was placed in the public realm through correspondence or publication and made accessible to others who had the tools to understand the texts, should be regarded as a major access-cost-reducing cultural development (Dasgupta & David 1994; David 2008).

[30] The invention of such "external storage systems" has been credited by Merlin Donald (1991: 308–312, 356) as the taproot of modern technological culture.

[31] Elizabeth Eisenstein (1979) has argued that the advent of printing created the background on which the progress of science and technology rests. In her view, printing created a "bridge over the gap between town and gown" as early as the sixteenth century, and while she concedes that "the effect of early printed technical literature on science and technology is open to question," she still contends that print made it possible to publicize "socially useful techniques" (pp. 558, 559).

Innovation and Inertia

Evolution is inherently conservative. In all evolutionary systems, technological systems included, there is considerable inertia and constraints on change (Nelson 1995: 54). In evolutionary models of technology, because of the dynamic structure of evolution in which knowledge depends on past knowledge, technical innovations (that is, additions to λ) are likely to be extensions and modifications of existing techniques. Most inventors and technological historians have thought of innovation as largely a set of new combinations of existing knowledge.[32] Weitzman (1996) sets up a model in which invention is essentially nothing but a recombination of existing technology. Yet this seems incomplete at second thought: it is not just the techniques *themselves* (or the artifacts in which they are embedded) that are combined as much as the knowledge underlying them. This may appear a distinction without a difference. It should be noted that complementarity rarely involves "similarity," and the elements to be recombined often come from what Adam Smith in the famous first chapter of *The Wealth of Nations* already called "the most distant and dissimilar objects" – in my terminology totally different subsets of Ω, for instance, software and hardware, or the electrical components of an automobile with the mechanical elements of transmission.

For whatever reason, some evolutionary systems change rapidly and frequently while others remain in stasis for very long periods. In biology we observe periods of very rapid change, known sometimes as "adaptive radiation." Even when such rapid change occurs, for whatever reason, it is important to realize that the genetic structure of living beings is subject to inertive mechanisms, which all evolutionary systems need to have unless they are to slide into chaotic mode. These inertive mechanisms are set up to resist change; without them, the system would clearly become unstable and likely to end up in what Stuart Kauffman (1995) has called the hypercritical region in which change becomes uncontrollable and unrestrained.

In biology the resistance shows up first in the absence (or extreme rarity) of anything that resembles a Lamarckian mechanism. A genotype

---

[32] Usher (1929: 11) felt that "invention finds its distinctive feature in the constructive assimilation of pre-existing elements into new syntheses," but in the revised (1954) edition of his book admitted that strategic inventions "comprise both old and new elements" (p. 68).

is set upon meiosis. If Lamarckian change could occur, the rate of change of an evolutionary system would be vastly more rapid, and stability would be unthinkable.[33] Within the Weismannian constraints change is very rare, and resistance to change is built in at any stage.[34] While such genetic cohesion has, of course, not precluded the well-known adaptive radiations that created different species, these explosions of variety are little more than ad hoc variations on a single *bauplan* or structural type. This cohesion, while not wholly understood, is essential to the development of the world of living species: the key to success is to strike a compromise between excessive conservatism and excessive malleability. Evolutionary systems, whether biological or other, that are too conservative will end up in complete stasis; too much receptivity to change will result in chaos (Kauffman 1995: 73).

Such resistance also exists in knowledge systems. Technological resistance has a number of different sources and mechanisms but it is a property of *all* evolutionary systems, including cultural ones. Consider language: grammatical errors and spelling mistakes are weeded out mercilessly by the red pencils of English teachers and copyeditors. Yet neologisms, new usages, novel forms of spelling, and even changed grammatical rules do eventually make it through, or languages would remain immutable over long periods. It is just that only the tiniest fraction of them ever have a chance, and of those another very tiny fraction gets selected. In technology it is a direct consequence of superfecundity in the set λ: a lot of new ways to carry out a particular production are "proposed" or "occur to individuals," but unless the vast majority of such suggestions are rejected, the cost of continuous experimentation and change would become unbearably large.

Even for unequivocally superior techniques, however, resistance is likely because given the finiteness of the number of techniques in use, they are likely to replace and displace existing techniques. In

---

[33] I am indebted to my late colleague David Hull for this insight.

[34] As Mayr (1991: 160–161) has explained,

> "Just exactly what controls this cohesion is still largely unknown, but its existence is abundantly documented ... during the pre-Cambrian period, when the cohesion of eukaryote genotype was still very loose, seventy or more morphological types (phyla) formed. Throughout evolution there has been a tendency for a progressive 'congealing' of the genotype so that deviation from a long-established morphological type has become more and more difficult."

knowledge systems, existing techniques are embodied in agents using them, and these agents operate as intentional and rational agents. Incumbent agents will sustain losses if the new techniques are adopted through the devaluation of their human and physical capital, and they are likely to resist. Even at the level of Ω it is conceivable to think of cases in which resistance to innovation occurred because of "vested interests." For instance, a complex religious culture in which some elements are out of tune with perceived reality may either adapt to reflect new beliefs or cling to increasingly antiquated beliefs (Benabou, Ticchi, & Vindigni 2014). The power structure within the organizations that depend on these beliefs (as is the case with the Catholic Church today) may either dig in and fiercely resist change, or it can adapt. Yet when there are few direct interests at stake, and when rhetorical devices such as mathematical proof, statistical significance, and experimental evidence are well developed and widely accepted, resistance to new knowledge about nature that meets those rhetorical tests tends to be short-lived and moribund. While Copernicus, Lavoisier, and Darwin all ran into well-determined and well-organized resistance, the outcome was never in doubt. This is much less true for new techniques. In part, techniques could be untight, in the sense that it is difficult to establish their superiority. But there is far more involved.

As a first approximation, the struggle against nature is not a social activity. One can imagine a solitary individual with a certain knowledge available to her, who maps from it to solve the material problems of survival. While almost immediately one can think of social dimensions of this game, the control and manipulation of nature in what we call "production" is in the first instance not a social activity but an environmental one. Once we admit, however, that in any kind of organized group technological activity becomes something that involves others as well through cooperation, coordination, and the sharing of knowledge, there are new opportunities but also new constraints on individual action. In part, technology becomes something of a social consensus, "the way we do things," and the individual must face up to the fact that when she wants to deviate from this norm, some measure of consent and cooperation from others has to be secured.

Every act of major technological innovation, then, is an act of *rebellion* not just against conventional wisdom but against existing practices and vested interests, and thus will normally lead to some kind of resistance.[35] In what follows I will discuss the latter in an attempt to assess the historical sources of resistance to technological innovation. In the history of technology we can distinguish a number of different sources of resistance. None of these have *exact* counterparts in evolutionary biology, nor should we expect there to be any; what matters is that there is resistance to change.

1. *Economically motivated resistance*: Groups or individuals with a stake in the incumbent technology may resist change because a switch to a newcomer may benefit other groups at their expense. Workers in danger of losing their jobs, facing changes in their work environment, or fearing that their human capital will depreciate are one example of this, but many others can be mentioned as well. In the Benabou, Ticchi, and Vindigni (2014) framework, scientific progress leads to technological progress, but at a cost: it erodes religious beliefs, and that reduces the utility and rents of those who were vested in religion; in their model, there is a state that has the option to either permit such innovations to spread, or can try to censor them and prevent them from spreading.

2. *Ideologically motivated resistance*: These include various sources of political resistance that are not fueled by direct economic motivation: technophobia, neophobia, a sense that meddling too much with the creation and nature is in some way sinful, or a high degree of risk aversion with particular high cost associated with low-probability catastrophic events such as nuclear accidents. Much of the resistance to nuclear reactors, GMOs, stem cell research, and cloning can be read this way, as do attitudes such as "we should not play God," or "if it ain't broke, don't fix it." The most obvious form such resistance takes, then, is as an ideology of *conformism* in which deviancy – whether technological, political, religious, or ethnic – is actively discouraged.

3. *Epistemological resistance*: The flip side of the relationship discussed earlier between knowledge of nature and its manipulation implies that techniques might be resisted when they are seemingly contradicted by an element in Ω that currently enjoys "accepted"

---

[35] The literature on the subject has been growing rapidly in recent years. For a useful collection, see Bauer, (1995). A more recent addition is Juma (2016); A one-sided and popularized account is Sale (1995). See also Mokyr (1994, 1998, 2002: 218–283).

status, especially when it does not have a strong base in Ω itself. Thus when quinine was first introduced into Europe, it was resisted for a number of reasons, at least one of them being that it did not mesh with accepted Galenian practice (Duran-Reynals 1946: 45–53). Smallpox vaccination was resisted strongly, and antivaccination movements sprung up (Knapp 1989: 265–266). The public, after all, had good reason to be suspicious of the recommendations of doctors, and it took decades and a determined propaganda campaign to convince a reluctant populace of the blessings of vaccination. Similarly, Dr. Barry Marshall's suggestion in the 1980s that peptic ulcers were caused by bacteria was resisted because "accepted" knowledge suggested that bacteria could not survive in the acidic stomach lining. Such resistance can be overcome, and often is when the techniques are sufficiently tight so that results can be readily demonstrated to conform to the rhetorical conventions of persuasion, as was the case with smallpox vaccination. In many cases in the history of technology the "proof of the pudding was in the eating," and simple observation and experimentation were enough to persuade skeptics that even if an invention flew in the face of accepted knowledge, it worked better and too bad for accepted knowledge. But when techniques are untight, such as acupuncture, astrology, mind reading, and other techniques not firmly based on an accepted part of Ω, they are still regarded with great skepticism by most selectors even if they are widely used by others. An especially telling example is the polygraph machine which relies on a questionable foundation in natural knowledge and whose actual effectiveness, much like homeopathic medicine, is controversial yet remains in wide use (Alder 2007).

4. *Strategic complementarities:* A considerable number of technological breakthroughs in history failed to gain widespread implementation because of the absence of strategic technological complementarities. Without the right tools, the right materials, and the necessary skilled workmanship, good ideas simply could not make it from the drawing table to the prototype and certainly not from the prototype to mass production. The difference between James Watt and Leonardo Da Vinci, both enormously original and creative technological geniuses, was that Watt had first-rate instrument makers and cylinder drillers at his disposal.

Hot-air ballooning could not become an effective means of transportation until lightweight sources of motive power could be made that solved the problem of direction; electrical power could not become a widespread means of energy transmission until the problem of cheap generation through self-excitation was resolved. Often an invention depends on the solution of subproblems. If these remain unsolved, an invention will be stillborn (e.g., Arthur 2009: 116–119).

5. A similar phenomenon occurs in the presence of *systemic resistance*. As long as technology consists of individual components that can be optimized independently, changes in individual techniques depend on those of others only through the price mechanism. In other words, a change in a particular technique will drive up demand for complements and reduce that for substitutes. As long as there are no strong network externalities, it may not matter what happens to other techniques. But such externalities have always existed, even if their extent may have been limited.[36] If the costs and benefits of the adoption of a technique depend on the technique's ability to match with existing components of a given platform, the process of innovation has to take this into consideration. Technological change in a "system" becomes a coordination game which may have multiple stable solutions. Once settled on a solution, it may require a substantial cost advantage for the system to move to a different one (Witt 1997b; Loch & Huberman 1999). In our own age, network externalities (broadly defined) place serious limits on the degree and direction in which technology can change at any given time. The concept of a "lock-in" into an existing outcome is the most extreme case. Normally all that occurs is that a finite but considerable cost has to be paid to make the switch. A new technology will need either to fit in with the existing system or be able to create a "gateway" technology that will

---

[36] It is sometimes thought that "technological systems" in T. P. Hughes's celebrated definition did not come into being until the Industrial Revolution (see for instance Edward Tenner's (1997) otherwise brilliant book, p. 13). Yet open-field agriculture was clearly a complex system in which individual components such as crop choice could not be optimized independently of the whole. The same is true for the sailing ships, a complex entity in which rigging, masting, hull, and steering all depended on each other and jointly determined the parameters of the vessel.

somehow create a bridge between it and existing components.[37] Software has to be "Windows-compatible," electrical tools require 115 V, car engines are constrained to gasoline and diesel fuels. As noted, such standardization problems can be overcome, but they impose a high transition cost and thus a constraint on new techniques and constitute a source of resistance. At times, such situations lead to ex post inefficient outcomes believed to require government intervention.

6. *Frequency dependence:* In many cases, the rate of technological change and the rate of adoption depend on the number of users. Frequency dependence is a prime example of systems with positive feedback (Arthur 1994) and exhibit certain nonergodic properties more common in evolutionary systems than in standard economics. Economies of scale (within a firm), external economies (among different firms), and learning by doing effects fall into that category, as do all models with network economies in communication, such as fax machines, instant messaging, and social media (thus blending with systemic properties in category 5). Frequency dependence is also more likely to play a role in technological change when the technique is untight so that the benefits of an innovation are hard to observe. Selectors will look at what their neighbors do and emulate them, trying to save information costs.

In short, resistance to the new exists at various levels, and if innovations are to occur at all, they have to overcome these barriers. Much like mutations, then, innovation should thus be regarded as a three-stage process, or a "pyramid of causality" (as Arthur 2009: 124 has called it). First, will the new techniques occur at all? Second, if the innovation does take place, does it overcome the initial resistance? Third, if it survives, it will be tested on the merits of its own traits – will it become fixed in the population or at least carve out a sustainable niche? The question that needs to be asked is not why is there no more innovation, but why does innovation occur at all – how does it succeed in overcoming the first- and second-stage barriers? There is no single answer to that question, of course. There have been inventions in history that have been so truly overwhelming in their superiority that no effective resistance could be put up. The mechanical

[37] For an interesting historical example see Puffert (2009).

clock and moveable type, a quarter of a millennium apart, simply swept Europe off its feet. Both of them were "macroinventions" by the standards described earlier. Among the nineteenth-century inventions, the telegraph, the photographic camera aniline purple dyes, and x-ray photography were of that nature. These advances were all quite tight: the improvement in the desired traits were easily verified and all but impossible to dispute. They did not need to fit into an existing system. But many other breakthroughs encountered resistance of one form or another. In our own age, nuclear power, high-definition TV, and genetically modified organisms are noted examples (though the roots of resistance to each of those is quite different). The economic historian, stimulated perhaps by other cases in which evolutionary systems overcame resistance and produced sudden spurts of rapid evolutionary change, should continually ask what kind of environment and what type of community tend to be conducive to such sea changes?

Conclusions

The use of evolutionary models in economic history, despite many calls for it, has yet to materialize. While important work has been written using Darwinian ideas to explain economic history, they have relied on standard population dynamics rather than on the much more promising area of evolutionary epistemology (Galor & Moav 2002). The application of evolutionary thinking to the economic history of technology was pioneered by the now-canonical work of Walter Vincenti (1990) and Edward Constant (1980). Despite its many attractions described earlier, it has yet to make a serious impact.

With the growing interest of economics in culture and cultural factors in economic growth (e.g., Fernández 2011; Alesina & Giuliano 2016), evolutionary thinking may become increasingly interesting to economists because of its obvious applicability to cultural dynamics. For economic historians, this should be particularly interesting because of the centrality of scientific and technological progress in modern economic growth and because science and technology are, in the final analysis, things we know and believe and thus cultural phenomena. If we accept that "useful knowledge" consists of cultural variants in which innovations struggled to be accepted in a Darwinian competitive "red in tooth and claw" environment, its full implications for the emergence of a modern economy are obvious. Specifically, it helps us understand how, in the critical centuries between Columbus and Newton, the selection environment in the European market for ideas changed in a way that made it more receptive to new ideas and in which the fitness of cultural variants was redefined to create a world in which "progress" itself became a successful cultural item (Mokyr 2016).

None of this suggests that concepts from biology can and should be adopted in unaltered form into economic history, or any other field in economics. But the power of evolutionary thinking in understanding how cultural dynamics and the progress of science and technology to change our economies stands undiminished. Above all, it teaches us the hazards of hindsight bias and strong contingent nature of some of the central developments in economic history, in contrast with materialist modes of thinking. And yet, it also warns us that history is not a sequence of random accidents. Contingency should not be overdone, and evolutionary theory, while making substantial allowances for contingency, does not imply sheer randomness. We can make sense of the past.[38]

References

Alder, K. 2007. *The Lie Detectors: The History of an American Obsession.* New York: Free Press.

Aldrich, H. E., Hodgson, G. M., Hull, D. L., Knudsen, T., Mokyr, J., and Vanberg, V. J. 2008. In Defence of Generalized Darwinism. *Journal of Evolutionary Economics*, 18, 577–596.

Alesina, A. and Giuliano, P. 2016. Culture and Institutions. *Journal of Economic Literature*, 53, 898–944.

Allen, P. M. 1988. Evolution, Innovation and Economics. In: Dosi, G. (ed.) *Technical Change and Economic Theory*. London and New York: Pinter Publishers, 95–119.

Allen, R. C. 2009. *The British Industrial Revolution in Global Perspective.* Cambridge: Cambridge University Press.

---

[38] Joseph Needham, originally trained in biological science, warned that to attribute "the origin of modern science" entirely to accidental factors would be tantamount to admitting the bankruptcy "of history as a form of enlightenment" (1969: 216).

Arthur, W. B. 1994. *Increasing Returns and Path Dependence in the Economy*. Ann Arbor: University of Michigan Press.

2009. *The Nature of Technology*. New York: Free Press.

Bauer, M. 1995. *Resistance to New Technology*. Cambridge: Cambridge University Press.

Benabou, R., Ticchi, D., and Vindigni, A. 2013. Forbidden Fruits: The Political Economy of Science, Religion and Growth. *Unpublished working paper*. Princeton University.

Bisin, A. and Verdier, T. 2011. The Economics of Cultural Transmission and Socialization. In: Benhabib, J., Bisin, A., and Jackson, M. O. (eds.) *Handbook of Social Economics*. Amsterdam: North-Holland, 339–416.

Blackmore, S. 1999. *The Meme Machine*. Oxford: Oxford University Press.

Bowles, S. 2004. *Microeconomics: Behavior, Institutions, and Evolution*. Princeton: Princeton University Press.

Bowles, S. and Gintis, H. 2011. *A Cooperative Species: Human Reciprocity and Its Evolution*. Princeton: Princeton University Press.

Boyd, R. and Richerson, P. J. 1985. *Culture and the Evolutionary Process*. Chicago: University of Chicago Press.

2005. *The Origins and Evolution of Cultures*. Oxford: Oxford University Press.

Boyd, R., Richerson, P. J., and Henrich, J. 2013. The Cultural Evolution of Technology. In: Richerson, P. J. and Christiansen, M. H. (eds.) *Cultural Evolution: Society, Technology, Language, and Religion*. Cambridge, MA: MIT Press, 119–142.

Campbell, D. T. 1987. Blind Variation and Selective Retention in Creative Thought as in Other Knowledge Processes. In: Radnitzky, G. and Bartley III, W. W. (eds.) *Evolutionary Epistemology, Rationality, and the Sociology of Knowledge*. La Salle, IL: Open Court, 91–114.

Cavalli-Sforza, L. L. and Feldman, M. W. 1981. *Cultural Transmission and Evolution: A Quantitative Approach*. Princeton: Princeton University Press.

Clark, J. C. D. 1985. *English Society 1688–1832*. Cambridge: Cambridge University Press.

Clark, G. 2007. *A Farewell to Alms*. Princeton: Princeton University Press.

Cohen, H. F. 2012. *How Modern Science Came into the World*. Amsterdam: Amsterdam University Press.

Cohen, J. and Stewart, I. 1994. *The Collapse of Chaos: Discovering Simplicity in a Complex World*. Harmondsworth, England: Penguin.

Constant, E. W. 1980. *The Origins of the Turbojet Revolution*. Baltimore, MD: Johns Hopkins Press.

Dasgupta, P. and David, P. A. 1994. Toward a New Economics of Science. *Research Policy*, 23, 487–521.

David, P. A. 1997. Path Dependence and the Quest for Historical Economics. *University of Oxford Discussion Papers in Economic and Social History*, No. 20 (November), Oxford. Oxford: Oxford University Press.

2008. The Historical Origins of "Open Science": An Essay on Patronage, Reputation and Common Agency Contracting in the Scientific Revolution. *Capitalism and Society*, 3, 1–103.

Dawkins, R. 1976. *The Selfish Gene*. Oxford: Oxford University Press.

Dennett, D. C. 1995. *Darwin's Dangerous Idea: Evolution and the Meanings of Life*. New York: Simon and Schuster.

de la Croix, D., Doepke, M., and Mokyr, J. 2018. Clans, Guilds, and Markets: Apprenticeship Institutions and Growth in the Pre-Industrial Economy. *The Quarterly Journal of Economics*, 133, 1–70.

Doepke, M. and Zilibotti, F. 2008. Occupational Choice and the Spirit of Capitalism. *The Quarterly Journal of Economics*, 123, 747–793.

Donald, M. 1991. *Origins of the Modern Mind*. Cambridge, MA: Harvard University Press.

Duran-Reynals, M. L. 1946. *The Fever Bark Tree: The Pageant of Quinine*. New York: Doubleday.

Dyson, G. B. 1997. *Darwin among the Machines: The Evolution of Global Intelligence*. Reading, MA: Addison Wesley.

Edgerton, D. 2007. *The Shock of the Old: Technology and Global History since 1900*. Oxford: Oxford University Press.

Eisenstein, E. 1979. *The Printing Press as an Agent of Change*. Cambridge: Cambridge University Press.

Elliott, E. D. 1985. The Evolutionary Tradition in Jurisprudence. *Columbia Law Review*, 85, 38–94.

Fernández, R. 2011. Does Culture Matter? In: Benhabib, J., Jackson, M. O., and Bisin, A. (eds.) *Handbook of Social Economics*. Amsterdam: North-Holland, 481–510.

Galor, O. 2011. *Unified Growth Theory*. Princeton: Princeton University Press.

Galor, O. and Moav, O. 2002. Natural Selection and the Origin of Economic Growth. *The Quarterly Journal of Economics*, 117, 1133–1191.

Goldschmidt, R. B. 1940. *The Material Basis of Evolution*. New Haven, CT: Yale University Press.

Gould, S. J. and Vrba, E. S. 1982. Exaptation: A Missing Term in the Science of Form. *Paleobiology*, 8, 4–15.

Helpman, E. 2004. *The Mystery of Economic Growth*. Cambridge, MA: Harvard University Press.

Henrich, J. 2009. The Evolution of Innovation-Enhancing Institutions. In: Shennan, S. and O'Brien, M. (eds.) *Innovation in Cultural Systems: Contributions from Evolutionary Anthropology. Altenberg Workshops in Theoretical Biology*. Cambridge, MA: MIT Press.

Hodgson, G. and Knudsen, T. 2010. *Darwin's Conjecture: The Search for General Principles of Social and Economic Evolution*. Chicago: University of Chicago Press.

Hull, D. L. 1988. *Science as a Process*. Chicago: University of Chicago Press.

Jablonka, E. and Lamb, M. J. 2005. *Evolution in Four Dimensions: Genetic, Epigenetic, Behavioral, and Symbolic Variation in the History of Life*. Cambridge, MA: MIT Press.

Jones, E. 2002. *The Record of Global Economic Development*. Cheltenham: Edward Elgar.

2006. *Cultures Merging: A Historical and Economic Critique of Culture*. Princeton, NJ: University Press.

Juma, C. 2016. *Innovations and its Enemies: Why People Resist New Technologies*. New York: Oxford University Press.

Kauffman, S. A. 1995. *At Home in the Universe: The Search for the Laws of Self-Organization and Complexity*. New York: Oxford University Press.

Kelly, M., Mokyr, J., and Ó Gráda, C. 2014. Precocious Albion: A New Interpretation of the British Industrial Revolution. *Annual Review of Economics*, 6, 363–391.

Knapp, V. J. 1989. *Disease and Its Impact on Modern European History*. Lewiston, NY: The Edwin Mellen Press.

LeCoq, A.-M. 2001. *La Querelle des Anciens et des Modernes*. Paris: Éditions Gallimard.

Liebowitz, S. J. and Margolis, S. E. 1995. Path Dependency, Lock-In, and History. *Journal of Law, Economics, and Organization*, 11, 205–226.

Loasby, B. J. 1996. The Organization of Industry and the Growth of Knowledge. Lectiones Jenensis, Jena: Max Planck Institute of Economics.

Loch, C. H. and Huberman, B. A. 1999. A Punctuated-Equilibrium Model of Technology Diffusion. *Management Science*, 45, 160–177.

Marshall, A. 1920[1890]. *Principles of Economics*. London: Macmillan & Co.

Mayr, E. 1982. *The Growth of Biological Thought*. Cambridge, MA: Harvard University Press.

1989. Speciational Evolution or Punctuated Equilibria. In: Somit, A. and Peterson, S. A. (eds.) *The Dynamics of Evolution*. Ithaca, NY: Cornell University Press, 21–53.

1991. *One Long Argument: Charles Darwin and the Genesis of Modern Evolutionary Thought*. Cambridge, MA: Harvard University Press.

McCloskey, D. 2010. *Bourgeois Dignity: Why Economics Can't Explain the Modern World*. Chicago: University of Chicago Press.

McElreath, R. and Henrich, J. 2007. Modeling Cultural Evolution. In: Barrett, L. and Dunbar, R. (eds.) *Oxford Handbook of Evolutionary Psychology*. Oxford: Oxford University Press, 555–570.

Mesoudi, A. 2011. *Cultural Evolution*. Chicago: University of Chicago Press.

Mesoudi, A., Laland, K. N., Boyd, R., Buchanan, B., Flynn, E., Mccauley, R. N., Renn, J., Reyes-García, V., Shennan, S., Stout, D., and Tennie, C. 2013. Cultural Evolution. In: Richerson, P. J. and Christiansen, M. H. (eds.) *Cultural Evolution: Society, Technology, Language, and Religion*. Cambridge, MA: MIT Press, 193–216.

Mokyr, J. 1990a. *The Lever of Riches: Technological Creativity and Economic Progress*. New York: Oxford University Press.

1990b. Punctuated Equilibria and Technological Progress. *The American Economic Review*, 80, 350–354.

1992. Is Economic Change Optimal? *Australian Economic History Review*, XXXII, 3–23.

1994. Progress and Inertia in Technological Change. In: James, J. and Thomas, M. (eds.) *Capitalism in Context: Essays in Honor of R. M. Hartwell*. Chicago: University of Chicago Press, 230–253.

1998. The Political Economy of Technological Change: Resistance and Innovation in Economic History. In: Berg, M. and Bruland, K. (eds.) *Technological Revolutions in Europe*. Cheltenham: Edward Elgar, 39–64.

2002. *The Gifts of Athena*. Princeton: Princeton University Press.

2016. *A Culture of Growth: Origins of the Modern Economy*. Princeton: Princeton University Press.

Monod, J. 1971. *Chance and Necessity: An Essay on the Natural Philosophy of Modern Biology*. New York: Alfred A. Knopf.

Needham, J. 1969. *The Grand Titration*. Toronto: University of Toronto Press.

Nelson, R. R. 1995. Recent Evolutionary Theorizing About Economic Change. *Journal of Economic Literature*, XXXIII 48–90.

North, D. C. 1990. *Institutions, Institutional Change, and Economic Performance*. Cambridge: Cambridge University Press.

Polanyi, M. 1962. *Personal Knowledge: Towards a Post-Critical Philosophy*. Chicago: Chicago University Press.

Puffert, D. J. 2009. *Tracks across Continents, Paths through History: The Economic Dynamics of Standardization in Railway Gauge*. Chicago: University of Chicago Press.

Raffaelli, T. 2003. *Marshall's Evolutionary Economics*. Abingdon: Routledge.

Rankine, W. J. M. 1873[1859]. *A Manual of the Steam Engine and Other Prime Movers.* London: Charles Griffin.

Richards, R. J. 1987. *Darwin and the Emergence of Evolutionary Theories of Mind and Behavior.* Chicago: University of Chicago Press.

Richerson, P. J. and Boyd, R. 2005. *Not by Genes Alone: How Culture Transformed Human Evolution.* Chicago: University of Chicago Press.

Richerson, P. J. and Christiansen, M. H. 2013. *Cultural Evolution: Society, Technology, Language, and Religion.* Cambridge, MA: MIT Press.

Ryle, G. 1949. *The Concept of Mind.* Chicago: University of Chicago Press.

Sale, K. 1995. *Rebels against the Future: The Luddites and Their War on the Industrial Revolution.* Reading, MA: Addison Wesley.

Saviotti, P. P. 1996. *Technological Evolution, Variety, and the Economy* Cheltenham: Edward Elgar.

Shennan, S. 2013. Long-Term Trajectories of Technological Change. In: Richerson, P. J. and Christiansen, M. H. (eds.) *Cultural Evolution: Society, Technology, Language, and Religion.* Cambridge, MA: MIT Press, 143–155.

Sperber, D. 1996. *Explaining Culture: A Naturalistic Approach.* Oxford: Blackwell's.

Stebbins, G. L. 1969. *The Basis of Progressive Evolution.* Chapel Hill: North Carolina University Press.

Teece, D. J., Winter, S., Rumelt, R., and Dosi, G. 1994. Understanding Corporate Coherence: Theory and Evidence. *Journal of Economic Behavior and Organization,* 23, 1–30.

Tenner, E. 1997. *Why Things Bite Back: Technology and the Revenge of Unintended Consequences.* New York: Alfred A. Knopf.

Tetlock, P., Lebow, N., and Parker, G. 2006. *Unmaking the West: "What-If?" Scenarios That Rewrite World History.* Ann Arbor, MI: Michigan University Press.

Usher, A. P. 1929. *A History of Mechanical Inventions.* New York: McGraw Hill.

Vermeij, G. J. 1995. Economics, Volcanoes, and Phanerozoic Revolutions. *Paleobiology,* 21, 125–152.

Vermeij, G. 2004. *Nature: An Economic History.* Princeton: Princeton University Press.

Vincenti, W. 1990. *What Engineers Know and How They Know It.* Baltimore, MD: Johns Hopkins Press.

Vries, P. 2013. *The Escape from Poverty.* Vienna: Vienna University Press.

Weitzman, M. L. 1996. Hybridizing Growth Theory. *The American Economic Review,* 86, 207–213.

Wesson, R. 1991. *Beyond Natural Selection.* Cambridge, MA: MIT Press.

Witt, U. 1997a. Economics and Darwinism. In: Aruka, Y. (ed.) *Evolutionary Controversies in Economics: A New Transdisciplinary Approach.* Tokyo: Springer Verlag, 41–55.

1997b. "Lock-in" vs. "Critical Masses" – Industrial Change under Network Externalities. *International Journal of Industrial Organization,* 15, 753–773.

2009. Propositions about Novelty. *Journal of Economic Behavior and Organization,* 70, 311–320.

Ziman, J. 2000. Selectionism and Complexity. In: Ziman, J. (ed.) *Technological Innovation as an Evolutionary Process.* Cambridge: Cambridge University Press, 41–51.

4 | Generalized Darwinism in Evolutionary Economics
The Devil Is in the Detail

JACK VROMEN

Introduction

This chapter is a follow-up on two earlier debates I contributed to. One debate is documented in a special issue of *The Journal of Economic Methodology* (2004) edited by Matthias Klaes, called *Symposium: Ontological Issues in Evolutionary Economics* (2004). The other one is reported in a special issue of *The Journal of Evolutionary Economics* edited by Ulrich Witt, called *Evolutionary Concepts in Economics and Biology* (2006), which is (as Witt notes in his editorial) mainly about the appropriateness and fruitfulness of Universal Darwinism (following Hodgson and Knudsen, I henceforth refer not to Universal Darwinism, but to Generalized Darwinism) in and for evolutionary economics.[1] The present chapter is meant to be a further contribution to this latter debate.

My own initial stance on Generalized Darwinism was to give it, at least for the time being, the benefit of the doubt. I recommended to suspend judgment, to wait and see until it was worked out into a full-fledged theory and only then assess it on the basis of usual criteria for theory assessment. This was based on a negative argument only: don't reject the project of Generalized Darwinism before it is given a fair chance to prove itself. No positive argument was given to contribute actively to making the project of Generalized Darwinism a success. It is one thing not to reject or dismiss a new theoretical project out of hand; it is quite another thing, of course, to actually help in letting the project succeed.

My thanks go to Caterina Marchionni, Jan-Willem Stoelhorst, Ulrich Witt and an anonymous referee for useful comments on earlier drafts. The usual caveat applies.
[1] Discussions of Universal Darwinism have found their way even to popularizations of economic theory (see, e.g., Coyle 2007 and Ferguson 2008).

One needs a positive reason or motivation to actively promote (or advocate) Generalized Darwinism, to contribute to its further development, to elaborate on it and so on. Such a positive reason could indeed be ontological in kind. Indeed, as we shall see both proponents and opponents of Generalized Darwinism do advance ontological considerations to back up their stance. After weighing the ontological arguments pro and con for Generalized Darwinism, I shall conclude that valid ontological arguments can be given to support it. But I shall also argue that the sort of Generalized Darwinism that can be defended on such grounds is so general and abstract that it is emptied of almost all content. Indeed, it becomes so empty that it is of very little, if any, use for further theory development (see also Levit, Hossfeld, & Witt 2011 and Vromen 2012).[2] Thus, the ontological battle won is a Pyrrhic victory really: the sort of Darwinism left does not give much guidance in constructing a full-fledged theory on its basis.

Hodgson and Knudsen's Case for Generalized Darwinism

In a nutshell, Hodgson and Knudsen's position with respect to Generalized Darwinism (Hodgson & Knudsen 2006a, 2010,[3] 2012; Aldrich et al. 2008) is as follows: If understood at a sufficiently high level of generality and abstraction, sociocultural evolution (and, in particular, economic evolution) is Darwinian. The Darwinian principles of variation, inheritance and selection are just as real in economic systems and populations as they are in biological populations. The presence of these three principles is sufficient for Darwinian evolution to occur. Thus we have Darwinian evolution occurring not only in the biological but also in the economic domain. It is not just that there is Darwinian evolution going on in the economic domain, Hodgson and Knudsen argue, we cannot have satisfactory explanations of how economic systems evolve that do not refer to these three Darwinian principles. This is not to say that biological and economic evolution are the same *tout court*, however. Though the three principles of Generalized Darwinism just stated are domain-general (in the sense that they are not only working in the biological domain but also in other domains such as

---

[2] For discussions of problems with using Generalized Darwinism to shed light on more concrete phenomena from a more applied perspective, see Breslin (2011); Buenstorf (2006); Pelikan (2011); Schubert (2014) or Stoelhorst (2009).

[3] See Vromen (2012) for a book review of Hodgson and Knudsen (2010).

the economic domain), the *details* of the mechanisms underlying the generation of new variants and underlying inheritance (or replication) and selection in the economic domain are very different from those working in the biological domain. Invoking the three principles of Generalized Darwinism is therefore necessary but not sufficient in explaining processes of economic evolution.[4] Auxiliary domain-specific hypotheses have to be added to arrive at explanatory powerful theories. Among other things this entails that replicators and interactors have to be identified in the economic domain. Hodgson and Knudsen identify individual habits and organizational routines as paradigmatic examples of ("social") replicators and firms as paradigmatic examples of ("social") interactors in the economic domain.

Thus Hodgson and Knudsen's case for Generalized Darwinism involves not just a *description* of what Generalized Darwinism entails: the three general principles of variation, inheritance (or replication) and selection. It also involves the *claim* that these principles are not only applicable to economic evolution (and other forms of nonbiological evolution) but are mandatory in any study of evolving systems. And, finally, it also involves a *program* (or project): more is needed than the application of just the three principles to have a satisfactory study of economic evolution. Domain-specific hypotheses and data have to be added to arrive at explanatory theories.

There is much in Hodgson and Knudsen's case for Generalized Darwinism that I agree with. Hodgson and Knudsen are right in arguing, I think, that introducing a Darwinian explanatory framework in economics does not imply endorsement of genetic determinism or biological reductionism. Accepting the three Darwinian principles stated earlier does not commit one to hold that genes are in charge of economic behavior, for example. There is no inconsistency in accepting a Generalized Darwinian explanatory framework and at the same time denying that genes are in charge of economic behavior. Likewise, accepting a Darwinian explanatory framework in economics does not make economic evolution a subset of biological evolution. And neither does it imply that phenomena at the social level and at the level of individual agents are reducible to phenomena at the cellular and molecular level. Thus rejection of genetic determinism and

---

[4] This is aptly stated, for example, in the title of their 2006b paper: "Why we need a generalized Darwinism, and why generalized Darwinism is not enough".

of biological reductionism (which Hodgson and Knudsen believe should be rejected) should not be taken to provide a good reason to reject Generalized Darwinism (which Hodgson and Knudsen take to be an ill-taken rejection).

Resisting Generalized Darwinism in economics on the ground that cultural evolution, and economic evolution in particular, are Lamarckian, where "Lamarckian" is taken to mean that acquired characteristics can be inherited, is also misguided. Generalized Darwinism does not rule out the inheritance of acquired characteristics. This belief rests on the misunderstanding that there is only one sort of inheritance: genetic inheritance. Such a misunderstanding is curious. For if there is one thing Generalized Darwinism wants to bring out, it is exactly that genetic inheritance is just one particular mode of inheritance among several and possibly many others. Generalized Darwinism stresses that there might be (and probably actually are) other replicators than genes. If nongenetic modes of inheritance are taken into consideration, it is easy to see how acquired characteristics can be inherited. Through learning and instruction parents can transmit the skills they themselves have learned to their children (and also to nonkin), for example. A suitably Generalized Darwinism has no problem with accommodating this.

What Hodgson and Knudsen stress, in short, is that a suitably generalized and abstract version of Darwinism is able to meet many, if not all, of the *prima facie* cogent objections against developing an evolutionary theory in economics that is strictly analogous to Darwinian evolutionary biology. The objections mostly pertain to purported disanalogies between biological and economic systems. Generalized Darwinism's ambition precisely is to abstract from those specific elements (or "details") in Darwinian evolutionary biology that do not have counterparts or analogues in economic systems, so that what is left after the abstractions are made – Generalized Darwinism – contains only general principles that biological systems share with other systems (including economic systems). The project of Generalized Darwinism would falter in the eyes of its proponents if its formulation were to involve references to peculiarities in biological evolution that are lacking in evolutionary processes in other domains. If it were pointed out that some particular attempt to formulate a suitable Generalized Darwinism contains references to such peculiarities in biological evolution, then this need not necessarily undermine the project of Generalized

Darwinism. It possibly would only show that the particular formulation
under consideration is not yet general and abstract enough to serve as a
correct formulation of Generalized Darwinism.

This also explains the general strategy that Hodgson and Knudsen
adopt in countering objections against Generalized Darwinism: to
show that the objections only have force against nongeneralized (or
not suitably generalized) versions of Darwinism (especially those that
have been worked out in evolutionary biology). Hodgson and
Knudsen set out to show that the objections fail to hit their generalized version of Darwinism. It is to be noted that Hodgson and
Knudsen seem to agree with some of the disanalogies between biological and economic systems identified by critics of "the biological
analogy (or metaphor)" (cf. Foster 1997; Witt 1999). One such
disanalogy is that there is not something like inheritance going on in
processes of economic change. Another objection opponents raised
against importing the biological metaphor was that it would introduce a *selectionist bias* in economic theorizing. Something akin to
natural selection would thereby be put center stage, at the expense of
other possible evolutionary forces and agents that might be more central to processes of economic change (such as self-transformation).
Thus Hodgson and Knudsen acknowledge that there are real and significant differences between biological and economic systems. But
they argue that the differences relate to domain-specific details rather
than to the general principles stated in Generalized Darwinism. I
think that this is the best, if not only, available strategy to follow in
making their case. As we shall later see, however, this strategy
also has a serious drawback. But before I come to that, I first want to
discuss the role that *ontology* is supposed to play here.

Different Clusters of Ontological Issues

Hodgson and Knudsen argue that applying Generalized Darwinism in
(evolutionary) economics is a matter of ontology rather than analogy:

This is not essentially a matter of analogy; it is a partial description and
analysis of reality. Social evolution is Darwinian by virtue of (social) ontology, not (biological) analogy. (Hodgson & Knudsen 2006a: 16)[5]

[5] See also "It is not that social evolution is *analogous* to evolution in the natural
world; it is that at a high level of abstraction, social and biological evolution
share these general principles. In this sense, social evolution *is* Darwinian"
(Hodgson and Knudsen 2006b: 14).

I am tempted to argue that Hodgson and Knudsen invoke a false opposition here of social evolution being Darwinian in virtue either of analogy or of ontology.[6] But let me resist this temptation and ask instead what sense of ontology is implied here. Many things have been discussed under the rubric of "ontology" that are so different that they'd better be kept distinct. In fact, the things Hodgson (2002) explicitly discusses under the rubric of "ontology" are not related (or at least not clearly related) to the issue of whether or not economic systems exhibit the Darwinian features of variation, inheritance and selection. The most prominent ontological issue discussed by Hodgson is the Darwinian rejection of *"uncaused causes"* (Hodgson 2002: 268). Darwinism is argued to be committed to the view that intentionality, the capacity to act on one's intentions, is a cause of action that is itself caused by other prior causes. Accordingly, Darwinism sets out to explain how this capacity has (or could have) evolved. Another issue that Hodgson brings up under the rubric of ontology is that of *a multilayered ontology*. The idea here is that Darwinism acknowledges that there are adjacent layers (or levels) of organization in reality. There is not just one basic or ultimate layer in reality, say at the molecular level (of genes, for example) or even further down at the (sub) atomic level, to which all existing phenomena can be reduced. Instead we have several layers of organization in reality, Hodgson argues, with emergent properties featuring at all layers (except, perhaps, the most basic one). Thus human beings have properties that cannot be reduced to properties of any of their parts. And social reality in turn has properties that cannot be reduced to those of individual agents.

Following a classification I introduced elsewhere (Vromen 2004), I suggest the "ontological issues" mentioned here belong to three different clusters that should be clearly distinguished from one another. The issue of whether the three principles of Generalized Darwinism are adequate for studying economic evolution belongs to the *first cluster* of issues. What is at stake here are what significant features (if any) evolutionary processes in different domains have in common.

---

[6] I would argue that applying Generalized Darwinism to evolutionary economics is a matter of both analogy and ontology. Generalized Darwinism posits similarities in general principles between biological and nonbiological evolution (and economic evolution, in particular, which makes it a matter of analogy) and is based on the ontological claim that economic evolution actually exhibits these principles.

Hodgson and Knudsen argue that both biological systems and socio-cultural (such as economic) systems exhibit variation, replication and selection and that therefore Darwinian evolution occurs in economic systems (Hodgson & Knudsen 2006a: 6). This provides the ontological basis for their claim that the same general Darwinian framework can be applied in attempts to explain phenomena both in the biological and sociocultural domain.

The issue of whether there are (or can be) uncaused causes belongs to the *second cluster*. What is at stake here is whether there is one giant unbroken, continuous causal chain running (like an all-encompassing tree of life) from the origin of first life on earth (or even earlier, from the Big Bang) to, say, ongoing processes of economic evolution that does not involve divine (or, more generally, non-natural) interventions. It is clear that the existence of such an all-encompassing causal chain would rule out the existence of uncaused causes. What is not immediately clear is what light such a causal chain would shed on ongoing processes of economic evolution. For example, is it possible, as Jon Elster once suggested,[7] that we human beings are evolved creatures that, as the sorcerer's apprentice, are capable of transcending (and even annihilating) the very forces (such as natural selection) that produced us?

The issue of a multilayered ontology belongs to the *third cluster*. It is here that the traditional question alluded to earlier, about the stuff or substance that reality is ultimately made of, is posed. At stake here is whether entities and their properties at higher levels of organization have a life of their own, or that their existence and operations are merely derived from what is happening at lower levels of organization. Do firms and their properties (such as their organization forms and routines) exist *sui generis*, for example, or do they have a derived existence only, stemming from the interactions of the individuals partaking in their operations?[8] Is, in the end, all of life (including "economic life") ultimately a matter of subatomic particles swerving in the void? If Hodgson is right in believing that emergent properties exist at higher levels of organization, such a "reductionist" view is fundamentally mistaken. The issue of the levels of organization at which replicators and interactors in evolutionary processes are to be situated

---

[7] "We may say that in *creating man natural selection has transcended itself*" Elster (1979:16).
[8] See Vromen (2006) for an ontological analysis of organizational routines of this kind.

also clearly belongs to this third cluster. Hodgson and Knudsen follow Hull (1981, 1988) in distinguishing replicators from interactors in evolutionary processes. As Hull observes, interactors in evolutionary processes (such as individual organisms) might be situated at a higher level of organization than replicators (such as genes).[9]

The point of insisting on clearly distinguishing the three clusters of issues is partly that the issues in the clusters are really different and, hence, should not be confused or conflated. Sometimes theses or claims are presented as if they were competitors addressing the same issues, whereas in fact they are compatible stances taken on issues belonging to different clusters. Christian Cordes (2006), for example, treats Generalized Darwinism and the so-called Continuity Thesis as competitors that address the same issues. The Continuity Thesis, as defended by Witt (2003), is in line with Hodgson's endorsement of the Darwinian principle that there are no uncaused causes.[10] The Continuity Thesis roughly states that currently ongoing processes on economic evolution proceed on the basis of outcomes of prior evolutionary processes (both biological and cultural), that these outcomes causally affect ongoing economic evolution and that therefore these outcomes should be taken into account when studying ongoing economic evolution. Cordes compares the strengths and weaknesses of Generalized Darwinism and the Continuity Thesis with each other and concludes that the research project inspired by the Continuity Thesis is more promising than the project inspired by Generalized Darwinism.

Cordes might be right that the Continuity Thesis inspires a more promising research project than Generalized Darwinism. But his argument is flawed, as he erroneously assumes that the issues the Continuity Thesis and Generalized Darwinism are dealing with are the same. They are not. As argued earlier, Generalized Darwinism deals with issues belonging to the first cluster. It is about general features that evolutionary processes in all domains allegedly have in

---

[9] Mesoudi, Whiten, and Laland (2006) show what it could mean to argue that we should move *beyond analogy* to ontology: we should investigate whether neuroscience gives us reason to believe that information is processed and stored roughly in the way that Generalized Darwinism suggests it is (this belongs to cluster III: multilayered ontology).

[10] As a matter of fact, Hodgson also subscribes to (what he calls) the Continuity Hypothesis.

common and about the explanatory framework adequate to account for these features. By contrast, the issues the Continuity Thesis deals with belong to the second cluster. It is about causal processes and about how the products of past evolutionary processes influence ongoing processes of economic evolution. The Continuity Thesis does not necessarily undermine a generalized version of Darwinism, as Hodgson rightly recognizes. Granting not just that intentionality is a product of past evolutionary processes but also that intentionality plays a crucial role in economic evolution is compatible with a sufficiently Generalized Darwinism, for example.[11]

Thus, *pace* Cordes, the Continuity Thesis and Generalized Darwinism need not imply taking contradicting stances on the same set of issues. But what Cordes does seem to be right about is that starting either from Generalized Darwinism or from the Continuity Thesis might steer you in different research directions. As different points of departure for further research, Generalized Darwinism and the Continuity Thesis have *different heuristics*. They draw our attention to different features, elements or aspects in evolutionary processes. Generalized Darwinism spurs us to look for relevant variants, selection pressures and processes and inheritance (or replication) processes in some given domain of enquiry. The Continuity Thesis directs our attention to past evolutionary processes and their outcomes. Generalized Darwinism and the Continuity Thesis also present different agendas for further research. Generalized Darwinism invites us to look more closely into how, for example, new variants are generated in some given domain, whereas the Continuity Thesis invites us to look more closely into how precisely the products of past evolutionary processes causally affect ongoing evolutionary processes.

Noncausal Explanations of Causal Processes

Clearly distinguishing the clusters can also help us see more clearly that, sometimes contrary to first appearances, some particular stance taken in one cluster does not imply a commitment to taking a particular position in other clusters. Consider once again the Darwinist

---

[11] Cordes also seems to criticize a form of Generalized Darwinism that is less general and abstract than the form Hodgson and Knudsen are willing to defend.

rejection of uncaused causes in the second cluster. Hodgson suggests that this implies that Darwinism sets out to give causal explanations of phenomena and processes. I take it that giving causal explanations means that attempts are made to reconstruct (at least part of) the actual causal history behind the phenomena and processes in a step-by-step fashion. The ideal in Darwinism would be to provide what Sterelny (1996) calls *actual-sequence explanations*, explanations that aim to get right the actual sequence of causes and effects in the production of some particular phenomena and processes. But in fact no such thing follows from the recognition of the nonexistence of uncaused causes. There is no inconsistency in denying the existence of uncaused causes and at the same time to engage in attempts to give explanations that are not causal. In particular, one can try to explain some phenomenon (that almost all firms in an industry have the same organization form, for example) by showing that it is an instantiation of a more general explanatory pattern that has already been observed elsewhere. When we succeed in doing so, Philip Kitcher argues, we have put our finger on what (to wit, the *general* explanatory pattern) unites the phenomenon with other phenomena (which we already have shown to be instantiations of the same pattern). Hence, on this view explanation is *unification*.[12] The more phenomena we can show to be instantiations of the same general pattern, the greater the explanatory power of the pattern. Giving explanations is here thought of as providing arguments or inferences rather than as identifying causal relations. The general pattern from which the phenomenon to be explained is inferred might be, but need not be, indicative of a generic causal mechanism.

What is interesting is that in his famous case study of unification-as-explanation, "Darwin's Achievement," Kitcher (1985) focuses precisely on the explanatory pattern constituted by Generalized Darwinism's three principles (variation, inheritance and selection).[13] Kitcher

---

[12] Some remarks of Hodgson also seem to point in this direction (e.g., Generalized Darwinism provides an "encompassing framework", Hodgson 2002: 272, or a "universal metatheory", Hodgson 2002: 278).

[13] Note, though, that Kitcher only discusses the explanatory power of the three principles in their original biological domain. Furthermore, to be fully accurate, Kitcher (following Darwin) argues that the third principle is not selection, but the struggle for existence. Evolution by natural selection follows from the three principles working in tandem.

explicitly contrasts his notion of unification-as-explanation with received notions of causal explanation (such as Wesley Salmon's). Thus, for Kitcher explanations in which the three Darwinian principles are invoked are not instances of causal explanations but of unifications-as-explanations. What this shows is that one can accept Hodgson and Knudsen's claim that the three principles of Generalized Darwinism should be invoked in any satisfactory explanation of evolution in complex systems without drawing their conclusion that it is causal explanation that we should be after. It is one thing that there is one huge causal chain running from the Big Bang (or, if you prefer, from the moment things started to evolve) and that there are no supernatural interventions (or skyhooks) in this chain. It is quite another thing that the goal in all of science must be to engage in causal explanation, meaning that attempts must be made to depict causal processes realistically and faithfully (as meticulously as possible) that gave rise to the phenomena we want to explain. We might accept the first and reject the second without running into inconsistencies.

Kitcher's rendering of the explanatory power of the three principles of variation, inheritance and differential fitness suggests that Generalized Darwinism's explanatory potential might not lie so much in being a first, indispensable step in working out minute accounts of how many *particular* things evolved as in presenting a unifying framework for seeing *general* patterns in many seemingly disparate and disconnected phenomena across several domains. By showing that the same pattern underlies instances of organized complexity and of adaptive fit not only in the biological but also in the economic domain, for example, we get an appreciation and better understanding of how organized complexity and adaptive fit *in general* (across different domains) comes about.[14] Rather than being interested in particular evolutionary processes, evolutionary theorists might be interested more in general patterns in and across domains (see D'Arms, Batterman, & Gorny 1998 for an insightful discussion of the debate between "particularists" and "generalists" in evolutionary theorizing). Whereas evolutionary generalists typically marvel at the usefulness, if not indispensability, of simple, tractable formal models, evolutionary particularists tend to stress the limits and shortcomings

---

[14] Alternatively, evolutionary economists might be interested more in general reasons that prevent ideal adaptive fit from being actually realized.

of such models in dealing with the richness and complexities in actual evolutionary processes.

Boyd and Richerson (1987) likewise argue that one of the great attractions of adopting an explicit Darwinian framework in studying nonbiological evolutionary processes (in their case: cultural evolution) is that it gives us insightful, simple abstract models. The goal of such models is not to present true historical narratives of events. Instead, simple abstract models, even though they are deliberately unrealistic (Boyd & Richerson 2005: 98), enable us to detect general patterns; patterns that easily delude us if we are entangled in the nitty-gritty details of actual historical processes. As such, simple abstract models and rich historical explanation are complementary, rather than competing (Boyd & Richerson 2005: 94–96). Another service that simple abstract models render to us, Boyd and Richerson argue, is that they school our intuitions. Unaided by such models, our intuitions often lead us astray. From the observation that cultural transmission is biased by (what Dan Sperber calls) psychological attractors, for example, we tend to infer that "therefore" Darwinian models do not apply. As Henrich and Boyd (2002) point out, however, no such conclusion follows from the observation. Paradoxically, what Henrich and Boyd show in particular is that replicator dynamics can be observed at the population level, especially if the psychological attractors are strong.[15]

Kitcher's notion of unification-as-explanation also provides a different perspective on Hodgson's argument that Generalized Darwinism explains little on its own (Hodgson 2002: 273; see also Hodgson & Knudsen 2004: 285). Does it? It depends on what we are after in our explanation. If it is "detailed" causal explanation that we are after, if we want to trace the causal histories or etiologies of the phenomena we want to explain, then Hodgson is right that Generalized Darwinism explains little on its own. We then need much more information than is provided in Generalized Darwinism. But if it is explanatory unification we are after, then, if advocates of Generalized Darwinism are right, Generalized Darwinism has huge explanatory power of its own. If Hodgson and other advocates of Generalized Darwinism are right, the

---

[15] But see Claidière and Sperber (2007), who argue that Henrich and Boyd fail to make a convincing case because their result is based on an inaccurate modeling of attraction.

scope of phenomena that can be explained with just the three general and abstract principles of Generalized Darwinism is enormous. Indeed, it is virtually unbounded. The economy or efficiency in the ratio between the number of phenomena that can be explained (i.e., that can be seen as instantiations of the Darwinian pattern or schema; the *explananda*) and the number of explanatory principles needed (the *explanantia*) would be nothing less than stupendous.

What More Is Needed Than Generalized Darwinism to Arrive at Causal Explanations?

It is clear that Hodgson and Knudsen hold both that we need Generalized Darwinism in evolutionary economics and that Generalized Darwinism is not enough to arrive at fully satisfactory theories in evolutionary economics. What is not entirely clear, however, is precisely what contribution Generalized Darwinism is supposed to make in the construction of fully satisfactory theories and exactly what more is needed in addition to the three principles of Generalized Darwinism to arrive at such theories.[16] Hodgson and Knudsen mention the "inspiring, framing and organizing" (Hodgson & Knudsen 2006a: 16) role that Generalized Darwinism could play.[17] Hodgson and Knudsen (2008) argue that Generalized Darwinism can serve as constructive principles for theory development. This suggests that the three principles of Generalized Darwinism are supposed to serve a *heuristic function* and provide guidance in theory construction (see also Darden & Cain 1989: 125). What is not entirely clear, however, is how Generalized Darwinism is supposed to serve this heuristic function.

Here again, I submit, Kitcher's discussion of Darwin's great achievement in biology is helpful. According to Kitcher, Darwin's major innovation consisted in the formulation of a few general explanatory principles that served at least two heuristic functions (Kitcher

---

[16] See Stoelhorst and Hensgens (2007) for constructive proposals.

[17] Similarly, Nelson argues that general principles of evolution in theory can enhance the clarity, power and rigor of theorizing (Nelson 2007: 92). Nelson also stresses, however, that much of the interesting empirically oriented evolutionary theorizing in the social sciences is done independently of such general principles. In these cases general evolutionary principles served not to inspire and guide theory construction, but to organize and structure the discussion only after the evolutionary theories were already constructed.

1993: 32). Not only did Darwin make biologists look specifically for instances of heritable variation and of selective pressures in explaining the occurrence of some particular trait in the individuals of some species (or population), Darwin also identified the questions that biologists should address. In particular, Darwin made biologists search for theoretical accounts of processes of heritable transmission and of the origination and maintenance of variation. In short, with his development of a general explanatory scheme, Darwin to a large extent set the research agenda for the next generations of evolutionary biologists to come.

Kitcher's characterization of Darwin's great achievement also sheds light on what more is needed in addition to the three principles of Generalized Darwinism to arrive at satisfactory full-fledged theories. Darwin's general explanatory scheme can be said to be abstract in that its scope is not restricted to particular groups of individuals with particular properties. Its scope includes all groups of individuals with properties that evolved by natural selection. This is why Kitcher's representation of Darwin's explanatory scheme contains dummy letters such as G for groups of individuals and P for their (heritable) properties. The first heuristic function of Darwin's explanatory scheme is that it makes biologists look for particular instantiations of it. Thus we might be interested in why a certain group of finches evolved particularly shaped beaks. This involves first substituting the dummy letters for nonlogical expressions and then looking for historical evidence that, given the then-prevailing ecological conditions (or selective pressure), ancestors of the present group of finches were fitter than then-living finches with other-shaped beaks. The replacement of the dummy letters by nonlogical expressions, if we apply the general abstract scheme to explain particular groups of individuals with particular properties, can be called a *concretization* of the scheme.

The second heuristic function of the scheme is that it makes biologists search for theoretical accounts of things that are presupposed in the scheme. In particular, it spurs biologists to investigate how heritable transmission works and how variation originates and is maintained. If these accounts involve specifying the mechanisms or processes underlying heritable transmission and the emergence and maintenance of new variants, we might say that this amounts to *specifications* of underlying mechanisms. In short, Kitcher's discussion suggests that whatever more is needed to get from the general principles of Generalized Darwinism to full-fledged causal theories, this at any rate requires first concretization(s) and then specification(s).

As noted before, Hodgson and Knudsen do not spell out exactly what more is needed than the three principles of Generalized Darwinism to arrive at satisfactory full-fledged causal theories about the evolution of economic phenomena. They talk about domain-specific auxiliary hypotheses and domain-specific empirical material that have to be added to the three principles. They do not explicate what exactly they have in mind here and how such hypotheses and empirical material have to be fitted together with the three principles. What is clear, however, is that they believe that concretizations and specifications of the three principles are also needed. More specifically, they identify firms (rather than individuals) as *interactors* and habits and routines (rather than genes) as *replicators* as concretizations that are specific for the economic domain. They also repeatedly stress that the *details of the specific mechanisms* at work in the economic domain differ from those in the biological domain (Hodgson 2002: 273, 272; Hodgson & Knudsen 2006a: 3). Thus Hodgson and Knudsen hold that the specifications of the mechanisms underlying the processes of interaction and of replication in the economic domain are different than the specifications of these mechanisms in the biological domain. Unfortunately, Hodgson and Knudsen leave it at this. They do not elaborate on what specifications of the mechanisms in the economic domain they have in mind.

Summing up now, we saw that Hodgson and Knudsen are looking for a generalization of Darwinism that meets two *desiderata*. First it should be general and broad enough to cover evolutionary processes in all complex systems, including notably economic systems. It is here that Hodgson and Knudsen see the main difference with earlier pleas to found evolutionary economics on "the biological metaphor." The problem with such pleas was that "the biological metaphor" was not sufficiently domain-unspecific; it involved taking features on board that are specific of the biological domain. The second *desideratum* is that the generalization of Darwinism should be helpful in guiding the construction of theories that causally explain specific evolutionary processes in particular domains (again including notably specific evolutionary processes in the economic domain). As Hodgson and Knudsen argue, their own generalization of Darwinism explains little on its own. Starting with Generalized Darwinism, additional steps are to be taken to arrive at causal theories with great explanatory power. Whatever more this entails, it at any rate involves concretizations of the principles and specifications of the mechanisms underlying them.

Hodgson and Knudsen's discussion of Generalized Darwinism suggests that the two *desiderata* can and should be met in sequential order. Their discussion of "the biological metaphor" indicates that generalizing Darwinism primarily (if not wholly) is a matter of *abstracting* from all features in Darwinian evolutionary biology that pertain only to the biological domain. Only by shrugging off elements that are specific to the biological domain can we retain elements that are truly general in the sense of domain-unspecific. To put the same point in negative terms: a form of Darwinism that is unable to leave behind peculiarities of the biological domain is doomed to fail from the start. Hodgson and Knudsen clearly believe that their own generalization of Darwinism (their own Generalized Darwinism) in terms of the three principles of variation, inheritance and selection meets this first *desideratum*. Subsequently Hodgson and Knudsen take additional first steps to show that their version of Generalized Darwinism is also able to meet the second *desideratum*: to construct an economic evolutionary theory on the basis that it is able to causally explain specific evolutionary processes in the economic domain. To this end they first assume that, in an acceptable economic evolutionary theory, replicators and interactors have to be identified, and they then identify firms as economic interactors and habits and routines as economic replicators.

This can be represented as follows (Figure 4.1).

What this figure is meant to bring out primarily is that different levels of abstraction can be discerned in Hodgson and Knudsen's view. The three principles of Hodgson and Knudsen's Generalized Darwinism at level A are supposed to be the most abstract principles in the figure; the identification of firms as social interactors and habits and routines as social replicators at level C is supposed to be the most concrete part in the figure. If we think of the figure as a tree, making abstractions means that we ascend the tree, and making concretizations and adding specifications means that we descend the tree. I take it that Hodgson and Knudsen hold that both Generalized Darwinism's principles at level A and the depiction of Darwinian evolutionary processes at level B are domain-unspecific. Domain-specific elements only enter the picture at level C. I also take it that Hodgson

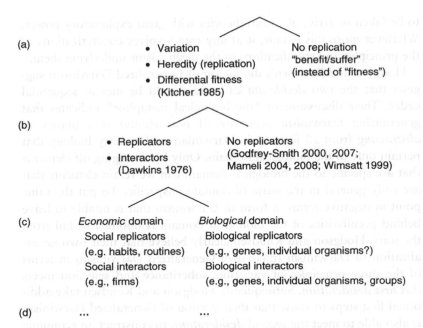

(a)
- Variation
- Heredity (replication)
- Differential fitness
 (Kitcher 1985)

No replication
"benefit/suffer"
(instead of "fitness")

(b)
- Replicators
- Interactors
 (Dawkins 1976)

No replicators
(Godfrey-Smith 2000, 2007;
Mameli 2004, 2008; Wimsatt 1999)

(c)
Economic domain
Social replicators
(e.g. habits, routines)
Social interactors
(e.g. firms)

Biological domain
Biological replicators
(e.g., genes, individual organisms?)
Biological interactors
(e.g., genes, individual organisms, groups)

(d)
...   ...

Figure 4.1 Adjacent levels of abstraction in Hodgson and Knudsen's Generalized Darwinism

and Knudsen hold that more domain-specific auxiliary hypotheses have to be added to arrive at satisfactory causal theories than just identifying firms as social interactors and habits and routines as social replicators at level C. This means that further concretizations, specifications and additions are needed that will introduce additional levels beyond level C.

Other Optional Routes Not Taken

As Hodgson and Knudsen realize, the specific concretizations of the three principles of generalized Darwinism that they propose do not follow logically from the principles. Far from being forced moves, they are optional choices. Starting from Generalized Darwinism's three principles at level A, there are other options that Hodgson and Knudsen might have chosen. In particular, acceptance of the principle of inheritance (or replication) does not imply that the existence of replicators has to be granted at level B.[18] As several commentators have pointed out, strictly speaking, no particle-like entities such as genes that are transmitted from parents to offspring need to exist for Darwinian evolution by natural selection to occur (cf. Mesoudi, Whiten, & Laland 2004: 1). All that is needed is that existing variants are more or less reliably transmitted to the subsequent generation. Parents and their offspring should be more similar in the relevant respects than randomly drawn individuals (Godfrey-Smith 2000; see also Wimsatt 1999).[19] There can be replication in this sense without replicators. So starting with the three principles of variation, replication and selection, further steps could be taken in the direction of a full-fledged economic evolutionary theory that do not involve the identification of replicators.

Are Replication and Interaction Two Separate Processes in Nonbiological Evolution?

As already noted earlier, Figure 4.1 does not present a complete picture of what, according to Hodgson and Knudsen, is to be done to arrive at a full-fledged economic evolutionary theory. What is missing at any rate is a specification of the processes of replication and of interaction in economic systems. Thus far Hodgson and Knudsen have not provided such a specification.[20] But the fact that they posit

[18] It goes without saying, I hope, that nothing in the concept of social (or economic) interactors prescribes that firms (rather than groups, for example) should be identified as social interactors (and likewise for habit and routines as social replicators). To foreclose misunderstanding, note that my point here is only that descending the tree is not a matter of fleshing out logical implications and not that no good reasons can be given for the choices that Hodgson and Knudsen make.
[19] See also "All that may be required is a process that retains features of interactors (event or object) across generations in a lineage" (Hull, Langman, & Glenn 2001: 525). Interestingly, Hodgson and Knudsen refer to both Godfrey-Smith (2000) and Wimsatt (1999) to support their case. For the issue at hand, however, the two papers undermine rather than support their case. Note also that in the case of cultural and economic evolution, talking of generations and lineages might be farfetched in the first place, as transmission might proceed "horizontally" (e.g., between peers or role models in the same generation).
[20] Hodgson and Knudsen do argue, however, that habits of behavior (as social replicators) do not directly make copies of themselves, but replicate indirectly, by means of their behavioral expressions (cf. Hodgson and Knudsen 2007). As far as I can see, insofar as it is appropriate at all to call this replication, it is likely to have low fidelity (see Sperber's incisive critique later).

replicators and interactors at level B strongly suggests that they hold that there are two processes going on: replication and interaction. On this account, Darwinian evolution by natural selection is not a single process but the result of the interaction of two separate processes. As Hull, Langman, and Glenn (2001) cogently argue in their attempt to give a general characterization of selection processes[21]:

> The most fundamental distinction made in this paper is between passing on information via replication and the biasing of this replication because of environmental interaction. As we have argued at some length, selection is not a single process but composed of two processes – replication and environmental interaction. As a result, the issue of the levels at which selection occurs must be subdivided into two questions: at what levels does replication take place and at what levels does environmental interaction take place.
>
> (Hull, Langman, & Glenn 2001: 527)[22]

Other commentators agree (cf. Mameli 2004, 2008). The bottom line, or most minimal requirement for evolution by natural selection to occur, they argue, is that there are two separate (and independent) processes[23]:

1. A process taking care of *"heritable" variation* – the minimal requirement here is that the correlation of relevant properties between parents (or role models) and offspring should exceed that of randomly drawn individuals in the population.[24]

---

[21] If there is one person who inspired Hodgson and Knudsen to formulate and defend a version of Generalized Darwinism, it is David Hull. Hodgson and Knudsen dedicate their most elaborate defense of Generalized Darwinism to date (Hodgson & Knudsen 2006b) to him.

[22] See also "we define selection as repeated cycles of replication, variation, and environmental interaction so structured that environmental interaction causes replication to be differential" (ibid., 513).

[23] There are other (and perhaps for the economic domain more promising) formulations of Universal (or Generalized) Darwinism in terms of "blind variation and selective retention" (Campbell 1974; Plotkin 1994; Cziko 1995). This formulation omits "replication" (and "parents" and "offspring") altogether. Because this is not the formulation of Darwinism Hodgson and Knudsen opt for, I will not go into this here. See Stoelhorst (2008) for further discussion.

[24] One might wish to distinguish between "real" inheritance (or replication) processes on the one hand, as in the case of parents, and dissemination processes, as in the case of role models, on the other hand. In the latter case there are not really successive generations (I owe this observation to Ulrich Witt – personal communication – see also Note 19).

2. A process taking care of *differential reproduction* – individuals with higher "fitness" are leaving more offspring than individuals with lower "fitness." Paraphrased in terms of interaction, this means that interactors interact as cohesive wholes with their environment in such a way that this environmental interaction causes replication to be differential.

The joint operation of the two processes yields the result that the "heritable" properties of the "fitter" individuals spread in the population at the expense of those of the individuals with lower "fitness."

Hodgson and Knudsen apparently believe that they are on safe ground in arguing that the decomposition of evolutionary processes into the two processes of replication and interaction is general enough to cover also processes of cultural (or social) evolution and of economic evolution in particular. But are they? Wimsatt convincingly argues that in cultural evolution processes of inheritance (replication) and of selection (interaction) cannot be separated. In biological evolution, it makes sense to distinguish (analytically, if not physically) stages (or processes; mechanisms) of inheritance, development and selection. But this does not make sense in cultural evolution: "development and selection ... both impinge upon cultural heredity in a constitutive way" (Wimsatt 1999: 290). The three are totally inseparable in cultural evolution (ibid.).

To see why, let us look at what generally is believed to be one of the most advanced Darwinian treatments of cultural evolution to date: Boyd and Richerson (1985) and Boyd and Richerson (2005). Like Hodgson and Knudsen and other Darwinists, Boyd and Richerson distinguish between inheritance (or transmission) and selection in cultural evolution. In cultural evolution, Boyd and Richerson argue, the transmission of behaviorally relevant traits (such as skills and social norms) is nongenetic and notably involves imitation of cultural "parents" (who need not coincide with the biological parents) by cultural "offspring." If selection in cultural evolution ("cultural selection") were strictly analogous to natural selection in biological evolution, one would expect the relative fitness of the culturally transmitted traits to determine subsequently which traits spread in the population. But this is not how Boyd and Richerson (and other leading anthropologists working on cultural evolution, such as Dan Sperber; see also Mesoudi, Whiten, & Laland 2004: 2) conceive of selection in cultural evolution.

Selection in cultural evolution rather refers to the selection of whom to imitate. It is a choice made (consciously or not) by imitators that is supposed to predate cultural transmission processes.[25] First comes the decision of whom to imitate, and only after this decision is made it remains to be seen what the imitator takes over (or wants to take over) from the person(s) imitated.

Thus Wimsatt is right in arguing that selection is constitutive of the replication process in cultural evolution. The replication process involves not only the identification of what is transmitted from parents to offspring and how it is transmitted, we could say, but also the identification of who are the parents and who are their offspring. If we want to know what is replicated, the first thing we need to know is who are the models for replication (the parents) for the offspring. In biological evolution, we know the latter independently from selection. The identification of parents and their offspring is independent of selection. Selection here only affects whether individuals have offspring, not what sort of offspring they have. In cultural evolution, this is different. Selection here means that certain particular "parents" are selected by imitators (the "offspring") as models for imitation. Thus the identification of parents and their offspring depends on selection. This implies that selection is an integral part of replication in cultural evolution, and as such selection is inseparable from replication in cultural evolution.[26]

Why Replication Is a Nonstarter in Cultural Transmission in the First Place

It could be objected that this difference in parent–offspring relation between biological and cultural evolution is insignificant for the reliability and fidelity in the process of replication. The fact that in cultural

---

[25] For similar reasons Godfrey-Smith (2014: 48) argues that cultural evolution is less Darwinian than biological evolution: in cultural evolution, the retention of successful variants does not occur through reproduction by variants, as in biological evolution, but by a more centralized mechanism (such as the mind or brain of imitators).

[26] Although Boyd and Richerson (2005) retain the analytical distinction between cultural selection and replication (or transmission), they recognize that the dividing line between them is hard to draw if cultural transmission is biased (which they take to be the rule, rather than the exception), and in particular if the bias involved is model-based (as in the case of conformist transmission, for example; Boyd and Richerson 2005: 79).

evolution (prospective) children choose their parents on the basis of their pre-evolved psychological mechanisms, whereas there is not such a choice in biological evolution does not make a significant difference, it can be argued. The significant thing arguably is that despite this difference the end result in both biological and cultural evolution is the same: after the parent–offspring transmission, the offspring resembles their parents in the relevant respects (at least more so than they resemble other individuals in the population), so that condition 1 stated earlier (of "heritable variation") is met. But is this condition really met in cultural evolution? So far we did not question that imitation leads to more or less faithful and reliable transmission of traits. Yet there seem to be good reasons to call this in question.

As some of its leading advocates readily acknowledge, the image invoked in notions such as "replication" and "inheritance" is one of *copying*: "Replication is inherently a copying process. Successive variations must in some sense be retained and then passed on" (Hull, Langman, & Glenn 2001: 514). As incisive critics such as Maurice Bloch (2000) and in particular Dan Sperber (1996, 2000) argue, when it comes to thinking about cultural transmission, this image is seriously misleading (for a balanced treatment, see Sterelny 2006). Rather than being critical only of the notion of meme and being engaged in an attempt to develop a generalized account of replication that does justice to cultural transmission (as is suggested by Hodgson 2006: 211; see also Hodgson & Knudsen 2008: 4), Sperber wants to dispense with the notion of replication altogether. Sperber argues that it would be misleading even to keep something like high-fidelity copying as a reference point, which is what we do in saying that cultural transmission often or typically leads to failures to replicate, mutations or noise. For this would get the essence of cultural transmission completely wrong. The goal of acquisition in cultural transmission is generally not to acquire a replica of other people's variants. Cultural transmission rather is a constructive process in which the goal is to acquire a piece of knowledge or a skill that suits the individual's own dispositions and preferences. This explains why we should consider acquired pieces of knowledge and skills that deviate from the pieces of knowledge and skills transmitted to be normal and functional rather than accidents or malfunctions.

In acquiring some piece of knowledge or skill from some role model, people bring their own pre-evolved cognitive machinery and in particular their pre-evolved psychological mechanisms with them. The operation of these mechanisms will normally lead to a transformation of the input (such as public expressions of knowledge and skills) in the production process (within the people acquiring the knowledge and skills) leading to output (in the form of acquired knowledge and skills, or overt behavior). Even if people are explicitly asked to reproduce a drawing as accurately as possible ten minutes after they have been shown the drawing (for some ten seconds), for example, transformations will occur. One might think that the transformations and modifications of the information incessantly brought about by the workings of psychological mechanisms produce quite some variety between individuals in the things they acquire and also erratic changes in what is acquired by individuals over time. But Sperber argues that generally this is not the case. One of the main reasons for this is that individuals happen to have many pre-evolved psychological mechanisms in common with each other and that these mechanisms tend to be stable in time.[27] Sperber calls such shared and stable pre-evolved psychological mechanisms *attractors*. The bias in cultural transmission produced by attractors is systematic (in the sense both of individual-unspecific and stable in time), rather than random or erratic. In short, attractors, rather than high fidelity in replication, see to it that there is some macro-level stability in cultural entities within whole populations over time.

Although Sperber's objections may not be equally forceful against all forms of cultural transmission (Sterelny 2006), I think they are rightly widely considered to be powerful and convincing. The upshot is that studying cultural transmission in terms of replication is a non-starter. Far from being a copying process, cultural transmission is a constructive process in which deviations from the model are the rule rather than the exception. It might be more fruitful to conceive of cultural transmission as part of a learning process in which acquired pieces of knowledge and skills are retained only if they suit the individual's dispositions and preferences. That is, only if the acquired pieces turn out to be beneficial or useful for the individual in question when they are acted upon, will the pieces be retained.

---

[27] Another reason Sperber gives is that environmental constraints and affordances might be acting as gravitational forces in cultural transmission.

To sum up, in processes of nonbiological evolution it seems artificial and contrived, if not seriously misleading, first to maintain that we have two component processes (replication and interaction) instead of one process and then to conceive of the first component process (replication) in terms of copying. If we want to do justice to the peculiarities of nonbiological evolution, it seems we'd better dispense not just with the notion of a replicator but also with the notion of replication. The upshot of all this is that Hodgson and Knudsen's formulation of Generalized Darwinism is not general enough to do justice to evolutionary processes in nonbiological domains (and to cultural evolution, in particular). Thus Hodgson and Knudsen's formulation of Generalized Darwinism does not meet their first *desideratum*. It seems we need a version of Darwinism that is even more general than Hodgson and Knudsen's Generalized Darwinism. In the image of the tree we introduced earlier, it seems we have to ascend beyond Hodgson and Knudsen's Generalized Darwinism. What version of Darwinism could we possibly move to?

Selection Type Theories as an Even More General Version of Darwinism

A promising candidate is Darden and Cain's (1989) *selection type theories*. Darden and Cain (1989: 108) argue that they have to move to an even more abstract level than the one Kitcher's schemas is situated on, precisely for the reason Generalized (or Universal) Darwinism is constructed for: to find a formulation of Darwinism that is sufficiently general and abstract to accommodate processes of selection in several domains.[28] Just like Universal Darwinists, Darden and Cain pick out immunology (to be more precise: clonal selection theory for antibody formation) and Edelman's neural Darwinism as theories in the nonbiological domain that their own notion of selection type theories should be able to cover.

Darden and Cain's "selection type theory" is more abstract, and hence more general, than Kitcher's depiction of Darwin's general explanatory scheme in biology, in that its scope is not confined to cases in which superior (or inferior) outcomes result in more offspring

---

[28] See also Skipper (1999), who embraces Darden and Cain's notion of selection type theories.

via a reproduction step. Their selection type theory is also applicable to cases in which the beneficial property is not inherited by offspring. The beneficial property should somehow spread in the population (relative to nonbeneficial properties) also in their selection type theory, but the way in which this is realized need not be through survival and inheritance (or replication).[29]

Like Kitcher and Hodgson and Knudsen, Darden and Cain also emphasize the *heuristic function* of their selection type theory in theory construction. But they also draw attention to the fact that selection type theory can serve a *diagnostic function* in spotting gaps and lacunas in attempts to actually work out selection type theories in some specific nonbiological domain. One of the crucial things any worked out selection type theory has to specify, Darden and Cain argue, are the *critical factors* in some past environment that determine what particular sorts of individuals benefit and what other sorts suffer. Critical factors might be associated with a shortage of food or water, but also with the existence of predators or with the availability of fertile mating partners, for example. The specific sort of critical factor that shapes the extant selection pressure also determines what variant properties are relevant to the benefiting or suffering of the individuals with the properties from the selective interactions. So any worked out selection type theory should identify and specify the relevant critical factors in the environment and the related relevant properties in the individuals that are exposed to the critical factors. It is in this respect that Darden and Cain find Edelman's neural Darwinism wanting. More precisely, Edelman's neural Darwinism tells too little about what the critical factors are in signal configurations and hence also about why certain particular neuron connections are better able to cope with the critical factors than others (ibid., 123). This is a gap in Edelman's neural Darwinism that needs to be filled in further theory construction.

Note that Darden and Cain do not set out to develop an abstract and general account of evolutionary theories. They confine their attention to selection theories within a possibly wider category of

---

[29] Darden and Cain suggest that theories lacking a reproduction step might be called "election" rather than "selection" theories (Darden & Cain 1989: 118), because successful variants might be consciously elected by individuals rather than selected for by some environmental constraints. Peter Godfrey-Smith (2007) is reluctant to call such a generalization "Darwinian."

evolutionary theories. Contrary to what Hodgson and Knudsen maintain, just like Darden and Cain's selection type theories their own version of Generalized Darwinism belongs to a family of attempts to generalize Darwinism that exhibit a *selection bias*. They all cling to the idea that the frequency (or proportion) of the properties that make individuals benefit (or rather suffer) increases (or rather decreases) in the population over time. In this respect Hodgson and Knudsen's version of Generalized Darwinism is not so different after all from earlier attempts to base evolutionary economics on "the biological metaphor," as Hodgson and Knudsen want us to believe. One of the main reasons for opponents to resist "the biological metaphor" was its purportedly unjustified emphasis on the evolutionary force of selection at the expense of other possible evolutionary forces such as drift, migration, recombination and especially self-organization and self-transformation. Hodgson and Knudsen distance themselves from earlier advocates of "the biological metaphor" because they believe that "the biological metaphor" takes on too many features that are specific for the biological domain. But it seems that with the formulation of their own favored Generalized Darwinism they have not been able to shake off the selection bias in "the biological metaphor".

If we want to dispense with the selection bias, we should ascend to an even higher level of abstraction than the level at which Darden and Cain's selection type theories are located. *Population thinking* might be a good candidate (cf. Godfrey-Smith 2009). As Boyd and Richerson (2005) put it, population thinking involves that "we keep track of the different variants, independent little bits or big complexes as the case may be, present in a population, and try to understand what processes cause some variants to increase and others to decline" (Boyd & Richerson 2005: 91). In population thinking, it is not presupposed that natural selection (or some other form of selection) is the dominant, let alone only, process causing changes in population frequencies of variants. These might be caused by altogether different processes, such as drift, migration, recombination or self-organization.

The Devil Is in the Details

Hodgson and Knudsen might object that in identifying variation, inheritance and selection as the three general principles of Generalized Darwinism, they need not, do not want to and as a matter of fact do not actually take on board any of the connotations discussed earlier (to wit, the selectionist bias, replication as copying, the separateness and independence of mechanisms of replication and interaction). Their adherence to the general principles of variation, inheritance (replication) and selection to a general discussion of Darwinian evolutionary processes in terms of replication and interaction, and to a general discussion of such processes in terms of replicators and interactors, suggests that they hold that the connotations also apply to the sociocultural domain. But they might deny that any of these connotations fit the sociocultural domain. They might hold that these connotations are specific for, and hence confined to, the biological domain. If so,[30] the foregoing arguments that the connotations do not fit sociocultural evolution do not undermine Hodgson and Knudsen's position. Rather than countering the arguments, Hodgson and Knudsen would happily embrace them.

What would follow from this? It in fact would imply that the sort of Darwinism Hodgson and Knudsen endorse is to be situated higher in the tree than where I situated it (at level A). Rather than endorsing selection type theories, what Hodgson and Knudsen would really advocate would be something like population thinking (at level II; see Figure 4.2[31]). If processes of biological and sociocultural evolution have features in common only at this high level of abstraction, even more domain-specific "details" have to be added to arrive at the sort of detailed causal theory that Hodgson and Knudsen seem to envisage as the final goal of Generalized Darwinism in evolutionary economics. But the specific shape and contents that Darwinism got in evolutionary biology (and to which the earlier connotations do apply) cannot give any guidance in adding such details. The highly general and abstract principles of Generalized Darwinism do not give much structure and guidance for doing this either. This means that there is much work still to be done. If this can be called a matter of adding details, *the devil surely is in the details!*

Recall that Hodgson and Knudsen see their version of Generalized Darwinism as the first step only in the construction of a theory that is able to give detailed causal explanations of processes of economic

---

[30] If this is really what Hodgson and Knudsen hold, then I urge them to speak out more clearly on these issues.

[31] For a similar view, see Godfrey-Smith (2009: 148). For further discussion, see Vromen (2011).

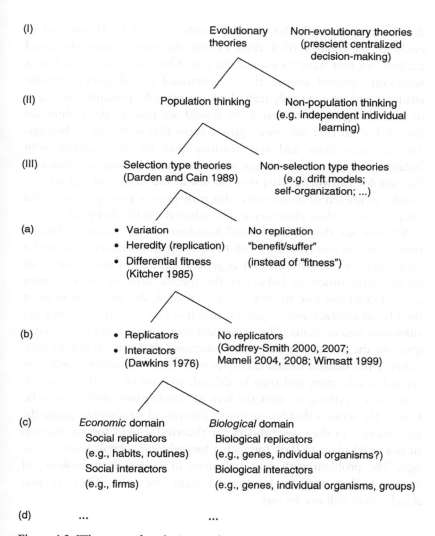

(I)   Evolutionary   Non-evolutionary theories
           theories   (prescient centralized
                             decision-making)

(II)   Population thinking   Non-population thinking
                            (e.g. independent individual
                                    learning)

(III)   Selection type theories   Non-selection type theories
        (Darden and Cain 1989)   (e.g. drift models;
                                 self-organization; ...)

(a)   • Variation   No replication
       • Heredity (replication)   "benefit/suffer"
       • Differential fitness   (instead of "fitness")
         (Kitcher 1985)

(b)   • Replicators   No replicators
       • Interactors   (Godfrey-Smith 2000, 2007;
         (Dawkins 1976)   Mameli 2004, 2008; Wimsatt 1999)

(c)   *Economic* domain   *Biological* domain
        Social replicators   Biological replicators
        (e.g., habits, routines)   (e.g., genes, individual organisms?)
        Social interactors   Biological interactors
        (e.g., firms)   (e.g., genes, individual organisms, groups)

(d)   ...   ...

Figure 4.2 What sort of evolutionary theory is general and abstract enough to fit both the biological and the cultural domain?

evolution. Their version should not only be general enough to cover evolutionary processes in all domains (their first *desideratum*), it should also be helpful and instrumental in constructing such a causal theory (their second *desideratum*). In my image of a tree, this means that if we start with the domain-specific version of Darwinism in evolutionary biology (that does exhibit the connotations discussed earlier), we first have to ascend the tree. Once we have settled on a sufficiently general version that has brushed off all domain-specific elements and retained only truly domain-unspecific principles, we have to descend again. But what steps should we take in descending the tree? It is clear that we cannot go the route that is specific to biology. The concretizations and specifications that we are familiar with because they got some coinage in evolutionary biology are blocked. For ontological worries that they do not fit the subject matter of economics prompted us in our search for truly general principles to ascend the tree further than Hodgson and Knudsen do in the first place.

We now see that Hodgson and Knudsen are caught in a dilemma here. If we do everything we can to meet the first *desideratum*: find a formulation of Darwinism that is general enough to do justice to all evolutionary processes (whatever the specific domain), this requires us to ascend the tree to eerie heights. Indeed, the formulation must then be so abstract and so general that it is bereft of much (if not all) substance and contents. The theoretical structure and guidance that it gives to the search for the many additions that are needed to construct a full-fledged causal theory is next to nil. In other words, the second *desideratum* will then be difficult to meet (if at all). However, if we do everything to meet the second *desideratum*: find a formulation of Darwinism that has sufficient theoretical structure to guide the construction of the causal theory (or theories) sought for, the natural (if not only) place to look for such a formulation is evolutionary biology. The problem with causal theories in evolutionary biology, of course, is that they are far from domain-unspecific. Thus the first *desideratum* will not be met.

Conclusions

Hodgson and Knudsen deserve praise for their advocacy of Generalized Darwinism. They defend Darwinism in studying sociocultural (and, in particular, economic) evolution in the most (and perhaps only) sensible way: to find a formulation of Darwinism that is abstract and general enough to do justice to the special features of sociocultural evolution. Hodgson and Knudsen also deserve credit for not mixing up different sorts of ontological issues. They rightly argue in particular that Generalized Darwinism is compatible with the Continuity Thesis.

The ontological considerations at stake in Hodgson and Knudsen's case for Generalized Darwinism amount to the issue of whether there are significant features that processes of sociocultural evolution have in common (at an appropriate abstract level) with processes of biological evolution. Ontological considerations of this kind also played a major role in the earlier debate about the accuracy of the biological metaphor. What is more, we found that roughly the same ontological objections that were raised against the biological metaphor can be (and actually are) raised again against Generalized Darwinism. The ideas behind these objections seem to be sound and seem to be shared by friends and foes of Darwinism in nonbiological domains alike. Taking the objections seriously, it was argued, necessitates finding a formulation of Darwinism that is even more general and abstract than Hodgson and Knudsen's Generalized Darwinism.

Hodgson and Knudsen want their version of Generalized Darwinism to play a constructive role in the development of theories in evolutionary economics that can explain actual historical processes in a detailed way. They recognize that this entails that domain-specific hypotheses have to be added to Generalized Darwinism. If the version of Darwinism that is able to do justice to nonbiological evolution is to be even more general than Hodgson and Knudsen's Generalized Darwinism, even more hypotheses have to be added than Hodgson and Knudsen envisage to arrive at detailed causal theories. Given that the specific concretizations and specifications of such an even more Generalized Darwinism that are given in evolutionary biology are blocked, the guidance given in this by an even more Generalized Darwinism is pretty poor. In fact, it is next to nil. This seems to suggest that if we stick to the function Hodgson and Knudsen want Generalized Darwinism to serve, it is best not to waste more time with discussing the merits and demerits of Generalized Darwinism and go to the investigation and specification of the details right away.[32]

---

[32] In fact, in the ten years that passed since I wrote the first version of this paper that this chapter is based on, no real progress has been made on this front. Rather than engaging in a search for additional domain-specific hypotheses, subsequent work of Hodgson and Knudsen (e.g., Hodgson & Knudsen 2010) continued to concentrate on foundational issues.

It might be a more promising avenue to defend Generalized Darwinism on other grounds. The main function and explanatory power of Generalized Darwinism might lie elsewhere. It may serve altogether different functions than providing heuristics for the development of theories that can give causal explanations of the actual evolution of economic phenomena. Formulation of some generalized version of Darwinism might facilitate cross-disciplinary transfer (Mesoudi, Whiten, & Laland 2006) of modeling techniques (Boyd & Richerson 1985), for example. As Henrich and Boyd (2002) suggest, borrowing sophisticated modeling techniques from evolutionary biologists might be warranted even in the face of obvious differences between biological and cultural evolution. Even if "replication" is a nonstarter in cultural evolution, replication dynamics might still apply in cultural evolution at the population level. This is an interesting and remarkable result. But if the model applied becomes so disconnected from the actual causal process in the real world as it is in Henrich and Boyd's case, one might rightly remain skeptical of the model's explanatory power (Sober 1991).

References

Aldrich, H. E., Hodgson, G. M., Hull, D. L., Knudsen, T., Mokyr, J., and Vanberg, V. J. 2008. In Defence of Generalized Darwinism. *Journal of Evolutionary Economics*, 18, 577–596.

Bloch, M. 2000. A Well-Disposed Social Anthropologist's Problem with Memes. In: Aunger, R. (ed.) *Darwinizing Culture*. Oxford: Oxford University Press.

Boyd, R. and Richerson, P. 1985. *Culture and the Evolutionary Process*. Chicago: Chicago University Press.

Boyd, R. and Richerson, P. J. 1987. The Evolution of Ethnic Markers. *Cultural Anthropology*, 2, 65–79.

Boyd, R. and Richerson, P. T. 2005. *The Origin and Evolution of Cultures*. New York: Oxford University Press.

Breslin, D. 2011. Reviewing a Generalized Darwinist Approach to Studying Socio-economic Change. *International Journal of Management Reviews*, 13, 218–235.

Buenstorf, G. 2006. How Useful Is Generalized Darwinism as a Framework to Study Competition and Industrial Evolution? *Journal of Evolutionary Economics*, 16, 511–527.

Campbell, D. T. 1974. The Philosophy of Karl Popper. In: Schilp, P. A. (ed.) *The Library of Living Philosophers*. La Salle, IL: Open Court.

Claidière, N. and Sperber, D. 2007. The Role of Attraction in Cultural Evolution. *Journal of Cognition and Culture*, 7, 89–111.

Cordes, C. 2006. Darwinism in Economics: From Analogy to Continuity. *Journal of Evolutionary Economics*, 16, 529–541.

Coyle, D. 2007. *A Soulful Science: What Economists Really Do and Why It Matters*. Princeton, NJ: Princeton University Press.

Cziko, G. 1995. *Without Miracles*. Cambridge, MA: MIT Press.

D'arms, J., Batterman, R., and Gorny, K. 1998. Game Theoretic Explanations and the Evolution of Justice. *Philosophy of Science*, 65, 76–102.

Darden, L. and Cain, J. A. 1989. Selection Type Theories. *Philosophy of Science*, 56, 106–129.

Elster, J. 1979. *Ulysses and the Sirens: Studies in Rationality and Irrationality*. Revised Edition. Cambridge: Cambridge University Press.

Ferguson, N. 2008. *The Ascent of Money: A Financial History of the World*. New York: Penguin.

Foster, J. 1997. The Analytical Foundations of Evolutionary Economics: From Biological Analogy to Economic Self-organization. *Structural Change and Economic Dynamics*, 8, 427–451.

Godfrey-Smith, P. 2000. The Replicator in Retrospect. *Biology and Philosophy*, 15, 403–423.

2007. *Population Thinking, Darwinism, and Cultural Change* [Online]. Available: www.interdisciplines.org/adaptation/papers/14

2009. *Darwinian Populations and Natural Selection*. Oxford: Oxford University Press.

2014. *Philosophy of Biology*. Princeton, NJ: Princeton University Press.

Henrich, J. and Boyd, R. 2002. On Modeling Cognition and Culture: Why Replicators Are Not Necessary for Cultural Evolution. *Journal of Cognition and Culture*, 2, 87–112.

Hodgson, G. M. 2002. Darwinism in Economics: From Analogy to Ontology. *Journal of Evolutionary Economics*, 12, 259–281.

2006. *Economics in the Shadows of Darwin and Marx: Essays on Institutional and Evolutionary Themes*. Cheltenham, UK: Edward Elgar.

Hodgson, G. M. and Knudsen, T. 2004. The Complex Evolution of a Simple Traffic Convention: The Functions and Implications of Habit. *Journal of Economic Behavior and Organization*, 54, 19–47.

2006a. Dismantling Lamarckism: Why Descriptions of Socio-economic Evolution as Lamarckian Are Misleading. *Journal of Evolutionary Economics*, 16, 343–366.

2006b. Why We Need a Generalized Darwinism, and Why Generalized Darwinism Is Not Enough. *Journal of Economic Behavior and Organization*, 61, 1–19.

2008. Information, Complexity and Generative Replication. *Biology and Philosophy*, 23, 47–65.

2010. *Darwin's Conjecture: The Search for General Principles of Social and Economic Evolution*. Chicago: University of Chicago Press.

2012. Underqualified – Maximal Generality in Darwinian Explanation: A Response to Matt Gers. *Biology and Philosophy*, 27, 607–614.

Hull, D. L. 1981. Units of Evolution: A Metaphysical Essay. In: Jensen, U. J. and Harré, R. (eds.) *The Philosophy of Evolution*. New York: St. Martin's Press, 23–44.

1988. *Science as a Process: An Evolutionary Account of the Social and Conceptual Development of Science*. Chicago: Chicago University Press.

Hull, D. L., Langman, R. E., and Glenn, S. S. 2001. A General Account of Selection: Biology, Immunology, and Behavior. *Behavioral and Brain Sciences*, 24, 511–528.

Kitcher, P. 1985. *Vaulting Ambition: Sociobiology and the Quest for Human Nature*. Cambridge: MIT Press.

1993. *The Advancement of Science: Science without Legend, Objectivity without Illusions*. Oxford: Oxford University Press.

Klaes, M. 2004. Ontological Issues in Evolutionary Economics: Introduction. *Journal of Economic Methodology*, 11, 121–163.

Levit, G. S., Hossfeld, U., and Witt, U. 2011. Can Darwinism Be "Generalized" and of What Use Would This Be? *Journal of Evolutionary Economics*, 21, 545–562.

Mameli, M. 2004. Nongenetic Selection and Nongenetic Inheritance. *The British Journal for the Philosophy of Science*, 55, 35–71.

2008. Understanding Culture: A Commentary on Richerson and Boyd's Not By Genes Alone. *Biology and Philosophy*, 23, 269–281.

Mesoudi, A., Whiten, A., and Laland, K. N. 2004. Perspective: Is Human Cultural Evolution Darwinian? Evidence from the Perspective of the Origin of Species. *Evolution*, 58, 1–11.

Mesoudi, A., Whiten, A., and Laland, K. N. 2006. Towards a Unified Science of Cultural Evolution. *Behavioral and Brain Sciences*, 29, 329–347.

Nelson, R. R. 2007. Universal Darwinism and Evolutionary Social Science. *Biology and Philosophy*, 22, 73–94.

Pelikan, P. 2011. Evolutionary Developmental Economics: How to Generalize Darwinism Fruitfully to Help Comprehend Economic Change. *Journal of Evolutionary Economics*, 21, 341–366.

Plotkin, H. 1994. *Darwin Machines and the Nature of Knowledge*. London: Penguin Books.

Schubert, C. 2014. "Generalized Darwinism" and the Quest for an Evolutionary Theory of Policy-making. *Journal of Evolutionary Economics*, 24, 479–513.

Skipper Jr., R. A. 1999. Selection and the Extent of Explanatory Unification. *Philosophy of Science*, 66, S196–S209.

Sober, E. 1991. *Core Questions in Philosophy: A Text with Readings*. New York: Macmillan.

Sperber, D. 1996. *Explaining Culture: A Naturalistic Approach*. Oxford: Basil Blackwell.

2000. An Objection to the Memetic Approach to Culture. In: Aunger, R. (ed.) *Darwinizing Culture*. Oxford University Press.

Sterelny, K. 1996. Explanatory Pluralism in Evolutionary Biology. *Biology and Philosophy*, 11, 193–214.

2006. Memes Revisited. *The British Journal for the Philosophy of Science*, 57, 145–165.

Stoelhorst, J. W. 2008. The Explanatory Logic and Ontological Commitments of Generalized Darwinism. *Journal of Economic Methodology*, 15, 343–363.

Stoelhorst, J. W. and Hensgens, R. 2006. On Applying Darwinism in Economics: From Meta-theory to Middle-range Theories, (paper presented at European Association for Evolutionary Political Economy Conference, Istanbul, November 2007).

Stoelhorst, J. W. 2009. The Naturalist View of Universal Darwinism: An Application to the Evolutionary Theory of the Firm. In: Hodgson, G. M. (ed.) *Darwinism and Economics*. Cheltenham: E. Elgar.

Stoelhorst, J. W. and Hensgens, R. 2007. On the Application of Darwinism to Economics: From Generalization to Middle-range Theories In: Amsterdam, U. o. (ed.) *Working Paper*. Amsterdam Business School, Amsterdam: University of Amsterdam.

Vromen, J. 2004. Conjectural Revisionary Economic Ontology: Outline of an Ambitious Research Agenda for Evolutionary Economics. *Journal of Economic Methodology*, 11, 213–264.

Vromen, J. J. 2006. Routines, Genes and Program-based Behavior. *Journal of Evolutionary Economics*, 16, 543–560.

2011. Heterogeneous Economic Evolution: A Different View on Darwinizing Evolutionary Economics. In: Davis, J. B. and Hands, D. W. (eds.) *The Elgar Companion to Recent Economic Methodology*. Cheltenham: Edward Elgar Publishing.

2012. How to Make a Convincing Case for Darwinizing the Social Sciences. (Review of Hodgson and Knudsen 2010). *Journal of Economic Methodology*, 19, 77–88.

Wimsatt, W. C. 1999. Genes, Memes, and Cultural Heredity. *Biology and Philosophy*, 14, 279–310.

Witt, U. 1999. Bioeconomics as Economics from a Darwinian Perspective. *Journal of Bioeconomics*, 1, 19–34.

2003. *The Evolving Economy: Essays on the Evolutionary Approach to Economics*. Cheltenham: Edward Elgar.

2006. Evolutionary Concepts in Economics and Biology. *Journal of Evolutionary Economics*, 16, 473–476.

PART III

Perspectives on Evolutionary Macroeconomics

5 Macroeconomic Evolution
Long-Run Development and Short-Run Policy

RICHARD H. DAY

Introduction

My early work on economic dynamics focused on the development of models that could be calibrated using empirical data; that were amenable to numerical solution; and that could mimic production, investment, technological change, and resource allocation in agricultural regions and industrial sectors. From the beginning I took it as fact that economizing, viewed as a human activity, occurs locally, that it is based on available but limited information, and when consciously rational involves behaviorally constrained optima of what are in effect mental models; these mental models can only approximate the total conditions that will ultimately influence both actions and results. Also central to my approach was the view that agents tend to respond to perceived opportunities with a lag, and their conceptions of opportunity and of the constraints limiting their possibilities were adapted, period by period, to their unfolding experience.

Correspondingly, my theoretical agents were adaptive economizers. In the course of pursuing profit opportunities, they behaved in ways that, in the aggregate and with the passage of time, brought about vast changes out of equilibrium in technology, resource utilization, and labor utilization; changes vast enough so that the terms "structural change" and "evolution" aptly describe the process as a whole. Technically, they traced out growth in terms of switching phases (or stages) of technology and resource utilization.[1]

---

[1] Examples of this work can be found in Day (1967) and (1978). I first developed the theory for multiple-phase dynamics in a course on economic dynamics at the University of Wisconsin in the early 1970s. In 1978 Jerry Sablov organized an advanced seminar at the Center for American Studies in Santa Fe involving archaeologists M. Aldenderfer, L. Cordell, G. Low, C. Renfrew, and E. Zubrow; mathematician K. Cooke; a philosopher J. Bell; and myself. The goal was to see how the fascinating prehistory of our species that had been so patiently constructed by archaeologists in the preceding hundred years could be

As this work progressed, I devoted increasing effort to constructing a general framework, abstract enough to apply to virtually any economy, yet concrete enough to incorporate salient features of human economic behavior as we know it. This work was carried out at the Mathematic Research Center at the University of Wisconsin and was presented first at the Marschak Colloquium at UCLA.[2] The paper I gave at this colloquium became a contribution to a conference which led to a volume edited jointly with Theodore Groves (Day & Groves 1975). Many brilliant people participated in the venture, including Masanao Aoki, J. P. Aubin, Richard Cyert, Morris DeGroot, Sanford Grossman, Alan Kirman, Mukul Majumdar, Hukukane Nikaido, Michael Rothschild, Martin Shubik, and Sidney Winter. It seemed that we were on the verge of a major breakthrough in economic science. Subsequent developments, however, were obscured by the avalanche of extensions and refinements of equilibrium theory.

Progress was nonetheless ongoing, and by now a number of modeling approaches have been developed involving adaptive games, complexity theory, nonlinear dynamics, multiple-phase dynamics, and so on, that together may contribute to the breakthrough we had anticipated. The micro theory of adaptive, out-of-equilibrium adjustments is necessarily complicated, however, and I began to consider how some of its central features could be mobilized in a macroeconomic approach that would be much simpler yet still help explain salient features of economic development in the very long run.[3] The remainder

understood in formal terms and simulated numerically. It was not until I came across Ester Boserup (1981), quite by serendipity, that I actually set down in writing my theory of macroeconomic evolution delivered at the conference on Evolutionary Dynamics and Nonlinear Economics in 1989 at Ilya Prigogine's Center for Statistical Mechanics, in Austin, see Day (1993); see also Day and Walter (1989).

[2] The day before my talk, while Professor Marschak drove me around Westwood and Santa Monica, we exchanged views on economic theory and methodology. He ardently espoused the expected utility theory as the proper basis for economics, but with characteristic generosity of spirit acknowledged interest in my behavioral approach and put me on to a literature that was closely related to the ideas I was attempting to develop. I knew of Simon's early papers, but Marschak suggested writings in general systems theory. References are given in Day (1975).

[3] I should also mention here the provocative and stimulating interaction with Arthur Iberall's interdisciplinary group centered here at UCLA with R. Baum and D. Wilkerson (political scientists), A. Moore and D. White (anthropologists), and L. Goldberg (biologist).

of this chapter summarizes the resulting theory, discusses its empirical relevance, and outlines its implications for contemporary public policy.

The Theory of Macroeconomic Evolution

The Classical Story

Consider the classical time unit of a human generation, a quarter century, say. Each period is represented by a population of adults and their children who inherit the adult world in the next generation. Assume that each generation must provide its own capital goods, which only last the period. The output possible is then a function of the number of adults. The number of children who survive (that is, who become adults in the next period) depends on the per capita production of goods. This relationship I call a family function, which can, in principle, be derived from the expansion path of an appropriate household preference function.

Putting these ingredients together we obtain the standard classical results: population, beginning at a small enough level, rises at an exponential rate during a phase of relative abundance, then, as diminishing returns lowers the marginal and average productivity of labor, switches to a regime of scarcity. Population growth slows and converges to a stationary state at which the level of well-being is sufficient to motivate and sustain the formation of families just big enough to replace themselves generation after generation. If a continuous advance in labor augmenting productivity is incorporated, then the steady state gives way to "geometric growth." The iron law of wages is postponed indefinitely and output converges to an exponential, technology-driven trend.

Suppose now there exists a positive standard of living below which no children survive to adulthood. Such a survival threshold exists for physiological reasons alone, and its empirical relevance is evident whenever famine or social conflicts become severe. It is easy to show that a positive survival threshold is sufficient to induce fluctuations in output, income, and population numbers.[4]

---

[4] It must also be recognized that at high levels of income birth rates appear to decline. As this phenomenon does not change the results of the present analysis in a significant way, we may set it aside.

Internal Diseconomies

The classical economists recognized that production within a given economy must eventually exhibit diminishing returns to variable factors due to the scarcity of land, water, and other material resources. Diseconomies also accrue because of the increasing complexity of planning, communicating, and coordinating production activity as the economy grows. The ability to overcome them depends on the administrative technology (an apt term introduced by Ester Boserup 1981) and on the "social space" which depends on this technology. If there is "social slack," then more people can be easily accommodated within the economy. As social space is "used up," cooperation becomes increasingly more difficult, social conflict increases, and productivity declines. These *internal diseconomies* can yield absolutely diminishing returns to population within an economy.

A negative sloping segment in production cannot occur if resources are freely disposable but *people* are not freely disposable, so that the "free disposal axiom" is not germane. It could be argued that people would never reproduce to such an extent as to depress absolute production, but this is a view supported more by faith than by facts. Overpopulation within the context of a given administrative technology or given stage of development seems to have occurred, and very likely *is* occurring in a number of places, so that its analysis would seem relevant indeed. Economists sometimes argue that such problems can easily be solved merely by paying people not to work. Indeed, such a solution has been widely practiced in Western countries. But a part of the effect is to alienate the unemployed, which leads to increased political and social conflict.

As in the case of the survival threshold, internal diseconomies – when important enough – are sufficient to cause fluctuations (cyclic or irregular) and, in the extreme, collapse; a prospect more dismal than envisaged in the iron law of wages. This possibility means that the conditions for an economy to persist cannot be taken for granted.

Infrastructure and Viability

Technology can only be effective if a part of the population forms a social infrastructure upon which the use of the given technology depends. As Douglas North (1981) put it, "The performance of an economy depends on its organizational structure."[5] Such an infrastructure mediates the human energy devoted to coordinating production and exchange. It provides social cohesion for effective cooperation, for training and inculturating the workforce, and for producing the public goods such as waste disposal and public safety, required for the well-being of the work force. The knowledge that makes this human infrastructure effective is the *administrative technology*. It must augment the production technology. Given that the social infrastructure requires a significant block of human resources, it follows that for an economy to be feasible with a fixed technology, population size must exceed a certain bound.

Combined with the possibility of absolute diseconomies introduced earlier, the problem of viability is clearly exacerbated. If the infrastructure and the administrative technology on which it is based is fixed or relatively fixed, then internal diseconomies must eventually overwhelm productivity, and the possibility of fluctuations or demise is more likely. In the extreme, population size can fall below the numbers required to keep the infrastructure intact. The system as a whole becomes inviable.

Growth and Decline through Replication and Merging

Growth, however, need not come to an end with such a bang – even within a fixed technological regime. At some point in the expansion of human numbers within an economy, the population may reach a level at which a new society with a newly constituted infrastructure can be split off in such a way as to increase welfare by overcoming the internal diseconomies of population size. Such a process can continue until the known world is full of such units.

To see what is meant by the term "full" to the *internal* diseconomies that operate within a given socioeconomic unit, take account of the *external* ones that derive from the total population of all the economies together. These are, for example, caused by the exhaustion of the environment's waste-absorbing capacity. This capacity can – for a given technology – be stated in terms of the environmental space available which, in turn, depends on the population density. In addition, as resources become scarce and the cost of extracting and

[5] See also Acemoglu, Johnson, and Robinson (2005).

refining them grows, diminishing absolute returns to the workforce can eventually come to pass as the total world population gets large. The internal diseconomies can be overcome by fission; the external ones cannot. Once the world is full in the sense that external diseconomies become important, the replication of economies with the same basic structure must come to an end.

If, when this state is attained, a collapse occurs due to a very powerful drop in productivity, the population may reorganize itself by eliminating some of the previous groups and fusing into a smaller number of economies. Then the stage is set for a new growth process, both through the internal growth of the individual economies and through a resumption of the fission process just described. Fluctuations in the numbers of economies (or societies), as well as in total population size, could ensue, perhaps in a highly irregular way for a very long time (Day, Kim, and Macunovich 1989).

Growth and Decline through Integration and Disintegration

Because of external diseconomies and in the absence of technological change, growth must ultimately be limited. But now consider the role of "ways of life," "development blocks," or distinct administrative and/or production technology *regimes*. Each of these is structurally distinct, depending on production and administrative technologies, and correspondingly with very different infrastructural requirements. Suppose that the regimes have a natural order so that each successive regime in the order requires a greater overhead of human capital in the infrastructure and has a higher attainable production and population level than its predecessors. For a more advanced regime to emerge, existing economies must be integrated and reorganized to form larger, more elaborate infrastructures.

But further growth in the total population is possible only if the external diseconomies are greatly diminished by such a change. Then for each successive regime a much larger worldwide population becomes possible before external diseconomies again become acute. Such a change in regime is unlikely to occur unless average productivity is enhanced by doing so. This does not mean that each successive technology is uniformly more productive than its predecessor, but only that at a given total population the switch to a new regime will enhance the standard of living at that population level. In other words, "local efficiency" is sufficient to drive the selection process of technological regime switching in much the same way that it drives the process of replication through fission. If, in the process of growth, productivity falls enough, existing economies could be forced to disintegrate into a larger number of units that require less elaborate infrastructures, in effect economizing on human capital by reverting to a less infrastructure-intensive regime.

Continuous Productivity Advance and the Ultimate Population Bound

Suppose that a productivity growth factor such as "learning by doing" or "learning by imitation" is incorporated so that as experience within a given regime accumulates, output per unit of labor increases. Suppose such a factor does *not* expand the ultimate limits on population allowed by the internal and external diseconomies described earlier. Then, as productivity is enhanced, the processes of output growth, fission, integration, and regime switching are accelerated. Over the long run, the system becomes more unstable. Development is less likely to get "stuck" within a given regime, and economies are more likely to split or jump. If there is an upper bound on the environmental capacity, then the collections of economies will bump up against an ultimate population limit sooner than before. The advancing regimes become progressively "squashed" against this ultimate bound, with ever greater speed; with an ever greater likelihood of collapse.

The "Grand" Dynamics

The classical theory has now been augmented by the following ingredients:

- A birth-welfare threshold
- Absolute internal diseconomies
- A selection criterion of local efficiency
- Infrastructural human capital
- Absolute external diseconomies
- The possibility of growth through replication and decline through merging
- Multiple technological regimes

- The possibility of growth through integration and switching to a more productive regime and decline through disintegration and reversion to a less productive regime
- Continuous productivity advance

These theoretical ingredients can be given specific mathematical forms such that a model is obtained that describes economic history in terms of a sequence of episodes, characterized in turn by various qualitative evolutionary scenarios.[6] To summarize:

1. Evolution in this theory is driven by an unstable, deterministic (intrinsic) process, not by a random shock (extrinsic) process. (Of course, random shocks could be introduced but I have wanted to isolate the intrinsic dynamics of the development process.)
2. The probabilities of various possible historical scenarios can be derived in terms of sequences of qualitative (regime switching) events due to replication/merging and integration/ disintegration.
3. If the socioeconomic menu is finite, then evolution in terms of continued progression to higher regimes eventually comes to an end.
4. If the model is unstable and closed, then its histories must involve endless fluctuations, eventually sticking with a given regime or cycling in a nonperiodic fashion through an endless sequence of regimes.
5. If there were a reachable regime with a stable stationary state, the model's histories could converge after possibly many periods of local chaos to a classical equilibrium.
6. If the model is not closed, then trajectories can escape the zone of definition and demise can take place.

Fact in Economic Theory and Economic Development in Fact

Economic science involves two distinctly different categories of fact: (1) facts about causality or how things work and (2) facts about how states of the world change. The first set of facts provides the basis for

---

[6] See Day and Walter (1989); Day and Pavlov (2001). The mathematical analysis of the model is intriguing, but because it requires a considerable amount of nomenclature to develop rigorously, it is not reproduced here. For an extensive discussion see Day (1999). Complexity is increased further when capital required for the infrastructure and for production and accumulation with multiple phases is also accounted for; see Day and Zou (1994) for a discussion.

a theory. A theory is then judged – from the scientific viewpoint – on how well it explains and predicts facts of the second kind. How well does the theory presented earlier reflect facts of the first kind? And can it "explain" and "predict" facts of the second kind? First, let us consider the broad picture of socioeconomic development over the span of time for which *Homo sapiens sapiens* are known to have roamed the earth. Then we will take a closer look at what happened within and between the stages of growth that are involved in this long run picture.

The Great Stages

Historians of the nineteenth century noticed that prior to the industrial take-off economies had passed through distinct stages of development characterized by differences in production technology and in the organization of exchange and governance. Archaeologists, aided by modern methods of dating materials, began extending this picture backwards in time. By now they have constructed an approximate but coherent chronology of major developments on a worldwide basis that stretches back to the earliest evidence of a human presence.

Briefly, the great variety of human societies can be roughly grouped into a relatively small number of stages based on production technology and social infrastructure. To describe the major developments throughout the entire span of *Homo sapiens sapiens* and to take advantage of the known archaeological information, a reasonable minimal specification would be:

1. Hunting and gathering
2. Quasi-settled agriculture and herding
3. Settled (village) agriculture
4. Complex societies and the city state (civilization)
5. Trading empires
6. Industrial economies and the nation-state
7. Global information economies

These names are, of course, only suggestive. It is not implied, for instance, that hunter-gatherers only hunt and forage or that agrarians never hunt or gather wild foods. Nor do we wish to imply by the term "city state" that citizens never engaged in hunting or that hunter-gatherers were entirely absent in later stages. The division merely reflects the roughly dominant forms of social organization and economic activity. The technology regimes incorporated in the theory are idealizations of these rough stages. The mechanisms of replication/merging and of integration/disintegration are also idealized and discretized reflections of historical fact.

In reality, various geographical areas traversed these stages at very different times, and the advance through them did not increase uniformly from lower to higher index. Rather, progress from one to another, especially in earlier times, was interrupted by reversions to lower-level stages. Moreover, fluctuations in income, population size, and capital have been typical. The overall picture is one of growth at fluctuating rates with sometimes smooth, sometimes turbulent transitions when jumps and reversions occurred until a "higher" stage became firmly established. But all of this is what our theory would "predict." That is, it can generate model histories like this broad historical record. In the works cited earlier, simulations of the model have been reported that exhibit these characteristics. Now let us consider behavior within epochs and in the transitions between them, beginning with hunting and food collecting and settled agriculture.

Hunting and Food Collecting and Settled Agriculture

It is well known that the diffusion of hunting and food collecting cultures throughout the world occurred through a process of fission and migration with relatively little elaboration of infrastructure but with advances of technology that involved a gradual improvement in utensils, weapons, and other material artifacts. Our theory both reflects and explains this fact.

The reason for the cessation of this expansion and the subsequent settlement of people into more or less fixed agricultural villages is less obvious and still debated. If Binford (1968); Cohen (1977); Boserup (1981), and others are right, then the regime switch was not due to the discovery of agriculture, which must have occurred long before the switch. Rather, it was due to the necessary decline in the productivity of the earlier way of life when the world became "full," which made farming relatively more efficient, given the population levels that had been reached. Our theory explains the early growth in terms of replication through fission, a well-established fact, and the switch to agriculture in terms of the reorganization of production due to the relatively greater productivity of labor in the new regime, given the large population.

Settled Agriculture and City States

The process of expanding agrarian settlement from 9000 to 3000 BC and the subsequent emergence of city states in the Ancient Near East have been described in meticulous terms by Nissen (1988). Of special interest is his explanation of the internal conflicts that led to a reversion back to individual village organizations and the continuing fluctuation between these forms for an extended period. Saggs (1989), in an equally fascinating survey of civilization before the classic period, explained why Egypt settled later because of the unusually favorable conditions for wild animals and plants along the Nile. He also describes how, as the population emerged, towns began to form from 5000 BC onward and then integrated to form a unified state, combining upper and lower Egypt in about 3000 BC.

Scarre (2005) observes how a similar transition occurred in Greece about 1800 BC when the cluster of villages making up Attica unified politically to form what eventually became the city state of Athens. Much is known about the vast extension in administrative infrastructure associated with the regime switches in Mesopotamia, Egypt, and Greece, developments only possible with sufficiently large and productive populations divided between production per se and administrative functions.

Of special interest to the present theory is the process of the repeated integration of villages to form the complex societies of Burundi and Polynesia and their disintegration back to collections of independent villages. This history, described by Sagan (1985), involves a switching and re-switching between levels of socioeconomic organization (see also Currie et al. 2010). Our model predicts these instabilities for well-defined conditions of infrastructural requirements and productivity.

Another possibility that occurs generically in our theory is that of collapse and demise, a developmental outcome known to have occurred at various times and places in the archaeological and historical records. Iseminger (1996) summarizes an example discovered relatively recently in the broad plain east of St. Louis. During the period 9500–9600 BC, hunter-gathers set up seasonal villages and later permanent settlements. By 1200 AD a substantial city known as Cahokia came to dominate the surrounding territory in what was essentially a city state (Fowler 1989). Two centuries later the city was abandoned, and no ties have been established between the great city and any historical tribe.[7]

The replication mechanism that played such an important role in the diffusion of the hunting and food collecting culture is dramatically evident in the diffusion of the city state. The classic description of the process is Herodatus's story of the division of Lydia's population and the subsequent colonization of North Africa and then Italy. He also relates the belief of people in a city near the Bosporus whose citizens claimed that they were founded by a colonial expedition from Egypt.

Trading Empires, the Industrial Nation-State, and the Global Information Economy

Throughout the world, trading empires eventually arose through the widespread political and economic domination of surrounding territories by larger, more powerfully organized, and more effectively coordinated agglomerations of people. We might include the historical period through the Renaissance in this epoch, which is distinguished by repeated integrations and disintegrations of smaller city states and principalities as empires rose and fell. All this can be explained in terms of the theory at hand and mimicked by computational simulations. One thinks of Egypt, Persia, Greece under Philip and Alexander, Rome, China, and India. Obviously, a great variety of geographical, social, and even psychological factors were involved in these examples, and none were alike in detail. Yet all the historical details had to work themselves out within a framework of interacting technological and demo-economic forces roughly modeled by the present theory.

The nation-states that emerged during the Industrial Revolution involved an even more vast expansion in the resources devoted to infrastructure: elaborate education and scientific establishments,

---

[7] Pollard (1995) simulated my model using data describing the reconstructed history of the Anasazi Indians in Chaco Canyon described by Lightfoot (1984). Her model traces these people through their initial "hunting and gardening," village agriculture and centralized (city state like) systems, the fluctuation between the first two regimes, and the ultimate collapse and disappearance.

multiple levels of representative government, bureaus for monitoring economic activities of many kinds (banking, trade, production, etc.), elaborate systems for adjudicating economic and social conflict, public goods for recreation, communication, transportation, and so on.

These infrastructural institutions reside in both public and private domains. The importance of the latter is sometimes overlooked. Large-scale corporations allocate roughly half their expenditures on educational, research, managerial, and administrative functions and roughly half on the production of goods and services. Although some economists would include such things in the category of intermediate goods used in the production process, it is worth distinguishing them because their individual productivity cannot be measured in the usual ways (output per hour expended). Their productivity, like that of the elements of public infrastructure, is only reflected in the productivity of the entire organization. That is to say, a productive public infrastructure will be reflected in some measure of aggregate accomplishment such as political, military, or economic dominance and/or a high level of culture and wide distribution of welfare. Likewise, a productive private infrastructure is reflected in the overall productivity of the organization as a whole. The contribution of individual scientists, teachers, managers, and accountants to the organization's success is impossible to measure except by profit comparisons among similar organizations.

Associated with the rise of the nation-state is an explosive increase in population and a considerable instability in the composition of the individual units. From the point of view of the present theory, it is not the business cycle that reflects this institutional instability, but rather the integration and disintegration of political units throughout the 19th and 20th centuries. Also noteworthy has been the vast elaboration of infrastructure on a global basis, both capital and institutional. We have in mind, for example, earth satellite systems; international courts; trade organizations; and world political organizations and their capacity for communications, negotiations, and so forth.

With the spread of jet aircraft, airport facilities, and satellite communications, we would have appeared to have entered a new era of the global information economy. There are no entirely independent economic or political units left. Rather, all are bound together by elaborate webs of transportation and communication. Further development will modify the infrastructural systems of administration and coordination, but unless a collapse occurs, we are unlikely to observe the re-emergence of essentially independent economies. But within this system of interconnected political units, reorganizations are occurring, the most dramatic of which is the disintegration of the Soviet Union and of the various republics that made up the Eastern Bloc.

As we get to this epoch, our grossly aggregative theory would seem to provide too coarse a sieve to filter out the salient features of modern history which involve such intricately elaborate and interconnected institutions among many levels of organization. Yet it seems to me the theory can provide some relevant and, indeed, extremely important insights that should enhance our understanding of what is going on and what might happen in the future. It tells us that there is a crucial link between infrastructure and productivity.

The productivity of a society by any measure (its wealth, political power, size, and distribution/welfare) depends on an effective workforce whose productivity depends in turn on the existence of an appropriately developed infrastructure with sufficient resources to sustain the population as a whole. As population grows, infrastructure must also. It is not just the size of the infrastructure but its functions and organization that must change, and *when a population begins to become excessive relative to its infrastructure, productivity must fall. To avoid fluctuations or even collapse, the population must be stabilized or the infrastructure transformed.* These implications of the theory seem to me to be amply borne out again and again in what is now the 100,000-year history of our species from the hunting and food collecting band to today's global information economy.

The Lessons

Although our theory explains economic evolution in the long run, its mechanisms of replication and merging, integration and disintegration, and regime switching take place within a generational time scale. When regimes jump or revert, they often do so within a fraction of a biblical life. It is for this reason that the multiple-phase theory of macroeconomic evolution in the very long run holds lessons for us now. If the facts about how the world works – not in detail, of course, but in some of its salient aspects – have been interpreted correctly, then we are entitled to draw implications for understanding events in our own time and for considering policies that will shape events in the future. I want to conclude this chapter with a few reflections of this kind.

The Transition

Consider disintegration of the former Soviet Union in the recent past. Here we saw something like the kind of reversion our theory predicts: a large, complexly organized economy falls apart and is succeeded by a number of smaller ones in what was a turbulent process with highly uncertain prospects. In the terms spelled out here, the causes are clear. The system outgrew the infrastructure required to continue growing in an effective manner. A population of such great size cannot persist within that kind of a regime. A new one is required, and that is what the transition is about.

By now, however, the big bangers have been discredited, along with their belief that a market economy could spontaneously arise from the socialist economy merely by destroying the socialist state and introducing private property. Indeed, private property and the market economy depend on the state – *the right kind of state* – one that has created the right kind of public infrastructure within which private initiative can thrive in a way that enhances the system as a whole. This means an accumulation of laws defining the rights, obligations, opportunities, and limitations on public and private actions; a system of courts for interpreting the law and adjudicating disputes about its application; an effective system of representative government to adjust the law in response to changing conditions so as to engage the willing participation of most of the people most of the time; a large scientific and educational establishment to provide competent participants in private and public institutions; a system of monitoring to ensure standards of quality on the basis of which specialized production and trade can flourish. Most of all, it needs institutions that create a sense of common purpose and commitment so that the population forms a cohesive body that spends most of its energies on symbiotic activity rather than on destructive social conflict.

We know of the great cultures that have accomplished enough of these things to have played a powerful role in shaping the world as we know it. We also know that most of them eventually failed in providing some of these crucial ingredients. In the midst of the transition from a culture that has failed to another regime, it is difficult indeed to anticipate the outcome. We know the turbulence of past transitions; we do *not* know if our own culture can outgrow the instabilities of the past.

The American Decline

In the midst of its spectacular transition into the global information economy, America's leadership in various technological areas has waxed and waned and waxed again. More important for predicting the future is the decline in the aspects of welfare by which the quality of life has been measured in America in the first half of the twentieth century: infant mortality, literacy, educational attainment, material well-being, longevity, and the sense of unlimited individual opportunity. The fact is that the situation has substantially worsened in these terms, both absolutely and relative to many other countries in the last quarter century or more (see, e.g., Friedman 2017). No doubt, many causes have contributed to these trends. The theory developed here suggests that we look at infrastructure and population size as key elements in an explanation.

Let us take one prominent example: the modern city state. Many cities in the world now exceed in size the population of entire nation-states of present and former times. A significant case in point is Los Angeles. Los Angeles has a population roughly the same magnitude as Denmark. Yet it has a single mayor, a single police chief, a single superintendent of schools; in short, a single layer of government. Denmark, by way of contrast, has several layers of government, many mayors, many police chiefs. In this sense, it has far more infrastructure than Los Angeles has. Or consider a historical comparison: when the first census of the United States of America was taken in 1790, the population of the country was about 4 million, roughly that of Los Angeles now. But the US population was divided into thirteen states with thirteen governors, thirteen legislatures, and thirteen state supreme courts, not to mention county and city governmental institutions – all this in addition to the institutions of the federal government.

Can it be that the United States has outgrown its governmental infrastructure and outgrown it by far? Is this the reason representative government is seen by a growing body of alienated citizens no longer to be representative? Can the basic problem facing the United States be one of *too little government* and not one of too much? Suppose the answer is yes. Then our theory suggests two possibilities. First, our most populous states could split into two or three, as some have already suggested. Second, in order to restore participatory government at the local level, counties, cities, and towns could be created within the new state borders with, say, a constitutional provision for towns to be rezoned so as to maintain a maximum limit of somewhere between 10,000 and 100,000 people. Local police, local fire departments, local schools, and all the local public services would be established. The police functions of the new state government would be limited to those of existing state governments. Many other functions would be reallocated from what is now the city to the new smaller city and town units.

Are There Limits For Growth?

Finally, we should ask if new administrative and production technologies can continue to be designed so as to enable growth to continue forever. Economists favor growth, politicians favor growth, and, indeed, almost everyone would like to envisage a long and healthy life for humankind. What, then, *are* the prospects for continual growth? Many scientists argue that there *is* some kind of bound, perhaps one much bigger than the present world population – but perhaps also smaller.[8] If so, continued growth could eventually lead to drastically strengthened externalities with all the attending instabilities and possibilities for collapse noted in our discussion. To prevent this squashing against the limits of growth, the previous theory identifies three key parameters for attention:

1. The externality-generating effects of aggregate population
2. The propensity for a greater than zero population growth rate of reproduction
3. The vast infrastructural complexities of advanced stages of development.

---

[8] Such an ultimate bound was suggested by a National Academy of Sciences panel convened as long ago as 1968 as lying somewhere between 6 and 25 billion people.

There would seem to be four corresponding policy objectives:

1. Pollution abatement and resource conservation
2. Lowering or eliminating population growth
3. Elaborating infrastructure so as to restore and augment public services at the local level that are essential for participatory democracy and private enterprise
4. Expanding research on new technologies, behavioral rules, and modes of organization that can arrest the debilitating aspects of growth

Without success in the pursuit of all these objectives, the likelihood of a collapse would seem to be very high. Because the current velocity of the process is so great, the urgency for action along these lines seems to be rising.

Conclusion

In this chapter an evolutionary theory of economic development has been outlined that explains why human evolution has not exhibited steady progress but, instead, fluctuating growth and changing forms, sometimes progressing to higher levels of complexity, sometimes reverting to earlier stages of organization. In terms of macroeconomic growth theory, it is convenient to think of the analysis as involving the "very long run." Key ingredients in the theory are infrastructure, internal and external diseconomies, and regime switching through replication/merging and integration/disintegration. Accumulated knowledge of human development throughout the entire history of our species provides evidence for the theory's explanatory power. As has been discussed, the theory also implies that the "very long run" is of great interest for interpreting events in the "very short run," in particular, the processes of integration and disintegration currently at work in the world. Moreover, important lessons for current national economic policy have been suggested that are of special relevance for reforming infrastructure in very large states in our time.

References

Acemoglu, D., Johnson, S., and Robinson, J. A. 2005. Institutions as a Fundamental Cause of Long-Run Growth. In: Aghion, P. and Durlauf, S. (eds.) *Handbook of Economic Growth*. Amsterdam: Elsevier.

Binford, L. 1968. Post Pleistocene Adaptations. In: Leane, M. (ed.) *New Perspectives in Archaeology*. Chicago: Aldine Publishers.

Boserup, E. 1981. *Population and Technological Change: A Study of Long-term Trends*. Chicago: Chicago University Press.

Cohen, M. 1977. *The Food Crisis in Prehistory*. New Haven, CT: Yale University Press.

Currie, T. E., Mace, R., Gray, R. D., Greenhill, S. J., and Hasegawa, T. 2010. Rise and Fall of Political Complexity in Island South-East Asia and the Pacific. *Nature*, 467, 801–804.

Day, R. H. 1967. The Economics of Technological Change and the Demise of the Sharecropper. *The American Economic Review*, 57, 427–449.

1975. Adaptive Processes and Economic Theory. In: Day, R. H. and Groves, T. (eds.) *Adaptive Economic Models*. New York: Academic Press.

1978. Modelling Economic Change: The Recursive Programming Approach. In: Day, R. (ed.) *Modeling Economic Change*. Amsterdam: Elsevier North-Holland.

1993. Nonlinear Dynamics and Evolutionary Economics. In: Day, R. and Chen, P. (eds.) *Nonlinear Dynamics and Evolutionary Economics*. New York: Oxford University Press.

1999. *Complex Economic Dynamics, Vol. II: An Introduction to Macroeconomic Dynamics*. Cambridge, MA: MIT Press.

Day, R. H. and Groves, T. 1975. *Adaptive Economic Models*. New York: Academic Press.

Day, R. H., Kim, K.-H., and Macunovich, D. 1989. Complex Demo-economic Dynamics. *Journal of Population Economics*, 2, 139–159.

Day, R. H. and Pavlov, O. 2001. Qualitative Dynamics and Macroeconomic Evolution in the Very Long Run. In: Punzo, L. (ed.) *Cycles, Growth and Structural Change*. London: Routledge.

Day, R. H. and Walter, J. L. 1989. Economic Growth in the Very Long Run: On the Multiple-Phase Interaction of Population, Technology, and Social Infrastructure. In: Barnett, W., Geweke, J., and Shell, K. (eds.) *Economic Complexity: Chaos, Sunspots, Bubbles and Nonlinearity*. Cambridge: Cambridge University Press.

Day, R. H. and Zou, G. 1994. Infrastructure, Restricted Factor Substitution and Economic Growth. *Journal of Economic Behavior and Organization*, 23, 149–166.

Fowler, M. L. 1989. *The Cahokia Atlas: A Historical Atlas of Cahokia Archaeology*. Springfield, IL: Historical Preservation Agency.

Friedman, B. M. 2017. Work and Consumption in an Era of Unbalanced Technological Advance. *Journal of Evolutionary Economics*, 27, 221–237.

Iseminger, W. R. 1996. Mighty Cahokia. *Archaeology*, 49, 30–35.

Lightfoot, K. G. 1984. *Prehistoric Political Dynamics*. Dekalb, IL: NIU Press.

Nissen, H. J. 1988. *The Early History of the Ancient Near East, 9000–2000 B.C.* Chicago: University of Chicago Press.

North, D. C. 1981. *Structure and Change in Economic History*. New York: W. W. Norton & Co.

Pollard, K. 1995. An Analysis of a Model for Socioeconomic Evolution Based on a Reading of Economic Growth in the Very Long Run by Richard Day and Jean-Luc Walter. *Working Paper*. Claremont College.

Sagan, E. 1985. *At the Dawn of Tyranny*. New York: Alfred A. Knopf.

Saggs, H. W. F. 1989. *Civilization before Greece and Rome*. New Haven, CT: Yale University Press.

Scarre, C. 2005. *The Human Past: World Prehistory and the Development of Human Societies*. London: Thames & Hudson.

6 | Evolutionary Micro-Founded Technical Change and the Kaldor-Verdoorn Law
Estimates from an Artificial World

ANDRÉ LORENTZ

Introduction

Understanding the sources of growth and long run development of economies is an age-old issue in economics. It is now widely acknowledged among economists that technical change is a major source of economic growth. Technological changes are usually considered as favouring growth by preventing decreasing returns. Among the possible explanations to be found in the literature, division of labour and technological innovation are the most widespread. The emergence of the New Growth Theory (NGT) brought back to light the role of increasing returns as a source for economic growth (see Romer 1986; Romer 1990) in an existing tradition of neo-classical endogenous growth models. The nature of these increasing returns considered in the NGT are in line with the traditional Marshallian scale effect, the agglomeration or spillover effects found in the New Economic Geography (Krugman 1997) or the network externalities literature (Arthur 1994), in that it remains contextual. The production technology, the localisation and the nature of knowledge or information allow for these increasing returns to occur, rather than the decision of economic agents.

Prior to the development of the NGT, some economists tried to consider the sources of these increasing returns as resulting from the economic activity itself. Kaldor develops a post-Keynesian approach to economic growth, accounting for technical change as the main source for increasing returns.

The author wishes to thank A. Coad, C. Cords, K. Frenken, U. Witt and T. Heinrich for their comments. This version also benefited from various discussions with T. Ciarli, M. Savona and M. Valente. The chapter largely draws on research conducted at the Max Planck Institute of Economics, Jena, Germany. Research assistant: Sebastian Mueller. The usual disclaimers apply.

For Kaldor, technical change is one of the key components of the cumulative causation mechanism underlying the growth process. Technical change within this framework cannot be disconnected from the existence of increasing returns: technical change constitutes a source for increasing returns, on the one hand, and increasing returns are a prerequisite for technical change to occur, on the other. These interconnections are twofold and occur both at the micro-economic and the macro-economic levels.

At the micro-economic level, technical change is inherent to the activity of the firm. Productivity gains do not just result from increasing returns induced by large-scale manufacturing activities, in line with Smith (or as reprised by Romer). These are mainly rooted in the renewal of production capacities through investments and capital accumulation. Capital deepening induces the adoption of more efficient machinery leading to productivity gains. These micro-level sources are captured in Kaldor's (1957) 'technical progress function'. Second, increasing returns are rooted in a macro-level division of labour. The latter increases the sectoral specialisation, generates novelty and therefore improves the efficiency of the economic activity. These increasing returns are intrinsically dynamic. Kaldor refers to Young (1928), who attributes these increasing returns to a large-scale division of labour.[1]

Kaldor (1966) supports this twofold explanation for the existence of increasing returns by re-interpreting the empirical evidence provided by Verdoorn (1949). Verdoorn's article initially aimed at proposing a statistical method to forecast changes in labour productivity. As a matter of fact, his empirical investigations stress the existence of a constant relationship between growth rates of labour productivity and the growth rate of output for both the pre- and the post-World War I periods for a selected number of countries.[2] Kaldor refers to this empirical relation as the 'Verdoorn Law'. In addition to his own

[1] 'In addition, as Allyn Young emphasized, increasing returns is a "macro-phenomenon" – just because so much of the economies of scale emerge as a result of increased differentiation, the emergence of new processes and new subsidiary industries, they cannot be "disconnected adequately by observing the effect of variations in the size of an individual firm or of a particular industry".' (Kaldor 1966: 9–10).

[2] Depending on the period, Verdoorn's country sample included Canada, Czechoslovakia, Estonia, Finland, Germany, Holland, Hungary, Italy, Japan, Norway, Poland, Switzerland, UK and United States.

estimation of the Verdoorn Law,[3] Kaldor (1966) investigates the relationship between the growth rate of employment and the growth rate of output as supporting evidence for the macro-level increasing returns. Both empirical relationships appear to be significant and robust, and since then it has become known as the Kaldor-Verdoorn Law:

- The Verdoorn specification of the law states that the growth rate of productivity increases with the growth rate of output; this increase should, according to Kaldor, remain less than proportional.[4]
- The Kaldor specification of the law also states that the growth rate of employment increases with the growth of output. This increase should, however, remain less than proportional to support the existence of increasing returns.[5]

The simplicity of the functional form of the law presents a handy alternative to forecasting productivity changes or quantifying the magnitude of the increasing returns. As already shown by Verdoorn (1949), the law is largely compatible with any common production function. It therefore prevents the 'abuse' of micro-level assumptions, either on the formal form of an aggregate production function or on the behaviour of economic agents. This might explain the relative popularity of the law. McCombie, Pugno, and Soro (2002) list about 80 major papers making use of the Kaldor-Verdoorn Law since the seminal paper by Verdoorn (1949). Most of these contributions concern applied empirical analysis, making use of the law to measure increasing returns for specific countries, regions or sectors and/or to account for differences among the latter. The Kaldor-Verdoorn Law per se does not provide any explanation for the mechanisms underlying technical change or the existence of these increasing returns. The theoretical foundations brought to the Kaldor-Verdoorn Law by Kaldor (1966) remain verbal.

[3] Kaldor (1966) estimates the Verdoorn's relationship for the period 1953–63 using a different sample of countries (Austria, Belgium, Canada, Denmark, France, West Germany, Italy, Japan, Netherlands, Norway, UK and United States).

[4] If the estimated coefficient exceeds 1, the labour productivity grows faster than the output and therefore generates a decline in employment. This limits the expansion of demand required to sustain cumulative growth.

[5] If the estimated coefficient exceeds 1, employment grows faster than the output. There is a decrease in labour productivity and therefore no increasing returns.

Only a few formal attempts to provide micro-foundations of the law can be found in the literature. Verdoorn (1949) initially shows that the relationship holds regardless of the functional form of the underlying aggregated production function. He, however, does not propose any formal explanation for the relationship per se. More recently, McCombie (2002) shows that under some specific assumptions on the production structure of industrial sectors, a Kaldor-Verdoorn Law appears in an NGT model. McCombie (2002) reverts to a modelling frame in line with Romer (1990) to provide a formal reprise of Young (1928). Within this framework, the introduction of intersectoral interactions allows for a Kaldor-Verdoorn-like relation at the macro level. It has to be noted that in this case increasing returns are assumed rather than micro-founded and the sectoral level interactions superimposed. The lack of further micro-foundations possibly resides in the fact that, in an equilibrium framework, such dynamic increasing returns have to be assumed. Second, as stated by Kaldor (1972), dynamic increasing returns, as measured by the law, can only be considered out of equilibrium and necessarily generates disequilibrium.

Metcalfe, Foster, and Ramlogan (2006) propose an alternative using an out-of-equilibrium approach. As for McCombie (2002), the author relies on the sectoral interactions within the economy to account for a Kaldor-Verdoorn-like relationship at the macro level. The authors assume a Fabricant Law[6] holding at the industry level as an engine for increasing returns. A macro-level Kaldor-Verdoorn Law results from the aggregation of the effect of the Fabricant Law and the structural changes. Hence, the transformation of the industrial structure of the economic activity leads to the diffusion of the micro-level increasing returns generating the emergence of increasing returns at the macro level. In this respect, Metcalfe, Foster, and Ramlogan (2006) propose a micro-foundation of the law based on the industrial structure and its changes, again assuming increasing returns to pre-exist at the industry level. Metcalfe, Foster, and Ramlogan (2006) explain the emergence of a Kaldor-Verdoorn Law to the adaptation and selection mechanisms at the core of economic dynamics, allowing

---

[6] Fabricant (1942) shows a similar robust relationship between the growth of output and the growth of productivity for various industrial sectors in the United States for the period 1899–1939.

for the diffusion of micro-level increasing returns to the aggregate level. The approach developed by Metcalfe, Foster, and Ramlogan (2006) is in direct line with the principles of evolutionary economics.

Alongside the post-Keynesian growth literature, evolutionary economics constitutes an alternative to the NGT in the analysis of technical change as a source for long run economic growth. Drawing on Schumpeter's legacy, it accounts for technical change as the trigger for an out-of-equilibrium economic dynamics. The evolutionary growth theory develops around the work of Nelson and Winter (1982). Part IV of their seminal book provides the foundations of the evolutionary modelling approach to economic growth. It gives a central position to technological change, whether radical or incremental. The sources of technical change are found in the firms' R&D investment behaviours and their learning capacities. Evolutionary economics considers population dynamics, following their namesake in theoretical biology, rather than the representative agent assumption of neo-classical economics or the macroscopic approach used by the post-Keynesians. These populations of agents are heterogeneous and evolve in highly uncertain environments. This uncertainty is due to the imperfection of information and of the perception of the technology dynamics of an intrinsically uneven nature. These uncertainties are incompatible with the substantial rationality found in mainstream economics and leads evolutionary economics to favour bounded rationality. The behaviours of economic agents are then confined to the application of decision routines such as fixed or adaptive decision rules. The economic dynamics are rooted in the interaction of these bounded rational agents with a selection mechanism. This process differentiates the heterogeneous agents, defining the survival or extinction of agents on the basis of given characteristics (i.e., competitiveness, profitability, etc.). To survive the selection process, heterogeneous agents have to mutate. These mutations are the technological changes at the core of economic dynamics. The continuous mutations in the population characteristics ensure the persistence of the selection process and therefore economic dynamics. The seminal contribution by Nelson and Winter (1982) opens the door to a highly heterogeneous literature.[7] The core of the evolutionary principles, such as

---

[7] See also Dosi et al. (1988); Kwasnicki (2003); Silverberg and Verspagen (2005) and Witt (2008) for more recent developments in this stream of literature.

heterogeneity, selection and mutation processes, or assumptions such as bounded rationality or the key role played by technological changes remain the common building blocks of these models. Among these various trajectories, the one proposed by Silverberg and Lehnert (1993) and reconsidered in Silverberg and Verspagen (1994, 1995, 1998) is of particular interest for the current chapter. These models share a common embodied conception of technical change with Kaldor. Technical progress is incorporated in capital vintages. Technical change is driven by the adoption of these capital vintages. The mechanisms at work here are those of Kaldor's technical progress function. The adoption of these capital vintages is a response to the selection mechanisms.

As argued in Llerena and Lorentz (2004a), the evolutionary approach to technical change provides a formal framework to micro-found the Kaldor-Verdoorn Law. Within the evolutionary economics framework, and following Schumpeter's precepts, technical change emerges at the micro level and diffuses into the economy. These mechanisms are at the core of economic dynamics. This chapter aims to show that a Kaldor-Verdoorn Law can emerge from the dynamics generated by an evolutionary model of technical change. In this sense, we aim at providing a formal micro-level explanation for the law complementary to the ones verbally provided by Kaldor (1966). The proposed micro-foundations of the Kaldor-Verdoorn Law do not aim at competing with but rather complementing the macro-level approach proposed by Metcalfe, Foster, and Ramlogan (2006).

The remainder of the chapter is organised as follows: the second section describes the model we use for the numerical simulations, whose results are presented and analysed in the third section. The fourth section concludes the chapter.

An Evolutionary Model of Technical Change

We develop a simple model of a firm-level technical change in line with the evolutionary literature, more specifically to the neo-Schumpeterian branch of evolutionary economics. Developed around the seminal work of Nelson and Winter (1982), this stream of literature proposes a formal representation of Schumpeter's thought: technical change, as a key factor for economic dynamics, emerges unevenly and unpredictably from firms' or entrepreneurs' behaviour.

It then diffuses across the economy, disrupting the established economic equilibrium.

The evolutionary interpretation of Schumpeter's analysis relies on formal analogies drawn from evolutionary biology. An economic system is composed of one (or more) population(s) of agents. The latter are defined by a set of heterogeneous characteristics. The characteristics of the population(s) are subject to mutations occurring unevenly among agents, generating and sustaining the heterogeneity within populations. The agents composing the population(s) are subject to selection mechanisms. The selection mechanism defines the level of performance of the agents and their survival. In the Neo-Schumpeterian literature, the selection mechanism is usually considered to represent (or alternatively to be represented by) market mechanisms. Following the traditional modelling strategies to be found in this stream of the evolutionary literature, the model is organised as follows:

1. A population of I firms, indexed $i \in \{1; ...; I\}$, characterised by a homogenous product but heterogeneous production processes leading to differences in productivity, price and profitability.
2. The selection mechanism shares the total demand among firms, favouring the best-performing firms. Selection acts here as a channel for the diffusion of the most efficient technologies, ruling out the least efficient firms from the market.
3. A firm's production process is subject to mutation through technological changes linked to their R&D activity. We choose here to distinguish two phases in this process:
   a. Exploration: Firms search for new production facilities, through innovation or imitation of existing production facilities. The outcome is uncertain and defines the efficiency (in terms of productivity) of the resulting vintage of capital goods.
   b. Exploitation of R&D outcome: This stage requires firms to invest in incorporating the outcome of research in the production process. This second stage is funded by firms' sales and is directly dependent on the success of previous investments.

The firms are bounded rational. Firms do not directly respond to the selection mechanism but revert to simple decision rules to set their prices, their investment and technological strategies. The aggregated dynamics analysed in the third part of this chapter is derived from the combination of these microelements. Note that we focus here on the supply-side dynamics to put in a new light the technological mechanisms that can lead to the emergence of a Kaldor-Verdoorn Law. We therefore leave aside the mechanisms expanding aggregate demand, a complement of the Kaldor-Verdoorn Law in generating cumulative growth.[8]

The remainder of this section is organised as follows: we first characterise the agents composing our population, then describe the selection process and close with the presentation of the mutation mechanisms.

Defining the Population: Firms' Characteristics

In the short run (i.e., at each time step t), a given firm i is represented by a production function characterised by constant returns to scale. Firms' production processes use labour as a unique production factor. Capital enters indirectly into the production function. The level of labour productivity depends on the accumulation of capital vintages. Investments in the different vintages of capital goods increase labour productivity. The production function is represented as follows:

$$Y_{i,t} = A_{i,t-1} L_{i,t} \tag{6.1}$$

where $Y_{i,t}$ is the output of firm i at time t. $A_{i,t-1}$ represents the current level of labour productivity, and $L_{i,t}$ the labour force employed in the production process. The level of output is constrained by the demand for the firms' products. The aggregate demand (D_t) is assumed to grow at a fixed rate (δ). Each firm produces to cover a share $(z_{i,t})$ of the aggregate demand. This market share $(z_{i,t})$ results from the market selection mechanisms described in the next section. The level of production of each firm is computed as follows:

$$Y_{i,t} = z_{i,t} D_t \tag{6.2}$$

The firms set prices through a mark-up rule. This mark-up (μ) is applied to unit production costs. Formally, the pricing rule can be represented as follows:

$$p_{i,t} = (1 + \mu) \frac{w}{A_{i,t-1}} \tag{6.3}$$

---

[8] Models integrating such evolutionary micro-dynamics in a complete cumulative causation growth framework can be found, among others, in Verspagen (2002); Llerena and Lorentz (2004b); Ciarli et al. (2010); Lorentz and Savona (2010); Lorentz (2015a, b) and Lorentz et al. (2016).

where $p_{i,t}$ represents the price set by firm i at time t, μ the mark-up coefficient and w the nominal wage set exogenously. It should be noted that we assume here that the mark-up coefficient remains fixed for each firm. The profit level of firms is deduced from this mark-up rule and defined as follows:

$$\Pi_{i,t} = \mu \frac{w}{A_{i,t-1}} z_{i,t} D_t \tag{6.4}$$

In the model profits constitute the only financial resource for firms' investments. In other words, all the decisions made by the firms are constrained by their profits. Their ability to capture demand shares (i.e., their past performances) directly affects all their investment plans and their ability to increase their performance in the future.

Defining Firms' Performance: The Selection Mechanisms

In an evolutionary system, the selection mechanism represents the core of its dynamics. It sorts the various components of a population, creating motion in the system and allocating resources within the population. In evolutionary economics, the selection process usually corresponds to the competition mechanisms. We choose here to use replicator dynamics to model the selection mechanisms.[9] Replicator dynamics are usually considered a formal representation of Fisher's principle of natural selection. This principle can be summarised as follows: the share of each group of individuals in a population grows as long as their fitness level remains higher than the average of the overall population. This average level depends itself on the shares of every group, such that the selection mechanisms tend to favour the fittest components of a population. Formally, the replicator equation defines the increase (decrease) in the share of a group of individuals as a function of the distance between the fitness level of the group and the average fitness level: the larger the distance, the more the share grows.

We use this mechanism to model the competition among firms. The goods produced are homogeneous, and the firms compete on prices. The replicator dynamics define firms' market shares as a function of the firms' price competitiveness $(E_{i,t})$. The lower the price $(p_{i,t})$, the

[9] A comprehensive view on the use of replicator dynamics in economics can be found in Metcalfe (1998).

higher the price competitiveness: $E_{i,t} = \frac{1}{p_{i,t}}$. Formally, the replicator mechanism defines the firms' market shares $(z_{i,t})$ as a function of the price competitiveness $(E_{i,t})$ of the firm relative to the average competitiveness on the market $(\overline{E}_t)$[10]:

$$z_{i,t} = z_{i,t-1}\left(1 + \phi\left(\frac{E_{i,t}}{\overline{E}_t} - 1\right)\right) \tag{6.5}$$

The parameter ϕ measures the sensitivity to changes in competitiveness. Given that the competitiveness is solely a function of prices, this parameter can be assimilated to the price elasticity of the selection mechanism: the closer ϕ is to 0, the less the selection mechanism, and therefore the changes in markets shares are with respect to prices.

Firms exit the market if their market share falls below $\bar{z}$. The exiting firms are replaced by entrant firms whose characteristics are set according to the market averages, with an entry market share equal to $\bar{z}$. This ensures a constant number of firms on the market, as required by the replicator equation to ensure that all market shares sum to 1 and remain bounded between 0 and 1. Moreover, the exit of an innovator (imitator) firm is compensated by the entry of another innovator (imitator) firm. The proportion of innovators in the population of firms remains constant.[11]

Changes in Firms' Characteristics: The Mutation Mechanisms

The mutation mechanisms ensure that the system remains in motion, counterbalancing the selection mechanisms. The selection dynamics require some degrees of heterogeneity among the characteristics of the agents. Through time, selection limits the level of heterogeneity in the system. The mutation of agents' characteristics generates and sustains some degree of heterogeneity within the population.

---

[10] $\overline{E}_t$, the average competitiveness on the market is computed as the average of firms' competitiveness weighted by their market shares:

$$\overline{E}_t = \sum_{i=1}^{I} z_{i,t-1} E_{i,t}$$

[11] Note that this assumption has been made to ease the modelling of the simulation model but has no qualitative effect on the results, as long as at least one innovator exists.

In our model, mutation occurs at the level of the firms through changes in labour productivity. The process of technical improvement can be divided into two distinct phases: firms either explore new technological possibilities through local search (innovation) or capture external technological possibilities (imitation). This process leads to a production design (capital vintage) that can be exploited by firms in their production process. These new vintages are incorporated into the production technology during a second stage. The exploitation phase is financed by investments in capital goods, while the exploration phase is allowed by investments in R&D. We assume that priority is given to capital investments, and therefore the exploitation of already discovered technologies.

Labour productivity is deduced from the accumulation of capital goods through time. Each vintage of capital embodies a level of labour productivity $(a_{i,t})$. The more a firm invests in a vintage, the more its embodied labour productivity affects the production process. At every time step labour productivity can be expressed by the following equation:

$$A_{i,t} = \frac{I_{i,t}}{K_{i,t}} a_{i,t-1} + \frac{I_{i,t-1}}{K_{i,t}} A_{i,t-1} \tag{6.6}$$

where $a_{i,t-1}$ represents the level of labour productivity embodied in the vintage of capital goods developed by i during the period $t - 1$. $I_{i,t}$ represents the amount of investment in capital goods of the firm at time t, $K_{i,t}$, the stock of capital vintages accumulated so far by the firm.[12]

The amount of investments in capital goods $(I_{i,t})$ corresponds to a share (ι) of firms' sales $(Y_{i,t})$. For the sake of simplicity, this share is

---

[12] The stock of capital accumulated by a firm i is computed as follows: $K_{i,t} = \sum_{\tau=0}^{t} I_{i,\tau}$. Note that we assume here that the capital vintages already accumulated remain in use in the production process. Their weight in the overall production capacity of the firms declines with the firms' continuous investments in more recent capital vintages. In this respect, and for the sake of simplicity, we do not model an explicit mechanism of depreciation of capital. It can easily be shown that adding an explicit depreciation of capital would simply reinforce the selection mechanism among firms, favouring the successful firms, able to invest to (over-) compensate the depreciation process, while the declining firms would simply be pushed faster to exit the market, being unable to compensate for the depreciation process. The focus of the chapter being on the analysis of the aggregate outcome of the mutation and selection dynamics on aggregate productivity, we choose to overlook the depreciation mechanisms.

assumed to remain fixed. We exclude the possibility of investments to be adapted and used as a strategic variable, departing here from some pre-existing evolutionary models by Silverberg and Verspagen (1994, 1998).[13] This assumption also allows us to isolate the effect of ι on the Kaldor–Verdoorn Law. Investments are funded on the financial resources of firms and cannot exceed the actual sales: $\iota \in [0; 1]$. For the sake of simplicity we rule out the possibility of firms to revert to a financial sector to finance their investments. Firms are therefore constrained by their own profits to finance investments[14]:

$$I_{i,t} = \min\{\iota Y_{i,t}; \Pi_{i,t}\} \tag{6.7}$$

The resources available for investments depend on the firms' sales, a function of their competitiveness, their ability to invest and therefore their past performances. The model accounts for the endogenous building of the production capacities of firms through the accumulation of capital. This process is also constrained by the firms' past performances. The model includes in its evolutionary micro-foundation an additional 'neo-Austrian' flavour (Amendola & Gaffard 1998).

The level of investments in R&D corresponds to a share ρ of the sales $(Y_{i,t})$. For the sake of simplicity, this share remains fixed and cannot exceed the firm's own resources: $\rho \in [0; 1]$. R&D investments are constrained by the remaining available profits $(\Pi_{i,t})$ net of investments in capital goods $(I_{i,t})$. The R&D investments are used to hire workers $(R_{i,t})$ assigned to the R&D activity[15]:

$$R_{i,t} = \frac{1}{w}\min\{\rho Y_{i,t}; \Pi_{i,t} - I_{i,t}\} \tag{6.8}$$

In direct line with Nelson and Winter (1982), we consider the outcome of the R&D activity as uncertain: first, the probability of success

---

[13] Silverberg and Verspagen (1994) propose an evolutionary model with an adaptive decision rule on firms' investment behaviours. The paper shows that the evolutionary dynamics leads to a fixed share of sales being devoted to investments among the surviving firms. In Llerena and Lorentz (2004a), we considered investment behaviours as driven by adaptive decision rules. With such rules, however, surviving firms tend to apply fixed shares in the long run, while firms lagging too far behind do not manage to compensate for their gap and adapt their behaviour. The priority given to investments in capital then prevents any R&D investment.

[14] This assumption is required to ensure that within the numerical simulations, investments do not exceed the available resources.

[15] We assume here that firms' resources are either invested in capital or in R&D, so that along the simulation we set $\rho = 1 - \iota$.

of R&D is an increasing function of the R&D intensity of the firm $(R_{i,t}/Y_{i,t})$. Second, if successful, the outcome, in terms of the characteristics of the newly developed capital vintage, is itself stochastic. This R&D outcome results from either a process of 'local search' or imitation, depending on the nature of the firm. We model the R&D process, followed by each firm, according to the following algorithm:

1. A first random draw decides the success (or failure) of the R&D activity at time t. The probability of success of the R&D activity increases with the number of workers hired for the research activity. This probability is null if the ratio is null and tends to 1 if the firm uses all its resources for R&D.
2. If R&D is successful, the prototype of a new capital vintage is developed. The new vintage at t is characterised by the level of labour productivity it embodies $(a_{i,t})$. The firm exploits the prototype only if it embodies a higher level of labour productivity:

$$a_{i,t} = \max\{a_{i,t-1}; a_{i,t-1} + \varepsilon_{i,t}\} \tag{6.9}$$

The level of change in embodied productivity $(\varepsilon_{i,t})$ is drawn from a normal distribution:

$$\varepsilon_{i,t} \sim N(0; \sigma_{i,t}) \tag{6.10}$$

The value of $\sigma_{i,t}$ depends on the nature of the firm: if the firm is an innovator, $\sigma_{i,t}$ is fixed; if the firm is an imitator, $\sigma_{i,t}$ is a function of the firm's technological gap:

$$\sigma_{i,t} = \begin{cases} \sigma & \text{if the firm } i \text{ is an innovator} \\ \max\{\chi(\overline{a_t} - a_{i,t-1}); 0\} & \text{if the firm } i \text{ is an imitator} \end{cases} \tag{6.11}$$

$\overline{a_t}$ represents the average level of embodied productivity in the industry.[16] χ represents the degree of appropriability of technological spillovers.

For the innovators, the formal representation of the R&D activity can be assimilated to a 'local search', in line with Nelson and Winter (1982). The stochastic process is centred on the existing level of

---

[16] It is formally computed as follows:

$$\overline{a_t} = \sum_{i=1}^{I} z_{i,t} a_{i,t-1}$$

productivity, reflecting the firm's level of technical knowledge, and the potential improvements are limited. For the imitators, the R&D activity consists of filling the gap with the industry's average technological level.[17] In this respect, there exist knowledge spillovers as traditionally considered in the NGT. These, however, do not imply static increasing returns, but require firms to invest, and be sufficiently lucky to benefit from them.

Simulation Results

Our aim with this chapter is twofold: while accounting for the contribution of the micro-level mechanisms underlying the emergence and diffusion of technical change on dynamic increasing returns at the aggregate level, we propose an alternative micro-foundation to the Kaldor-Verdoorn Law in line with the evolutionary neo-Schumpeterian tradition. In the earlier presented model, firms experience constant returns to scale in the short run. Firms do not experience increasing returns in the traditional Marshallian view. At the industry/sector level, the knowledge/technological spillovers solely concern the imitating firms. Those allow the imitating firms to (partly) fill their technological gap. The spillovers do not allow innovating firms to benefit from any knowledge or information gathered by the imitating firms while filling their technological gap. In this respect, the model does not assume the existence of static increasing returns due to knowledge spillovers and proximity, as traditionally considered in the network or economic geography literature. Hence increasing returns, if they emerge, are here intrinsically dynamic and the result of the evolutionary micro-dynamics. The sole gains in efficiency at the industry-level, as measured by the Kaldor-Verdoorn coefficient, are therefore rooted in the micro-dynamics; in the interplay between the mutation mechanisms, allowing for investment to improve productivity at the firm level and the selection mechanisms, allowing for positive feedback, at the sector/industry level, between the allocation of resources to firms and past productivity

---

[17] In Llerena and Lorentz (2004a), firms can switch from imitative to innovative strategies (and reversely) depending on their technological gap. Fixing the R&D strategies of the firms, as in this chapter, does not affect qualitatively the results of the simulations. On the other hand, this allows us to isolate the effect of the diffusion of technologies through imitation from the diffusion within the population through selection.

gains. The improvement in the production capacities requires firms to have invested a part of their past income in R&D and a part of their current income in building up their production capacity using the outcome of R&D. To bring this result to light, we focus on three main phases of the micro-dynamics of technological change:

1. The emergence of technological shocks. This phase corresponds to the arrival of new capital vintages. It occurs at the level of the innovative firms as the outcome of the R&D process.
2. The adoption of the technological shocks. This phase corresponds to the introduction of the new capital vintages in the production process.
3. The diffusion of the shocks within the population. The diffusion phase occurs through two channels: first through imitation; second through the selection process that allocates more resources to the fittest firms.

In this respect, the model presented here proposes a complementary approach to the effect of increasing returns on productivity and technological change dynamics as the ones usually considered either in the NGT or in models with network externalities.

The model presented here is developed as an agent-based model. The analysis of the model is conducted through numerical simulations. The simulations are conducted and analysed as follows: we first discuss a set of preliminary results focusing on the main dynamics generated by the model, among which there are some known stylised facts. These results are presented first. The next section presents and discusses the effect of the micro-level parameters controlling the various phases of the technological change on productivity dynamics. The third section presents and discusses the effect of the same micro-level parameters on the estimates of the Kaldor-Verdoorn Law using the data generated by the numerical simulations. Our aim in this last section is to identify some key mechanisms to understand the effect of firm-level technical change on the dynamic increasing returns observed at the macro-economic level.

Main Model Dynamics and Kaldor's Stylized Facts

This first set of simulations aims at presenting and discussing the dynamic functioning of the model. The numerical simulations are conducted as follows: every simulation lasts 500 steps. This time span is large enough to ensure the stabilisation of the output of the model. Most of the dynamics actually occur within the first 250 steps. For each simulation, we consider a population of 50 firms. The first half of these firms are set to behave as innovators, while the second half are imitators. This distribution remains fixed. The size of the population is sufficiently large to reach significant and robust results and ensure reasonable computation times. A larger population of firms would not drastically modify the results. Finally, we apply the same initial conditions to all firms, for all simulation runs. The heterogeneity among firms emerges only from the endogenous mutation mechanism. Those dynamics are described within the model description section.

For this first set of simulations, we simulate 100 replications of a benchmark specification of the model. Table 6.1 presents the initial conditions and the parameter values for the benchmark simulation setting. This benchmark specification is then used as a reference point for the analysis of the parameter changes reported in the next sections. The results presented in this section report the outcome of these 100 replications. We tested the robustness of the outcome of the model over those 100 replications of the benchmark parameterisation.

Figure 6.1 presents the dynamics of the aggregate labour productivity (a), the capital/labour ratio (b), capital intensity (c) and the Herfindhal index in the firms' output for both the single 100 replications (dotted lines) and the average over the 100 replications. Despite the growing variance among the replications for the first variables, these remain in an acceptable range, and the outcome remains robust among replications.

More interestingly, the dynamics generated by the model for these variables shows the following. There is a constant increase in the labour productivity at the sector/industry level. There is a constant increase in the capital/labour ratio. Through the simulations, the model therefore generates both productivity gains and transformations in the production structure. These transformations lead to a mechanisation

Table 6.1. *Parameter settings (initial conditions and benchmark setting)*

ι	σ	δ	ϕ	χ	$a_{i,0}$	μ	w	$\bar{z}$	D_0	$z_{i,0}$	$A_{i,0}$
0.2	0.05	0.01	1	0.75	1	1	10	0.0001	10	0.05	1

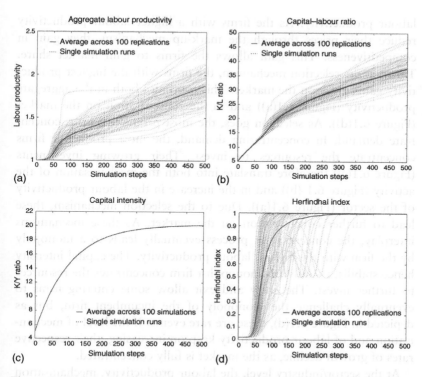

Figure 6.1 Labour productivity and capital/labour ratio over 500 simulation steps (benchmark setting)

of the activity. The capital intensity, if increasing, stabilises through time. The mechanisation of production is therefore sustained by the continuous increase in labour productivity. There is interplay between the mechanisation of the production and productivity gains through the investments in capital goods. These processes ought to be significant of the growth pattern of advanced economies, as pointed out by Kaldor (1957):

[I]nvestigations have also revealed that whilst in the course of economic progress the value of the capital equipment per worker (measured at constant price) and the value of the annual output per worker (also in constant price) are steadily rising.

(p. 260, as reprinted in Kaldor 1960)

As firms invest and adopt the more recent capital vintages, they increase the efficiency of the production process, thus increasing their labour productivity. As the firms with a higher labour productivity reduce their prices through the mark-up mechanism, they gain in competitiveness. This gain allows the firms to gain market share. Through the selection mechanism, the firms with the highest productivity gains grow on the market. This translates both in the aggregate productivity (Figure 6.1(a)) and in the concentration on the market (Figure 6.1(d)). As selection goes, the most productive firms concentrate demand. In concentrating demand, the most productive firms concentrate the resources to invest. Their growing investments (Figure 6.1(c)) therefore translate into both the mechanisation of the activity (Figure 6.1 (b)) and in the increase in the labour productivity of the sector (Figure 6.1(a)). Due to the selection mechanism, these lead to further concentration on the market. As these mechanisms interplay, the concentration process eventually leads to a monopoly by the firm with the highest labour productivity. The capital intensity hence stabilises – only the monopolist firm concentrates the resources to further invest. The entry and exit allow some entering firms to eventually challenge the monopoly of the incumbent firm, but as depicted in Figure 6.1(d), these are rare events. If the level of mechanisation and of labour productivity keep on increasing, their respective rates of growth decline, as the market is fully concentrated.

At the sector/industry level, the labour productivity, mechanisation and concentration appear strongly related to both the level of demand, and therefore the resources available to both invest in capital and R&D, and to the actual realisation of those investments. Table 6.2 reports the respective correlations between the level of labour productivity (A_t), capital deepening (K/L_t) and market concentration (H_t) with the level of market demand[18] (Y_t) and capital intensity (K/Y_t). These correlations are computed using least absolute deviation (LAD) estimation with 500 bootstraps.

---

[18] As discussed in the model description, the demand at the market level grows at a fixed and exogenous rate δ. Therefore, we avoid any endogeneity issue with regard to the estimation of the correlations with the level of market demand. In order to focus here on the technological change mechanisms, we choose to neutralise the effect of technological change on market demand. Evolutionary growth models accounting for the feedback effects between technological change and demand on the line of the Kaldorian literature can be found in Verspagen (2002); Llerena and Lorentz (2004b); Lorentz and Savona (2010); Ciarli et al. (2010); Lorentz (2015a, b) and Lorentz et al. (2016), among others.

Table 6.2. *Labour productivity, capital–output ratio and Herfindahl index correlations to output and capital intensity* (LAD)

	A_t	K/L_t	K/L_t	H_t	H_t
Y_t	0.0005*** (2.76e-05)	0.0141*** (0.5190)	2.4517*** (0.0802)	5.05e-05*** (5.77e-06)	0.0700*** (0.0033)
K/Y_t	0.0510*** (0.0013)		-16.7445*** (1.4874)		
Constant	1.3954*** (0.0124)	0.43179*** (0.0179)	24.3781*** (0.53499)	0.9592*** (0.0035)	-0.371*** (0.1376)
Observations	500	500	500	500	500

Standard errors in parentheses: *** $p < 0.01$.

Labour productivity, capital deepening and market concentration turn out to be highly correlated to both the level of market demand and capital intensity. As demand rises, the firms' resources to invest in both developing capital goods through R&D and adopting these capital goods grow. Both translate to an increase in the aggregated productivity on the market. Both productivity gains and the increase in capital intensity favours capital deepening and the mechanisation of the sector/industry. As resources are used by firms to invest, generating uneven productivity gains among firms, the market selection mechanisms reinforces the concentration on the market, explaining therefore the strong correlation between the size of demand and the concentration index. These mechanisms, moreover, tend to reinforce each other. Table 6.3 reports the Vector Autoregression (VAR) estimates of the correlations between labour productivity, capital deepening and market concentration and with the level of market demand.[19]

The VAR estimates show a strong momentum in the dynamics of all three variables. The estimates also show the existence of a feedback mechanism between labour productivity and market concentration. These estimates are in line with the dynamic description of the model shown: as demand increases, the firms having experienced the highest productivity gain, which mechanically raises the aggregate productivity, gain in market share as a result of the selection mechanisms. This increases the concentration. These firms then appropriate the resources to invest. The investments translate into further capital deepening. With capital embodying productivity gains, this explains the significant lagged effect of capital deepening labour productivity. The initial investments were the result of prior concentrations, and these prior concentrations process the result of the selection mechanism, favouring initial increases in labour productivity.

The simulation results obtained with the benchmark dynamics are in line with Kaldor's analysis of technical change. The evolutionary micro-dynamics at both the firm and market level generate similar dynamics to the one described by Kaldor. In this respect, the model presented proposed an evolutionary reinterpretation of Kaldor's technical progress function. Focusing the analysis on the effect of some key

---

[19] Note that the VAR estimates reported here only account for the contemporaneous effect of the market demand on the variables. The lagged effect appears insignificant when estimated.

Table 6.3. *Labour productivity, capital–output ratio, Herfindahl index dynamic correlations (VAR estimates)*

	A_t	K/L_t	H_t
Y_t	2.52e-08*	−8.40e-06***	−2.90e-08***
	(1.39e-08)	(2.87e-06)	(9.01e-09)
A_{t-1}	2.2480***	0.0190	0.2157***
	(0.0467)	(9.6461)	(0.0303)
K/L_{t-1}	0.0004*	1.4571***	0.0003**
	(0.0002)	(0.0426)	(0.0001)
H_{t-1}	0.0818***	−2.7769	2.8604***
	(0.0119)	(2.4645)	(0.0077)
A_{t-2}	−1.4299***	6.0162	−0.3289***
	(0.0965)	(19.9312)	(0.0626)
K/L_{t-2}	−5.57e-05	−0.1250	−0.0001
	(0.0004)	(0.0783)	(0.0002)
H_{t-2}	−0.1869***	3.9490	−2.7534***
	(0.0234)	(4.8307)	(0.0152)
A_{t-3}	0.1815***	−5.8953	0.1135
	(0.0502)	(10.3671)	(0.0325)
K/L_{t-3}	−0.0003	−0.3369***	−0.0002*
	(0.0002)	(0.0417127)	(0.000130981)
H_{t-3}	0.1050	−1.1621	0.8931***
	(0.0116)	(2.3999)	(0.00754)
Constant	0.000199131**	−0.0816329***	−0.000337293***
	(9.88e-05)	(0.0204)	(6.40e-05)
Observations	500	500	500

Standard errors in parentheses: *** $p < 0.01$, ** $p < 0.05$, *$p < 0.1$.

parameters, the next section aims to account for the specific effects of each of these evolutionary micro-dynamics on labour productivity.

Technological Parameters and Productivity Gains

This section discusses the role of a selected number of parameters characterising the three phases of the micro-dynamics of technical change, presented earlier. The remaining simulations are then conducted in order to stress the effect of these parameters. The numerical simulations are conducted as follows: every simulation lasts 500 steps. This time span is large enough to ensure the stabilisation of the output of the model. Most of the dynamics actually occurs within the first 250 steps. Each parameter setting is replicated at least 20 times.[20] The results presented in this section correspond to averages across the replications of the considered parameter setting. By doing so, we ensure the robustness of the results presented. We focus here on the analysis of five parameters affecting the three main mechanisms of technical change at work in the model, namely, the emergence, the adoption and the diffusion of technological shocks.

ι is defined in the previous section as the share of firms' resources devoted to investments in capital goods. This parameter controls the speed of adoption of the technological shock generated by the R&D activity and embodied into the capital vintages. Moreover, we assume through the simulations procedure that ρ, the share of resources devoted to finance the R&D activity, is set equal to $(1 - \iota)$. ι also controls the frequency of technological changes, affecting directly the probability of success of R&D. The parameter is set so that: $\iota \in [0; 1]$. As ι tends to 1, the allocation of resources by firms favours the adoption of existing technologies. As ι tends to 0, the allocation of resources favours the development of new technologies. Note that for extreme values, no productivity gains are possible: on the one hand, if all the resources are devoted to the adoption of existing technologies, this prevents the R&D financing necessary for further advances in production technologies. On the other hand, if ι is null, all the resources are used to develop capital vintages that are never adopted by the firm.

σ corresponds to the standard deviation of the stochastic process defining the outcome of the R&D process for the innovator. This parameter controls the amplitude of the technological shocks resulting from the R&D activity of the firms. As σ increases, the potential jump in embodied productivity increases. Simultaneously, as firms adopt only the positive jumps, increasing σ also increases the unevenness of the technological shocks. This parameter therefore affects both the amplitude of technical changes at the firm level and the degree of heterogeneity among firms.

χ measures the appropriability of technological spillovers by imitators. This parameter controls the diffusion of technological shocks

---

[20] The robustness of the model to stochastic shocks has been tested over 100 replicates for the benchmark setting.

resulting from innovative firms to the imitative firms. The larger $\chi \in [0; 1]$, the higher the spillovers, and the faster the imitators reduce their technological gap.

ϕ defines the sensitiveness of the replicator dynamics. This parameter directly controls the strength of selection. Through market selection, the available resources (aggregate demand) are allocated to firms. These resources are used for developing and adopting production technologies. Increasing ϕ, first increases the uneven distribution of resources resulting from the productivity differences among firms. Second, it reinforces the uneven technological endowments of firms, favouring the access to resources for the high-productivity firms. Finally, ϕ affects the diffusion of the best technologies within the economy.

δ defines the rate of growth of aggregate demand, constraining directly the level of the resources available for firms. As we focus in this chapter on the technological mechanisms underlying the Kaldor-Verdoorn Law, we choose to assume a fixed rate of growth.[21] δ, therefore, controls the overall amount of resources to be distributed to firms. For a given distribution of resources among firms, and a given allocation of resources between capital and R&D investments within firms, increasing δ amplifies both the emergence of technological change through R&D investments and the adoption of technologies by firms through capital investments.

The first two parameters, ι and σ, allow us to identify the effect linked to both the emergence and the adoption of technological shocks at the firm level. The parameters ϕ and χ allow us to isolate the effect of the phase of diffusion of these shocks among the population and to the economy as a whole. The parameter δ amplifies these mechanisms. The detailed parameter values used for the simulations are reported in Table 6.4. We focus in this section on the effect of the various parameters, controlling for the three phases of technical changes on productivity dynamics. We do so to ease the comprehension of the effect of these parameters on the estimated increasing returns reported in the next section. We choose to measure productivity growth rates over the 50, 100 and 250 first simulation steps.

---

[21] The parameter also allows us to control the total level of output in our population of firms. This appears useful to avoid any problem of endogeneity in the explanatory variable while estimating the coefficients of the Kaldor-Verdoorn Law in the second part of the analysis.

Table 6.4. *Parameter settings (default values in bold)*

ι	0	0.02	0.04	0.06	0.08	0.1	0.12	0.14	0.16	0.18
	0.2	0.22	0.24	0.26	0.28	0.3	0.32	0.34	0.36	0.38
	0.4	0.5	0.6	0.7	0.8	0.9	1			
σ	0.01	0.015	0.02	0.025	0.03	0.035	0.04	0.045	**0.05**	0.06
	0.07	0.08	0.09	0.1						
δ	0.001	0.002	0.003	0.004	0.005	0.006	0.007	0.008	0.009	**0.01**
	0.011	0.012	0.013	0.014	0.015	0.016	0.017	0.018	0.010	0.02
	0.021	0.022	0.023	0.024	0.025	0.026	0.027	0.028	0.029	0.03
	0.031	0.032	0.033	0.034	0.035	0.036	0.037	0.038	0.039	0.04
	0.041	0.042	0.043	0.044	0.045	0.046	0.047	0.048	0.049	0.05
φ	0	0.25	0.5	**0.75**	1	1.25				
χ	0	0.25	0.5	**0.75**	1					

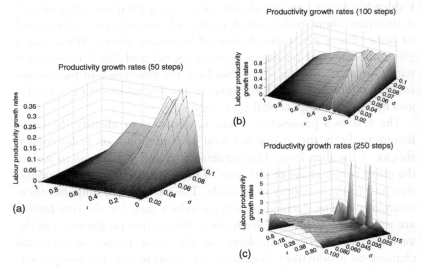

Figure 6.2 Labour productivity growth rate: ι vs. σ

Figure 6.2 presents the effect on aggregate productivity growth rates of changes in the values of ι and σ over selected time periods. Simulations show that both parameters have a clear effect on productivity dynamics: higher values of ι tend to decrease productivity growth, while increasing σ increases productivity growth. On the one hand, the more resources are devoted to R&D, the higher the productivity growth. This effect is amplified as σ increases. On the other hand, the higher the amplitude of technical change, the higher the productivity growth. This effect is amplified for low values of ι (see Figure 6.2(a)). Similar patterns emerge for the various time periods considered. However, the amplitude of these effects seems to gradually vanish with time (see Figure 6.2(b) and (c)). With the probability of success of R&D being directly correlated with the share of resources devoted to R&D, the lower the ι, the higher the probability of technical change occurring. More frequent novel capital goods arising hence favour productivity growth. However, if ι is too low ($\iota = 0$), firms do not invest in capital to exploit these changes. Favouring the emergence phase increases productivity growth but requires a minimum of resources to be devoted to the adoption to be effective. The parameter σ controls the potential productivity jumps between two capital vintages. Increasing the amplitude of the shock then mechanically favours the productivity growth rate. This effect is reinforced as the frequency of the shocks is increased, with greater shares of resources devoted to R&D. These two parameters affect directly the emergence phase and adoption of technological change. The higher the frequency of the technological shocks, the higher the productivity growth. Second, the higher the amplitude of the technological change induced by these shocks, the higher the productivity growth rates. On the one hand, the more firms favour the emergence of new capital vintages, the higher the aggregate productivity growth. On the other, adoption constrains the actual effect of technical change on productivity growth. If no resources are devoted to the adoption of these vintages, the effect of technical change on productivity disappears.

The second set of simulations focuses on the effect of changes in χ and ϕ on the productivity dynamics. These parameters favour the diffusion of the shocks through imitation. Figure 6.3(a) presents the outcome of the changes in these parameters on the productivity growth rates over 50 simulation steps. Strengthening the selection mechanism positively affects the productivity dynamics: the higher the ϕ, the stronger the selection mechanisms and the faster the diffusion of the technological shocks. Modifying χ, on the other hand, only slightly increases productivity. These effects even vanish when considering productivity growth over a larger time span (Figure 6.3(b) and (c)).

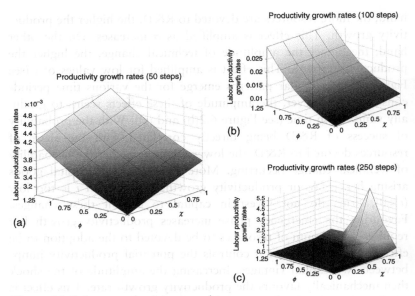

Figure 6.3 Labour productivity growth rate: χ vs. ϕ

In the latter cases, firms have time to imitate explaining the productivity growth picks for the high values of χ. The influence of the selection mechanism is only transitory. This is due to the nature of the selection mechanisms. The replicator dynamics necessarily leads the system to a monopoly situation. The aggregate dynamics is only due to the productivity changes of the monopolistic firm, and the underlying Schumpeterian micro-dynamics stabilise. The factors favouring diffusion then become marginal. This result is directly linked to some assumptions made to keep the model simple: including changes in technological trajectories or large-scale division of labour could prevent the Schumpeterian dynamics from stabilising.[22] We can briefly summarise the results found as follows: first, the factors favouring the emergence of technical shocks at the firm level seem to dominate all the other mechanisms. Second, as selection mechanisms go, all the effects tend to gradually disappear, with technical change becoming less likely. Third, in all cases, the effect of these parameters on productivity dynamics vanishes through time.

---

[22] We can observe this, for instance, in Ciarli et al. (2010); Lorentz and Savona (2010) and Lorentz et al. (2016).

Evolutionary Micro-Dynamics and the Kaldor-Verdoorn Law

The last section of the simulation analysis investigates the effect of the micro-dynamics of technological change on the emergence of a Kaldor-Verdoorn Law at the aggregate level. As discussed in the previous sections, the model developed in this chapter proposes an approach to technological change as a mutation process occurring at the firm level. The model diverts from the static approach to increasing returns linked to scale effects and externalities developed in the mainstream literature. In line with both Kaldor's *technical progress function*, and the principles of the neo-Schumpeterian evolutionary literature, technological change is driven by the micro-decisions of firms. The improvement of the production capacities of firms is driven by their investment behaviours and constrained by their past performances. In this respect, increasing returns at the micro level are intrinsically dynamic. At the macro level, increasing returns therefore results from the interplay of these micro-dynamics and the industrial dynamics driven by the selection mechanism. The aim of this section is to analyse the effect of these micro-dynamics on the macro level increasing returns as measured by the Kaldor-Verdoorn Law. We estimate the Verdoorn specification of the law as follows:

$$\frac{A_{t_1} - A_{t_0}}{A_{t_0}} = \lambda \frac{Y_{t_1} - Y_{t_0}}{Y_{t_0}} + \alpha$$

A_t is the aggregate level of productivity as generated by the simulations, and Y_t measures the aggregate output. This equation is then estimated using the data generated by the simulation model.

The data set is built as follows: The aggregate output is defined by aggregate demand. Aggregate demand grows at an exogenous growth rate. We use exactly the same values of this growth rate for all the parameter settings. The data set for aggregate productivity is generated by the various replications of the simulation for different values of the parameters. A first set of estimations is conducted with the data generated using the benchmark configuration, with 20 replications of each of the 50 values of δ reported in Table 6.4. We estimate this relationship using a simple ordinary least squares (OLS) over a cross-section of replications of the benchmark setting for average growth rates over different time spans: for the whole simulation period, as well as for 50 steps long sub-periods. These results are reported in Table 6.5. If the estimations of the law appear significant for the average growth rates

Table 6.5. *Kaldor-Verdoorn Law estimates (OLS)*

		$\Delta Y(500)/Y(1)$	Const.	R^2	Obs.
(6.1)	$\Delta A(500)/A(1)$	2.008e-12*	0.0018***	0.0034	1000
		(1.086e-12)	(1.616e-05)		
		$\Delta Y(50)/Y(1)$	Const.	R^2	Obs.
(6.2)	$\Delta A(50)/A(1)$	0.0066***	0.0014***	0.0975	1000
		(0.00006)	(5.79e-05)		
		$\Delta Y(100)/Y(50)$	Const.	R^2	Obs.
(6.3)	$\Delta A(100)/A(50)$	−0.0039***	0.004***	0.0255	1000
		(0.0008)	(6.96e-05)		
		$\Delta Y(150)/Y(100)$	Const.	R^2	Obs.
(6.4)	$\Delta A(150)/A(100)$	0.0033***	0.0013***	0.0056	1000
		(0.0014)	(0.0001)		
		$\Delta Y(200)/Y(150)$	Const.	R^2	Obs.
(6.5)	$\Delta A(200)/A(150)$	0.0023***	0.0010***	0.0254	1000
		(0.0004)	(4.02e-05)		
		$\Delta Y(250)/Y(200)$	Const.	R^2	Obs.
(6.6)	$\Delta A(250)/A(200)$	0.0019***	0.009***	0.0203	1000
		(0.0004)	(3.78e-05)		
		$\Delta Y(300)/Y(250)$	Const.	R^2	Obs.
(6.7)	$\Delta A(300)/A(250)$	0.0018***	0.0008***	0.0289	1000
		(0.0003)	(3.07e-05)		
		$\Delta Y(350)/Y(300)$	Const.	R^2	Obs.
(6.8)	$\Delta A(350)/A(300)$	0.0010***	0.0008***	0.0117	1000
		(0.0003)	(2.70e-05)		
		$\Delta Y(400)/Y(350)$	Const.	R^2	Obs.
(6.9)	$\Delta A(400)/A(350)$	0.0005*	0.0008***	0.0035	1000
		(0.0003)	(2.63e-05)		
		$\Delta Y(450)/Y(400)$	Const.	R^2	Obs.
(6.10)	$\Delta A(450)/A(400)$	0.0006**	0.0008***	0.0054	1000
		(0.0003)	(2.38e-05)		
		$\Delta Y(500)/Y(1)$	Const.	R^2	Obs.
(6.11)	$\Delta A(500)/A(450)$	0.0001	0.0008***	0.0000	1000
		(0.0002)	(2.3e-05)		

Standard errors in parentheses: *** $p < 0.01$, ** $p < 0.05$, * $p < 0.1$.

over the entire simulation period (6.1), its significance remains low. Slicing the simulations into 50 steps long sub-periods, on the other hand, we observe that the Kaldor-Verdoorn Law can be found significant for most of the subperiods. The amplitude of the increasing returns, as measured by the Verdoorn coefficient, gradually reduces within the course of the simulations. It reaches low levels of significance over the last periods – (6.9) and (6.10) – becoming nonsignificant for the last subperiod (6.11). This result can be explained by the interplay of the mutation and the selection mechanisms at the microeconomic level: As selection goes, mutation first accelerates due to the reallocation of resources towards the best-performing firms. This results in a high concentration. Further productivity gains become uneven and rare, as the number of firms with the resources to innovate drops. The macro-level increasing returns gradually reduce and disappear. Another notable exception concerns the estimate for the subperiod 50 to 100. In this case, the estimated coefficient appears negative. This subperiod of the simulation runs corresponds to the one experiencing a high occurrence of technological shocks, while at the same time, the selection mechanism hasn't completely stabilised. This generates a high volatility in the aggregate productivity growth rates over that subperiod, explaining the negative correlation.

Result 1: *The evolutionary micro-dynamics of technological change are able to generate a Kaldor-Verdoorn Law relationship at the aggregate level. With the course of selection, however, and the concentration of the activity, the relationship fades away.*

In a second set of simulations, we estimate the Kaldor-Verdoorn Law for the various specifications of the micro-level parameters considered in the previous section. We analyse the effect of the changes in the values of these parameters on the estimated value of the Verdoorn coefficient and its significance level. The significance level is measured using student t and the corrected R^2. We focus here on the estimates realised for the 50 steps' growth rates. In all cases, estimates of the Verdoorn coefficient are significant (except for extreme values of the parameters). In other words, a Kaldor-Verdoorn Law emerges, regardless of the parameter settings. In this respect our micro-founded model is able to generate significant dynamic increasing returns as an emergent property of the micro-dynamics, confirming the statement made in Result 1.

We first focus on the parameters controlling the emergence of the technological shocks. The results of these estimates are presented in Figure 6.4. Figure 6.4(a) presents the estimated values of the Verdoorn coefficient for the different settings of ι and σ. These parameters influence the frequency and the amplitude of technological shocks and positively affect the level of the increasing returns, respectively. First, increasing the value of σ significantly increases the value of the

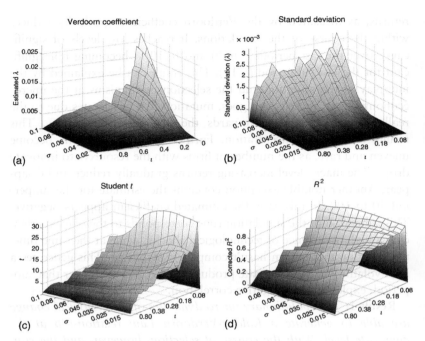

Figure 6.4 Estimates and statistics for the Verdoorn coefficient: ι vs. σ

Verdoorn coefficient. Second, increasing the values of ι, reducing the frequency of the technological shocks, reduces the value of the coefficient. Figure 6.4(c) shows a decrease in the student's t when increasing both ι and σ. We focus on this statistic to measure the effect of the changes in the parameters on the significance level of the estimated coefficient. The decrease is so that for high values of σ only few of the estimated coefficients remain significant. If an increase in the amplitude of the technological shocks increases the value of the Verdoorn coefficient, it tends to lower its significance. Figure 6.4(d), which presents the corrected R^2 of the estimations, also confirms this tendency. This result is due to the stochastic nature of the technological change: increasing σ enlarges the potential productivity gains at the cost of more uneven gains. These increases in the variability of the technological shocks explain the loss of significance in the estimated relationship.

Result 2: *The higher the amplitude of innovation (σ), the higher the Verdoorn coefficient, therefore, the higher the increasing returns. Simultaneously, the estimated coefficients lose their significance. The*

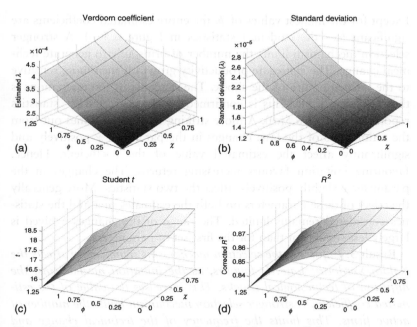

Figure 6.5 Estimates and statistics for the Verdoorn coefficient: ϕ vs. χ

higher the investments in R&D (lower ι), the higher the increasing returns. Higher investments in R&D preserve the significance of the law for high values of σ.

The last set of estimations focuses on the parameters affecting the diffusion of the technological shocks. We consider the analysis on the effect of changes in the strength of the selection mechanisms (ϕ) and the appropriability of the spillovers (χ) on the estimated value of the Verdoorn coefficient. Figure 6.5 presents the estimated value of the Verdoorn coefficient, its student t statistic and the corrected R^2, respectively, for the various specifications of the two parameters.

The previous section highlights the significant but transitory effect of strengthening the selection mechanisms on productivity dynamics. As shown by Figure 6.5(a), increasing the sensitiveness of the selection process has a positive effect on the estimated values of the coefficient of the law. A strong selection process mechanically increases the aggregate productivity dynamics, giving more weight to the most dynamic firms. This effect is then disclosed, through the estimates of the Kaldor-Verdoorn Law, into a higher level of increasing returns.

Except for the highest values of ϕ, the entire estimated coefficients are significant (see the student t statistics in Figure 6.5(c)). A stronger selection mechanism limits the number of firms able to generate technical change. The aggregate productivity growth is then more sensitive to the uneven nature of the shock. The outcome of the estimations is then less significant. This is confirmed by the corrected R^2 statistics reported in Figure 6.5(d)). A more striking result also comes out from the estimations of the law: changes in the parameter χ positively and significantly affect the estimated value of the coefficient. Hence, favouring imitation favours increasing returns. The changes in the parameter χ slightly positively affect the two statistics. More generally the effect of these parameters on both the estimates of λ and the statistics considered remains limited. The range of the changes evolved is largely less significant than for the first set of parameters.

Result 3: *Enforcing the selection mechanisms significantly affects the Kaldor-Verdoorn Law. It favours, as the imitation mechanisms, the diffusion of technological shocks. This increases the value of the estimated coefficient. A stronger selection mechanism limits the number of active firms. This limits the frequency of the technical change and therefore reduces the significance and explanatory power of the law.*

The estimations realised over this artificial data set lead to the following results (as summarised in Table 6.6): On the one hand, the frequency and the persistence of technological shocks favour both value and significance of the dynamic increasing returns, strengthening the Kaldor-Verdoorn Law. On the other hand, the factors favouring the amplitude and the diffusion of the shocks positively affect the level of increasing returns, although to the detriment of the significance of the coefficient, thereby weakening the Kaldor-Verdoorn Law.

In other words, dynamic increasing returns require frequent technical shocks to occur. The more frequent these shocks, the higher the returns.

Table 6.6. *Main simulation results*

	ι	σ	ϕ	χ
Verdoorn coefficient	−	+	+	+
Standard deviation	−	+	+	+
Student t	−	−	−	+
Corrected R^2	−	−	−	+

However, the amplitude of these shocks might prevent these returns from being significant. Too large productivity jumps at the firm levels are detrimental for the aggregate-level increasing returns. This also happens when market pressures are too important. These results seem in line with recent empirical estimations of the Kaldor-Verdoorn Law (see, among others, Knell 2004, Lorentz 2005): the sectors experiencing higher (and/or significant) dynamic increasing returns are mainly activities (both in manufacturing and services) characterised by established technologies and/or constant technical improvements. For sectors experiencing important technical changes or technological breakthroughs (as information and communication technology [ICT]-related industries and services or aircraft and spacecraft industries in Lorentz 2005), the Kaldor-Verdoorn Law is more rarely observed.

These results somehow relativise the predominant role of technological breakthrough as explaining economic growth as usually put forward in the Schumpeterian literature. More frequent incremental improvements along a given technological trajectory seem more favourable to increasing returns then a rugged technological trajectory. These breakthroughs remain important in favouring the emergence of new trajectories which cannot be accounted for in our model. These results also show that the accumulation of capital cannot, by itself, explain the existence of increasing returns. The accumulation of capital affects increasing returns only as a vessel for novelty. This brings us back to the very essence of Kaldor (1957)'s *'technical progress function'*.

Concluding Remarks

This chapter develops a simple micro-founded model of technological change inspired by the evolutionary literature. We aim at identifying some micro-economic sources of dynamic increasing returns put forward by Kaldor (1966). In this respect, we analyse the effects of changes in various micro-characteristics of the model on the productivity dynamics. This analysis highlights the importance of the frequency and amplitude of the technological shocks in shaping the aggregate productivity dynamics. Second, the simulations show that the resources devoted to the adoption of these shocks only transitorily affect these dynamics. Similarly, the factors favouring the diffusion of these shocks, and particularly the selection mechanism, have a significant but transitory effect on productivity dynamics.

We estimate the Kaldor-Verdoorn Law using the data generated by the simulations for the various specifications of the parameters. The law is verified in most of the cases. Moreover, the estimation showed that some of the micro-characteristics affect the value and significance level of the Verdoorn coefficient. On the one hand, increasing the amplitude of the shocks and the strength of the selection mechanisms increases the values but decreases the significance of the coefficient. These losses in significance are due to the increase in the unevenness of the shocks and/or a reduction in the frequency of the shocks, respectively. On the other hand, increasing the resources devoted to R&D affects the frequency of the shocks, affecting positively the value and significance of the shocks. The results from these estimations therefore show the limited impact that breakthrough technical change can possibly have on the aggregate productivity dynamics.

We showed in this chapter that Schumpeterian micro-dynamics constitutes an alternative explanation for the emergence of a Kaldor-Verdoorn Law. The various components of these micro-dynamics have a rather complex effect on the law: reinforcing the increasing returns and, in some cases, simultaneously limiting their significance due to higher unevenness in technological changes. These results, however, are only transitory; as the Schumpeterian dynamics stabilises, the law is no longer observable. This can be explained by some of the assumptions made in designing the model: Technological changes are only 'local'; there is no change of trajectory or emergence of new paradigms that would prevent the stabilisation of the Schumpeterian dynamics. Furthermore, the model does not account for large-scale division of labour, either through the emergence of new sectors or the externalisation of parts of a firm's activities. Such considerations require us to rethink the formalisation of the production process beyond what the evolutionary literature proposes, opening the door for future developments.

References

Amendola, M. and Gaffard, J. 1998. *Out of Equilibrium*. Oxford: Clarendon Press.

Arthur, B. 1994. *Increasing Returns and Path Dependence in the Economy*. Ann Arbor, MI: University of Michigan Press.

Ciarli, T., Lorentz, A., Savona, M., and Valente, M. 2010. The Effect of Consumption and Production Structure on Growth and Distribution. A Micro to Macro Model. *Metroeconomica*, 61(1), 180–218.

Dosi, G., Freeman, C., Nelson, R., Silverberg, G., and Soete, L. 1988, *Technical Change and Economic Theory*. Pinter: London.

Fabricant, S. 1942. Employment in manufacturing, 1899–1939: An analysis of its relation to the volume of production, Technical report, NBER.

Kaldor, N. 1957. A Model of Economic Growth. *Economic Journal*, 67(268) December, 591–624.

1960. *Essays on Economic Stability and Growth*. Glenchoe: Free Press.

1966. *Causes of the Slow Rate of Growth in the United Kingdom*. Cambridge: Cambridge University Press.

1972. The Irrelevance of Equilibrium Economics. *Economic Journal*, 82(328), 1237–1255.

Knell, M. 2004. Structural Change and the Kaldor-Verdoorn Law in the 1990s. *Revue d'Economie Industrielle*, 105, 71–84.

Krugman, P. 1997. *Development, Geography and Economic Theory*. Cambridge: MIT Press.

Kwasnicki, W. 2003. Evolutionary Models' Comparative Analysis. Methodology Proposition Based on Selected Neo-Schumpeterian Models of Industrial Dynamics. *The ICFAI Journal of Managerial Economics* 1(2).

Llerena, P. and Lorentz, A. 2004a. Co-evolution of Macro-dynamics and Technical Change: An Alternative View on Growth. *Revue d'Economie Industrielle*, 105, 47–70.

2004b. Cumulative Causation and Evolutionary Micro-founded Technical Change: On the Determinants of Growth Rates Differences. *Revue Economique*, 55(6), 1191–1214.

Lorentz, A. 2005. *Essays on the Determinants of Growth Rates Differences among Economies: Bringing Together Evolutionary and Post-Keynesian Growth Theories*, PhD dissertation, University Louis Pasteur, Strasbourg and Sant'Anna School for Advance Studies, Pisa.

2015a. Sectoral Specialisation in an Evolutionary Growth Model with a Kaldorian Flavour. *International Journal of Computational Economics and Econometrics*, 5(3), 319–344.

2015b. Structural Change, Sectoral Specialisation and Growth Rates Differences in an Evolutionary Growth Model with Demand Shocks. *Journal of Innovation Economics and Management*, 16, 217–248.

Lorentz, A., Ciarli, T., Savona, M., and Valente, M. 2016. The Effect of Demand-Driven Structural Transformations on Growth and Technological Change. *Journal of Evolutionary Economics*, 26(1), 219–246.

Lorentz, A. and Savona, M. 2010. *Structural Change and Business Cycles: An Evolutionary Approach, Papers on Economics and Evolution*. Jena: Max Planck Institute of Economics.

McCombie, J. 2002. Increasing Returns and the Verdoorn Law from a Kaldorian Perspective. In: McCombie, J., Pugno, M., and Soro, B. (eds.) *Productivity Growth and Economic Performance: Essays on the Verdoorn's Law*. London: MacMillan, 64–114.

McCombie, J., Pugno, M., and Soro, B. 2002. *Productivity Growth and Economic Performance: Essays on the Verdoorn's Law*. London: MacMillan.

Metcalfe, J. 1998. *Evolutionary Economics and Creative Destruction*. London: Routledge.

Metcalfe, S., Foster, J., and Ramlogan, R. 2006. Adaptive Economic Growth. *Cambridge Journal of Economics*, 30, 7–32.

Nelson, R. and Winter, S. 1982. *An Evolutionary Theory of Economic Change*. Cambridge: Harvard University Press.

Romer, P. M. 1986. Increasing Returns and Long-Run Growth. *Journal of Political Economy*, 94, 1002–1037.

1990. Endogenous Technological Change. *Journal of Political Economy*, 5(98), S71–S102.

Silverberg, G. and Lehnert, D. 1993. Long Waves and "Evolutionary Chaos" in a Simple Schumpeterian Model of Embodied Technical Change. *Structural Change and Economic Dynamics*, 4(1), 9–37.

Silverberg, G. and Verspagen, B. 1994. Learning, Innovation and Economic Growth: A Long Run Model of Industrial Dynamics. *Industrial and Corporate Change*, 3(1), 199–223.

1995. An Evolutionary Model of Long-Term Cyclical Variations of Catching-Up and Falling Behind. *Journal of Evolutionary Economics*, 5(3), 209–227.

1998. Economic Growth as an Evolutionary Process. In: Lesourne, J., and Orlean, A. (eds.) *Advances in Self-Organization and Evolutionary Economics*. Washington: Brooking Institutions Press.

2005. Evolutionary Theorizing on Economic Growth. In: Dopfer, K. (ed.) *The Evolutionary Foundations of Economics*. Cambridge: Cambridge University Press, 506–539.

Verdoorn, P. 1949. Fattori che regolano lo svilluppo della produttivitá del lavoro. *L'Industria*, 1, 45–53.

Verspagen, B. 2002. Evolutionary Macroeconomics: A Synthesis between Neo-Schumpeterian and Post-Keynesian Lines of Thought. *The Electronic Journal of Evolutionary Modelling and Economic Dynamics* n1007.

Witt, U. 2008. What Is Specific about Evolutionary Economics? *Journal of Evolutionary Economics*, 18(5), 547–575.

Young, A. 1928. Increasing Returns and Economic Progress. *Economic Journal*, 38, 527–554.

PART IV

Advances in Explaining and Assessing Institutional Evolution

7 | Democracy, Rationality and Religion

DENNIS C. MUELLER

Introduction

An often implicit assumption in the argument for democracy is that citizens are rational actors, that they are *capable* of deciding for the community. This assumption also underlies the public-choice approach to studying political institutions. Unfortunately, a good deal of empirical and experimental evidence puts this assumption into question. Most pertinently, a truly *rational* citizen in a large electorate would never vote, since the probability of her vote affecting the outcome is infinitesimal. Yet millions of people do vote, which implies either that they are *not rational* or that they have some other motive for voting.

One explanation that has been put forward is that citizens regard voting as an ethical act – democracy functions better if all citizens vote; therefore, it is a civic or moral duty for a citizen to vote. This argument links the efficacy of democracy to the civic morality of citizens. It implies that two important conditions must be fulfilled for a successful democracy: citizens must be sufficiently intelligent and rational so that they are *capable* of making good collective decisions, and they must be sufficiently ethically motivated that they are *willing* to devote time and effort to become informed about collective issues and to participate in the democratic process. These links among democracy, rationality and ethics are the focus of this chapter.

I begin by describing the *psychology* of individual decision making and the extent to which it can be characterized as rational. The second section describes how human psychology has evolved and with it human capacities for rational thought, culminating in the development of a scientific method to explain natural phenomena. The third section describes an alternative theoretical structure for explaining natural phenomena, namely superstitions and religions. These alternative theoretical structures characterize modern and traditional societies and are contrasted in the fourth section. The fifth section reviews how

215

modern, theoretic cultures came to triumph over traditional, mythic cultures. The importance of citizenship for a well-functioning democracy is discussed in the sixth section. The seventh section considers why religion and democracy are to some extent incompatible. Conclusions are drawn in the final section.

The Psychology of Individuals

Behavioral

Perhaps the simplest of all models of human psychology is that of *behavioral* psychology or operant behaviorism.[1] Operant behaviorism provides a theory of learning that is quite similar to the selfish gene account of natural selection. This theory assumes that nature randomly distributes genes across individuals. Genes that increase fitness and reproductive success are selected over those that do not. Operant behaviorism assumes that individuals randomly undertake actions. Actions followed by rewards increase in frequency; actions followed by punishments decline in frequency. In the one case, the environment selects for genes; in the other, for actions. Operant behaviorism takes the assumption of narrow self-interest to the extreme. Individuals are assumed to be pure hedonists seeking rewards and avoiding pains. In this regard, the premises of behavioral psychology are quite compatible with those underlying the philosophies of Hobbes and Bentham.

Operant conditioning relies on a rather primitive cause-and-effect association in people's minds. Action *A* is followed by reward *B* and action *A* is associated with the reward and repeated. When action *A* does in fact *cause* reward *B*, this behavior is functional and thus accords with what we would expect a rational person, as conventionally defined, to do. Thus, well-conditioned individuals might behave *as if* they were *choosing* actions to maximize an objective or utility function. The well-conditioned consumer buys more of a good at a lower price because she has been rewarded for such actions in the past. Rats in the laboratory behave as if they were maximizing a utility function that includes water as an argument. Rats, like humans, have negative sloped demand curves (Staddon 1983).

---

[1] Operant behaviorism is the term used to describe the branch of psychology launched by B. F. Skinner. See Catania and Harnad (1988).

Correlation does not always imply causation, however, and some actions are followed by rewards that they did not bring about. This possibility can explain why some habits are not functional or are even harmful. A football player unconsciously dons nonmatching socks on a day when he scores three goals, and from then on consciously chooses to wear nonmatching socks. Millions of people consult the horoscope sections of their newspapers every day to see what the stars have in store for them. On any given day, some of them will experience the good fortune forecast for them in the morning paper. They will "thank their lucky stars," and the habit of reading their horoscope will be reinforced and sustained.

Thus, operant behaviorism offers a plausible account for much animal and human behavior. Its explanation for why people cooperate in prisoners' dilemma situations would be that they have been rewarded for such cooperative behavior in the past. The most successful strategy to induce cooperation in a repeated prisoners' dilemma appears to be the TIT FOR TAT strategy (Axelrod 1984) – reward cooperation in one period by cooperating in the next, punish noncooperation in one period by not cooperating in the next. The TIT FOR TAT strategy might have been developed in one of B. F. Skinner's laboratories.

Cognitive

Operant behaviorism does not appear to be able to explain all human actions, however. Although climbing a tree to escape a grizzly bear would be rewarded by staying alive, how would the first person who confronted a grizzly have known to climb and not to run? Many actions appear not to be the result of past rewards, but a result of a reasoning process in which the actor *foresees* the consequences of the action. An individual learns not to hold her hand in a fire the first time she does so. But how does she know to run or to move her camp when she sees smoke from a brush fire in the distance? She seems to deduce that the smoke is caused by a fire, that the wind is blowing the fire in her direction, and that she had better move if she wishes to escape the fire. Humans are capable of cognitive processes far more complex than those presumed under the operant behavioral model. Any model of human behavior must allow for these cognitive processes.

Evolutionary

The most dramatic difference between humans and other animals – even other primates – is the relatively large size of the human brain. "The brain is a biological organ just like the pancreas, the liver, or any other specialized organ" (Ramachandran 1990: 24), and like these other organs it has evolved to serve specific functions (Barkow, Tooby & Cosmides 1982: 7). Its main function is to process information, which could be used to help humans survive during the Pleistocene (Barkow, Tooby & Cosmides 1982: 66). It owes its size to the fact that during its evolution it has added one functional capacity to another – the ability to see and to recognize depth of field, the ability to sense danger (approaching a precipice, a snake), to recognize faces, to imitate and learn from others, and numerous more.[2] Thus, both its size and the way in which it functions are products of natural selection.

An extremely important cognitive development was the ability to understand complex causal relationships and to generalize about them. The advantages for survival from such an understanding are obvious. The first person who stuck a stick into a desert cactus and obtained water must have been quite surprised. The action of piercing cacti to obtain water would be positively reinforced and beneficial for survival. But so, too, would the capacity to generalize and deduce that if cacti contain liquids, probably other plants and trees do too, and that some of these might also be tapped and put to good use.

An important complement to the brain's development was the development of language. The ability to communicate complex thoughts and commands with other individuals must have greatly facilitated cooperation among tribe members in hunting and warfare. Those with the biggest brains and the most sophisticated powers of reasoning would have had the highest probabilities of survival, and thus natural selection would favor large brains and genetically determined processes of reasoning within these brains.[3]

Of course, the reasoning processes that would have been favored would have increased survival chances in a hunter/gather society.

---

[2] See, Barkow, Tooby and Cosmides (1982: 113) and Pinker (1997: 183–184, 193–194).

[3] For discussions of the brain's evolution see, the essays in Barkow, Tooby and Cosmides (1982), and again Pinker (1997: 175–186).

Much has been written about a human proclivity to cooperate being partially genetically determined. Cooperation in hunting large animals or fighting other tribes could obviously increase chances for success and probabilities of survival. A genetic disposition to cooperate has been given as an explanation for individuals' seemingly "irrational" proclivity to cooperate in prisoners' dilemma situations.[4]

Unfortunately, not all mental processes that aid survival in tribal societies on the African savanna have positive value in the 21st century. An instinctive reaction to a pickpocket's taking your wallet is irate rage. Many people give chase to pickpockets, risking their lives from either a heart attack or a knife or bullet, even though the financial loss from the theft is rather modest. "It's not the money, but the principle of the thing." Having one's pocket picked or apartment burgled sets off in most people a violent reaction. They feel personally "violated," and they often react with violence. They often overreact. For people living on the edge of survival, theft can be very costly, and overreactions might well deter theft, free riding and other noncooperative behavior, thereby increasing survival chances. Such instinctive and uncontrollable reactions to theft are likely to be genetically triggered.[5]

A willingness to fight for, kill for, and if need be die for one's tribe would have increased the probabilities of the tribe's success in battle with other tribes and to the survival of its members. Loyalty to one's tribe and animosity toward members of other tribes is also in part genetically determined. But, of course, before one can defend one's fellow tribe members, one must be able to recognize who they are. This would have been easy 50,000 years ago on the savannas of Africa, but is less so in our polyglot societies of today. Race is an obvious clue, as is language and religion, and history is replete with wars between societies that differ on the basis of race, language and religion. But even more subtle differences between groups can lead to strife. Dividing boys attending a summer camp into two groups for the purpose of sports and other activities can lead to animosity and violent confrontations between those who were arbitrarily assigned

---

[4] See Dawkins (1976/1989); Axelrod (1984); Trivers (1985); Barkow, Tooby and Cosmides (1982) and Pinker (1997: 502–506).
[5] See Trivers (1971, 1985) and Pinker (1997: 404–405).

red jerseys and those assigned blue. Even separating people by a coin flip can lead to strong loyalties among "the heads."[6]

Most students of politics are familiar with James Madison's discussion of the evils of "factions" in *Federalist 10*. Madison's analysis was preceded, however, by David Hume.

As much as legislators and founders of states ought to be honoured and respected among men, as much ought the founders of sects and factions to be detested and hated; being that the cause and influence of faction is directly contrary to that of laws. Factions subvert government, render laws impotent, and beget the fiercest animosities among men of the same nation, who ought to give mutual assistance and protection to each other. And what should render the founders of parties more odious is, the difficulty of extirpating these weeds, when once they have taken root in any state. (Hume 1758: 55)

Hume goes on to say that

Factions may be divided into PERSONAL and REAL; that is, into factions, founded on personal friendship or animosity among such as compose the contending parties, and into those founded on some real difference of sentiment or interest. (Hume 1758: 56)

As examples of factions based on personal differences, Hume cited "the remarkable dissension between two [Roman] tribes, the POLLIA and PAPIRIA, which continued for the space of near three hundred years" (p. 57) and "the civil wars which arose some few years ago in MOROCCO, between the *blacks* and *whites*, merely on account of their complexion" (p. 59, emphasis in original). Anticipating experiments conducted more than 200 years later, Hume noted,

When men are once enlisted on opposite sides, they contract an affection to the persons with whom they are united, and an animosity against their antagonists: And these passions they often transmit to their prosperity. (Hume 1758: 58)

In addition to a psychological identification to a group, Hume listed the following motivations and passions to which humans are susceptible: "the intolerant adherence to abstract principle, inherited animosity, love of imitation, psychological infatuation with a leader ... craving for approval, anger, envy, fear, grief, shame, depression,

---

[6] See discussion and references in Pinker (1997: 513–517).

melancholy, and anxiety."[7] Virtually every item in this list is likely to be in part genetically driven.

Our genetic heritage can thus be regarded as somewhat of a mixed bag. On the positive side, we find our evolved big brains and cognitive abilities. We *are* capable of reasoning in a manner that justifies the assumptions of rational actor models, and the accumulated miracles of science attest to the scope of these abilities. Further on the plus side are our innate tendencies to cooperate and behave altruistically. But our genetic baggage also has its darker, more problematic side. Group loyalties, cravings for approval, love of imitation and infatuation with leaders make us prone to racist and bigoted behavior, willing to follow a leader who tells us that we are better than others and to march off into war to prove our superiority. The challenge humans face today is the same one that they have always faced: how to harness the creative powers of the brain to make our lives better, while at the same time avoiding the self-destructive impulses that we all share? Social mores play an important role in constraining destructive behavior, and religion is often thought to provide the foundation for social mores. Thus, we shall devote considerable space to examining the main characteristics of religions. But first we briefly sketch the evolutionary stages of human psychological development.

The Evolution of Human Psychology

Merlin Donald (1991) divides the evolution of "the modern mind" into four stages.

Episodic Culture

All primates, including humans, live in groups. To survive in groups, primates must learn when a particular action is likely to bring forth a hostile response by another member of the group and when it will bring forth a friendly response, which chimpanzees will reciprocate acts of grooming and which will not, what the male hierarchy is and so on. Migratory groups would have to learn when certain trees would bear fruit, when water holes would be dry and so on. The power to

[7] I have taken this list from Holmes (1995: 55), who cites several of Hume's works.

recognize and respond to these situational clues Donald (1991: ch. 5) is called episodic culture. Both birds and mammals have these capabilities, and they are most highly developed in the great apes.

The learning process that characterizes episodic culture is well characterized by behavioral psychology. Animals respond to stimuli and learn what actions will be rewarded and punished. The advantages of acquiring this kind of knowledge for survival are obvious. *Some* human behavior resembles that of the great apes and can be classified as part of the episodic culture. Characteristics that are useful for survival do not disappear as a species evolves – they get complemented by additional useful characteristics. Humans evolved beyond the stage of apes by acquiring greater cognitive powers.

Mimetic Culture

Prior to the invention of language, humans acquired the ability to communicate with one another by *acting out* their thoughts. Donald refers to this as *mimetic skill.*

Mimetic skill or mimesis rests on the ability to produce conscious, self-initiated, representational acts that are intentional but not linguistic. These mimetic acts are defined primarily in terms of their representational function ... mimesis is fundamentally different from imitation and mimicry in that it involves the *invention* of intentional representations. When there is an audience to interpret the action, mimesis also serves the purpose of communication. However, mimesis may simply represent the event to oneself, for the purpose of rehearsing and refining a skill. (Donald 1991: 168–169, emphasis in original)

Mimetic culture appears during the period in which *Homo erectus* lived, starting roughly 1.5 million years ago. Mimesis would have been used to coordinate actions in hunting and fighting with other groups; to teach making fires, huts, weapons and tools; to teach fighting and hunting; and in ritual dancing and game playing. Thus, by the end of the period in which *Homo erectus* lived, his communities would have had many of the characteristics that we associate with human society except for an elaborately developed language. Felipe Fernández-Armesto (2004) argues forcefully that *Homo sapiens* cannot be separated from other primates like chimpanzees and the great apes, because they, too, make limited use of tools, engage in coordinated activities and even make various sounds to communicate with one another.

Although this is true, the cognitive achievements of *Homo sapiens* and the complexity of their social structures have far surpassed those of the other primates, making it legitimate to claim that the other primates alive today live *largely* within an episodic culture.

Mythic Culture

Somewhere between 200,000 and 100,000 years ago modern man, *Homo sapiens*, appeared. *Homo sapiens* possessed several important evolutionary advantages over *Homo erectus*, most importantly a 20 percent larger brain than *Homo erectus* and a supralaryngeal vocal apparatus, which contained a soft palate and a highly flexible tongue. This vocal apparatus differentiated *Homo sapiens* from both *Homo erectus* and the Neanderthals, who existed alongside of *Homo sapiens* until their extinction around 35,000 years ago. Both *Homo erectus* and the Neanderthals must have possessed some capabilities for oral communication. Indeed, the selection process that resulted in *Homo sapiens* must have built on these capabilities. The Neanderthal brain was comparable in size or even slightly larger than that of *Homo sapiens*, but the shape and positioning of their larynx and other features of their vocal apparatus would have made oral communication much more limited than that of *Homo sapiens*, and one surmises that this may have been a contributing factor to their extinction (Lieberman 1975; Donald 1991: 115–119, 204–208). Once again Fernández-Armesto (2004) underplays this difference between the Neanderthals and *Homo sapiens*.

Speech gave humans a tremendous evolutionary advantage over their predecessor, *Homo erectus*. Although *Homo erectus* had succeeded through the use of mimesis to engage in a great deal of coordinated social activities – hunting, gathering, tool making, etc. – speech made "humans ... better and faster at everything: social coordination, tool manufacture, systemic war, finding and building shelter, gathering and hunting food" (Donald 1991: 210).

Simultaneously with the appearance of speech there appeared a whole constellation of thought skills that are associated with language and are, broadly speaking, linear, analytic, rule-governed, and segmented. Semiotic cultures also triggered completely new forms of information processing and storage: semantic memory, propositional memory, discourse comprehension, analytic thought, induction, and verification, among others. (Donald 1991: 212)

The increasing complexity of social life and the difficulty of expressing complex thoughts through mimesis must have spurred the invention of language. Each word is a symbol for some thing, action or attribute, and thus language's invention also entailed the invention of many symbols. "The invention of a symbol requires a capacity for thought," and their existence extends the boundaries for rational thought (Donald 1991: 219). The invention of language thus brought with it a great expansion in humans' capacity to *reason.*

As Mokyr (2002: 16) observes, "curiosity [is] an essential human trait without which no historical theory of useful knowledge makes sense." Of particular importance for the acquisition of knowledge is curiosity about causal relationships. Within the episodic culture, an understanding of causal relationships could have been acquired through the recognition of sequences of events. Act *A* is followed by reward *R.* The expansion of humans' cognitive powers that accompanied the invention of language expanded their ability to recognize more complex causal relationships.

It is natural to assume that every event has a cause. The fire cooks the meat; water extinguishes the fire. When obvious causes are unavailable, more remote causes must be sought. It is in this way that myths and superstitions first arose in the early *Homo sapiens* who invented languages. Donald describes the role played by myths for the !Kung of Africa:

As in most early religions, their god myths are closely tied to their idea of causality: gods cause pain and death, create life and the heavens, cause rain and thunder. The eland, identified with [the] moon through the creation myth, was also important in the ceremonial celebration of a young girl's first menstruation, since they knew of the correlation between the duration of the menstrual cycle and the lunar cycle. (Donald 1991: 214)

Their mythical thought, in our terms, might be regarded as a unified,

collectively held system of explanatory and regulatory metaphors. The mind has expanded its reach beyond the episodic perception of events, beyond the mimetic reconstruction of episodes, to a comprehensive modeling of the entire human universe. Causal explanation, prediction, control – myth constitutes an attempt at all three, and every aspect of life is permeated by myth. (Donald 1991: 214)

All known hunter and gatherer communities possess such myths; all possess language. An important function of language in early

Homo sapiens societies was to allow them "to construct conceptual models of the human universe." Donald (1991: 215) claims that this use of language was initially more important than its role in creating new social technologies and organizational structures. So important is the role of myth in the cultures of the first talking humans that Donald names this stage in human development the *mythic culture*.

Theoretic Culture

While all human groups developed speech and language, only a few societies succeeded in inventing writing. The Sumerians appear to be the first with the earliest written symbols, dating back about 10,000 years (Donald 1991: 285). The first use of writing was to record transactions – numbers of sheep traded, quantities of wheat and barley stored. Eventually, however, humans learned how to express words and ideas through writing and developed mathematical symbols, geometry, maps and other ways of storing information.

The advent of writing greatly expanded humans' capacity to store data and information. Although its invention was not accompanied by any further expansion of the brain's size, the use of visual symbols would have required changes in human cognition at least comparable to those accompanying the invention of language (Donald 1991: ch. 8). The advent of writing also allowed humans to extend the length of a chain of reasoning. Written ideas can be examined one by one, modified or replaced, supplemented, their order changed and so on. Such manipulations without the aid of visual representations of the ideas are severely limited by the mind's capacity to retain and recall ideas. Thus, the invention of writing and other means of visual representation of ideas allowed humans to expand their ability to reason. They facilitated the construction of abstract models of natural phenomenon and eventually the development of what we now call scientific method, which is why Donald names this phase in human evolution the *theoretic culture*.

Superstition and Religion

Religion and Causality

Two tribesmen are chasing an antelope across the plains of Africa. It is hot and they have been running a long time. Suddenly, one of them

falls to the ground clutching his chest and complaining of pain. In a
few minutes he is dead. What caused his death? There must be a
cause. People do not simply fall over dead for no reason. The dead
man had not eaten or drunk anything just before dying; there is no
sign of a deadly snake or spider. The surviving hunter has seen men
die when a spear enters their chests. Since the dead hunter clutched his
chest in pain, something must have entered his chest and caused the
man's pain and death. But what could have entered it? There is no cut
or hole or other sign of anything entering. Something invisible must
have entered his chest – an evil spirit. But why did it choose to enter
his chest and not that of the surviving hunter? Ah, the survivor donned
a necklace that morning made of the horns of an antelope that he
killed last week. The necklace protected him from the evil spirit. Our
surviving hunter is well on his way to inventing a theory about spirits
that kill hunters, and a protection against these evil spirits.

This example illustrates how myths and superstitions can arise.
Our minds are always seeking causal explanations for events. Had
the hunter been bitten by a poisonous snake or attacked by a lion,
the cause of death would have been obvious. But lacking such a visi-
ble cause, the second hunter invents an invisible cause. His first
thought was of an evil spirit, but he could have hypothesized many
other causes. If he had seen a blackbird watching them from a nearby
tree, he might have hypothesized that the bird killed his companion
with an evil look, or perhaps by launching an invisible, internal organ
that penetrated the chest.[8] The number of possible causes of death
that the surviving hunter could imagine is quite large, and thus we
might not expect any two hunters to hit upon exactly the same cause.
This superabundance of possible causes helps explain the many vari-
eties of religion that are found. In some cases, the invisible spirits and
gods take on a human form; in others they are animals or birds. One
thing we can say with considerable certainty, however, is that the
hunter would not have hypothesized that a nearby stone killed his
companion. Stones are inanimate objects. They do not move, are not
alive and presumably do not think. Events like the death of a companion must be caused by some *intentional being*, like a human or some

---

[8] An African tribe called the Fang believes that some people possess an internal
organ called an *evur*, which allows them to launch invisible attacks on other
people (Boyer 2001: 66–67).

other type of animal, an intentional being that *wanted* to kill the hunter. Someone – some invisible one – intended that the hunter die, and the second hunter must guess who or what this invisible someone was. This example also illustrates the importance of language in the propagation of religions. The two men would have been able to coordinate their actions in hunting during the mimetic period, and the same event might have taken place then. The surviving hunter might have suspected that something entered the other hunter's chest, but it would be difficult to communicate this belief to other tribe members. He could have acted out what happened, but it would have been difficult to convey his hypothesis about the cause of the hunter's death in the absence of language. With language he could describe the suspicious-looking blackbird and his hypothesis that it killed his companion. A myth about evil blackbirds would be started. If another misfortune occurred in the presence of a blackbird, the myth would be reinforced. With enough such coincidences, a belief in the evil powers of blackbirds would become part of this tribe's religion.

Religion and Death

The ritualization of death appears even to predate language (Boyer 2001: 203). Losing someone dear is a traumatic emotional experience, and has presumably always been so. Our minds recognize other people as both living animals or beings and as unique persons with specific personalities. When someone dies, we recognize that this person has stopped breathing, stopped living and soon will begin to decay like all other animals. Our built-in aversion to pollution tells us that the deceased's body must be disposed of before it begins to rot, but at the same time our mind finds it difficult to accept that the *person* we knew is no more. Our mind tells us that the *spirit* of this person must still exist somewhere. Thus, arises the notion of *dualism* – that we possess a body and a soul, and that they are two separate things. The body dies, but the soul lives on forever. Spirits of the dead are the most common form of supernatural agents across all cultures (Boyer 2001: 227).

In many communities, the spirits of the dead are assumed to watch over the community and intervene in its daily activity. In these communities, religion takes the form of ancestor worship. Prayers and sacrifices are offered to the ancestors to induce them to intervene for the benefit of the community or for specific individuals. These prayers and sacrifices always must be performed in particular ways to be effective. Thus arises the need for intermediaries – shamans and priests – who are experts in performing the rituals.

Ghosts of the dead, other forms of spirits like angels and devils and gods all share common characteristics. They are conscious, intentional agents, and thus it is possible to make inferences about what they are thinking, their intentions and what it takes to please them or offend them. Unlike ordinary intentional agents, however, spirits and gods inevitably possess some supernatural property – they are immortal, omniscient, invisible, can pass through brick walls and so on. The combination of their being both familiar agents whom we can understand and communicate with and at the same time having wondrous attributes makes a vivid impression in the mind, a lasting impression.

Religion and Morality

No one has recorded how notions of gods and spirits developed among our earliest ancestors. Did someone first hypothesize the existence of an invisible spirt to explain a perplexing event, and later the tribe hit upon the idea that these spirits were the ghosts of deceased tribe members, or did the tribe first imagine that people's souls lived on after their bodies died and these living souls were the invisible causes of puzzling events? Conceivably, spirits were invented for one reason in some tribes and for another in others. Once invented, however, the spirits take on an active role in all tribal societies. They intervene in the daily lives of tribal members. Individuals believe that they see the spirits occasionally, communicate with them and do things that please or anger the spirits.

The challenge of surviving in the Pleistocene placed a premium on cooperative behavior. As in all communities, children would learn from their parents and elders which actions are right and which are wrong. Guilt feelings from doing something wrong and pride from doing good appear to be part of our inherited emotional response kit (Boyer 2001: ch. 5). All people thus grow up believing that their elders know right from wrong and that they punish and reward our actions. It is quite natural, therefore, to assume that our elders remain concerned about what we are doing after they die. Thus, we find that the spirits of ancestors are preoccupied with observing the behavior of tribal members. Moreover, unlike parents and living elders, ancestor spirits see *everything* that we do, and thus it is impossible "to get away with" an immoral act without being caught. Thus it is that the link between religion and morality arises. Although spirits and ghosts were perhaps invented for other reasons, once invented they take up the task of monitoring the behavior of the living to ensure that they behave morally, that they behave in ways that benefit the community and not just themselves.

To the untrained in mathematics, the concept of chance is difficult to comprehend.[9] Why did *my* daughter get struck by lightning during a summer storm, and not a tree, or my neighbor's son, or me? She must have done something wrong. But she is too young and innocent to have done something wrong. *I* must have done something wrong.

The need for a causal explanation for every event, a lack of understanding of the concept of chance, plus the belief that our ancestors or the gods are watching our every move, combine to produce the belief in a direct link between our actions on earth, the spirits' and gods' responses to these actions and subsequent events on earth. The fear of punishment (hope for reward) from the spirits leads people to behave morally and to interpret good fortune as a reward for good deeds and misfortune as a punishment for wrong-doing.

Religion as an Exchange Relationship

Humans are endowed with intuitive notions of fairness. Our tribal ancestors would have had a good understanding of fairness and would, like we do today, have known that you usually do not get something for nothing. It would be natural for tribe members to think, therefore, that their spirit-ancestors would want something in exchange for doing them a favor – the performance of a prayer, a dance, the sacrifice of a lamb.

---

[9] Boyer (2001: 195–196) challenges the idea that tribal societies do not understand the concept of chance: "anthropologists know that people the world over are rather good at detecting statistical regularities in their environment." He then goes on, however, to give examples indicating that individuals *do not* in fact understand pure chance. The African tribe Fang, for example, understands that people die of biological causes like tuberculosis but still want to know why a particular person "was chosen" to die of this disease (Boyer 2001: 196). Dennett (2006) observes that people have difficulty with the concept of pure chance.

All religions have this exchange-relationship characteristic. The community facing a drought prays for rain, the expectant father for a healthy baby, the terminal cancer patient to be taken into heaven. A tribe sacrifices a goat for success in battle. If the spirits and gods could not "deliver the goods," there would not be much point in praying to them.

Religious rituals always have a particular goal behind them – success in battle, success in love, success in the hunt, a happy afterlife. To be effective, religious rituals must typically be performed in certain ways. The ancestors would not be pleased to have just any old goat sacrificed. It must be a pure white goat washed three times by a virgin and so on.[10] The complexity of the rituals often required certain persons to perform them – a shaman, witch doctor or priest. Each shaman had to have a certain bag of "Wizard-of-Oz tricks" to impress his clients. Because religious rituals require a belief in the supernatural, shamans, witch doctors and priests must themselves be *un*natural in some way. When an epileptic has a seizure, he behaves in a most unnatural way, as if perhaps he were seized by a spirit. Epileptics frequently became shamans. Others became shamans because they could put themselves into a trance or feign entering one. As religions evolved, shamans were replaced by priests who obtained their "powers of magic" through training and performing certain rituals.

Summary of Local Religions

Rather than use a possibly pejorative term like tribal or primitive religions, I call early religions *local* religions in contrast to the universal religions to be discussed next. Early religions were truly local in that the nature of the spirits and gods, and a tribe's beliefs about them would typically differ from one tribe to the next. Some beliefs were

---

[10] See discussion in Boyer (2001: ch. 7). Boyer (2001: 238–239) notes the similarities between the behavior prescribed in religious rituals and the behavior of people with obsessive-compulsive behavior (think of Jack Nicholson in *As Good as It Gets*). In both cases there is often a great fear of pollution, and thus ritualistic washing of the hands; a mindless repetition of certain actions; and a fear of great danger should the acts not be performed properly – the goat has not been washed three times, the obsessive-compulsive steps on a crack in the sidewalk.

common to almost all local religions, however, and are also found in modern states (Boyer 1994: 5).

1. The belief that "a nonphysical component of persons can survive after death and remain an intentional being."
2. The belief that "certain people are especially likely to receive direct inspiration or messages from extra-natural agencies, such as gods and spirits."
3. The belief that "performing certain ritual 'recipes' in the exact way and order prescribed can bring about changes in physical states of affairs."

These beliefs arise as attempts to explain events that cannot be explained with the information and knowledge at hand. Once again the chance juxtaposition of events may lead to an inference of causality. A tribe has good luck hunting by a full moon and begins to pray to the moon. Hunting tribes frequently have had moon gods. Since hunting was carried out by the men, moon gods were typically male. Tribes dependent on farming had sun gods, since the sun is more important than the moon for growing plants. Since tending crops and gathering grains and berries was carried out by the women of the tribe, sun gods have generally been female.[11]

Universal Religions

Local religions are oriented toward the present life. They explain certain events, help people cope with the trauma of death and reinforce the mores of the community. Although a tribe's members may expect to join their ancestors when they die, they typically have vague ideas about what this afterlife will be like. The ancestors are not presumed to have a particularly happy afterlife, and the actions of tribe members are not motivated toward rewards in the afterlife.

In contrast, universal religions are heavily focused on the afterlife and the rewards and punishments that await one there. The first of Buddhism's Four Noble Truths, for example, emphasizes human suffering (*dukkha*). All humans are caught in a cycle of life and rebirth that entails much suffering. The second Noble Truth deals with the *cause* of human suffering. Here we see a direct correspondence with

---

[11] See, Quigley (1979: 176–177).

local religions. The spirits and gods of local religions offer explanations for certain, often tragic, events. Buddhism offers an explanation for why we have been chosen to suffer. The third and fourth Noble Truths, however, offer hope. The cycle of suffering can be broken by following the Eightfold Path of (1) right views, (2) right intentions, (3) right speech, (4) right conduct, (5) right livelihood, (6) right effort, (7) right mindfulness and (8) right concentration. Following this path is no easy thing, however. Besides faith (*saddha*), one needs training in concentration and meditation (*samadhi*) and various ethical and disciplinary practices (*samadhi*). Those who follow the Eightfold Path successfully are able to break the cycle of suffering and enter into *nirvana*.

The Ten Commandments are also a set of proscriptions forbidding certain actions on earth with the promise of Heaven for those who obey the Commandments. Much speculation and theorizing in Christianity has centered on life in Heaven – or in Hell. At first glance, Islam might be thought to be an exception in this regard, since the Koran is not otherworldly oriented, but rather is minutely focused on life on this earth and what we should do here. The word *Islam* means *submission*, however, and the Koran describes in great detail what each individual should and should not do in her daily life. Many of its prescriptions, from praying five times a day to fasting during the Ramadan, require the sacrifice of certain earthly pleasures with, as with Christianity and Buddhism, the promise of rewards after death. In this respect, Islam is like the other major universal religions.

As knowledge advanced and societies became more complex and sophisticated, understanding of causality increased and the need to invent supernatural causes for events declined. As trade and communication expanded, individuals came into contact with other religions and began to notice the strange, if not bizarre, beliefs of some other groups. These developments favored the invention of universal religions.

A universal religion must, by definition, be essentially the same in every community where it is practiced – in farming as well as in hunting communities. A universal religion cannot easily accommodate local peculiarities and conditions therefore. It could not offer a female sun god to a farming community and a male moon god to a hunting community. Replacing the multitude of gods and spirits with a single or small number of gods is thus a necessary step in the creation of a universal religion.

Heterogeneity across communities also makes it difficult to orient a universal religion toward providing rewards and penalties in this life, since the needs of communities differ greatly. It is also likely, as knowledge and understanding of causality and chance grew, that individuals in more complex societies became skeptical about the powers of shamans and priests to cure diseases, chase away evil spirits and bring success in battle. Thus, another logical step in the development of a universal religion is to reorient exchange relationships between gods and humans away from providing rewards on earth to providing them in the afterlife. This shift in orientation also has the advantage of making verification of the receipt of the rewards impossible.

Although universal religions are less concerned with explaining inexplicable events in daily life than are local religions, they, too, have their miracles that account for certain wondrous events on earth, many of which occur when the religion's founder lived. But universal religions place much more emphasis on explaining the causes of more momentous events – like the creation of the universe and of man. These religious claims again have the advantage of being unverifiable.[12]

Thus, universal religions have all of the salient characteristics of local religions. They provide answers to puzzling questions; proscribe certain immoral actions and prescribe certain moral actions; contain rituals, which allow individuals to obtain rewards and avoid punishments; and are greatly concerned with death and the passage into the afterlife. Equally important, however, is the way in which universal and local religions differ. Universal religions provide answers for different sorts of questions – who created the earth? They replace all-knowing ancestors and spirits with all-knowing gods. Where rewards and punishments meted out by the ancestors alter individuals' lives on earth, a universal religion's rewards and punishments are experienced in the afterlife.

The death of a founder of a universal religion – Buddha, Christ, Mohammed – creates a crisis for his followers: how to continue and to spread the teachings of the founder. Compilations of his teaching are then put together, and his followers set out to convert others to

---

[12] Dennett (2006: 164) stresses the importance of propositions in religion that cannot be refuted.

the religion. Out of this group of initial missionaries emerges a set of experts on the religion, which Boyer refers to as a *guild*.[13] Guild members become the official interpreters of the religion's doctrines and performers of its rituals. Like all guilds, religious guilds abhor competition, and thus set out to eliminate it. It is no accident that the First of the Ten Commandments prohibits belief in "false" gods. Each universal religion claims that it alone can provide salvation, nirvana or other forms of eternal happiness, and thus encourages people to join the *true* faith and discourages defection.

Local religions' shamans and priests are assumed to be born with mystical powers or to receive them from the spirits. In contrast, the priests of universal religions acquire their powers through study. Since in principle *anyone* could study and become a priest,[14] guild members are very vulnerable to entry and competition. Thus, religious guilds inevitably seek protection from competition by teaming up with the state.

One effective way to protect a monopoly is to create a *brand* image. Religious brands take the form of specific doctrines. Thus, doctrine plays a great role in universal religions, while being largely absent from local religions. Religious doctrines are easier to standardize and promulgate if they can be written down. Thus, the emergence of both universal religions and writing and literacy in more complex societies is not an accident. Without a written version of a religious doctrine, it would not be possible to guarantee that it was the same in every community. Passing a religious doctrine on by word of mouth would inevitably lead to alterations in content. With writing one can ensure that the same doctrines are taught and the same rituals performed in every community. Thus, universal religions can be regarded as the first form of brand creation and franchising. Just as a McDonald's customer can expect the same size and quality of a Big Mac in China, Austria and California, a Catholic can expect the ritual of the mass to be the same in China, Austria and California.

Although all universal religions seek to be monopolies, none has succeeded.[15] One reason for this is that no founder of a universal religion had the time or inclination to codify his teachings. Codifications

---

[13] See discussion in Boyer (2001: ch. 8).
[14] In several religions, this anyone must be a male.
[15] For an interesting discussion of the Catholic Church's efforts to maintain and exploit a monopoly position, see Ekelund et al. (1997).

came *after* a founder's death and were undertaken by his followers. Since different followers had different recollections and interpretations of the founder's teachings, disagreement over the exact wording of the religion's authentic doctrine was inevitable. *All* universal religions have thus been plagued by schisms.

In addition to competition from within, universal religions face competition from without – from other universal religions and from local religions. Many religious doctrines are rather abstract – think of the doctrine of the Holy Trinity, that there is one God but he consists of three parts, two of which have a father–son relationship. Although accounts of events in the lives of Buddha, Christ and Mohammed are inspiring when first heard, these, too, may lose their power to excite over time. Behavioral psychology teaches us that habits are more easily established and maintained when rewards immediately follow actions than when they are delayed. A problem all universal religions face is that their greatest rewards are delayed until after death. The rewards individuals perceive that they get from local religions, on the other hand, occur here on earth. Thus, it is that universal religions often have to bend to accommodate local religious customs. Boyer gives the following account.

[M]any Hindu scholars contrast what they call *shastrik* elements of the religion, the belief and practices supposed to be the definition of Hinduism, with the *lautik* or local, popular and contextual versions. The *shastrik* elements should apply everywhere ... People always add to or distort doctrine. The same phenomenon is found in Buddhism, where scholars are scandalized by the many pagan practices they must witness, tolerate and in which they are sometimes forced to participate. The history of early Christianity also includes many difficult conflicts between the competing claims of a still fragile Church with considerable political backing and a host of local cults that somehow deviate from doctrine ... In some ways, Hinduism achieved a more balanced equilibrium between the general, literate version and the inevitable local variants and additions. This was realized mostly through the convenient division between great gods of cosmic significance and local deities, more generally goddesses, that were mainly relevant at the local level. More or less every settlement has its own goddess who is specially concerned with the inhabitants of that special place. (Boyer 2001: 281–282)

Today many Italian towns and cities have their particular saint whose birthday is celebrated each year with a parade and festival. According to Na Honoun, a voodoo priestess, Christians in Benin go to church on Sunday but visit the voodoo priests and priestesses the rest of the week (*Economist* Jan. 28, 2006). In Benin, day-to-day exchange relationships with the spirits appear just as or even more important than the relationship with the more remote Christian God.

Contrasting the Theoretical Systems of Modern and Traditional Societies

In an interesting essay, Robin Horton contrasted the theoretical systems of "modern" and "traditional" societies. Modern societies make considerable use of scientific methods to achieve an understanding of causal relationships, whereas traditional societies rely to a great degree on abductive methods. Both modern and traditional societies, however, possess "theoretical systems whose basic *raison d'être* [is] the extension of the magnificent but none the less limited causal vision of everyday commonsense thinking" (Horton 1982: 201).[16]

Both types of theoretical systems can be divided into two parts. *Primary* theory refers to the commonsense causal relationships people infer from the close juxtaposition of natural events, what Boyer (1994) refers to as abductive theory. *Secondary* theory consists of mental constructs to explain those phenomena that cannot be explained by primary theory. Whereas primary theories are similar across cultures, secondary theories "possess startling differences ... between community and community, culture and culture" (p. 228). In one important respect they are similar, however: both types of secondary theory rely on entities and processes that are "hidden" to the human observer, while these entities and processes are directly observable in the primary theories (p. 229).

The hidden entities in the secondary theories of traditional societies are ghosts, spirits and gods and thus are *personal* in the sense that they are assumed to be intentional beings like humans and animals. In contrast, the hidden entities in the secondary theories of modern Western society are inanimate objects and thus *impersonal* or *mechanistic* – atoms, electrons, sound waves and gravitational forces (p. 229).

Horton also notes the following important differences between cultures: traditionalist versus progressive; consensual versus competitive

---

[16] All page references in this section are to Horton (1982) unless otherwise noted.

(pp. 238–248). In a traditionalist society, people believe that wisdom was discovered by the ancients and has been passed down to the present. This wisdom provides a true picture of the world, first because it has the authority of the ancients behind it, and second because it has "withstood the test of time." Its account of events is not so out of line with experience as to call the wisdom of the ancients into question. Edmund Burke, awkwardly born into the Enlightenment, was the perfect embodiment of a traditionalist.

Progressives place little stock in the teachings of the past. We know more today than we did yesterday; we will know more tomorrow than we do today. Thus, progressives are inherently optimistic about man's ability to acquire knowledge and about the future. Immanuel Kant's (1795) *World Peace* captures this optimism perfectly.

A consensual society reinforces the conservatism of a traditional society. With all members of society sharing a common set of beliefs, a common *Weltanschauung*, there is no one to point out inconsistencies in these beliefs and failures to account for certain phenomena. Where belief systems and theoretical models compete, proponents of one system will be continually pointing out the inadequacies of their competitors, and all competitors will be striving to improve the performance of their theories in explaining and predicting events. A more rapid accumulation of knowledge can thus be expected in a progressive and competitive system than in a traditionalist, consensual system. Horton goes on to claim that cultural homogeneity, as existed in pre-colonial Africa and medieval Europe, is more conducive of traditionalism than the kind of melting pot, frontier societies that existed in sixth-century BC Greece or the Netherlands at the beginning of the Scientific Revolution (pp. 254–256).

Horton's traditional societies belong to Donald's mythic culture. They possess language and the capability to reason, but lack writing and thus are unable to store and accumulate knowledge to the same degree that modern societies can. "Theories" of traditional societies about the origins of humans, life after death, whether dead people reappear as ghosts and the like are stories made up to fill in gaps in their knowledge of the world. The invention of writing and symbols allowed humans to replace these myths and stories, with hypotheses involving abstract concepts like gravity. Models of nature could be constructed and predictions made and verified. Scientific theories of the modern age could replace the mythic stories of traditional societies. In some places, this development led eventually to wealth and prosperity and to the rise of democracy, but not everywhere.

The "Triumph" of the Theoretic over the Mythic Culture

State and Religion: The Sumerian State

At some time during the fifth or fourth millennia BC, the Sumerians migrated into Mesopotamia, "the land between the two rivers," where they established the first known state. One might expect that its bureaucracy, being the first in history, would be loosely organized and inefficient. Such was not the case. In the Sumerian city-states, bureaucracy developed to a high degree and controlled nearly every aspect of economic and social life. The entire society shared a set of morals and beliefs, which were determined by the religion as interpreted by the class of priests. The priests had evolved from being shamans who claimed to be able to predict the future by reading the stars. The state was an absolute monarchy with religion for an ideology. The king was god's representative on earth, and immediately beneath him were the priests. Together they ran the state with the help of a fairly large bureaucracy and a small number of scribes. The role of the masses was to serve god, which in effect meant to serve the king, since he was god's representative on earth. The power of the king was absolute.

The economy was based on agriculture. The class of priests, with the help of the bureaucracy, directed the planting and harvesting of crops. Harvested crops were taken to the temples to be stored and redistributed. Outside of the class of priests there was no private ownership of land or much in the way of other private property and little trade. The economy of the Sumerian city-state was what we would today call a command economy.

Carroll Quigley (1979: 193) described the Sumerians as "the most important group of humans who ever lived." There is much evidence to back up this claim. In addition to writing, the Sumerians either invented or made important advances in agriculture (irrigation, the plow, wheeled carts, draft animals), metallurgy (brass and copper smelting), pottery manufacturing (the potter's wheel), transportation (the sailboat), astronomy and, of course, the state. These inventions largely constitute progress at the level of *primary* theory – observations made about natural phenomena. The secondary theory of the

Sumerians was still based on religious beliefs, and thus can be said to have been largely personal as in less developed, tribal societies.

The Sumerian city-state survived anywhere from 800 to 1500 years depending upon one's choice of starting and ending points (Finer 1997: 127–128). Finer (1997: 29) attributes longevity in a state to a congruence between a society's belief system and its social and political structure. In the Sumerian city-state this congruence was as close as it could possibly come. "In no other antique society did religion occupy such a prominent position ... the religious ideas promoted by the Sumerians played an extraordinary part in the public and private life of the Mesopotamians, modeling their institutions, colouring their works of art and literature, pervading every form of activity."[17]

The State without Religion: The Greek City-State

The salient characteristics of the Sumerian city-state were also found in Egypt, Persia and other states of the ancient world – innovations in metallurgy, farming, engineering and the practical arts coupled with an autocratic and bureaucratic state in which state leadership and religion were fused. While knowledge of the causal relationships that govern the natural world progressed and were exploited, fear and awe of the supernatural world remained strong and were exploited by the state's leaders, who often claimed to be gods.

The great and unexpected rupture with this pattern occurred in ancient Greece. A society emerged around the Aegean Sea at about 800 BC that was unlike any that had come before and in many ways unlike any that has come since, a society which "had a totally new conception of what human life was for, and showed for the first time what the human mind was for" (Kitto 1957: 7). They organized themselves into city-states, but except for their territoriality, they bore no resemblance to the city-states of Mesopotamia. They were democratic to a degree unknown until that time and almost unknown since.

Importance of Rational Thought

A distinguishing feature of the Greeks was their "firm belief in Reason" (Kitto 1957: 176). In ancient Greece, rational thought

---

[17] Roux (1980: 91) as quoted in Finer (1997: 115).

moved to center stage. We can identify the development of two quite different variants of rational thought processes. The first approach places great faith in the power of *a priori* reasoning. Truth can be found by reasoning alone, and "knowledge" gained from the senses, from observing the real world, would only lead one away from the truth. Underlying the apparent complexity and variety that one observes in the real world lay a few simple, universal laws which, when understood, would explain the workings of the universe. This line of reasoning led to the development of the fields of both metaphysics and mathematics and to major contributions in each field. One need only mention the names of a few proponents of this approach – Euclid, Zeno, Pythagoras, Socrates and Plato – to realize the extent of its development and the importance of its achievements.

The other variant of a rational thought process that can be attributed to the Greeks is what we call today the scientific method – a succession of hypothesis formulation, testing, reformulation and further testing – logical inference informed by observing and gathering data. The first name here would be that of Aristotle.

The "Greeks, practical men that they were, had a passion for asking useless questions" (Kitto 1957: 178). Where did we come from? What is the world made of? What is virtue? Truth? Although other peoples had posed such questions before, none had posed so many or pursued the answers as far as the Greeks. Moreover, they did not seek answers to these questions through hypotheses about spirits and gods. Greek society can be said to have had the first *modern* system of thought, in that the elements in their secondary theories were inanimate objects and forces from the natural word, not spirits from a supernatural world. To cite one example, Thales posed in typical Greek style the question, "what is the world made of." His answer "was based on nothing but abstract reasoning ... [completely free] from any form of religious mysticism, such as one might reasonably expect from a thinker whose predecessors had all expressed themselves in mythological terms" (Kitto 1957: 179–180). Although Thales's answer – water – has not withstood the test of time, the way in which he approached the question certainly has.

The Greeks had religion, of course, a form of polytheism. Its form stemmed from the fact that the Greeks were an amalgam of different peoples who had simply taken over the various gods of the peoples absorbed into their culture. Greek myths and gods offered answers to questions concerning the origin of the Greeks, the sun, the sea – questions that cannot be answered by simply observing nature, and for which the supernatural has often been invoked.

Greek gods were not Supreme Beings who did no wrong and had to be obeyed unquestioningly. They were "bigger than life" humans with human passions and foibles. Being human-like, their actions could be measured by the same powers of reasoning as applied to man. "This form of religion induced the thinking Greek into something that Egyptians, Sumerians, Babylonians, Assyrians, and Jews were incapable of: applying rational and indeed secular calculation to nature and to man himself" (Finer 1997: 328).

Greek religion reflected human weaknesses. It provided the Greeks with a theology of sorts, and some of the gods were concerned with morality. But for answers to the great moral questions, the Greeks were more likely to turn to their great thinkers like Homer, Aeschylus, Socrates, Plato and Aristotle than to the gods. In this respect it is legitimate to call Athens a *secular* state, for religion played little role in its public decisions. The secular nature of ancient Athens is nicely illustrated in Pericles's funeral oration to commemorate those who had fallen in battle. On such an occasion today, no American president could fail to mention God and perhaps the afterlife. In the more than seven pages that Thucydides (1943) devotes to the oration, however, there is no mention of a god or the afterlife. Instead, Pericles uses the occasion to remind his listeners of what it means to be a citizen of Athens and why those commemorated died to defend it (see also the further discussion later).

The Invention of Democracy

The Greeks' penchant for asking questions helps to explain why it was they who invented democracy. Prior to the Greeks "states had just evolved ... [and] it was natural that authority should be 'traditional'. In ... [Greece] nothing was less obvious, and every change was questioned and its legitimacy challenged. The *polis* was an artifact and man was its measurer" (Finer 1997: 329). This confidence in man's ability to be the measurer of all things, to be capable of answering the questions that a society must answer, is an essential presumption underlying democracy. No people have ever had greater confidence in man's ability to fulfill these demands than the Greeks.

The Greeks thought of themselves as different from all other peoples, different not in the sense that they had a privileged relationship to God, as the Hebrews thought they had, but in the sense that they had a privileged relationship to one another – they were Greeks and not barbarians (non-Greeks). And what was distinctive about being a Greek? He was a free man, free not necessarily in living in a democracy, but in the sense of being a citizen who had certain rights, who was ruled by laws. "Greek Tragedy is built on the faith that in human affairs it is Law that reigns, not chance" (Kitto 1957: 176). Moreover, the laws that reigned were not dictated from above by a God or a sacred king, but arose from the collective decisions of the citizens themselves. The Greek citizen was free to seek redress from the courts if he felt that he had been injured and to defend himself in front of the courts if he was accused of injuring someone else. And there he would be tried by juries of his citizen peers.[18]

Appraisal

"This [the Greek] polity is extraordinary. It was a miracle of ingenuity and design, one of the most successful, perhaps the most successful, of political artefacts in the history of government" (Finer 1997: 367–368). It is difficult not to share Finer's judgment. Cleisthenes's constitution was one of the great "political artefacts" of all time. When one contemplates the additional contributions that the Greeks made to architecture, astronomy, mathematics, philosophy, science, sculpture, arts in general and theater, one stands in awe. All of these can be explained by the fact that for the first time in human history, man's mind was freed to follow whatever path it chose, free from the constraints imposed by superstition and religion. Of all the Greek contributions to human history, the most important was the demonstration of the potential of rational thought, the power of *reason*.

The Athenian society personifies the modern society in its progressiveness and competitiveness. The Greeks were optimistic about the potential of man to reason and about his potential for self-government. Today the United States epitomizes in many respects the triumph of Western modernism in its democratic and capitalist institutions, in its scientific and technological progress. Yet the suggestion

---

[18] See, Kitto (1957: 7–9) and Finer (1997: 354–357).

that the knowledge of political institutions possessed by the present generation should allow it to write a better constitution than the forefathers wrote over 200 years ago is generally greeted with much skepticism – *particularly among political scientists.* For the Greeks, the novelty of Cleisthenes's constitution was, if anything, a point in its favor, such was the confidence of the Greeks in the creative powers of the human mind and enthusiasm for that which was new (Kitto 1957: 106–107).

The progressivism of the Greeks was equally matched by their competitiveness, particularly in the realm of ideas. The Platonists, Aristotelians, Stoics, Epicureans and Skeptics all competed in offering answers to the great questions of who we are and how we should live. The practitioner of pure, abstract reasoning competed with the empiricist in trying to explain the natural world. The vibrance and innovativeness of intellectual life in ancient Greece is symbolized by the fact that so many of our words for these bodies of thought – metaphysics, stoicism, empiricism – are of Greek origin.

The Rediscovery of Reasoning

During the first millennium following Christ, Christianity became the dominant religion in Europe. Its souls, saints, angels and devils replaced the evil spirits, ghosts, fairies, cherubim, demons and jinni of early religions. Its three gods rolled into one replaced the multiple gods of the pagan Greek and Roman religions. The celebration of the mass with the distribution of the Eucharist and wine replaces the animal sacrifices and redistribution of food in early Judaism (Harris 1989: 441).

Christianity's secondary theory is animistic and personal, like that of almost all religions, and thus with its rise the kind of reasoning introduced by the Greeks disappears. The Europe of the first millennium is a traditionalist society looking backwards at the wisdom of the Bible, Christ and the Apostles. There is no competition among schools of thought. One ideology – Christianity – dominates. Such reasoning as took place, as for example, among the Scholastics of the Middle Ages focused not on how to improve life on earth, but on the nature of life in heaven.

Then around 1200 AD an awakening begins to take place. The writings of the ancient Greeks are rediscovered. Scholarly attention shifts to understanding nature and life on this planet. Technological advances, like the development of the telescope, confirm glaring disparities between what can be observed and Church dogma. Undoubtedly, the intellectual awakening of the Renaissance was fueled in part by the spread of commerce and increasing mobility in Europe. Venetian, Genovese, Portuguese and Dutch traders were sailing to all corners of the globe and being exposed to new technologies and ideas. Representatives of different religions were coming into contact in southern Spain.

Naturally, the Church resisted this onslaught against its dogmas. Copernicus's theory that the earth circles the sun was opposed by the Church, and Galileo famously was forced to recant this theory. But, once released, the onslaught of intellectual activity could not be held back. Eventually it even entered the realm of metaphysics. One scholar after another – Descartes, Spinoza, Berkeley – offered up a new proof of the existence of God. Descartes's contribution was truly revolutionary. If a thinking man sitting in front of the fire in his bedroom could prove to himself by logical reasoning that God exists, then God exists. No appeal to a holy book or the wisdom of a long-dead holy man was needed.

Once competing theories of God's existence began to appear, it would not be long before proofs of his nonexistence began to appear. By the Enlightenment, Hume, Voltaire and its other great thinkers were using their analytical powers to cast doubt on virtually all of the teachings of the Church – the existence of miracles, angels and devils, saints and souls.

The Enlightenment has also been aptly named the Age of Reason. At no other time in history, and no other place than Europe and the North American colonies, has trust in the powers of reason, trust in the potential of the human mind, been so strong – except perhaps for ancient Greece. Although democracy first reappeared, appropriately enough, in Renaissance Italy, it was not to take firm root again until the Enlightenment. The boldest break with tradition and clearest assertion of man's right to and capability for self-government occurred in revolutionary France. But it was the Americans who actually designed and implemented a set of political institutions that allowed citizens to govern themselves (Commager 1978).

It was also during the Enlightenment that the systematic application of scientific methodology to the study of human behavior can be said to have begun with the writings of David Hume and, most importantly, Adam Smith. Once launched, economics developed rapidly during the 19th century and was eventually joined by the other social sciences.

The Enlightenment can also be said to have given birth to *liberalism*, although some of the great contributions to liberal thought, like Mill's essay *On Liberty*, came after the peak of the Enlightenment. Once the belief is established that humans are capable of rational thought, capable of transacting in the marketplace, capable of participating in the democratic process and making collective decisions for the community, it is a short step to the belief that humans should be free to do what they choose so long as it does not harm others.

Citizenship and Democracy

In 1785, the Marquis de Condorcet published a proof of a remarkable theorem. It rests on the following assumptions. A community must make a binary choice, as, for example, whether X has committed a particular crime or not. All members of the community have the same goal – to find X guilty if she committed the crime, and innocent if she did not. No one knows whether X is guilty, but each person has a probability p of being correct in deciding guilt or innocence, $p > 0.5$. The theorem states that if the community decides guilt using the simple majority rule, the probability that it makes the correct choice approaches 1 as the community's size increases.[19]

The theorem obviously is a defense of the simple majority rule, but it can also be regarded as a defense of democracy itself. In this context, the assumptions underlying it are very important. All citizens are assumed to have the same goal – correctly deciding guilt, improving the welfare of all citizens. Moreover, the probability that any one citizen makes the correct choice is greater than ½. Citizens do not simply flip coins to decide how to vote. They gather enough information to raise the probability of being correct above a coin flip.

All successful democracies require that similar conditions be fulfilled. Since all citizens consume the same set of publicly provided goods and services, their provision is more likely to improve citizens' welfare, if they agree on the ends of the state. If individual preferences are diametrically opposed, collective decisions benefiting all will be

[19] See Young (1997) and Mueller (2003: 128–133).

impossible. All successful democracies require that citizens take their duties seriously by participating in the process as voters, but also by becoming sufficiently well informed to contribute to the community's making *correct* decisions. Outputs from a democracy cannot be any better than its inputs.

The importance of these conditions is illustrated by the histories of the most successful democracies. Athenians believed that "the *polis* exists to express and secure the good of its citizens,"[20] and thus had the same normative view of the state as public-choice scholars like Wicksell (1896) and Buchanan (1986) have had. Moreover, no people have ever taken citizenship more seriously than the ancient Greeks.[21] The same word in Greek, *politeia*, stood for citizenship, the body of all citizens and the constitution. The state and its citizens were synonymous; the quality of the state (polis) depended on the quality of the citizens. This symbiosis between citizenship and constitution was to Isocrates the *soul* of the polis.[22]

Citizenship was cherished by the Greeks and was not bestowed lightly, at least not when Greek democracy was most vibrant. Citizenship could be withdrawn *in toto* or in part by taking away some of a citizen's rights. Thus, several levels of citizenship existed, with the highest level carrying with it the right to participate in the public assembly *and* to hold public office. Sons of Greek citizens would generally become citizens in time, but this was not automatic. Foreigners could acquire citizenship by service to the state. Even slaves sometimes were granted citizenship in exchange for fighting in a war. Citizenship carried with it the obligation to serve in the army and to equip oneself for battle.

Thus, in Athens obligations to the state and benefits from it were closely entwined. Being a Greek meant being a citizen with all of the rights and obligations that this involved. This aspect of Greek citizenship is nicely illustrated in the following passage attributed to Pericles by Thucydides (1943, II, §37):

For our government is not copied from those of our neighbors: we are an example to them rather than they to us. Our constitution is named a

[20] Farrar (1992: 17).
[21] The discussion in the next few paragraphs draws heavily from Ehrenberg (1969: 38–48) and MacDowell (1978: 67–83). See also Kitto (1957).
[22] Isocrates (1929, VII at 13, 14).

democracy, because it is in the hands not of the few but of the many. But our laws secure equal justice for all in their private disputes, and our public opinion welcomes and honours talent in every branch of achievement, not for any sectional reason but on grounds of excellence alone. And as we give free play to all in our public life, so we carry the same spirit into our daily relations with one another. We have no black looks or angry words for our neighbor if he enjoys himself in his own way, and we abstain from the little acts of churlishness, though they leave no mark, yet cause annoyance to whoso notes them. Open and friendly in our private intercourse, in our public acts we keep strictly within the control of law. We acknowledge the restraint of reverence; we are obedient to whomsoever is set in authority, and to the laws, more especially to those which offer protection to the oppressed and those unwritten ordinances whose transgression brings admitted shame.

What is particularly striking in this paragraph is the way Pericles intertwines a description of the democratic institutions of Athens and the cultural traits that, by implication, foster and are fostered by them. No distinction was made between a citizen's private and public life, the "man who holds aloof from public life" was regarded as "useless" (Thucydides 1943: 113).

Contained in this notion of citizenship was the assumption that a citizen was *capable* of exercising his public duties. This assumption was explicit in the obligation to serve in the military and to be able to equip oneself for battle, but was also implicit in the obligation to serve in the assembly or the Council of Five Hundred – *and to do so intelligently and conscientiously.* Thus, implicit in the notion of Greek citizenship and the creation of Greek democracy was an assumption that citizens had the capacity to not only make decisions for themselves in their private lives but also to make decisions for the community, decisions that would "express and secure the good of its citizens." Thus, it is no coincidence that democracy first appears in the society that was the first to be capable of engaging in the kind of rational thinking that we associate with modern scientific thinking and that this society invented an alphabet, which extended to a far greater fraction of the population the power to read and to reflect upon what one has read. At its zenith, Athenian democracy came as close to embodying the fundamental attributes of democracy as any political system has. What we should learn from this first flowering of democracy is that good government does not come cheaply. It requires the active participation of a body of citizens who possess the mental capacities to carry out their responsibilities as citizens and who are willing to bear the costs in time, money and energy of discharging these responsibilities.

By today's standards, the Venetian Republic was not a democracy, since the voting franchise was restricted to a group of aristocratic families making up only 10 percent or so of the population. Nevertheless, the Venetian city-state *"was* the best [government] in the world" (Finer 1997: 1016). Its citizens possessed rights to association, mobility, free speech and religious tolerance and enjoyed equality before the law, aristocrat and commoner alike. "The justice of Venice was famous throughout the whole of Europe" (Finer 1997: 1017). It was also one of the richest states in Europe. Although double-entry bookkeeping was not invented in Venice, it soon found its way there and then became known as "Venetian bookkeeping" and spread across Europe (Gleeson-White 2011). Venice became the financial hub of Europe, with the Rialto Bridge becoming a kind of Wall Street for engaging in financial transactions. Pugla and Trefler (2014) cast a shadow on Venice's economic success with evidence that the richest families sought to stifle competition and thus created significant inequality. Nevertheless, Venice's government appears to have been popularly supported. Although citizen uprisings against ruling aristocracies were common in other European city-states, they did not take place in Venice, and the government needed no standing army or large police force to maintain order. If the goal of a democracy is to protect and advance the welfare of its citizens, then Venice, with its limited franchise, fulfilled this goal to a measure that few, if any, other states have accomplished – and it did so for some 500 years.

How come? An important part of the answer lies in the fact that the voting franchise was restricted to a minority of highly qualified people, who had not only their own interests in mind, but those of the entire community. "The high offices in Venice were regularly occupied by men who were peers both socially and economically" (Martines 1988: 159). Although the electorate constituted a small fraction of the total citizenry, it was far too large to mold easily into a tight coalition bent on exploiting the nonvoting population. Large numbers of the Great Council must have always existed who would have opposed such moves. On the other hand, the Great Council was small enough to overcome free-riding. The fate of Venice lay in the hands of a permanent group of families; the physical scale of Venice was such that they would have known most other members personally. Here one must add in the Venetian's "civic sense, ... tenacious patriotism, [and] ... sense of solidarity under the laws" (Finer 1997: 992), which would supply the *intrinsic* motivation to govern wisely and fairly for all members of the Venetian community. These qualities of character existed in Athens at the height of its democratic republic and in Rome at the height of its republic; they are essential qualities in a citizenry for creating a successful democracy.[23]

It is also worth emphasizing that Venice was essentially a secular state. The Venetians were Catholics to be sure, but they did not let their religious beliefs color their judgments on civic matters, a fact of which Pope Pius II lamented, "they [the Venetians] are hypocrites. They wish to appear Christian before the world but in reality they never think of God and, except for the state, which they regard as a deity, they hold nothing sacred, nothing holy."[24] The separation of church and state was also a key feature of the US Constitution and has been a central feature of French democracy since the time of the revolution. We regard it as an essential element of successful democracy.

Religion and Democracy

In a typical public good experiment, each participant is given, say, 10 units of currency. If all participants voluntarily contribute 10 to the provision of the public good, each gets back, say, 20. If all but one contribute 10 and one participant contributes nothing, all participants – including the free rider – receive 19, giving the free rider a total payoff of 29. Free riding is the optimal strategy for all in a single play of the game. When the experiments are run, however, most participants contribute neither 0 nor 10, but something in between, with average contributions tending to be around 5.[25] One explanation for this seemingly irrational behavior is that the participants sense that they are in a situation in which cooperation is expected, and their genetically conditioned propensity to cooperate induces them to contribute more on average than is selfishly optimal.

[23] On the similarity between Venice and Rome, when "the [Roman] Republic was at its best," see Finer (1997: 993).
[24] Taken from Finer (1997: 1019), original source Gilbert (1968: 467, n. 3).
[25] For a survey of this literature, see Ledyard (1995).

This explains voluntary contributions in such situations, but it would appear something more than our genetic proclivities to cooperate is needed to bring about the optimal degree of cooperation. The moral codes embedded in religions might fill this need. David Sloan Wilson (2002) has argued that religions are so ubiquitous throughout history because they induce cooperative behavior with beneficial effects for all members of the community. Sumer fits Wilson's hypothesis nicely. The society prospered by developing an elaborate irrigation system whose construction and maintenance required the coordinated effort of a large fraction of the community. As noted earlier, religion played an important role in cementing the community together. Wilson (2002: 126–133) describes a similar example of religion's role in Bali helping to coordinate the elaborate irrigation system of that island. Norenzayan et al. (2014) develop this line of reasoning further, claiming that the prosocial religions came into existence to induce cooperation as societies grew larger. They present empirical, historical and experimental evidence in support of this hypothesis.

I find these arguments and evidence persuasive. When large-scale cooperation is necessary for a community to survive and prosper, religion *may* induce the additional cooperative behavior needed beyond that which our genetic heritage can supply. But there are also many examples of communities overcoming social dilemmas *without* the aid of religion. Elinor Ostrom (1990: 69–88) describes community-organized irrigation systems in Spain and the Philippines that have survived for centuries without relying on religious beliefs. Fieldwork has uncovered literally hundreds of other examples of communities cooperating in social dilemma situations (Ostrom 2000). What appears to be necessary are clearly defined rules regarding who has access to the common resource, the obligations of all members of the community to maintain the system, monitoring to detect individuals breaking the rules and (typically mild) sanctions imposed on rule breakers.

On a larger scale, ancient Athens and the Venetian Republic were highly successful states in which religion does not seem to have contributed much to their success. Instead of religious virtue being the stimulus inducing cooperation, *civic* virtue was. In both a "tenacious patriotism" led citizens to make sacrifices for the benefit of the entire community. De Tocqueville (1945[1840]: 129–130) also recognized the importance of civic virtue for the success of the American experiment in democracy. I contend that all democracies require some degree of patriotism and civic virtue among their citizenries if they are to succeed fully in advancing the interests of their citizens. Moreover, where such civic virtue exists, religion may not be necessary to induce a community to solve its various social dilemmas.

One might argue that an intelligent, well-informed citizenry is not necessary for having a well-functioning democracy – all that is needed is that citizens cooperate and adhere to a set of social norms. In simpler times this might have been true. Today, however, we live in a complicated world. The issues confronting us – global warming, the spread of AIDS, possible other world epidemics, terrorism, how to finance the needs of the elderly in aging societies – are complex and may require complex solutions. If citizens are to decide these issues, either directly or by selecting representatives to decide them, then they must possess sufficient intelligence to understand the issues and be willing to acquire sufficient knowledge to make the correct choices. Much of this knowledge is of a scientific character. Here religion may stand in the way of successful democracy. Religions substitute beliefs in religious doctrines for scientific knowledge. Throughout the last two millennia Christianity has doggedly questioned and opposed scientific advances. To give but one current example, AIDS has been one of the greatest health problems facing the world in recent times. A simple and effective preventative is the use of condoms, yet the Catholic Church opposes their use, because its interpretation of the Bible implies that God forbids the use of birth control devices. Global warming would be a far less serious problem today if the world's population were not constantly growing. Here again religious beliefs about the morality of birth control prevent some governments from taking the proper steps to curb population growth.

The constitution of an ideal liberal democracy both *allows* its citizens the maximum liberty to pursue their own goals and lifestyles in the private sphere, so long as this pursuit does not impose significant costs on the rest of the community, and *protects their rights* to do so. It also protects the rights of citizens to think and say what they choose. Here we confront a conflict between religion and *liberal* democracy. Studies going back to the 1950s have found a negative correlation between tolerance of dissent or civil liberties and the strength of one's religious beliefs, a correlation that gets weaker the more education a person has.[26] Unquestioning fundamentalism appears to be particularly antithetical to democratic values.

[P]rejudice and anti-democratic sentiments are not associated with religion *per se*, but with certain aspects of religion that are bound up with intellectual rigidity, closed-mindedness, and social conformity. (Klosko 2000: 94)

Democracy might function quite well in a religious community, where all members hold the same religious beliefs. In such a community, agreement on what actions should be banned or required, restrictions on dress and speech and the like should be noncontroversial. Conflict between religion and liberal democratic values can arise, however, when *different* religious groups are present in the same community. Here our genetic heritage comes into play again. In a homogeneous religious community, our instincts for group loyalty bind us to other members of the community, and the adherence to social norms reinforced by religion produces benefits for all members of the community. Ensminger (1997) presents evidence that the spread of Islam in Africa created greater trust and cooperation in the tribes that converted to it, thereby stimulating trade and economic success. Norenzayan et al. (2014) cite her in support of their thesis. Although religion can induce *intragroup* cooperation to the benefit of a community, it can also lead to *intergroup* conflicts by triggering perceptions of tribal differences. Nigeria is 50 percent Muslim, 40 percent Christian, with the remainder of the population following various local religions. It has been plagued by religious conflict throughout its history. In 1967 a civil war broke out between the Muslims and Christians, and the eastern part of the country composed of mostly Christian members of the Igbo tribe broke away and formed the independent state of Biafra. Anywhere from 1 to 3 million people died during the conflict. Today, Boko Haram, an Islamist group in northeast Nigeria, has killed tens of thousands of people while waging jihad. Muslim Somalis launch periodic attacks into largely Christian Kenya. More examples could be given. Although Africa may illustrate the beneficial effects of the spread of prosocial religions, it also demonstrates the potential costs.

---

[26] See Stouffer (1955: ch. 4), discussion and references in Klosko (2000: 44–50) and Putnam and Campbell (2010: 479–489).

Conclusions

The biological evolution of humans has consisted of an expansion of both brain size and the functional capability of the brain to process information and understand causal relationships. Over time theoretical models of the relationships of inanimate objects have displaced early theories that postulated animate causes of events like spirits, ghosts and gods. Scientific reasoning has – in some parts of the world – largely displaced myth and superstition.

The institutional history of humans has witnessed the creation of the state – at first dictatorial and oppressive – and, with many reverses and false turns, eventually the at least partial triumph of the democratic state. The two developments are related. Successful democracy requires an educated citizenry sufficiently capable of making collective decisions that improve the welfare of the community. It also requires a civic ethic that induces citizens to carry out their civic duties responsibly.

Within the evolutionary baggage that humans possess is an instinct to be loyal to one's tribe and to defend it against other tribes. Such instincts can strengthen democratic institutions if they can be channeled in such a way that citizens identify with their polity and are loyal to it and to their fellow citizens. Such an identification existed in ancient Greece, where being an Athenian meant, first of all, being a citizen, and there was no higher status one could obtain. It existed in Venice with its strong "civic sense, ... tenacious patriotism, [and] ... sense of solidarity under the laws" (Finer 1997: 992). And it exists today in Switzerland. Like the Greeks, the Swiss expect much from their citizens – repeated trips to the polls to vote on referenda, a preparedness to fight for their country if called. Like the Greeks, the Swiss are fond of direct democracy. I know of no other country in which the outcomes from the democratic process come closer to matching citizens' preferences than in Switzerland.

In this chapter I have stressed the tension between democracy and religion. Religion can be another clue as to a person's tribe. When different religions coexist within a country, they can be a source of conflict, which undermines civic-mindedness and loyalty to the state. Northern Ireland has been torn apart by religion since it came into existence. Religious differences in the United States have polarized its society and poisoned its politics. The inept intervention of the United States in Iraq unleashed a sectarian civil war between Shiites and Sunnis.

What lessons can we draw? Political correctness today requires religious tolerance. Religion is good, and all religions are equally good. In Europe, such political correctness risks allowing – indeed encouraging and subsidizing – fundamentalist religious groups, which threaten its liberal, democratic societies. In Europe the chief danger is posed by Islam. "About a third of French schoolchildren of Muslim origin see their faith rather than a passport or skin colour as the main thing that defines them. Young British Muslims are inclined to see Islam (rather than the United Kingdom, or the city where they live) as their true home" (*Economist* June 24, 2006). Such divided loyalties pose a threat to democratic institutions and civil liberties in Western Europe. Given a choice between acting as a good French or British citizen or as a good Muslim following the call to *jihad,* some young Muslims in Europe have chosen jihad. The train bombings in Madrid, underground bombings in London, the assassinations of movie director Theo Van Gogh in the Netherlands and cartoonists at the magazine *Charlie Hebdo* in Paris indicate that radical Islam, when transplanted to Western Europe, poses a threat to its liberal democratic institutions.

Much the same can be said for extremist movements in other religions. In the United States it is Christian extremists (fundamentalists) who have helped polarize the country and made its democratic institutions, at least at the national level, largely dysfunctional. The increasing political power of religious conservatives in Israel appears to be having a polarizing effect on its politics. Pakistan is a mostly Muslim country with reasonably fair democratic elections, but it is racked by violence mostly stimulated by religious differences. India has been a democracy for over 60 years with steadily rising voter participation. For many, rising voter participation would signal a *strengthening* of India's democracy. But as participation levels have risen, the average education level of Indian voters has fallen, with the result that India "has become less tolerant, less secular, less law-abiding, less liberal" (Zakaria 2003: 106). In India, it has been the Muslim community which has borne the brunt of the rise of intolerance.

The lesson to be learned from these examples is that simply putting out ballot boxes, holding fair elections and allowing everyone to vote is no guarantee that the outcomes of the elections will advance the collective interests of the community. Indeed, in heterogeneous communities, there may not exist *collective* interests in a meaningful sense. Religious differences can be an important source for heterogeneity and conflict. Beyond shared goals successful democracy requires a citizenry capable of making well-informed collective decisions. Here again the beliefs and prejudices that religions foster may be a hindrance to successful democracy.

References

Axelrod, R. 1984. *The Evolution of Cooperation*. New York: Basic Books.

Barkow, J. H., Cosmides, L., and Tooby, J. 1982. *Adapted Mind*. Oxford: Oxford University Press.

Boyer, P. 1994. *The Naturalness of Religious Ideas*. Berkeley, CA: University of California Press.

2001. *Religion Explained*. New York: Basic Books.

Buchanan, J. M. 1986. *Liberty Market and State*. New York: New York University Press.

Catania, A. C. and Harnad, S. 1988. *The Selection of Behavior: The Operant Behaviorism of B.F. Skinner: Comments and Consequences*. Cambridge: Cambridge University Press.

Commager, H. S. 1978. *The Empire of Reason: How Europe Imagined and America Realized the Enlightenment*. London: Weidenfeld & Nicolson.

Dawkins, R. 1976. *The Selfish Gene*. Oxford: Oxford University Press.

Dennett, D. C. 2006. *Breaking the Spell*. London: Allen Lane.

De Tocqueville, A. [1840] 1945. *Democracy in America*, Vol. 2. New York: Vintage Books.

Donald, M. 1991. *Origins of the Modern Mind*. Cambridge, MA: Harvard University Press.

Economist. 2006. Islam, America and Europe. Economist [Online]. Available: www.economist.com/node/7081343

Ehrenberg, V. 1969. *The Greek State*. London: Methuen.

Ekelund, R. B., Hébert, Robert F., Tollison, R. D., Anderson, G. M., and Davidson, A. B. 1997. *Sacred Trust: The Medieval Church as an Economic Firm*. Oxford: Oxford University Press.

Ensminger, Jeseses. 1997. Transaction Costs and Islam: Explaining Conversion in Africa. *Journal of Institutional and Theoretical Economics*, 153, 4–29.

Farrar, C. 1992. Ancient Greek Political Theory as a Response to Democracy. In: Dunn, J. (ed.) *Democracy: The Unfinished Journey 508 BC to 1993 AD*. Oxford: Oxford University Press.

Fernández-Armesto, F. 2004. *So You Think You're Human?* Oxford: Oxford University Press.

Finer, S. E. 1997. *The History of Government, vols. I, II, and III.* Oxford: Oxford University Press.

Gilbert, F. 1968. The Venetian Constitution in Florentine Political Thought. In: Rubinstein, N. (ed.) *Florentine Studies: Politics and Society in Renaissance Florence.* London: Faber & Faber.

Gleeson-White, J. 2011. *Double Entry: How the Merchants of Venice Created Modern Finance.* London: Allen & Unwin.

Harris, M. 1989. *Our Kind.* New York: Harper & Row.

Holmes, S. 1995. *Passions and Constraint.* Chicago, IL: Chicago University Press.

Horton, R. 1982. Tradition and Modernity Revisited. In: Hollis, M. and Lukes, S. (eds.) *Rationality and Relativism.* Oxford: Basil Blackwell.

Hume, D. [1742] 1987. *Essays, Moral, Political and Literary.* Indiannapolis, IN: Liberty Fund.

Isocrates 1929. *Isocrates.* New York: W. Heinemann.

Kant, I. 1795. *Zum ewigen Frieden. Ein philosophischer Entwurf (Perpetual Peace: A Philosophical Sketch), Königsberg: Friedrich Nicolovius.*

Kitto, H. D. F. T. 1957. *The Greeks.* Harmondsworth: Penguin Books.

Klosko, G. 2000. *Democratic Procedures and Liberal Consensus.* Oxford: Oxford University Press.

Ledyard, J. O. 1995. Public Goods: A Survey of Experimental Research. In: Kagel, J. H. and Roth, A. E. (eds.) *The Handbook of Experimental Economics.* Princeton, NJ: Princeton University Press.

Lieberman, P. 1975. *On the Origins of Language: An Introduction to the Evolution of Human Speech.* New York: Macmillan.

Macdowell, D. M. 1978. *The Law in Classical Athens.* Ithaca, NY: Cornell University Press.

Martines, L. 1988. *Power and Imagination: City-States in Renaissance Italy.* Baltimore, MD: Johns Hopkins University Press.

Mokyr, J. 2002. *The Gifts of Athena.* Princeton, NJ: Princeton University Press.

Mueller, D. C. 2003. *Public Choice III.* Cambridge: Cambridge University Press.

Norenzayan, A., Shariff, A. F., Willard, A. K., et al. 2014. The Cultural Evolution of Prosocial Religions. *Behavioral and Brain Sciences,* 39, 1–65.

Ostrom, E. 1990. *Governing the Commons.* Cambridge: Cambridge University Press.

2000. Collective Action and the Evolution of Social Norms. *Journal of Economic Perspectives,* 14, 137–158.

Pinker, S. 1997. *How the Mind Works*. London: Penguin Books.

Pugla, D. and Trefler, D. 2014. International Trade and Institutional Change: Medieval Venice's Response to Globalization. *Quarterly Journal of Economics,* 129, 753–821.

Putnam, R. D. and Campbell, D. E. 2010. *American Grace*. New York: Simon & Schuster.

Quigley, C. 1979. *The Evolution of Civilizations*. Indianapolis, IN : Liberty Press.

Ramachandran, V. S. 1990. Visual Perception in People and Machines. In: Blake, A. and Troscianko, T. (eds.) *AI and the Eye*. Chichister, UK: Wiley.

Roux, G. 1980. *Ancient Iraq*. Harmondsworth: Penguin Books.

Staddon, J. E. R. 1983. *Adaptive Behavior and Learning*. Cambridge: Cambridge University Press.

Stouffer, S. A. 1955. *Communism, Conformity, and Civil Liberties*. Garden City, NY: Doubleday.

Thucydides 1943. *The History of the Peloponnesian War*. Oxford: Oxford University Press.

Trivers, R. L. 1971. The Evolution of Reciprocal Altruism. *Quarterly Review of Biology*, 46, 35–57.

1985. *Social Evolution*. Menlo Park: Benjamin Cummings.

Wicksell, K. [1896] 1967. A New Principle of Just Taxation, Finanztheoretische Untersuchungen. Jena: Fischer, English translation. In Musgrave, R. A. and Peacock, A. T. eds. *Classics in the Theory of Public Finance*. New York: St. Martin's Press, 72–118.

Wilson, D. S. 2002. *Darwin's Cathedral*. Chicago: Chicago University Press.

Young, H. P. 1997. Group Choice and Individual Judgments. In: Mueller, D. C. (ed.) *Perspectives on Public Choice*. Cambridge: Cambridge University Press.

Zakaria, F. 2003. *The Future of Freedom*. New York: W. W. Norton.

8 | On the Evolution of Organisational Governance
Divided Governance and Survival in the Long Run

ROGER D. CONGLETON

Introduction

Formal organisations are among the most important inventions of humankind. They allow groups of humans to produce and create far more than possible for the same individuals operating alone. This is not to deny the importance of other inventions such as the wheel, wedge, language, property rights, and markets; however, it is the organised "nodes" of production referred to as firms by economists that account for the great strides in production made in the past century or two. And it is the rule-creating and enforcing organisations that political scientists refer to as governments that account for the laws and infrastructure that allow markets to work as well as they do. Indeed, it can be argued that most of what separates humanity from the animal kingdom are consequences of the organisations formed to coordinate human activities and solve associated social dilemmas.

This is not to say that organisations are entirely consequences of design. Just as the wheel and wedge have been adapted to overcome a broad array of physical problems, the divisions of authority and standing procedures within organisations have been refined and extended to advance a wide range of human interests. Although many formal and informal rules are intentionally revised with the aim of more effectively undertaking preexisting and new tasks, many mistakes are made along the way. As the constitutional political economy literature makes clear, effective organisational design is a nontrivial task.

This chapter was written while a visiting fellow at the Max Planck Institute for Evolutionary Economics, whose support is gratefully acknowledged. The present version benefited from several helpful comments from Ulrich Witt, a reviewer, and conversations while at the institute with several of institute faculty, and comments received at annual meetings of the American and European public-choice societies in 2011.

Given the complexity of organisation design and the environments in which they operate, how do organisations sustain themselves in a changing world? Are they products of genius or survival? The simple answer is that both matter. Survival in a dynamic world requires constant adaptation. The adaptations that "work" tend to survive because the organisations using them do so as well. Both successes and failures are recognised by others and successful adaptations are copied and further refined.

This long process of trial and error has produced some obvious but neglected regularities in organisational design. These regularities and their contributions to organisational survival are the main focus of this chapter.

A major "output" of all organisations is rules, and these rules are chosen through processes that are themselves substantially rule bound. An organisation's internal rules help align the interests of team members with those of their organisation – which is often those of their formeteurs – but not all rules are equally effective in all environments. As a consequence, rules and procedures are revised from time to time, both in the day-to-day sense and in the quasi-constitutional sense by an organisation's "top decision makers," that is, by its government. By neglecting the creation and refinement of organisational rules, economic theories of economic and political organisations miss much that is important about the nature of existing organisations and dynamics of organisations. Indeed, the "governance" literature in economics is not about policy making by organisational governments but about internal systems of conditional reward and punishment.[1]

This chapter provides a general framework for understanding the founding and survival of organisations that sheds light on many of the core rules and procedures that most organisations rely upon. That

---

[1] Economists normally focus on the properties of particular reward and recruitment systems at a given moment in time or focus on the properties of spontaneous orders such as markets and political culture. Political scientists tend to focus on governmental organisations and neglect applications of their theories to nongovernmental organisations. The pool of existing organisations, services, and routines for making policy decisions are "given," rather than subjects of analysis. Organisational decision-making procedures are normally taken for granted. "Firms" maximise profits and "political parties" maximise votes or probability of electoral success. See, for example, Williamson's extensive work in this area (Williamson 1996, 2002). Vanberg (1992) provides rare exceptions to this mode of analysis.

organisations are founded by more or less rational formeteurs who confront many similar problems implies that there is much that can be deduced that tends to be true of all organisations: economic, political, religious, and recreational.[2] The common interests of formeteurs are reinforced in the long run by natural selection, which tends to weed out the least effective procedures for governance. As a consequence, contemporary organisations share many features, although a surprising number of these have been neglected by the economic literature on the nature of firms and other organisations[3] (Congleton 2007a, b).

The Origins, Governance, and Convergence of Organisational Rules

To begin with, organisations are normally founded by a small subset of their members. The person or persons who found organisations are called "formeteurs" in this chapter, and the other persons in their organisations are called team members. It is the formeteurs and the organisations that they create that solve the Olson (1965) problems of collective action for their team members.

That formal organisations are intentionally founded has a number of implications. For example, that organisations are founded by formeteurs, rather than team members, implies that organisations are designed to advance the purposes of formeteurs, rather than their members. Decision-making authority within an organisation tends to be initially distributed in a manner that maximises formeteur control over their new organisation. This is, of course, a type of governance familiar to economists as rule by an entrepreneur or committee of partners, and to political scientists as rule by a dictator or junta. However, in the long run, authority does not often remain so narrowly distributed.

In most cases, divided forms of governance tend to replace the initially authoritarian ones as organisations grow and marketlike shifts of authority take place. As developed later, it is often in the formeteurs' interest to trade and/or delegate some of their initial authority to others

---

[2] The arguments and models developed here extend and generalise those developed in part 1 of *Perfecting Parliament* (Congleton 2011). There is, of course, an extensive literature on governance and motivation in the management and law literatures. That literature is neglected here, although much of it is consistent with the analysis developed.

[3] There is, of course, a large literature on the evolution of institutions, and it arguably has gradually, but modestly, affected mainstream research. See, for example, Nelson and Winter (1982); Vanberg (1992); Witt (1998, 2006); and Wohlgemuth (2002) for a small sample of this literature.

in exchange for services and resources that advance their organisational interests. Contemporary economic organisations often raise capital by selling off voting rights, and medieval kings often traded parliamentary authority for new taxes. Indeed, the advantages of divided governance induce most formeteurs to adopt such institutions from the beginning in all but the smallest of organisations. These shifts of authority are not marked by physical transfers of resources, but rather by changes in the rules through which major and/or minor policy decisions are made – that is, through shifts of policy-making authority.

In mature organisations (and many new ones), policy-making authority is often shared by creating "external" boards of directors, who are elected or appointed by shareholders or other stakeholders in the organisation. For example, tribal governments often include a council of elders or the wise and a head of council or chief. Sharing authority in this manner improves the decisions reached, solves various transition problems associated with organisations that outlive their founders, and often brings additional resources to the organisation.

Organisations are not simply "clocks" that are wound up by formeteurs to run themselves after they are founded; rather, organisations require active management to modify an organisation's rule-governed practices as circumstances change. Although all organisations tend to be "rule bound," some flexibility is necessary to cope with dynamic social and natural settings. Well-designed (well-evolved) organisational governments provide that flexibility.

The Emergence of Rules for Conditional Rewards and Punishments

In order to understand the role that rules play in organisations, it is useful to show how a variety of rules can increase the productivity of an organisation. Two game matrices are presented in Table 8.1 to illustrate how rules can increase the output of a team. The game on the left is assumed to characterise the equilibrium of a preexisting or natural game. It has a relatively simple rule for sharing the teams' output, namely equal shares. The game on the right has a more sophisticated sharing rule that breaks the link between effort and reward in a manner that increases output. The game on the left may be thought of as production in a "natural cooperative" in which team members participate in a common venture (perhaps a hunt or harvest) and share the output produced. The game on the right may be thought of as one created by a formeteur who believes that alternative sharing rules could increase output and the formeteur's own income.

Table 8.1. *The shirking dilemma*

Game for natural cooperatives			Organisational solution		
Team member B			Team member B		
Work	Shirk	Exit (B)	Work	Shirk	Exit (B)
Work (A) 3, 3	1, 4	1.5, 1.5 Work (A)	R, R	R, P	1.5, 1.5
Shirk (A) 4, 1	2, 2	1.5, 1.5 Shirk (A)	P,R	P, P	1.5, 1.5
Exit (A) 1.5, 1.5	1.5, 1.5	1.5, 1.5 Exit (A)	1.5, 1.5	1.5, 1.5	1.5, 1.5

Note: The cell entries are utilities, the rank order of subjective payoffs for the team members (A, B).

Team members will naturally choose the organisation that maximises their own payoffs, which in some cases could be production alone.

The upper four cells of the left-hand game characterise the prisoner's dilemma (PD) game that emerges within organisations when rewards are uniform and unconditional. The payoffs illustrate a case in which team members will participate in the cooperative activities, rather than exit. In equilibrium, each participant receives more than he or she would obtain working alone ($2 > 1.5$). However, team members do not work as hard as required to maximise the cooperative's output. They "shirk," rather than "work." Nonetheless, the natural cooperative is viable, because it is more productive than working alone outside the organisation.

The fact that output is not maximised provides an opportunity for "formeteurs," whether inside or outside the initial cooperative. Such formeteurs may believe that production could be increased if sharing rules were modified. Team members in the "Organised Game" on the right have the same strategy sets as in the natural cooperative (work, shirk, exit), but they confront a conditional reward system that is designed to encourage "work" and to discourage "shirking." The formal reward system sets the conditional payoff for work at R and the conditional payoff associated with shirking at P. The members of the formal organisation will work to advance the organisational goals (work) if $R > P$. They will join the organisation if $R > 2$. (The payoffs include both the value of output shares and private value of leisure associated with various effort levels.)

The surplus requirements of formeteurs and the exit options of team members constrain the values of R and P that are compatible with organisational viability. Individuals join the new team only if R

is greater than 2; otherwise, they would be better off than at the natural cooperative.[4] The punishment system also affects decisions whether to join a formal organisation. If punishments are imposed in an arbitrary or inaccurate manner, potential team members may fear that they may occasionally receive P even when they are working hard, which reduces their average payoff from working.

Prospective team members are more likely to join and less likely to exit from an organisation if they believe that only "shirkers" will be punished. $R > 2$ is sufficient to discourage exit of productive team members only if the average level of rewards, including mistaken punishments, is greater at the new organisation than at the natural cooperative (adjusted for risk). Thus, the effective (just) enforcement of company rules can be as important as the rules themselves for the viability of organisations.

The sharing rules, however, cannot be completely stable unless all relevant features of the operating environment and goals of the organisation are also stable. In the initial setting illustrated earlier, the formeteur might pay team members $R = 2.1$ for work and $P = 1.6$ if they are found to be shirking. The team production equilibrium in this case is (work, work) and the organisation's total output is 6. The total cost of the reward system will be $2 \times 2.1 = 4.2$ and the organisational surplus is $6 - 4.2 = 1.8$ (minus a small amount for accurate monitoring of work effort). However, if team-member exit options improve from 2 to 2.5, a reward such as $R = 2.6$ becomes necessary and organisational surplus falls to $6 - 5.2 = 0.8$.[5]

---

[4] An interesting and somewhat counterintuitive property of this reward system is that it disconnects rewards from joint output. The reward in the organisational game is conditioned only on an individual team member's effort. Paying team members according to the marginal products indirectly links payment to the effort levels of fellow team members in a way that often encourages free riding rather than productive effort. An illustration of this effect for the Cobb-Douglas production function is developed in Congleton (1991).

[5] If one ignores exit options, severe punishments alone may be used to encourage "cooperation," if punishments are less expensive than rewards. Given an R sufficient for survival of the team member, any $P < R$ below that will induce cooperation. Evidently, the systems used to motivate slaves, who have very limited exit options, were centred on punishments, rather than rewards.

Fortunately, there are limits on a formeteur's ability to use penalties whenever team members are "volunteers," in the sense that they are free to exit and join other organisations or to work alone. In such cases, as illustrated earlier, the formeteur faces a prisoner's dilemma with exist (PDE) to solve, rather than PD problem. In the example, exit implies that the formeteur cannot have average payoffs below 2, given the existence of alternatives at the natural cooperative or below 1.5 without risking exit by some or all team members.

The organisational design sketched out here and used later rests on two assumptions. The first is that an organisation's formeteurs are able to create gamelike settings in which they determine the (subjective) payoffs for team members. In the illustration, they did so by creating rule-based rewards for working and shirking. The second is that formeteurs design their organisations with their own organisational objectives in mind.

These two assumptions, in turn, implicitly rest on others not focused on in this piece. For example, the assumption that a formeteur can create a game in which team members feel constrained to play by the rules implicitly assumes that formeteurs exercise control over the distribution of an organisation's output(s). This may be a matter of deference on the part of other team members, a product of the legal environment in which organisations are formed, or generated by the personal and physical traits of formeteurs. It also presumes that formeteurs can solve a variety of related problems, including ones associated with informational asymmetries to properly assign rewards and penalties.[6]

Composite Reward and Punishment Systems

Systems for recruiting, motivating, and compensating team members are often complex, because there are many combinations of pecuniary (output shares) and nonpecuniary rewards that will elicit the

---

[6] The assumption that formeteurs can affect subjective net payoffs, $U = R(B) - P(L)$, is equivalent to assuming that formeteurs can raise or lower objective benefit B and penalty L for their team members.

In some settings, the formeteur may do so by directly producing resources that can be used to affect R and P, as when praise and criticism can affect team members' welfare. In other cases, the formeteur may simply use the team's output as a source of rewards and punishments. In such cases, the formeteur's control over the team's output is itself a product of organisation. Formeteur control of team output in such cases may also be supported by widely accepted norms of deference to leaders or by other external sanctions, as provided by civil law.

It bears noting that I do not make the Hobbesian assumption about anarchy, as many do in this literature, which essentially rules out the formation of small teams in which organisational surplus can exist. In a setting without civil law, I assume that there are places where at least a few persons can escape from "the war of every man against every other." Here it bears noting that many animals have genetic predispositions to respect each other's territory, at least in the short run.

behaviour of interest (working). Formeteurs will adopt the combinations that they believe to be most cost-effective. These tend to vary with the economic environment in which the organisation operates, as noted earlier. The best specific methods also vary with the leadership skills and charisma of the formeteur(s), the pool of potential team members, cultural setting, and goals of the organisation, as developed later.

Reward systems are often this complex. Rewards in most organisations include praise, status, perks, and prizes in addition to pecuniary rewards (take-home salary, output shares). Here one may note the use of special badges, medals, and uniforms in military organisations to encourage extreme effort, sacrifice, and bravery. Nonpecuniary "perks" are also used to motivate team members of modern corporations and governments, where the relative size and location of offices, parking places, company cars, and titles are used to indicate position (status) and authority (importance). It is clear that punishments for shirking also tend to be multidimensional and may include disapproval, shame, fines, loss of perks, and banishment from the organisation.

Composite reward systems increase survivorship whenever they reduce incentive problems of team production at a lower cost than an entirely pecuniary system of rewards and punishments.[7] Survivorship, in turn, creates an evolving menu of reward systems from which most formeteurs make their selections. Every organisation can be said to be designed by their formeteur(s), but the designs tend to be chosen from preexisting templates that survived and advanced formeteur interests in the past.

That the same sorts of team-production problems are confronted by organisations with very different objectives allows formeteurs to benefit from a wide range of experience, most of which is not their own, when choosing a reward system. For example, businessmen may copy ideas from military and religious organisations by creating their own award ceremonies and medals of honour. Military and religious organisations may adopt organisational structures and compensation schemes (task assigning and output sharing rules) that have proven effective in economic enterprises.

---

[7] When an organisational culture is successful, it may indirectly affect the local external culture insofar as team members take their organisational norms home with them, apply them in other parts of life, and teach them to their children.

Minimising the cost of effective reward systems also implies that formeteurs (and their successors) will not create or enforce rules arbitrarily. Both formeteurs and team members benefit from rules that produce stable, predictable rewards and punishments. Insofar as evolution favours organisations with relatively larger organisational surpluses, evolution can thus be said to favour organisations with their own *internal rule of law*.[8]

Assembling the Best Team

The cost of motivating team members can also be reduced by recruiting members with predispositions that tend to make them effective team members. Persons with propensities for rule-following behaviour, an internal work ethic, promise keeping, and honesty are less likely to shirk than those with the opposite traits. In addition, some people have goals and norms that are "naturally" more aligned with the goals of a subset of organisations. Such persons are natural team players for those organisations, and weaker conditional rewards and penalties will be sufficient to fully align their interests with those of the organisation than of otherwise similar persons with different internalised norms or interests. (Volunteers, for example, may require only a bit of praise and encouragement to undertake strenuous tasks.)

Churches thus recruit believers, rather than atheists, for their organisational bureaucracies. Military organisations similarly recruit those who accept the necessity of violence in international relations, rather than pacifists. Governments normally prefer to recruit persons who signal loyalty to their organisations, rather than dissidents or persons from abroad. Commercial firms tend to hire those who have (or pretend to have) an interest in high incomes or are (or pretend to be) natural "team players," rather than stubborn antimaterialists and loners,

---

[8] If $U^e = f^*R(B) + (1 - f) P(B)$ is the expected net reward, where f is the probability of being wrongfully punished and B and L are objective rewards and penalties with subjective values, $R(B)$ and $P(L)$, respectively, then $f = 0$ allows average rewards (B) to be smaller than $f > 0$ whenever function u is strictly concave and monotone, increasing in control variable B and decreasing in L whenever team members have an exit option. To retain team members U^e *must exceed* X, the value of the exit option.

unless the latter have interests that are already well aligned with the organisation's objectives.[9]

There are evolutionary reasons to expect such persons to exist. For example, Congleton and Vanberg (1992, 2001) demonstrated that propensities to cooperate (conditionally) have survivorship value in environments where team production is productive and exit is possible. The evidence surveyed by Frey and Jegen (2001) suggests that increases in explicitly conditional forms of motivation tend to reduce (crowd out) self-motivation and so, surprisingly, may reduce productivity, rather than increase it.

After self-disciplined, self-motivated, simpatico team members, formeteurs will choose members who are easy to motivate because they have relatively large responses to punishments or rewards.

In general, easily motivated persons will be recruited over other, more skilful persons whose internalised norms or goals are less naturally aligned with organisational objectives, whenever the monitoring and motivational savings more than dominate their lower productivity. Skills directly associated with productivity clearly matter, as emphasised by educators and economists, but they are not always the most important type of human capital for determining a person's productivity on a given team.

Formeteurs and managers may also attempt to create stronger versions of local norms – an "internal organisational culture" – by encouraging loyalty, hard work, courage, and useful innovation. Awards might, for example, be given to persons who never miss a day of work, who are especially diligent, or whose service demonstrates exceptional loyalty to the organisation.[10]

The reward systems chosen by formeteurs tend to minimise the cost of the compensation provided to team members, but they have to be sufficient to attract and retain team members, to solve the team production problems, and to reward formeteurs for their efforts.

---

[9] Recruiting is partly a matter of the payoffs from team membership. For example, in Table 8.1 the punishment may be purposely set much higher than 2, so that persons who are "natural shirkers" (difficult to motivate) remain at the natural cooperative instead of joining the new organisation. This technique is feasible, however, only if team members believe that there is little chance of being wrongly punished.

[10] Congleton (1989, 1991) provides illustrations of how status games and an externally supported work ethic can increase output and productivity.

The Evolution and (Partial) Convergence of Internal Reward Systems

The first formeteurs had to imagine their entire reward systems, which consequently are likely to have been very simple ones based on physical "carrots," "sticks," family loyalty, and deference to authority figures. Later generations of formeteurs were able to observe the successes and failures of earlier ones, copy practices that work, and revise (slightly) those that did not work as well as they might have. It is only the successful systems of rules for reward and punishment that attract the attention of subsequent generations of formeteurs.

As time passes, the systems in place will reflect the experience and experiments of more and more formeteurs, whose organisations have advanced a wider and wider variety of goals in increasingly diverse circumstances. As a consequence, reward and recruiting systems tend to become more effective and robust through time in the sense that they increase organisational surplus and better solve team production problems in a wide variety of circumstances.

The use of proven "off the shelf" reward and recruiting systems allows formeteurs to form new organisations more rapidly with fewer risks and to focus more of their attention on other issues that affect the viability of their organisation. Using a preexisting template for their reward and recruiting systems tends to reduce hiring, training, and agency costs over "whole cloth" creation of new reward systems.

Causal observation and a wide reading in the history of governments and organisations suggest that the result tends to be increasingly fine-grained and rule-driven compensation schemes that generally tend to resemble one another.[11] Full convergence does not occur, however, because practices vary to some degree with formeteur foresight and the circumstances, local culture, and aims of the organisation.

Why Durable Organisations Need and Have a Government

If circumstances inside and outside organisations were entirely stable, it is possible that a perfectly adapted reward and recruiting system

---

[11] An example of fine-grained evolution of reward or sharing rules is provided in Bailey (1992), who reviews the complex methods of sharing and control used by North American aborigines, which he refers to as property rights, evidently because of their stability.

would eventually emerge. Such a system would simply be left in place to "run" without active monitoring and review by an organisational government. In such cases, the ones implicitly modelled by most economists, durable organisations would be rule-governed "perpetual clocks" that run themselves.

However, circumstances are never completely stable or predictable. Because no reward or recruiting system works equally well in all circumstances, organisations benefit from being able to adapt to changes in circumstances – that is, from appropriately modifying their internal rules. Indeed, this is necessary if they are to survive in the long run. Clearly, a fishing club that continues fishing at the same pond after most of the fish are gone would disappear as its members starve or leave for clubs that catch more fish. Similarly, a firm that remains focused entirely on products that became obsolete because of technological change (buggy whips, ice boxes, record players, slide rules, and rotary phones) tend to disintegrate as members leave to find employment at firms with higher wages, whether in kind or cash. And a national government that continued to use the last century's best defence measures, might well be annexed by its neighbours because of its inability to effectively repel or resist invasions.

To adapt to changing circumstances, an organisation must have routines for recognising new circumstances and for revising its objectives, conditional rewards, and recruiting system. Specialisation can increase the reliability of this process. A standing group of persons – its government – might be tasked with gathering information, evaluating alternatives, and making policy decisions (or recommendations). Because their decisions matter, evolutionary pressures also matter. The least effective systems of governance tend to disappear, leaving a menu of alternative governmental templates that work reasonably well, in the sense that the standing decision-making process increases the organisation's risk-adjusted organisational. As with reward systems, the similarity of problems faced by organisations induce considerable convergence among the types of governing bodies adopted, although not complete convergence. One such template is extraordinarily commonplace.

A very broad range of organisational governments have been and continue to be drawn from the "king and council" template. This is evidently because that architecture solves a variety of common governance problems. The king and council template divides policy-making authority between a king (a chief executive officer, chief, king, president, etc.) with a council (board of directors, council of wise men, cabinet, parliament, etc.). It is used by armies (commanding general and council of war), by religious organisations (pope and council of cardinals), by modern corporations (chief executive officer and board of directors), by aboriginal governments (chief and council of wise men), and by contemporary democratic governments (president or prime minister and congress or parliament).

The next four subsections of this chapter argue that the king and council template for governance solves a number of organisational governance problems. The analysis begins by pointing out the informational advantages of this system of governance, and then discusses how it can be used to solve other medium- and long-term problems.

Formeteur Rule, the Need for Advice, and the Dictator's Dilemma

Perhaps the most "natural" form of organisational governance is the one implicitly assumed by most economists and political theorists. Formeteurs may simply retain their initial authority to make and revise all major policy decisions within their organisations. If a single individual forms a new organisation, he or she may retain complete control over his or her new organisation. In cases in which a small group of formeteurs founds an organisation, a ruling committee or council of partners may retain control over their organisation's policies.

Such "authoritarian" decision-making procedures have many advantages for formeteurs and their organisations. Formeteurs know their own goals better than others and are likely to have leadership skills that allow them to form and motivate groups at lower costs than others. Formeteurs often have a superior understanding of organisational possibilities, which partially explains their initial investment of time and attention to assembling a team and devising methods to advance particular goals.

However, in practice, as organisations increase in size or cope with more complex circumstances, authority for standing policies tends to be more widely distributed. For example, informational, resource, and design problems become more complex. New team members and tasks may be added and others eliminated or merged into others. The external circumstances may change in unpredictable ways and require the organisation's goals and/or conditional reward system to be revised. Exit options for some team members may rise while others fall. More monitoring and refinement of team member performance and responsibilities may become necessary.

To assist in gathering information and evaluating alternatives, a formeteur will often find it useful to assemble a team of "advisors," who specialise in monitoring and other informational tasks. Unfortunately for formeteurs, a team of advisors does not automatically improve their ability to make organisational decisions.

Authoritarian governments confront what Wintrobe (2000) calls the "dictator's dilemma." It is often in the interest of "advisors" to simply tell the formeteurs what they want and expect to hear, especially when the rulers have complete control over organisational rewards. In such cases, an in-house council of advisors would not add much to an authoritarian organisational government's stock of information or improve its decisions. Indeed, it may worsen those decisions by inducing the formeteur to underestimate risks (to be overconfident).

As true of other positions within organisations, leadership positions also benefit from effective recruiting and rewards systems. Thus, many of the conclusions reached about reward systems for "ordinary" team production also apply to the "leadership" teams with responsibility for making organisation-wide policy decisions. The recruiting process will take account of both managerial talent and the ease with which such persons can be motivated to "work," rather than "shirk," at their positions in the organisational government. Reward systems will normally combine pecuniary and nonpecuniary rewards. Reducing the dictator's informational dilemma requires a system of conditional rewards that motivates effective "advice production."

There are, however, a number of differences between organisational governments (leadership teams) and ordinary production teams within an organisation. One obvious distinction is that the "output" of the leadership team is largely the rules that characterise the organisation itself, rather than a service or product to be sold or an idea to be disseminated to outsiders. Addressing the problems of governance thus involve fine-tuning the standing procedures of governance, in addition to the usual incentivising and recruiting systems.

Delegating Policy-Making Authority

It bears noting that advisory committees will have both direct and indirect influence over the policy decisions of the organisation. They often provide a list of alternatives and provide preliminary (or final) assessments of the relative merits of those options. As a consequence, the mere adoption of an advisory committee implies some division of policy-making authority.

A variety of methods can be used to determine the most relevant alternatives and to estimate their relative merits. For example, advisory committees may use majority rule to make their policy recommendations or to produce "consensus" recommendations. Under majority rule, median voter outcomes tend to emerge, and in the context of an advisory committee, the median member's advice can be thought of as a median estimator. Median estimators tend to be relatively robust and unbiased estimators. (Condorcet's well-known jury theorem relies implicitly on the estimation properties of median estimators, see Congleton 2007a.) Consensus forecasts, in contrast, tend to place greater emphasis on extremal opinions, insofar as each member of the advisory team has veto power over alternatives and estimates of their relative merits. Policy recommendations for which even the worst-case expectation is better than the status quo are very likely to be improvements.

To motivate the committee, it is often useful to explicitly delegate some decision-making authority to them. They may, for example, be granted explicit agenda control – the authority to make policy recommendations to the formeteur(s). This makes the committee partly responsible for the result, which makes it easier to punish mistakes and reward insightful decisions. Besides improving the quality of decisions, delegating some policy-making authority to advisory committees benefits formeteur(s) by freeing time and attention for other purposes, such as long-run planning, leisure, or forming new organisations.

The advantages of specialisation and team production are also sufficient for divided forms of the king and council template to emerge when small groups of formeteurs found an organisation. Similar, but slightly different, informational advantages can induce councils of formeteurs (partnerships) to employ "kings" (chief executive or chief operating officer) and to delegate some authority to them.

A formeteur team has a variety of informational advantages over a single formeteur insofar as they can pool information and average their individual estimates to create an accurate consensus forecast. However, members of the council may free-ride on monitoring, research, and analysis. They receive only part of the benefits from better management and decisions and bear all the cost of their own efforts to improve organisational outcomes.

To encourage useful advice, especially concerning day-to-day operations, founding partners may hire a chief executive officer and delegate to that officeholder the authority to make a subset of day-to-day operational decisions and to mete out punishments and rewards to other team members. A properly incentivised CEO or COO can improve day-to-day policy making by improving operating decisions. CEOs will be recruited for both their skills as managers and the ease with which their interests can be aligned with those of the formeteur team. Delegation again improves results and frees time for the partners to focus on long-term strategy and other matters of personal interest.

Informational advantages alone provide a sufficient rationale for "kings" to have "councils" and for "councils" to have "kings." However, that is not the only advantage that this template for governance provides.

On the Value Added by Flexible Forms of Governance

When formeteurs adopt governance, recruiting, and reward templates from other organisations, they are implicitly acknowledging their limits as organisational designers. Many of the functional aspects of their organisations remain unknown and unanalysed, in part because of limits in time and attention and in part because of lack of training and ability. This implies that some aspects of a formeteur's organisation will be "spontaneous" in the sense that, although they anticipate "good" results, they do not fully understand the economic, psychological, and social effects of their systems that produce those results.

Acknowledging the unanalysed and poorly understood aspects of reward and recruiting systems implies that there are risks to experimenting with the templates adopted. If the various components of reward systems are not entirely independent of one another, adjusting even one parameter in a plausible manner may produce unexpected results. There are good reasons to "leave well enough alone" in a setting in which choices are not fully informed. This "rational institutional conservatism" tends to increase both the convergence of organisational systems and their stability.

The problems of organisational governance tend to be more similar than the specific production problems of teams, so governing institutions tend to be more similar than team production methods. All organisations need to collect information and to accurately assess internal and external opportunities and risks. All organisations need to determine which possible responses will advance organisational and/or formeteur goals at an acceptable risk.

Nonetheless, as in other aspects of organisational design, the procedures of governance may need adjustment from time to time as circumstances change; that is, durable organisations normally have amendment procedures. It is this that allows organisational governance an evolutionary character at both the level of a single organisation and as a social phenomenon. Modifications of an organisational government are not simply a consequence of blind trial and error but the results of a reform, although the actual results may not be fully anticipated results. Insofar as modifications to a system of governance are more difficult to reverse than many other changes, more caution is naturally called for.

Together, the advantages of flexibility and stability and limits of organisational knowledge imply that reforms will tend to be relatively "small" but discrete amendments to existing procedures in which most procedures and rewards are little affected. Here one may note that the basic technologies and organisational strategies for vegetable sellers and churches are often stable for hundreds of years at a time. A similar stability is evident in the most common general templates for governance, although the division and extent of authority within those templates are modestly adjusted through time (especially at points of succession). The best response to a new circumstance is often to slightly alter the decision-making procedures of the organisation or the distribution of decision-making authority.

The reform of governance requires that assignments of responsibilities and the decision process be incrementally adjustable. The decision-making procedures should also be robust in the sense that the departure of a small group of decision makers does not undermine the effectiveness of the organisation's government. In proprietorships, this is not always the case, and small- and medium-sized businesses often fail or are sold off when their founders retire.

The template allows a continuum of adjustments in decision-making procedures and domains of responsibility between the king and council, as, for example, with various voting rules within the advisory council (council of directors) and between the council and the CEO. Selection methods for the various posts can also be revised incrementally.

Overall the "king and council" template provides such an adjustable and robust template for governance. Again evolution (survivorship) will play a role in the most common assignments of authority and decision-making processes. The least effective divisions will tend to disappear from the menu of alternatives readily available to formeteurs and their successors.

Internal and External Markets for Authority

The term "power," or policy-making authority, is normally used as if authority is single-dimensional, in which case reallocations of authority that make all or most parties better off are impossible. However, if authority is multidimensional, then it can be traded in essentially the same manner as ordinary goods and services. Such quasiconstitutional exchanges are possible because the preexisting distribution of policy-making authority creates political property rights that can be bought and sold, much like control over ordinary goods and services.[12] For example, as noted earlier, granting some policy-making authority to an advisory council or CEO can be used to both compensate and motivate officeholders. That is to say, authority may substitute for or complement other forms of compensation.

Constitutional Gains to Trade

Table 8.2 illustrates one of many patterns of risk and reward that can induce authority-sharing agreements. The initial state is the one characterised by the upper left-hand cell in which a resource of interest to the formeteur(s) is entirely controlled by a nonteam member. The organisation's leadership is better off if it obtains complete control over that person's or group's resources than if it obtains shared or no control (14 > 12 > 10). The prospective team member is better off with shared control than with complete or no control. Retaining

---

[12] Congleton (2013) points out that the exchange of goods in ordinary private markets can be thought of as changes in the distribution of authority. When person A trades person B some apples for oranges, A gives up his authority over apples in exchange for new authority over oranges, and B receives new authority over apples in exchange for giving up authority over oranges.

Table 8.2. *Mutual gains from sharing authority*

		Organisational leadership		
		No authority	Shared authority	Complete authority
Owner of useful resource	Complete authority	8, 10	–	–
	Shared authority	–	10, 12	–
	No authority	–	–	6, 14

complete control requires sacrificing advantages from team production, whereas giving up complete control places his or her resources at greater risk than under shared control (10 > 8 > 6).

In cases like the one illustrated here, there are potential gains to trade, and realising them requires sharing policy-making authority with a particular subdomain of each organisation's activities.

Such authority-sharing regimes help to mitigate risks associated with even temporary transfers of control over a resource, while extending opportunities for each organisation. For example, teams of cherry pickers who are especially adept at climbing trees or own ladders may fear that their talents or ladders will be abused by the other organisation's leadership. Such persons and their ladders may always be assigned to the most dangerous trees. They would be more willing to participate in a coordinated annual harvest if they had some veto authority over the trees to which they are assigned. Their risks (broken legs and ladders) are reduced by limited veto power over the use of their ladders and/or assignments to particular treetops.

Similarly, a regional government that confronts an external threat from pirates or neighbouring navies may benefit from the use of commercial ships in defence of their territory. The owners of commercial ships may expect to benefit from that defence but may be unwilling to allow their ships to be under the command of the regional government. They might fear that the government would assign their ships to the most dangerous missions, while holding the government's own ships in reserve. Granting the commercial ship owners some authority to veto or at least influence how their ships will be used may make them more willing to allow their ships to be used for regional defence, benefiting both the kingdom and the ship owners.

Entrepreneurs of commercial organisations engage in similar transactions when they sell shares of stock (as in an initial public offering) to investors, who provide capital in exchange for claims against future profits and some control (voting rights) over major firm decisions. The capital investment is at risk to poor business decisions, yet properly employed could increase investor profits. To obtain a share of those additional profits, a firm's formeteurs often voluntarily transfer some (but not all) authority to shareholders or to a council elected by the new shareholders (board of directors). How much authority is transferred depends partly on risk assessments of capital owners, which determine their demand for control, and formeteur assessment of the cost of reduced control. For relatively larger infusions of capital, more control is normally given up. Major capital providers may be offered seats on the board of directors or special voting rights on policy issues involving dividends or senior appointments.[13]

It bears noting that threats of violence are not necessary for shifts of authority (power) to take place. For economists, this should be obvious, as ordinary market exchange also involves shifts of authority. When A trades money to obtain apples from B, A gives up authority over money in exchange for authority over apples. B does the reverse.

The King and Council Template Can Be Used to Reduce Unproductive Conflict

A related but somewhat different form of constitutional exchange may occur in settings in which two or more parties struggle to control a given resource. Table 8.3 illustrates a contest that may be said to

---

[13] In medieval and early modern Europe, kings engaged in similar constitutional bargains when they traded policy-making authority to towns or regional governments in exchange for new tax revenues Authority could also be "repurchased" from the council by trading royal lands for additional authority over particular areas of policy or territories.

Other transactions involved the balance of authority between the king and council. For example, in some cases a seat in parliament or elevation to the nobility might be traded for support on public policy decisions of interest. In other cases, kings granted parliament new authority in exchange for support on important issues and new tax authority (Congleton 2011: Part II).

Table 8.3. *Asymmetric conflict*

	Stronger party		
Weaker party	Little aggression	Moderate aggression	Intense aggression
Little resistance	6, 14	3, 16	0, 18
Moderate resistance	7, 10	4, 12	1, 14
Intense resistance	8, 8	5, 10	2, 12

waste resources because the joint payoffs fall as conflict intensifies. The Nash equilibrium produces lower payoffs than would have been the case with less intense conflict. Conflict often reduces the extent to which the contested resources can be used for other, more productive purposes. As in the previous cases, unrealised potential gains can be realised through improved institutional design.

One possible solution to external conflict and internal rent-seeking problems is to induce shifts to a less resource-intensive method of collective choice. For example, replacing "uncivil" with "civil" procedures tends to reduce the extent to which resources are consumed by the process of conflict and so can be an effective way to reduce losses. The king and council template can be used for this purpose, because it provides a broad range of possible divisions of authority.

Within markets, mergers often include provisions for power sharing after joint control is established. Shares and voting rights are defined and distributed among the existing shareholders; senior posts in the new organisational government are also typically shared. Similar gains from sharing authority exist when communities decide to merge their governments to realise economies of scale, diversify risks, or reduce transaction costs. In such cases, sharing policy-making authority allows the interests of the merging organisations or communities to be protected against rent extraction by the other, while the additional joint output or reduced risks make governmental officeholders and residents better off.

In cases in which more than two parties are involved, the king and council template also allows policy-making authority to be reallocated between the king and council and within the council in a manner that potentially replicates the expected payoff ratios of an uncertain military or political contest, while reducing the extent of the resources consumed by conflict.[14]

All this is not to say that authority is never concentrated in the hands of a single person but that many situations exist in which power can be (and is) voluntarily transferred from one party to another where the final assignment of authority reflects mutual gains from trade in the circumstances at hand.

Succession and the King and Council Template

Because durable organisations outlive their founders and effective governance contributes to an organisation's survival, a systematic method for replacing successive generations of leaders tends to increase an organisation's long-run survival prospects.

The king and council template provides a number of possible procedures for successive generations of policy makers to be replaced and also reduces the probability that governance will be totally disrupted by the unexpected departure or death of a member of government. It is unlikely that both the king and the council will simultaneously disappear in an unexpected manner, although the king or individual members of the council may do so.

Replacements for the king may be selected by the council, and other procedures for replacement may be monitored by them. Similarly, council members can be replaced by the king and/or surviving council members. Such choices tend to be fairly good ones, because both CEOs and surviving council members normally have the long-term interests of the organisation in mind and are relatively well informed about the qualities that contribute to good decision making at the council and executive levels.

To facilitate this process of selection, productive forms of competition for seats in the organisation's government can be encouraged. Council seats may, for example, be reserved for persons who have provided extraordinary service to the organisation, community, or kingdom. Challenging examinations on matters relevant for

---

[14] The various power indices demonstrate how dividing up the authority within an active board of directors or community government can do so. See Leech (2002) for an overview of the properties and assumptions behind these indices of the probability of membership in majority coalitions.

councillor or royal duties can also be contrived. Elections for office among an informed electorate may be conducted.[15]

In large organisations, competition for higher positions in a hierarchical structure can also be used to assess loyalty and demonstrate talent for making policy decisions by inducing productive forms of competition among persons for promotion to higher ones. Such assessment procedures create contests that serve as indirect "auctions" for future seats at higher levels of organisational governance, which allows the current generation of government officials to extract surplus (rents) from the next one.[16]

Such extractive contests indirectly reinforce the current generation of officeholders' interest in their organisation's long-term success. The better the future prospects appear to be, the more the next generation of leaders will be willing to "pay" (sacrifice) for leadership posts in the future.

Other institutional solutions are necessary if it is not possible to constrain rivals for high office to "play by the rules" or align the interests of senior staff with those of the organisation.[17] For example, to reduce unproductive conflict, some or all of the top positions in government may be assigned through some mechanical mechanism, as for example by lottery or inheritance. To mitigate risks from such procedures, various eligibility requirements or veto possibilities might be introduced. For example, the persons holding positions in the council or as king may be able to pass their positions along to their children (hereditary succession), unless this is vetoed by a supermajority of council members (and/or the king). Such compound systems reduce conflict by

---

[15] Unfortunately, it is often difficult to encourage all rivals for high office to play by the rules devised. Such problems can be reduced by imposing severe punishments on those that violate the rules of successional contests.

[16] Note that the king and council templates are scalable and can be used hierarchically. In divided hierarchical organisations, many centres of policy-making authority may exist, with some able to countermand the decisions of others and/or to appoint a subset of its members. This creates a hierarchical division of authority, which can itself be adjusted through bargaining. Intra-organisational polycentrism can improve decision making in large organisations for several reasons, including informational ones that improve responses to unanticipated problems.

[17] See Hillman and Katz (1987) for a model of conflict within an organisation over its surplus. They demonstrate that, in the limit, the entire surplus may be consumed by conflict over it. Congleton (1984) suggests that the use of committees and sharing rules can reduce those losses.

reducing the number of potential successors and protecting against negative genetic shocks and other forms of bad luck.

The Long-Term Evolution of Organisational Governance

There are both internal and external "markets for authority," and both these markets have effects on the balance of authority within a given organisation in both the short and the long run. For example, a new, especially talented team member may bargain for greater authority than usually held by persons in a given position. A technological innovation may reduce the relative importance of a particular area of production or distribution and lead to reforms that reduce their influence over policy. A corporation's stock may be bought up to replace the officials holding seats of authority or to change the existing balance of authority (Manne 1965).

External shocks can affect organisational governance and future policies through differential effects on what might be called the excess demand and supply of authority (Congleton 2007a, 2011). Such "demand shocks" may occur in a more or less uniformly distributed manner, in which case, policy-making authority would tend to follow a random walk, with the initial point determined by the formeteur(s) and their objectives. If the distribution of authority does not substantially affect the magnitude or variance of organisational surplus, a wide variety of organisational governments based on the king and council could emerge through time and be implemented in an approximately efficient organisational surplus-maximising manner.

A single organisation could experience periods as a sole proprietorship, a partnership, a shareholder-dominated firm, or even a cooperative, as adjustments to the preexisting template are negotiated and agreed to by the parties or centres of authority involved in response to external demand shocks, input price shocks, etc. Existential crises such as those created by threats of violence or natural disasters are not prerequisites to constitutional bargaining, although such events can also induce constitutional bargaining and exchange.

If some objectives are more effectively advanced in a given environment with a particular balance of authority, governance of the distribution of organisational governments that survive would tend to converge to that balance or be eliminated through competition with organisations with more effective governors. The menus confronted by subsequent formeteurs would tend to narrow, probably more so than it would in a dynamic environment. In stable settings, the balance of authority would also tend to be stable and clustered around the most efficient ones (from the perspective of formeteur interests), as both formeteur choices and survivorship converge toward best-known practices.

It bears noting that many of the adjustments that take place in dynamic settings – not simply intertemporal settings, but ones in which significant uncertainties exist – are often invisible to outsiders. Both shifts in authority and their effects are often small and subtle. The effects of shifts in authority between the king and the council are most evident when the king and the council represent different intra- or extra-organisational interests, and with the advantage of hindsight. A series of minor reforms can greatly alter the balance of authority within a given organisation.

For example, within a commercial enterprise, greater representation of shareholder interests on boards of directors may lead to higher dividends or lower salaries for organisational leaders. Greater representation of engineers may lead to higher capital investments, greater representation of marketing experts may induce larger investments in advertising campaigns and product styling, and greater representation of labour interests may produce shorter work days or more holidays. Overall, the flexibility of the king and council template, recruiting procedures, and conditional reward systems provide a good deal of potential for evolution and adaptation within a single general framework of organizational governance.

Conclusions

This chapter provides a general framework for describing and analysing the evolution of organisational governments. In general, it suggests that organisations have been systematically improving through time as the procedures for governance have been revised to cope with new circumstances. This process is substantially experimental. Not all experiments are successful ones, so differences in institutional efficiency will exist at every moment, although the general trend is toward greater efficiency in the sense that formeteur interests tend to be more and more effectively advanced by their organisations. Many, perhaps most, innovations in organisational governance have been modifications of various implementations of the king and council template.

The analysis has developed several general predictions about the kinds of organisations, governance institutions, and institutional adjustments that are observed. Many of these will appear to be common sense, although most are missing from mainstream economic analysis of organisations. It suggests that (1) most organisations are founded by small groups of formeteurs. (2) The common interests and problems of formeteurs imply that the templates for organisational governance share a number of properties, a subset of which have been identified and analysed in this chapter.

(3) Every durable organisation will have a body of internal procedures for making policy decisions that serves as its charter or constitution for governance. (4) The standing rules normally specify the officeholders who participate in major decisions and the manner in which those officials interact to make decisions, as with voting rules. (5) The latter may include specific architectures for policy making that group and/or assign tasks to centres of authority. (6) The standing procedures of long-lived organisations include rules governing selection and succession of officeholders and (7) formal and informal procedures for modifying the organisation's charter. (8) The governmental templates that attract formeteur adoption collect and use information relatively efficiently and (9) produce decisions that increase the viability of their organisation, while advancing their organisational interests.

(10) The founding charters (constitutions) of organisations favour formeteur interests, because formeteurs draft their organisation's founding documents and the organisations are founded to advance formeteur interests. (11) Improvements tend to concentrate organisational surplus in the hands of governmental leaders, especially formeteurs. (12) The evolution of organisational structures also tends to favour formeteurs, rather than employees or shareholders, which explains the reward structures of many large contemporary economic enterprises in which senior executives (its government) realise very high salaries relative to other team members.

(13) Governance, reward, and recruiting systems tend to converge, insofar as the same "best practices" can be applied by a variety of organisations. For example, similar reward structures have often been associated with governments and religious organisations.

(14) The salary predictions of this theory are rarely the same as those associated with marginal productivity theory, namely in cases in which exit costs are trivial and members are narrowly interested in pecuniary

rewards. (15) In all other cases, team-member salaries will reflect bargaining ability and exit options, with marginal productivity as the upper bound for team member compensation rather than its expected value. Equally productive persons with different exit costs are predicted to receive different salaries. (16) The analysis predicts that salaries normally consist of mixtures of pecuniary and nonpecuniary rewards rather than cash payments alone. (17) Organisations will both encourage internal norms and make use of persons who have internalised norms that make them more productive team members, because doing so can reduce the wage bill for the organisation of interest.

(18) The marginal product of formeteurs is largely organisational. However, choosing goals and creating an organisation often requires innovation, insight, and risk taking as in the theories of entrepreneurship developed by Knight (1921), Schumpeter (1934), Williamson (1967), and Kirzner (1978). Organisations are founded with purposes, often economic ones, that partially determine their success. However, it is the formeteur's governance skills that contribute the most to longterm success. Teams of innovators, speculators, and product designers are productive only if their various motivational and informational problems have been solved. Edison, Ford, Jobs, Gates, and Page would be unknown tinkerers and programmers were it not for the efficient organisations that they created to develop and sell their products.

(19) Most formeteurs will acknowledge their limits as institutional innovators and so use preexisting templates for governance that include provisions for revising the standing procedures of governance as problems and opportunities are recognised. (20) In all but the smallest of organisations, the "king and council template" for governance is likely to be used for choosing and refining policies, because it addresses a variety of short-, medium-, and long-term governance problems. (21) The division of authority within a given implementation of the king and council template will be adjusted in the long run in response to changes in internal and external conditions.

(22) As in other aspects of organisational design, formeteurs choose their organisation's formal governance and amendment procedures with their own interests in mind. (23) Organisational governance thus tends to be rule based, rather than arbitrary and capricious. An organisation's system of governance and its reward system tend to be stable and predictable because organisations tend to make better decisions and be better able to retain and train their teams.

(24) Gains from experimentation and constitutional exchange emerge from time to time, and the amendment procedures that allow such gains to be realised tend to produce more robust organisations in the long run. (25) Constitutional exchange takes place when particular changes in the distribution of authority advance the interests of office-holders with the authority to amend their organisational charter. Shifts in the long-term interests of organisational leaders and technologies of production have to be accounted for; adjustments to a variety of standing procedures of governance may be required to take advantage of new more or less permanent conditions. (26) Insofar as small reforms are easier to assess and implement than large reforms, both institutional refinements and amendment procedures tend to favour "piece-wise" reforms that address particular problems, rather than "reinventing" the entire organisation. Such modest reforms preserve advantages associated with stable procedures and help to avoid unforeseen costs generated by experimental failures. They also increase the predictability of reward and recruiting systems, which tends to reduce the cost of those systems and increase organisational surplus.

(27) That most formeteurs rely upon templates that have produced successful organisations in the past implies that much about the design and functioning of organisations is a product of evolution, rather than careful analysis by the formeteurs themselves. (28) Pressures to adopt best practices vary among organisations in the short run, as the natural conservatism of successors tends to favour continuation of existing routines over innovation. (29) However, survivorship pressures in the long run tend to induce reforms that increase organisational surplus; thus, all the organisational systems (governance, compensation, and recruiting) tend to improve through time. (30) Economic enterprises thus tend to maximise profits, partly because this is the intent of most of their founders and partly because the institutions of economic organisations have evolved to facilitate this objective.

References

Bailey, M. J. 1992. Approximate Optimality of Aboriginal Property Rights. *Journal of Law and Economics*, 35, 183–198.
Congleton, R. D. 1984. Committees and Rent-Seeking Effort. *Journal of Public Economics*, 25, 197–209.

1989. Efficient Status Seeking: Externalities, and the Evolution of Status Games. *Journal of Economic Behavior and Organization*, 11, 175–190.

1991. The Economic Role of a Work Ethic. *Journal of Economic Behavior and Organization*, 15, 365–385.

2007a. From Royal to Parliamentary Rule without Revolution: The Economics of Constitutional Exchange within Divided Governments. *European Journal of Political Economy*, 23, 261–284.

2007b. Informational Limits to Democratic Public Policy: The Jury Theorem, Yardstick Competition, and Ignorance. *Public Choice*, 132, 333–352.

2011. *Perfecting Parliament: Constitutional Reform, Liberalism, and the Rise of Western Democracy.* Cambridge: Cambridge University Press.

2013. On the Inevitability of Divided Government and Improbability of a Complete Separation of Powers. *Constitutional Political Economy*, 24, 177–198.

Congleton, R. D. and Vanberg, V. J. 2001. Help, Harm or Avoid? On the Personal Advantage of Dispositions to Cooperate and Punish in Multilateral PD Games with Exit. *Journal of Economic Behavior and Organization*, 44, 145–167.

Frey, B. S. and Jegen, R. 2001. Motivation Crowding Theory. *Journal of Economic Surveys*, 15, 589–611.

Hillman, A. L. and Katz, E. 1987. Hierarchical Structure and the Social Costs of Bribes and Transfers. *Journal of Public Economics*, 34, 129–142.

Kirzner, I. M. 1978. *Competition and Entrepreneurship.* Chicago: University of Chicago Press.

Knight, F. H. 1921. *Risk, Uncertainty and Profit.* Boston: Houghton Mifflin.

Leech, D. 2002. An Empirical Comparison of the Performance of Classical Power Indices. *Political Studies*, 50, 1–22.

Manne, H. G. 1965. Merges and the Market for Corporate Control. *Journal of Political Economy*, 73, 110–120.

Nelson, R. R. and Winter, S. G. 1982. *An Evolutionary Theory of Economic Change.* Cambridge, MA: Harvard University Press.

Olson, M. 1965. *The Logic of Collective Action: Public Goods and the Theory of Groups.* Cambridge, MA: Harvard University Press.

Schumpeter, J. A. 1934. *The Theory of Economic Development: An Inquiry into Profits, Capital, Credit, Interest, and the Business Cycle.* Cambridge, MA: Harvard University Press.

Vanberg, V. J. 1992. Organizations as Constitutional Systems. *Constitutional Political Economy*, 3, 223–253.

Vanberg, V. J. and Congleton, R. D. 1992. Rationality, Morality, and Exit. *The American Political Science Review*, 86, 418–431.

Williamson, O. 1967. Hierarchical Control and Optimal Firm Size. *Journal of Political Economy* 75, 123–138.

Williamson, O. E. 1996. *The Mechanisms of Governance.* New York: Oxford University Press.

2002. The Theory of the Firm as Governance Structure: From Choice to Contract. *The Journal of Economic Perspectives,* 16, 171–195.

Wintrobe, R. 2000. *The Political Economy of Dictatorship.* Cambridge, UK: Cambridge University Press.

Witt, U. 1998. Imagination and Leadership – The Neglected Dimension of an Evolutionary Theory of the Firm. *Journal of Economic Behavior and Organization,* 35, 161–177.

2006. *The Evolving Economy: Essays on the Evolutionary Approach to Economics.* Cheltenham: Edward Elgar.

Wohlgemuth, M. 2002. Evolutionary Approaches to Politics. *Kyklos,* 55, 223–246.

9 | *Strategic Interaction and Externalities*
FD-Games and Pollution

REINOUD JOOSTEN

Introduction

We study a(n environmental) social trap, that is, a social dilemma resulting from strategic interaction which may induce negative externalities over time. Dawes (1980) states that two properties define a social dilemma: (a) each individual receives a higher payoff for a socially defective choice than for a socially cooperative choice, no matter what other individuals in society do, and (b) all individuals are better off if all cooperate than if all defect. In a social trap, certain behavior leads to small positive outcomes, which are immediate, and large negative delayed outcomes (e.g., Hamburger (1973); Platt (1973); Liebrand (1983); Komorita & Parks (1994)).

Inspired by Aumann (2008), we engineer 'Bathroom Games', describing stylized externality problems by pollution in a minimally sized society of two players. Each has two actions, 'to clean up' or 'not to clean up', at each stage. The latter action payoff dominates the former for both, that is, it gives a strictly higher immediate payoff (utility) to either player, regardless of the choice made by the opponent and the state of the bathroom. There also exists, however, strategic interaction on a different time-scale, through externalities which become evident after some time. The less often the bathroom is cleaned up, the lower the stage payoffs (utilities). An essential feature is that cleaning up becomes more burdensome relative to not cleaning up the more polluted the bathroom is. The reason why this may occur is that the disutilities (e.g., costs) of cleaning up increase in the presence of more pollution, but also emotional factors such as disgust, indignation or irritation[1] may decrease utilities.

I thank Ulrich Witt, Werner Güth and Georg von Wangenheim for suggestions. Comments of an anonymous referee helped considerably to improve and focus the material.
[1] With the term *bathroom* we invoke an image of a real-life situation in which cleaning up other people's pollution would be rather revolting.

Bathroom Games are metaphors for real-life situations where divergence of stage payoffs in favor of precisely the action causing the social trap occurs. We briefly mention two such settings: shallow lakes and fisheries. In one version of shallow lakes problems, nutrients from fertilizers, which could have been prevented from reaching a lake or could have been removed from it at moderate costs, accumulate gradually in its sediments. This may after some time with only minor effects on the lake's condition, suddenly lead to an environmental catastrophe reducing stage payoffs significantly and quickly (e.g., Scheffer 1998; Carpenter, Ludwig, & Brock 1999; Scheffer et al. 2001; Mäler, Xepapadeas, & De Zeeuw 2003). Cleaning up after the nutrients have settled down in the sediments must be considered very costly, and the subsequent return to the pre-catastrophe state after new pollution has been curbed must be considered as remote in time. Capturing the latter is not our aim here, but it is the focal topic of Joosten and Meijboom (2010).

A stylized fact in fisheries is that fishermen tend to behave more socially cooperatively in well-preserved resources but turn to more socially defective behavior once the resource is found in bad shape, thus aggravating sustainability problems. Different branches of science offer a plethora of interpretations for this phenomenon.[2] Yet this can only be rationalized if the socially defective choice becomes more attractive over the socially cooperative one as the resource deteriorates. For instance, Hillis and Wheelan (1994) attribute the impatience of fishermen to great uncertainty about future landings (see also Döring 2006). Several factors may contribute to uncertainty in a resource system, for instance, stochastic resource dynamics, weather

---

[2] For psychological explanations, see Steg (2003). Deutsch (1978) forwards skepticism that 'good' own behavior will lead to the desired outcome. Dawes (1980), Dawes and Messick (2000) and Edney (1980, 1981) forward the expectation of nonreciprocation of cooperative behavior (cf., e.g., Brann & Foddy 1987). Trust might be an issue too, cf., e.g., Messick and Brewer (1983); Messick et al. (1983); Brann and Foddy (1987). Döring and Egelkraut (2008) connect long-term uncertainty to aggressive short-term behavior. Bjørndal and Gordon (1993) relate patience (and socially cooperative behavior) to absence or reduction of risk, and vice versa (cf., e.g., Edney & Harper 1978; Hanneson 1997; Boncoeur et al. 2000). Warner and Pleeter (2001) and Harrison, Lau, and Williams (2002) relate lack of patience to various factors 'perpendicular' to the ones mentioned already, but certainly aggravate this lack of patience if added.

or climatic conditions, spatial aspects, Allee effects,[3] the number of agents and legal and institutional settings of the resource system in isolation or even in combination. In a system close to exhaustion, the future might be more heavily discounted than one in which the resource is available at maximum capacity. This condition would induce the socially defective behavior, which complicates recovery or, alternatively, aggravates the danger of depletion.

Bathroom Games are special instances of FD-games, that is, games with frequency-dependent stage payoffs (Joosten, Brenner, & Witt 2003). The idea behind this notion stems from the work of the psychologist and economist Herrnstein on distributed choice[4] in which experimental stimuli changed depending on the choices made by the subjects (see e.g., Herrnstein 1997). Earlier, these effects had been examined primarily in 'one-person games' or 'games against nature' settings. The first contribution using the frequency-dependency concept in distributed choice in a (multiperson) strategic-interaction framework was Brenner and Witt (2003). Several applications to various themes almost monopolized by differential game-based analysis, cf., e.g., Haurie, Krawczyk, and Zaccour (2012); Long (2010) for overviews, have come to the fore, e.g., Joosten (2007a, b, 2009, 2014, 2015, 2016). Joosten, Brenner, and Witt (2003) analyzed FD-games quite extensively, adapting the analysis of repeated games to this subclass of stochastic games (introduced by Shapley 1953). The Folk Theorem-like results of Joosten, Brenner, and Witt (2003) imply that if the agents are sufficiently patient,[5] a large set of individually rational rewards can be supported by equilibria involving threats. We obtain rather similar results in the present chapter, but note a previously

---

[3] An Allee effect is a low-density phenomenon from biology. If the population density of a species gets below a critical level, only negative growth rates are possible. Hence, the species faces extinction. Especially problematic is that the critical level might be unknown completely or up to a certain degree!

[4] Similar mathematics can be used to model addiction in a two-player strategic interaction framework. One may assume that the addictive action gives a higher short-term utility, and as the addiction settles in, the addictive action is even more preferred than in the original nonaddicted state. Yet the overall (i.e., on all possible outcomes) utilities may be lower than even for the worst-case outcome in the nonaddicted state.

[5] Patient here means nonmyopic, interested in long-term outcomes. We formalize patience by taking the long-term average payoffs as evaluation criterion, known to be equivalent to taking a normalized sum of discounted future payoffs at rates going to unity.

unobserved fact that some feasible individually rational rewards cannot be obtained by the constructive methods underlying this type of analysis. We show that in almost every such equilibrium, the bathroom is cleaned up frequently, but not necessarily always. There is a unique Pareto-efficient equilibrium outcome in which the bathroom is cleaned each and every time it is used. If one player were to punish the other under a 'grim-trigger strategy', one of two situations may arise: either the punishee cleans up forever while the punisher never cleans up, or nobody ever cleans up again. Which situation arises depends on a parameter formalizing the size of the utility differences between polluting and cleaning up as pollution increases.

The richness of the strategy space allows us to deal partly with criticisms of the repeated game framework. We embark on this voyage because we wish to take away objections by practically inclined community members with regard to results from the more theoretically inclined. We replace 'grim-trigger' strategies with strategies which are (infinitely) forgiving in case of unilateral deviations. Moreover, these punishments, under the standard mild condition of full dimensionality, increase the limiting average rewards for the punisher, while decreasing those of the unilateral deviator, which solves the commitment issue regarding punishing often raised. This increases realism, as punishers have an incentive to punish indeed if significant deviation from an equilibrium path occurs, yet an insignificant sequence of 'mistakes' by a player does not induce maximal punishment. Finally, these more realistic strategies induce almost the set of subgame perfect equilibrium rewards.

The organization of this chapter is as follows. Next, we present the model. In the third section, we introduce restrictions on the strategies employed, and in the fourth section we focus on feasible rewards from them. In the fifth section, we present sets of rewards that can be connected to equilibria with threats. The sixth section deals with criticisms to the type of results obtained, and the final section is devoted to further reflections.

The Bathroom Game

We start by giving an illustration of the problem to be analyzed and present the main concepts as we go along. To keep our account tractable, we perform the analysis on the one-parameter family of Bathroom Games next.

The Bathroom Game: Aaron and Batsheva frequently use a bathroom. In each time interval, both visit the bathroom exactly one, and the order of visiting is random, that is, each period each player has a probability of $\frac{1}{2}$ to be the first visitor for that time interval. After each visit, each has two options: to clean up the mess made or not. The utility that either person derives from using the bathroom depends on its condition: the cleaner the bathroom, the higher the utilities. Cleaning up is burdensome, whereas the alternative requires no effort at all; moreover, cleaning up a tidy bathroom is less burdensome than cleaning up a soiled one. The following formalizes these ideas. The payoffs at stage t in state s_t are given by:

$$A(s_t) = \begin{bmatrix} 6 - 4(\rho_t^A + \rho_t^B) & 6 - 4(\rho_t^A + \rho_t^B) \\ 4 - \xi(\rho_t^A + \rho_t^B) & 4 - \xi(\rho_t^A + \rho_t^B) \end{bmatrix} = B(s_t)^{\mathrm{T}}$$

The row (column) player is Aaron (Batsheva), 'not cleaning up' ('cleaning up') is action 1 (2), and $A(s_t)$ $(B(s_t))$ denotes Aaron's (Batsheva's) payoff matrix in state s_t. As usual the top row (left column) corresponds to Aaron's (Batsheva's) action 1. The interpretation of the payoff matrices is that if Aaron uses action 1 (i.e., he does not clean up), and Batsheva uses action 2 (i.e., she cleans up), the immediate payoff to Aaron is $6 - 4(\rho_t^A + \rho_t^B)$ and the immediate payoff to Batsheva is $4 - \xi(\rho_t^A + \rho_t^B)$. Each player's stage payoff only depends on their own action. For our purposes it must hold that $\xi \geq 4$.

The state in which the game is at stage $s_t \equiv (\rho_t^A, \rho_t^B)$ where ρ_t^k is the relative frequency with which player $k = A, B$, played action 1 ('not cleaning up') until stage t. More precisely, for $k = A, B$, let $\rho_t^k = \dfrac{\#\{j_u^k = 1 | u < t\}}{t}$. Note that the bathroom's condition at stage t is measured by the sum of the average frequencies with which both players have not cleaned up until stage t, that is, $\rho_t^A + \rho_t^B$. This implies symmetry or anonymity, as it is quite irrelevant which player pollutes.

Since $\xi \geq 4$, stage payoffs to both players clearly decrease as the bathroom's condition deteriorates. Moreover, the difference between the utilities for cleaning up and not cleaning up increases as the condition of the bathroom deteriorates. Figure 9.1 illustrates the effects of the pollution on the stage payoffs.

So a Bathroom Game is played at discrete moments in time called stages, by two players, each having two actions; at each stage s_t each

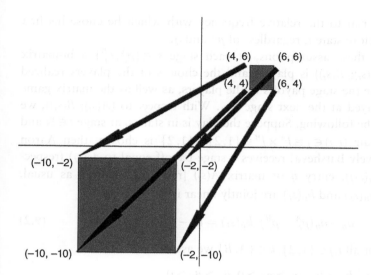

Figure 9.1 Stage payoffs for the Bathroom Game with $\xi = 7$

player chooses an action in a bi-matrix stage game $(A(s_t); B(s_t))$. The entries of the bi-matrices, that is, the payoffs at stage $t' \in \mathbb{N}$ of the play, depend on the relative frequencies of all action choices until then.[6]

Let $h_{t'}^A = (j_1^A, ..., j_{t'-1}^A)$ be the sequence of actions chosen by Aaron until state $t' \geq 2$ and let $q \geq 0$, then let $0 < \rho_t^A < 1$ for $t = 1$ and define ρ_t^A recursively for $1 < t \leq t'$ by

$$\rho_t^A = \begin{cases} \dfrac{q+t-1}{q+t}\rho_{t-1}^A + \dfrac{1}{q+t} \text{ if } j_{t-1}^A = 1, \\ \dfrac{q+t-1}{q+t}\rho_{t-1}^A \text{ if } j_{t-1}^A = 2 \end{cases} \tag{9.1}$$

Define ρ_t^B for Batsheva similarly. Taking large positive values for q serves to moderate 'early' effects. Recall that j_{t-1}^A denotes the action chosen by Aaron at stage $t - 1$, hence, the numbers ρ_t^A converge in

---

[6] This game extends the Littering Game of Brenner and Witt (2003) and Joosten, Brenner, and Witt (2003), also a two-person game. As in the traditional social dilemma/trap literature we used a dyadic choice model (cf., e.g., Schelling 1978; Komorita & Parks 1994). Cleaning up actually means that if the environment is quite polluted that it may take several consecutive periods to clean before its condition improves.

the long run to the relative frequency with which he chose his first action before state t, regardless of ρ^A and q.

Under these assumptions, at each stage $s_t \equiv (\rho_t^A, \rho_t^B)$ a bi-matrix game $(A(s_t); B(s_t))$ is played, and the choices of the players realized determine the stage payoffs to the players, as well as the matrix game to be played at the next stage s_{t+1}. With respect to $(A(s_t); B(s_t))$, we assume the following. Suppose the play is in state s_t at stage $t \in \mathbb{N}$ and action pair $(i,j) \in J \equiv J^A \times J^B \equiv \{1,2\} \times \{1,2\}$ is chosen, then Aaron (respectively Batsheva) receives a stage payoff equal to $a_{ij}(s_t)$ (respectively $b_{ij}(s_t)$), entry ij of matrix $A(s_t)$ [respectively $B(s_t)$] as usual. Entries $a_{ij}(s_t)$ and $b_{ij}(s_t)$ are jointly linear in ρ_t^A, ρ_t^B, that is,

$$a_{ij}(s_t) = a_{ij} - \alpha_{ij}(\rho_t^A + \rho_t^B), b_{ij}(s_t) = b_{ij} - \beta_{ij}(\rho_t^A + \rho_t^B) \tag{9.2}$$

where for all $i,j \in \{1,2\}, k \in \{A, B\}$ we assume

$$a_{1j} > a_{2j}, b_{i1} > b_{i2}, \alpha_{2j} \geq \alpha_{1j} \geq 0, \beta_{i2} \geq \beta_{i1} \geq 0$$

These restrictions ensure that in each stage game 'not cleaning up' strictly dominates 'cleaning up', that is, gives a strictly higher immediate utility than the alternative. Furthermore, choosing an action pair in a perfectly clean bathroom, that is, $\rho_t^A = \rho_t^B = 0$, yields higher utilities than choosing the same action pair for higher values of ρ_t^A and ρ_t^B. This reflects the idea that a deteriorating condition of the bathroom decreases utilities.

The more polluted the bathroom, the bigger the discrepancy between the stage-utilities of both actions is; cf., Figure 9.1, where the set of stage-payoffs moves from top-right for a clean bathroom to bottom-left for a polluted one as indicated by the arrows. Note that 'cleaning up' does not involve the entire bathroom; only a limited effort is made.

Strategies

At every stage t, both players know the current state and the history of play,[7] that is, the state visited and actions chosen at each stage before. A strategy prescribes at all stages, for any state and history, a mixed action to be used by a player. The sets of all strategies for

---

[7] Allowing, for instance, that Aaron cannot observe Batsheva's action(s) directly adds a layer of reality, but also several layers of complexity, see e.g., Hart (1985); Forges (1986).

Aaron (respectively Batsheva) will be denoted by $\aleph^A$ (respectively $\aleph^B$) and $\aleph \equiv \aleph^A \times \aleph^B$. The (stochastic) payoff to player k; $k = A,B$, at stage t, depends on the strategy-pair $(\pi, \sigma) \in \aleph$; the expected stage payoff is denoted by $R_t^k(\pi, \sigma)$.

It is not uncommon in the analysis of repeated or stochastic games to limit the scope of strategies on the one hand and to focus on rewards on the other. In the sequel, we do both: we focus on rewards from strategies that are pure and jointly convergent. Then we extend our analysis.

A strategy is pure if at each stage a pure action is chosen, that is, the action is chosen with probability 1. The set of pure strategies for player k is P^k and $P \equiv P^A \times P^B$. The strategy pair $(\pi, \sigma) \in \aleph$ is jointly convergent if and only if $z \in \Delta^{2\times2}$ exists such that for all $\varepsilon > 0$:

$$\lim \sup\nolimits_{t\to\infty} \mathrm{Pr}_{\pi,\sigma}\left[\left|\frac{\#\{j_u^A = i \text{ and } j_u^B = j | 1 \le u \le t\}}{t} - z_{ij}\right| \ge \varepsilon\right] = 0 \text{ for all } (i,j) \in J,$$

where $\Delta^{2\times2}$ denotes the set of all nonnegative 2×2-matrices such that the entries add up to 1, hence $z_{ij} \in [0, 1]$; $\mathrm{Pr}_{\pi,\sigma}$ denotes the probability under strategy-pair (π, σ). JC denotes the set of jointly convergent strategy pairs. Under a pair of jointly convergent strategies, the relative frequency of action pair $(i,j) \in J$ converges with probability 1 to z_{ij} in the terminology of Billingsley (1986: 274). Moreover, the empirical distribution of the past play by Aaron under such a pair of strategies converges with probability 1 to the vector given by the row-sums of the matrix z. The same holds for Batsheva. Hence, $\rho_t^A(\rho_t^B)$ converges with probability 1 to $Z^A(Z^B)$, defined as the sum of the top row (left column) elements of the matrix z.

Rewards

The players receive an infinite stream of stage payoffs during the play, and they are assumed to wish to maximize their average rewards. For a given pair of strategies (π, σ), player k's average reward, $k = A,B$, is given by

$$\gamma^k(\pi, \sigma) = \lim\nolimits_{T\to\infty} \inf \frac{1}{T} \sum_{t=1}^{T} R_t^k(\pi, \sigma); \gamma(\pi, \sigma) \equiv (\gamma^A(\pi, \sigma), \gamma^B(\pi, \sigma))$$

It may be quite hard to determine the set of feasible (average) rewards F, directly. Instead, we start the analysis by looking at what

can be obtained by restricting the scope of strategies under consideration and extend analysis from there. For this purpose, the set of
jointly convergent pure-strategy rewards is given by

$$P^{JC} \equiv cl\{(x^1, x^2) \in \mathbb{R}^2 \,|\, \exists_{(\pi,\sigma) \in P \cap JC} : (\gamma^A(\pi,\sigma), \gamma^B(\pi,\sigma)) = (x^1, x^2)\},$$

where $cl\,S$ is the closure of the set S: the interpretation of this definition is that for any pair of rewards in this set, we can find a pair of
jointly convergent pure strategies that yield rewards arbitrarily close
to them. P^{JC} can be determined rather conveniently, as we will show
now. With respect to jointly convergent strategies, Eq. (9.2) and the
arguments presented imply that

$$\lim_{t \to \infty} (a_{ij}(s_t), b_{ij}(s_t)) = \left(a_{ij} - \alpha_{ij}Z^A - \alpha_{ij}Z^B, b_{ij} - b_{ij}Z^A - \beta_{ij}Z^B\right).$$

So the matrices $A(s_t); B(s_t)$ 'converge' in the long run, too.

Denote $\varphi(z) = \sum_{(i,j) \in J} z_{ij}\left(a_{ij} - \alpha_{ij}(Z^A + Z^B), b_{ij} - \beta_{ij}(Z^A + Z^B)\right).$

The interpretation of $\varphi(z)$ is that under jointly convergent strategy
pair (π, σ) the relative frequency of action pair $(i, j) \in J$ being chosen
is z_{ij} and each time this occurs the players receive $(a_{ij}(s_t), b_{ij}(s_t))$ in
the long run. Hence, the players receive an average amount of $\varphi(z)$.
So, $\gamma(\pi, \sigma) = \varphi(z)$.

The following result has been proven in Joosten, Brenner, and Witt
(2003) for games with frequency-dependent stage payoffs. Less general ideas had been around earlier for the analysis of repeated games
with vanishing actions (cf., Joosten 1996, 2005; Schoenmakers,
Flesch, & Thuijsman 2002)

Lemma 9.1 *In the Bathroom Game, $P^{JC} = \cup_{z \in \Delta^{mon}}\varphi(z)$ and each
pair of rewards in $P' \equiv conv\ P^{JC}$, the convex hull of P^{JC}, is feasible.*

Figure 9.2 illustrates the influence of the parameter ξ (from the
matrices of stage-payoffs) on the geometric properties of the sets
of jointly convergent pure-strategy rewards for $\xi = 4$ (left), $\xi = 6$
(middle) and $\xi = 10$ (right).

Lemma 9.1 justifies convenient algorithms to determine P^{JC} and P'.
Figure 9.2 depicts the sets P^{JC} for different ξ's. The intuition behind
the changes in the geometric properties is that the upper left hand
and the lower right hand vertex move to the left respectively down-
wards, thereby changing the geometry of the boundaries. Figure 9.3

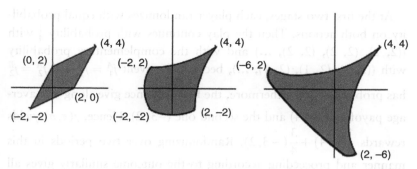

Figure 9.2 The sets of jointly convergent pure-strategy rewards for various values of ξ

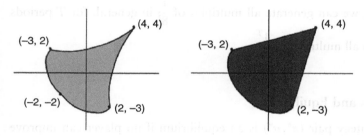

Figure 9.3 The set of jointly convergent pure-strategy rewards and its convex hull for $\xi = 7$

shows the link between P^{JC} and P'; both sets of rewards are feasible, cf. e.g., Joosten, Brenner, and Witt (2003).

To give the intuition on how to construct strategies that yield a convex combination of both rewards, we provide the following example.

The Bathroom Game (cont'd): Note that in Figure 9.2 (where $\xi = 7$) no strict convex combination of rewards $(-3,2)$ and $(4,4)$ can be achieved by a pair of jointly convergent pure strategies. Let (π, σ) be given by

$$\pi_t = \sigma_t = \left(\frac{1}{2}, \frac{1}{2}\right) \quad \text{for } t = 1, 2$$

$$\pi_t = \sigma_t = 2 \text{ for } t \geq 3 \quad \text{if } j_1^A = j_1^B \text{ and } j_2^A = j_2^B$$

$$\pi_t = \sigma_t = 1 \quad \text{otherwise}$$

At the first two stages, each player randomizes with equal probability on both actions. Then the play continues with probability $\frac{1}{4}$ with $((2, 2), (2, 2), (2, 2), ...)$ and with the complementary probability with $((2, 1), (2, 1), (2, 1), ...)$, because the event $j_1^A = j_1^B$ and $j_2^A = j_2^B$ has probability $\frac{1}{4}$. Furthermore, the first sequence gives long-run average payoffs of $(4, 4)$ and the second one $(-3, 2)$. Hence, $\gamma(\pi, \sigma)$ yields rewards $\frac{1}{4}(4,4) + \frac{3}{4}(-3,2)$. Randomizing over two periods in this manner and proceeding according to the outcome similarly gives all convex combinations of $(-3,2)$ and $(4,4)$ being multiples of $\frac{1}{4}$. Moreover, following the same procedure for a randomization of three periods, we can generate all multiples of $\frac{1}{8}$; in general, for T periods one gets all multiples of $\frac{1}{2}^T$.

Threats and Equilibria

The strategy pair (π^*, σ^*) is an equilibrium if no player can improve by unilateral deviation, that is, $\gamma^A(\pi^*, \sigma^*) \geq \gamma^A(\pi, \sigma^*), \gamma^B(\pi^*, \sigma^*) \geq \gamma^B(\pi^*, \sigma)$ for all $\pi \in \aleph^A, \sigma \in \aleph^B$. An equilibrium is subgame perfect if, for each possible state and history, the subsequent play corresponds to an equilibrium (i.e., no player can improve by deviating unilaterally from there on).

In the construction of equilibria for repeated games, 'threats' play an important role. A threat specifies the conditions under which one player will punish the other, as well as the subsequent measures. We call $v = (v^A, v^B)$ the threat point, where $v^A = \min_{\sigma \in \aleph^B} \max_{\pi \in \aleph^A} \gamma^A(\pi, \sigma)$, and $v^B = \min_{\pi \in \aleph^A} \max_{\sigma \in \aleph^B} \gamma^B(\pi, \sigma)$. So v^A is the highest amount Aaron can get if Batsheva tries to minimize his average payoffs. Under a pair of individually rational (feasible) rewards, each player receives at least the threat-point reward. Thus, the set of individually rational feasible rewards is

$$IR = \left\{ (x, y) \big| \exists_{(\pi, \sigma) \in \aleph} : x = \gamma^A(\pi, \sigma) \geq v^A, y = \gamma^B(\pi, \sigma) \geq v^B \right\}.$$

We have the following result on threat points in the Bathroom Game. The proof is quite technical but fortunately very short.

Lemma 9.2 *We have* $v = (v^A, v^B) = (\max\{-2, 4 - \xi\}, \max\{-2, 4 - \xi\})$

Proof: We only prove the case $v^A = \max\{-2, 4 - \xi\}$. If Aaron always plays his first action, then his stage payoffs converge to $(2 - 4\rho_t^B)$ in the long run and his rewards are at least -2; if he always plays the other action his stage payoffs converge to $(4 - \xi \rho_t^B)$ in the long run and his rewards are at least $(4 - \xi)$. Now, Batsheva can keep Aaron's maximal reward at max $\{-2, 4 - \xi\}$ by playing action 1 forever. In that case, his long-run stage payoffs are $(2 - 4\rho_t^A)$ for action 1 and $(4 - \xi - \xi \rho_t^A)$ for action 2. Hence, Aaron's long-run average payoffs converge to

$$\rho_t^A(2 - 4\rho_t^A) + (1 - \rho_t^A)(4 - \xi - \xi \rho_t^A) = (\xi - 4)(\rho_t^A)^2 - 2\rho_t^A + 4 - \xi.$$

It may be readily confirmed that on $[0, 1]$ this function has a maximum of $(4 - \xi)$ for $\rho_t^A = 0$ if $4 \leq \xi \leq 6$, and -2 for $\rho_t^A = 1$ if $\xi \geq 6$. So Aaron's rewards are, at most, max $\{-2, 4 - \xi\}$. Therefore, $v^A = \max\{-2, 4 - \xi\}$.

The Bathroom Game (continued): Consider the pair of strategies in which Aaron and Batsheva clean up alternately, starting with Aaron. This implies that $\rho^A = \rho^B = \frac{1}{2}$ in the long run. As Batsheva's long-run stage payoffs (for $\xi = 7$) are alternatively $6 - 4(\rho^A + \rho^B) = 2$ and $4 - 7(\rho^A + \rho^B) = -3$, her average stage payoffs converge to $-\frac{1}{2}$. A similar statement holds for Aaron.

Suppose Aaron were to deviate unilaterally and clean up exactly thrice every four stages. Then $\rho^A = \frac{1}{4}$ and $\rho^B = \frac{1}{2}$ in the long run. Aaron then receives once $6 - 4\left(\frac{1}{4} + \frac{1}{2}\right) = 3$ and thrice $4 - 7\left(\frac{1}{4} + \frac{1}{2}\right) = -\frac{5}{4}$ in every four stages. This leads to average stage payoffs of $\frac{1}{4} \cdot 3 + \frac{3}{4} \cdot -\frac{5}{4} = -\frac{3}{16} > -\frac{1}{2}$. Hence, Aaron can improve unilaterally against Batsheva's strategy.

Consider, however, the following pair of strategies. Aaron and Batsheva clean up alternately, starting with Aaron, as long as both players stick to cleaning up alternately. If one player deviates from this course of action, the other player is never to clean up again. This pair of strategies leads to exactly the same sequence of play: on odd stages

Aaron cleans up and on even stages Batsheva cleans up, inducing rewards $-\frac{1}{2}$ to both. If Aaron were to deviate only once, then Batsheva would 'punish' him by never cleaning up again, and Aaron's reward is, at most, -2. Hence, Aaron cannot improve unilaterally.

The 'threat' is that Batsheva will never clean up again if Aaron deviates even once from cleaning up on odd-numbered stages. Observe that in such an equilibrium involving threats, the play is such that the threats are never carried out.

To present the general idea of the next result of Joosten, Brenner, and Witt (2003), we adopt terms from Hart (1985) and Forges (1986). First, there is a 'master plan', which is followed by each player as long as the other does too; then there are 'punishments', which come into effect if a deviation from the master plan occurs. The master plan is a sequence of 'intra-play communications' between the players, the purpose of which is to decide by which equilibrium the play is to continue. The outcome of the communication period is determined by a 'jointly controlled lottery', that is, at each stage of the communication period the players randomize with equal probability on the first two actions; at the end of the communication period, one sequence of pairs of action choices materializes. Detection of deviation from the master plan after the communication period is easy, as both players use pure actions on the equilibrium path from then on. Deviation in the communication period by using another action than one of the first two actions can also be easily detected, but deviation by using an alternative randomization on the first two actions is impossible to detect. It can be shown that no alternative unilateral randomization yields a higher reward. So the outcome of the procedure is an equilibrium. For more details, we gladly refer to Joosten, Brenner, and Witt (2003).

Let $E \equiv IR \cap P^{JC}, \tilde{E} \equiv \{(x,y) \in E | x > v^A, y > v^B\}$ and E', $\tilde{E}'$ be the respective convex hulls. So $E(\tilde{E})$ is the set of individually rational rewards obtained by jointly convergent pure strategies (yielding strictly more to each player than his threat-point rewards). Now, we can efficiently present the following implication of the main results in Joosten, Brenner, and Witt (2003).

Corollary 9.1 *Each pair of rewards in E' (in $\tilde{E}'$) can be supported by an equilibrium (a subgame-perfect equilibrium).*

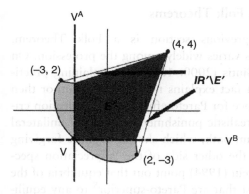

Figure 9.4 All rewards in E' are equilibrium rewards

The Bathroom Game (cont'd): Let $E' = conv\{(4 - \xi, 4 - \xi),$ $(4 - \xi, 2), (2, 4 - \xi, (4, 4)\}$ for $\xi \in [4, 6]$, and let furthermore for $\xi \geq 6 : E' = conv\left\{(-2, -2), \left(-2, -2 + \frac{48(\xi - 3)}{\xi^2}\right), \left(-2 + \frac{48(\xi - 3)}{\xi^2}, -2\right), (4, 4)\right\}$

Then, each pair of rewards in the set E' (in $\tilde{E}'$) can be supported by an equilibrium (a subgame-perfect equilibrium). Let $IR' = IR \cap P'$, then rewards exist that are feasible and individually rational, yet not in E'. Note that the set $IR' \backslash E'$ may be nonempty for Bathroom Games (cf., Figure 9.4), as in repeated games it must be empty by the (in)famous Folk Theorem. It is still an open question whether rewards in $IR' \backslash E'$ can be obtained by equilibrium strategies!

Corollary 9.1 hinges on the possibility of punishing unilateral deviations. So we need history-dependent strategies. To prevent misconception: there is no contradiction between strategies being both jointly convergent and history dependent.

Neither is there one between an equilibrium being jointly convergent and subgame perfect: if the equilibrium path in the terminology of Hart (1985) induces *convergence with probability 1*, the off-equilibrium part may be of arbitrary sophistication. Also, rewards in E' that do not belong to E can only be obtained by strategies that are *not* jointly convergent (see Joosten (2016) for a similar assessment).

Dealing with Criticism on Folk Theorems

The final result of the previous section is a Folk Theorem. Appreciation for such results varies widely among the profession. On the negative side we find Gintis (2000: 129): 'By explaining practically anything, the model in fact explains nothing'. The author then expresses a cautious preference for Pareto efficiency as a selection criterion, as well as for more realistic punishments in case of unilateral deviation from an equilibrium path, which should be more forgiving (e.g., allow for repair). On the other side of the 'appreciation spectrum', Osborne and Rubinstein (1994) point out that equilibria of the infinitely repeated game exist that are Pareto-superior[8] to any equilibrium of the associated one-shot game. In other words, strategies with threats may be necessary to obtain rewards that are better for all players involved.

From a theoretical point of view no value judgement seems possible on the issue of punishing unilateral deviations. Threats and punishments are possible in repeated games; removing these options seems artificial. However, the idea of punishments is hard to sell to the more practically oriented, despite the fact that in equilibrium threats are never acted out. The type of punishment that is often used in the construction of equilibria is of the grim-trigger type (see e.g., Van Damme 1991). Under such a strategy one deviation, even an inadvertent one, triggers the grimmest punishment possible to the deviating player, regardless of the consequences to the punisher. Of course, subgame-perfectness aims to take away this objection. After a unilateral deviation, the play is to continue with an equilibrium giving the deviating player a lower reward. However, if the threat-point rewards coincide with equilibrium rewards, the objection is still valid.

The richness of the strategy space allows us to accommodate several objections connected to equilibria involving threats. We construct subgame-perfect equilibria that are 'forgiving', that is, they allow many unilateral deviations (but such that their relative frequency goes to zero); 'mild', that is, the deviator is not punished maximally but merely by lowering his reward; and 'self-motivating', that is, the

---

[8] An outcome X is called Pareto-superior to outcome Y, if under X at least one agent is better off than under Y, while all others are equally well-off. A feasible outcome is Pareto-efficient if there exists no feasible outcome which is Pareto-superior to it.

punisher is not worse off afterwards. We give the proof immediately, hoping that checking the claims straight on is more convenient.

Theorem 9.1 *For any pair* $(a, b) \in \text{int}(E' \cap P^{JC})$ *a subgame-perfect equilibrium* (π, σ) *exists yielding rewards* (a, b), *which induces play such that*

- *if Aaron deviates from the equilibrium path 'too often', then play proceeds according to an equilibrium such that he receives strictly less than the amount a but more than* v^A *and Batsheva receives at least b;*
- *if Batsheva deviates from the equilibrium path 'too often', then play proceeds according to an equilibrium such that Batsheva receives strictly less than b but more than* v^B *and Aaron receives at least a.*

Proof: Let (x, y) be a pair of rewards in the interior of E'. Then numbers $\underline{x} < x < \overline{x}$ and $\underline{y} < x < \overline{y}$ exist such that $(\underline{x}, \overline{y}), (\overline{x}, \underline{y}) \in E'$. So equilibrium strategies (π^a, σ^b) with $(a, b) \in \{(x, y), (\underline{x}, \overline{y}), (\overline{x}, \underline{y})\}$ exist such that $\gamma(\pi^a, \sigma^b) = (a, b)$. Let $T^* \geq 0$ denote the length of the communication period of strategy pair (π^x, σ^y). For $T > T^*$, let the average number of deviations from equilibrium path (π^x, σ^y) be given by $AD^A_{\pi^x}(T) = \dfrac{\#\{j^A_t \neq \pi^x_t | T^* < t \leq T\}}{T - T^*}$, and $AD^A_{\sigma^y}(T) = \dfrac{\#\{j^B_t \neq \sigma^y_t | T^* < t \leq T\}}{T - T^*}$, respectively. Define (π, σ) as follows:

$$\pi_t = \pi^{\underline{x}}_{t-T'} \quad \sigma_t = \sigma^{\overline{y}}_{t-T'} \quad \text{if for some } T' > T^* : AD^A_{\pi^x}(T') > 1/\sqrt{T' - T^*}$$

$$\pi_t = \pi^{\overline{x}}_{t-T''} \quad \sigma_t = \sigma^{\underline{y}}_{t-T''} \quad \text{if for some } T'' > T^* : AD^B_{\sigma^y}(T'') > 1/\sqrt{T'' - T^*}$$

$$\pi_t = \pi^x_t \quad \sigma_t = \sigma^y_t \quad \text{otherwise}$$

Then, $\gamma(\pi, \sigma) = \gamma(\pi^x, \sigma^y) = (x, y)$, since in the long run deviations from the equilibrium path of (π^x, σ^y) go to zero in relative frequency. Now (π, σ) is an equilibrium because if, for example, Batsheva deviates more than Aaron does such that for some $T'' : AD^B_{\sigma^y}(T'') > 1/\sqrt{T'' - T^*}$, the play continues according to equilibrium $(\pi^{\overline{x}}, \sigma^{\underline{y}})$. Batsheva gets $\underline{y} < y$, while Aaron gets $\overline{x} < x$. A similar statement holds the other way around if Aaron deviates too much. So neither player can improve his rewards by deviating unilaterally as described.

The reader may confirm in the proof that the 'too often'-s in the statement of the theorem are well specified, as the relative frequency of the deviations in play away from the equilibrium path by any player must be smaller than an ever decreasing number as the play continues.

Conclusions

We engineered, in the spirit of Aumann (2008), Bathroom Games as a metaphor for a collection of real-world situations with runaway feedback or reinforcement in the following sense. One action payoff dominates all other ones, and the continued play of this dominating action causes the payoff or utility gap between itself and all other ones to increase over time. What makes the framework into a social trap setting is that all stage payoffs decrease over time if the dominating action is played exclusively (or for a sufficiently high proportion of the stages). Well-known environmental pollution problems, such as shallow lakes or global warming, exploitation of renewable resources such as fisheries or forestries, or intertemporal interactive decision-making problems with addiction features may be interesting applications of this admittedly rather stylized model.

We demonstrated how to proceed if there is sufficient interest of all agents for the long term. For the limiting average reward criterion we prove a Folk Theorem-like result: a continuum of rewards well above the threat-point rewards can be supported by an equilibrium. The threat-point rewards maximize a player's minimum long-turn average payoffs, taking an antagonistic perspective on the other. Many equilibria provide rewards considerably higher than these threat-point rewards. There is even a unique Pareto-efficient pair of rewards supported by an equilibrium in which both players never pollute. So sufficiently patient agents solve the social trap.

Folk Theorems are often criticized as unrealistic. We dealt with several critiques by proving that the richness of the strategy space allows under the mild condition of full dimensionality that essentially the same set of rewards can be supported by subgame-perfect equilibria, which are infinitely forgiving with respect to deviations from the equilibrium path, punish mildly in case deviations appear to be systematic and significant, and make punishments self-motivating in the sense that the punisher will improve his rewards while punishing his opponent.

Admittedly, we stacked the cards in favor of solving the social trap as we analyzed a minimal society of infinitely patient agents. Increasing the number of players is known to cause difficulties in achieving our good-news results (cf., e.g., Komorita & Parks 1994), as does impatience of these players (cf., e.g., Joosten 2014), and certainly more so if both are combined. Many of our improvements dealing with criticism to Folk Theorems presented can be upheld under slightly more restrictive assumptions. One can design an infinitely forgiving, mild and self-motivating punishment plan for arbitrary sets of players to stabilize any combination of individually rational, jointly convergent, pure-strategy rewards 'surrounded' by rewards of the same type. Every player required to punish can be counted on to do so as (s)he has an incentive to do so. What may change though and cause increased complexity in analysis is the level of the 'threat point' determining the set of individually rational, jointly convergent, pure-strategy rewards. More research on this topic may provide precise and definite insights.

References

Aumann, R. 2008. Game Engineering. In: Neogy, S., Bapat, R., Das, A., and Parthasarathy, T. (eds.) *Mathematical Programming and Game Theory for Decision Making*. Singapore: World Scientific. 279–285.

Billingsley, P. 1986. *Probability and Measure*. New York: John Wiley & Sons.

Bjørndal, T. and Gordon, D. V. 1993. The Opportunity Cost of Capital and Optimal Vessel Size in the Norwegian Fishing Fleet. *Land Economics*, 69, 98–107.

Boncoeur, J., Coglan, L., Le Gallic, B., and Pascoe, S. 2000. On the (Ir)relevance of Rates of Return Measures of Economic Performance to Small Boats. *Fisheries Research*, 49, 105–115.

Brann, P. and Foddy, M. 1987. Trust and the Consumption of a Deteriorating Common Resource. *The Journal of Conflict Resolution (1986–1998)*, 31, 615–630.

Brenner, T. and Witt, U. 2003. Melioration Learning in Games with Constant and Frequency-Dependent Pay-offs. *Journal of Economic Behavior and Organization*, 50, 429–448.

Carpenter, S. R., Ludwig, D., and Brock, W. A. 1999. Management of Eutrophication for Lakes Subject to Potentially Irreversible Change. *Ecological Applications*, 9, 751–771.

Dawes, R. M. 1980. Social Dilemmas. *The Annual Review of Psychology* 31, 169–92.

Dawes, R. M. and Messick, D. M. 2000. Social Dilemmas. *International Journal of Psychology*, 35, 111–116.

Deutsch, M. D. 1978. *The Resolution of Conflict*. New Haven, CT: Yale University Press.

Döring R. 2006. Investing in Natural Capital the Case of Fisheries. In: Sumaila, U. R. and Marsden, A. D. (eds.) *North American Association of Fisheries Economists Forum Proceedings*, 2006 Fisheries Centre, Univ BC, Vancouver, 49–64.

Döring, R. and Egelkraut, T. M. 2008. Investing in Natural Capital as Management Strategy in Fisheries: The Case of the Baltic Sea Cod Fishery. *Ecological Economics*, 64, 634–642.

Edney, J. J. 1980. The Commons Problem: Alternative Perspectives. *American Psychologist*, 35, 131–150.

  1981. Paradoxes on the Commons: Scarcity and the Problem of Equality. *Journal of Community Psychology*, 9, 3–34.

Edney, J. J. and Harper, C. S. 1978. The Effects of Information in a Resource Management Problem: A Social Trap Analysis. *Human Ecology*, 6, 387–395.

Forges, F. 1986. An Approach to Communication Equilibria. *Econometrica*, 54, 1375–1385.

Gintis, H. 2000. *Game Theory Evolving*. Princeton, NJ: Princeton University Press.

Hamburger, H. 1973. N-person Prisoner's Dilemma. *Journal of Mathematical Psychology*, 3, 27–48.

Hannesson, R. 1997. Fishing as a Supergame. *Journal of Environmental Economics and Management*, 32, 309–322.

Harrison, G. W., Lau, M. I., and Williams, M. B. 2002. Estimating Individual Discount Rates in Denmark: A Field Experiment. *The American Economic Review*, 92, 1606–1617.

Hart, S. 1985. Nonzero-Sum Two-Person Repeated Games with Incomplete Information. *Mathematics of Operations Research*, 10, 117–153.

Haurie, A., Krawczyk, J. B., and Zaccour, G. 2012. *Games and Dynamic Games*. Singapore: World Scientific.

Herrnstein, R. J. 1997. *The Matching Law: Papers in Psychology and Economics*. Cambridge, MA: Harvard University Press.

Hillis, J. F. and Wheelan, B. J. 1994. Fisherman's Time Discounting Rates and Other Actors to Be Taken into Account in Planning Rehabilitation of Depleted Fisheries. In: Antona, M., Catanzano, J., and Sutinen, J. G. (eds.) *Proceedings of the 6th Conference of the International*

Institute of Fisheries Economics and Trade, 1994 IIFET-Secretariat Paris. 657–670.

Joosten, R. 1996. *Dynamics, Equilibria, and Values*. PhD thesis, Maastricht University.

——— 2005. A Note on Repeated Games with Vanishing Actions. *International Game Theory Review*, 7, 107–115.

——— 2007a. Small Fish Wars and an Authority. In: Prinz, A., Steenge, A. E., and Schmidt, J. (eds.) *The Rules of the Game: Institutions, Law, and Economics*. Berlin: LiT Verlag. 131–162.

——— 2007b. Small Fish Wars: A New Class of Dynamic Fishery Management Games. *ICFAI Journal of Managerial Economics*, 5, 17–30.

——— 2009. Strategic Advertisement with Externalities: A New Dynamic Approach. In: Neogy, S. K., Das, A. K., and Bapat, R. B. (eds.) *Modeling, Computation and Optimization*. Singapore: World Scientific. 21–43.

——— 2014. Social Dilemmas, Time Preferences and Technology Adoption in a Commons Problem. *Journal of Bioeconomics*, 16, 239–258.

——— 2015. Long-run Strategic Advertisement and Short-run Bertrand Competition. *International Game Theory Review*, 17.

——— 2016. Strong and Weak Rarity Value: Resource Games with Complex Price–Scarcity Relationships. *Dynamic Games and Applications*, 6, 97–111.

Joosten, R., Brenner, T., and Witt, U. 2003. Games with Frequency-Dependent Stage Payoffs. *International Journal of Game Theory*, 31, 609–620.

Joosten, R. and Meijboom, R. 2010. *Stochastic Games with Endogenous Transitions*. In: Economics, M. P. I. o. (ed.) Papers on Economics and Evolution. Jena.

Komorita, S. S. and Parks, C. D. 1994. *Social Dilemmas*. Madison, WI: Brown & Benchmark.

Liebrand, W. B. G. 1983. A Classification of Social Dilemma Games. *Simulation and Games*, 14, 123–138.

Long, N. V. 2010. *A Survey of Dynamic Games in Economics*. Singapore: World Scientific.

Mäler, K. G., Xepapadeas, A., and De Zeeuw, A. J. 2003. The Economics of Shallow Lakes. *Environmental and Resource Economics*, 26, 603–624.

Messick, D. M. and Brewer, M. B. 1983. Solving Social Dilemmas: A Review. *Annual Review of Personality and Social Psychology*, 4, 11–43.

Messick, D. M., Wilke, H., Brewer, M. B., Kramer, P. M., Zemke, P. E., and Lui, L. 1983. Individual Adaptations and Structural Change as Solutions to Social Dilemmas. *Journal of Personality and Social Psychology*, 44, 294–309.

Osborne, M. J. and Rubinstein, A. 1994. A Course in Game Theory. Cambridge, MA: MIT Press.

Platt, J. 1973. Social Traps. *American Psychologist*, 28, 641–651.

Scheffer, M. 1998. *The Ecology of Shallow Lakes*. London: Chapman & Hall.

Scheffer, M., Carpenter, S., Foley, J. A., Folke, C., and Walker, B. 2001. Catastrophic Shifts in Ecosystems. *Nature*, 413, 591–596.

Schelling, T. C. 1978. *Micromotives and Macrobehavior*. New York: W. W. Norton & Company.

Schoenmakers, G., Flesch, J., and Thuijsman, F. 2002. Coordination Games with Vanishing Actions. *International Game Theory Review*, 4, 119–126.

Shapley, L. 1953. Stochastic Games. *Proceedings of the National Academy of Sciences*, 39, 1095–1100.

Steg, L. 2003. Motives and Behavior in Social Dilemmas Relevant to the Environment. In: Hendrickx, L., Jager, W., and Steg, L. (eds.) *Human Decision Making and Environmental Perception. Understanding and Assisting Human Decision Making in Real-Life Settings*. Liber Amicorum for Charles Vlek. Groningen: Groningen University.

Van Damme, E. E. C. 1991. *Stability and Perfection of Nash Equilibria*. Berlin: Springer.

Warner, J. T. and Pleeter, S. 2001. The Personal Discount Rate: Evidence from Military Downsizing Programs. *The American Economic Review*, 91, 33–53.

10 | Fairness in Urban Land Use
An Evolutionary Contribution to Law and Economics

CHRISTIAN SCHUBERT

Introduction

The question of how to regulate bilateral land use conflicts has been a classic home ground of orthodox law and economics theorizing since Coase's (1960) seminal contribution.[1] Coase proposed to view conflicts between neighboring cattle ranchers and wheat farmers or between urban confectioners and dentists as cases of reciprocally produced harm, indicating ill-specified and inefficiently allocated property rights as the actual *economic* or institutional (as opposed to purely physical) causes of "externalities" (Papandreou 2003: 285). Although his contribution revolutionized the way economists regarded these sorts of conflicts and paved the way for what originally was the home turf of lawyers, it left essential questions open. In this particular case, the gaps in the Coasean treatment of land use issues not only raised theoretical concerns but also impeded the practical use of the economic insights on the part of lawmakers and judges, a use that any law and economics approach naturally aims at.

These gaps can be attributed to two key aspects of the mainstream approach to land use conflicts: First, it is concerned exclusively with the static efficiency characteristics of alternative economic states (land use patterns), thereby not only excluding any dynamic perspective but also the question of how costs and benefits induced by land uses are distributed among the parties involved. In a nutshell, one might say that questions of (distributive and procedural) *fairness* are neglected. Second, the mainstream approach does not account for the deeper role of informal institutions (such as social norms), that is, normatively expected, locally enforced and generally known

---

[1] This chapter continues an argumentation first outlined in German, in Schubert (2006).

behavioral dispositions that not only shape the agents' subjective fairness perceptions but that also affect the judicial regulation of land use conflicts.[2]

This chapter attempts to show ways how these gaps may be closed. Moreover, it will advocate a general evolutionary perspective that may help to clarify the issues involved, thereby contributing to the construction of a conceptual framework within law and economics that is based on an evolutionary view of human behavior. So far, evolutionary economics perspectives have hardly been incorporated into law and economics (von Wangenheim 2011 is a notable exception). The need to adopt such a perspective is obvious if we take into account the fact that the regulation of land use conflicts – understood as an intervention into an ongoing process of endogenously changing land use patterns – generates patterns of land use that are partly regarded as "undesirable" in light of the fairness norms shared by the parties involved. An evolutionary perspective can shed light on the origins and nature of those fairness norms – an issue hitherto largely neglected in mainstream law and economics with its efficiency-focused neoclassical methodology.

The chapter is organized as follows: The second section briefly describes the mainstream instrumental law and economics approach to land use conflicts and taking decisions. The third section then shows where important theoretical and practical gaps remain and introduces the distributive and procedural fairness considerations on the background of an evolutionary-institutional perspective on economic behavior. The fourth section sketches some normative implications, followed by concluding remarks in the last section.

Urban Land Use Conflicts: The Orthodox View

"There is perhaps no more impenetrable jungle in the entire law than that which surrounds the word 'nuisance'." (William Lloyd Prosser)[3]

---

[2] To be sure, agents' fairness perceptions will often be biased, as research in behavioral economics has shown (e.g., Babcock & Loewenstein 1997 on the self-serving bias). For the application of behavioral economics insights in law and economics, see, e.g., Jolls, Sunstein, and Thaler (1998). For a critical discussion see Hayden and Ellis (2007).

[3] As quoted in Swanson and Kontoleon (2000: 382).

The Coasean Perspective

Economists typically view land use conflicts within densely populated urban areas as manifesting either materially ill-specified or inefficiently allocated property rights. This perspective differs from both the (maybe more intuitive) classical Pigouvian welfare view and from the traditional lawyer's perspective – the difference not only being one of theoretical interest but also resulting in markedly different legal policy implications.

The standard view is based on Coase's powerful insight into the reciprocal nature of externalities. Recall that Coase (1960; see also 1988) argued that with negligible transaction costs and in the absence of wealth and income effects,[4] decentralized bargaining makes sure that the initial legal allocation of property rights is irrelevant with respect to the rights' final allocation. Under those ideal conditions law matters only for the way the surplus is distributed among the parties involved. In other words, the "Coase Theorem" (Stigler 1966: 113) – henceforth CT – defines the sphere where law is relevant for allocative issues (hence, relevant for the orthodox economist), to wit, the sphere of positive transaction costs. Notice that whereas most neoclassical "Coaseans" were fascinated by the characteristics of a world of frictionless transactions, Coase himself was rather interested in the real world where judges and policy makers have to cope with the implications of positive friction. Although the major part of his classic piece (Coase 1960) dealt with the world of positive transaction costs, he later argued, referring to the neoclassical textbook setting, that "it would not seem worthwhile to spend much time investigating the properties of such a world ... [A] situation in which transaction costs ... are assumed to be zero ... is in any case but a preliminary to the development of an analytical system capable of tackling the problem posed by the real world of positive transaction costs" (Coase 1988: 15).

---

[4] "Negligible" relative to the total amount of gains from exchange potentially realized. Coase himself defined transaction costs simply as "the costs of carrying out market transactions," including the costs "to discover who it is one wishes to deal with, to inform people that one wishes to deal and on what terms, to conduct negotiations leading up to a bargain, to draw up the contract" (Coase 1960: 15). Cooter (1982: 16) defines transaction costs as "the cost of communicating among the parties ..., making side payments ..., and the cost of excluding people from sharing in the benefits exchanged by the parties."

The Coase Theorem has initiated an enormous amount of theoretical and (more recently) empirical research. It has also been an object of fierce criticism from many angles. The arguably most important one concerns the problem that in a bilateral bargaining situation, the distribution of the surplus is indeterminate, as the parties cannot be assumed to act like passive price takers (Cooter 1982). We will come back to that issue later. First, however, we will stick to the original theorem in order to prepare the ground for discussing the *instrumental* implications that have been derived from it. "Instrumental" statements are those that take some policy goal as given and describe the most effective means to reach that goal. Hence, they do not discuss the quality of the proposed goal itself. Instrumental statements serve as the main base from which concrete legal policy advice can be derived – a key concern for law and economics research from its inception.

According to the CT, then, under the ideal conditions sketched earlier, "the outcome of the bargaining process will be efficient, regardless of who is initially assigned the right" (Medema 1999: 213). Hence, efficiency or social welfare maximization is postulated as the relevant goal to be pursued by legal policy makers and judges. Coase (1960) himself referred to the maximization of the "total social product," but the mainstream of law and economics scholars (with the important exception of Posner 1979)[5] has not reduced the relevant goal to one that is measurable in monetary terms. Rather, utility remains the essential maximin in normative law and economics.[6]

The outcome of an ideal transaction cost-free bargaining process is thus generally taken to be the normative reference point for the efficient solution of land use conflicts. Starting from this premise, Calabresi and Melamed (1972) have established an instrumental rule to guide legal practitioners in coping with this sort of conflict. Their rule comprises two subrules that Cooter and Ulen (2011: ch. 4) refer to as the normative Coase Theorem and the normative Hobbes Theorem, respectively. According to the former, law should "develop a set of rules that promote the closest possible approximation to the world of zero transaction costs" (Epstein 1985: 556), that is, any impediment to bargaining should be removed in order to allow the

[5] See also Posner (2010: 13–16).
[6] See Kaplow and Shavell (2002) for a forceful defense of this.

parties involved to engage in a decentralized solution to the land use conflict they are facing. According to the latter theorem, if transaction costs turn out to be prohibitively high, the legal policy maker or judge should herself attempt to allocate the relevant property rights in a welfare-maximizing way by simulating the outcome of ideal bargaining (Posner 2010).

According to Calabresi and Melamed (1972), the policy maker or judge can facilitate decentralized bargaining under the normative CT by clearly assigning the property rights bundle in question to one of the parties involved and making it (i) tradable, as well as (ii) protecting it with a *property rule* or injunctive remedy that prohibits any infringement by a third party. In this context, differing costs of collective action should be taken into account: Realistically, parties consisting of hundreds of members (neighbors of a chemical plant, say) first have to organize themselves and aggregate their individual members' preferences before being able to engage in bargaining with another party. In other words, "internal transaction costs" may be asymmetric (Mishan 1971: 73). If transaction costs happen to be too high initially, the rights bundle should simply be assigned to the party that seems to value it the most. Then, however, the bundle should only be protected by a relatively weak *liability rule*, making sure that the other party can indeed obtain the rights if (and only if) her willingness to pay (i.e., damages) for them exceeds the first party's willingness to accept. Thus, both parties' subjective valuations may be revealed and the initial assignment may be corrected ex post, on the basis, however, of an implicit price (reflected in the damages) set by the policy maker or the court. Notice that price determines the distribution of the surplus that the reallocation of rights has produced.

Based on Calabresi and Melamed's approach, Posner (2010: 55 ff.) has proposed a rule that serves as an incentive-compatible revelation mechanism also under conditions of asymmetric information, as Kim and Kim (2004) demonstrate. Let A_D and A_P denote the avoidance costs of parties D (defendant) and P (plaintiff), and let V and H be the valuation of the relevant rights by D and P, respectively. Both parties inform the court about these values, that is, D reveals A_D and V, and P reveals A_P and H. If transaction costs are prohibitively high, the court should first compare these four values with each other, assigning the entitlement to P if V turns out to be the lowest value. If, however, H proves to be minimal, then party P should be held liable for any harm, with the value H defining the damages. If, on the other hand, A_D is the smallest value, then the court should hold party D responsible for avoiding any harm, and vice versa for party P if A_P should turn out to be minimal.[7]

The Calabresi/Melamed rule has been modified in order to account for cases of asymmetric information on the part of the court. If the court knows the value of the total harm produced but lacks reliable information on the parties' avoidance costs, then it should assign the rights to the plaintiff by using a liability rule approach. The defendant, that is, the party physically "causing" the harm, will reveal her private avoidance costs by her own action after the plaintiff has received the entitlement in question. If, on the other hand, the court knows the avoidance costs functions but not the harm produced, then it's efficient to assign the property rights to the defendant, protecting it with a liability rule (Kaplow & Shavell 1996: 14 f.). That means that the plaintiff, if she wishes the harmful activity to be stopped, has to pay the defendant for this, thereby revealing her true valuation of the rights in question.

Further problems arise, of course, if the court only has access to biased information on harm and/or avoidance cost functions. Mainstream law and economics, following Coase, never saw any good reason to venture into that territory. In the words of Swanson and Kontoleon (2000: 388), courts were typically regarded as having a comparative advantage in collecting the relevant information, because "judicial intervention ... can be an efficient method for accumulating and applying information on previous similar conflicts to current ones."[8] We will return to this assumption later. Notice, though, that it's not as ad hoc as it may appear at first sight, since it's implicitly based on theoretical premises quite similar to those that underlie the famous "efficiency thesis of the common law" that says

---

[7] Kim and Kim (2004) show that under asymmetric information, the incentive-incompatibility of this mechanism is only in question in the following case: If revelations to the court are sequential, with party D moving first, then, after D having revealed her values, P does have an incentive to exaggerate his own values if $H < V$, that is, if he values the property right lower than D does. P, however, will locate his reported value (H') strictly within the range $H < H' < V$. For with $H' > V$, the Posnerian court would order party D to stop her harmful activity, an order that would reduce P's payoff back to the level of H. Therefore, the reported ordinal ranking of the four values will not be biased.

[8] See also Ehrlich and Posner (1974).

that common law adjudication systematically selects for efficient over inefficient judgments (Aranson 1986; Posner 2010: 271–275).

What's a "Fair" Compensation?

Having described the central instrumental implications of the CT with respect to bilateral land use conflicts in general, let's now have a look at the second essential area where the Coasean approach has been applied, to wit, the area of governmental *takings*. Takings are the complete physical appropriation of single land parcels by a state agency. In contrast to ordinary land use regulation, they normally require monetary compensation. Law and economics has not only (i) examined the efficiency rationale of takings in general but also (ii) the question under which conditions compensation should be paid and (iii) the question of the efficient level of compensation that should be paid to the previous owner.

As to the efficiency rationale, most economists would agree that (a) the risk of strategic behavior ("hold-out") and (b) the costs of collective action may justify regulatory intervention. The hold-out problem is a straightforward consequence of the bilateral monopoly nature of the original Coasean bargaining (Cooter 1982; see also Demsetz 1972). If party A has a higher willingness to pay for some land parcels, if her willingness to pay refers to the whole package (think of some infrastructure project, say), and if the single parcels that make up the package are originally owned by separate agents, then any of those agents has an incentive to hold back her consent as long as possible in order to maximize her private share of the joint surplus. At the limit, these incentives may very well block the surplus from being produced at all. Hence, it may be efficient to step in and to enforce a "fair market price" by regulatory means. To be sure, principal–agent problems loom large here and may be at least partly solved by legal restrictions, such as the requirement that enforced takings only be allowed in order to realize a welfare-increasing public project.[9] The second rationale mentioned, viz., the problem of collective action costs, again refers to the realistic setting where at least one party consists of a multitude of agents, each with its own private interests.

---

[9] On the "public use" requirements see the arguments by Fischel (1995: 71–73) and Epstein (1985: ch. 12).

In that case, the agents may face prohibitive transaction costs for organizing themselves, and the state agency may intervene in order to act as the representative (the "agent" in principal–agent theory lingo). Here again, public choice issues have to be solved, of course, which may prove to be a tricky task in its own right.

Given that there is, in principle, a basic efficiency rationale for governmental takings, we now face the question of where the line should be drawn between regulation and outright takings of land: When should compensation be paid? In the literature, four criteria have been advanced. First, it has been argued that compensation should be due if the initial use of the parcel of land in question has been "reasonable" (as opposed to "injurious to the public welfare," given the local circumstances). This position is reflected in the *noxious use doctrine* of US land use law.[10] Fischel (1995: 154 f.) has proposed to model this doctrine as a "harm-benefit rule," according to which the state agency is allowed to prevent harmful activities, while it is barred from compelling, without compensation, private landowners to contribute to local public goods by using their property in some specified nonharmful way. Hence, in the latter case we are facing a genuine taking, where compensation is due. From an economic viewpoint, this rule is not completely convincing, since any harm can, of course, be interpreted as a benefit foregone and vice versa. Who defines "harm"? In the end, without further information, we are back at the efficiency calculus: Any land use that is inefficient may be labeled "harmful" and therefore made subject to uncompensated regulation.

Second, it can be argued that compensation should reasonably be restricted to those cases where the regulation-induced value loss is "excessive." This "diminution of value-test" has been introduced by Judge Holmes in the case of *Pennsylvania Coal* v. *Mahon* (1922) – it has later been modified in *Lucas* v. *South Carolina* (1992), ruling that the private landowner should be compensated if and only if she "has been called upon to sacrifice *all* economically beneficial uses in the name of the common good."[11] An analogous rule applies in German land use law (Papier 1994: Rn. 352 ff.). In the case of *Penn*

---

[10] This doctrine has been made operational in the famous case of *Penn Central Transportation Co.* v. *City of New York* (1978), where the court defined "public welfare" rather loosely as comprising aspects of "health, safety, morals, or general welfare."

[11] See *Lucas* v. *South Carolina Coastal Council* (1992) and Bromley (1997: 48).

Central v. *City of New York*, a similar rule has been advanced, specifying that only those regulatory interventions should qualify as takings that "so frustrate *distinct investment-backed expectations* as to amount to a taking."[12] Here the question is critical whether the intervention does indeed affect expectations on whose basis legitimate investment decisions have already been taken (Miceli & Segerson 2000: 344f.). Compare this rule to the slightly bizarre principle in German property law that denies compensation if the land use in question is one that "a landowner who takes into account the public welfare (sic!) and the concrete geographical situation and surroundings would not *reasonably* have chosen" (Wolf 2005: Rn. 68, my italics). Again, mainstream law and economics takes a shortcut by identifying the meaning of terms like "legitimate" and "reasonable" with "efficient."[13]

Third, one may argue that compensation should only be due if the regulatory intervention affects some private landowners in a *discriminating* way.[14] The rationale of this rule can best be seen from a contractarian perspective, where rules that restrict an individual's behavior can ideally be interpreted as a reciprocal exchange, generating a surplus for all parties voluntarily involved. Put differently, "each person whose property is taken by the regulation receives implicit benefits from the parallel takings imposed upon others" (Epstein 1985: 196). If rules discriminate, though, this reciprocity no longer holds, justifying extra compensation to the party that is negatively affected.

Fourth and finally, state agencies in both the United States and Germany have tried to go beyond statutory and judge-made law by making separate deals with private landowners in order to exchange land use restrictions against concessions. In other words, the state agency "buys" private contributions to local public goods. The extent of bargaining-induced (often in-kind) "compensation" has, however, been restricted by the courts.[15] According to the US Supreme Court, a contract between state agency and private landowner has to be based on a "material connection" between the *quid* and the *quo*. There has to be a verifiable "essential nexus" between the entitlements that are being exchanged. In a similar case – *Dolan* v. *City of Tigard* (1994) – the

---

[12] See *Penn Central* v. *City of New York* (1978: 127), my italics.
[13] See Miceli and Segerson (2000: 344 f.).
[14] See Papier (1994: Rn. 342f., 357 ff.) for the German land use law.
[15] See in particular *Nollan* v. *California Coastal Commission* (1987).

court ruled that there must be a "reasonable relationship" between the rights exchanged.[16] And again, we face the intricate question of how a "reasonable" relationship can be determined on the basis of economic logic. Notice that in most instances, there is a bilateral monopoly situation; hence, no innocent market price is available that could help in determining which compensation could plausibly be accepted as "reasonable" by the private landowner.

Finally, we have to determine the amount of compensation to be paid to the landowners affected. German property law (Article 14 of the German constitution) stipulates that compensation has to be determined by a "fair balancing of the public's and the involved parties' interests."[17] Analogously, the Fifth Amendment to the US Constitution requires that "private property [shall not] be taken for public use, without just compensation." Thus, we have two key notions – "fair" and "just" – whose meaning have to be determined before the level of compensation can be properly set. Not surprisingly, law and economics sees the meaning of these two notions through the lens of efficiency considerations – its implications are, however, somewhat tricky in this case.

Consider, first, the intuitively appealing idea of using market prices ("fair market value") as a proxy for the proper amount of compensation. Given that the owner's (unfortunately unobservable) subjective valuation of her land parcel tends to be significantly higher than the market price, this proxy would systematically underrate the welfare losses of takings and, consequently, their social opportunity costs. Hence, the state agency, suffering from fiscal illusion, would tend to engage in excessive takings (Miceli & Segerson 2000: 331). If, on the other hand, the landowner gets a compensation that perfectly covers her losses, inefficient incentives would result as well, if the amount of compensation is made a function of market values. For in that case, she could influence the amount of compensation by adapting her own behavior – a genuine case of moral hazard, causing excessive private

---

[16] According to the court, "no precise mathematical calculation is required, but the city must make some sort of individualized determination that the required dedication is related both in nature and extent to the impact of the development," as quoted by Healey, Purdue, and Ennis (1995: 232). See Grigoleit (2000) for an analogous German rule.

[17] See Papier (1994: Rn. 344 f.).

investment in the value of land (Blume, Rubinfeld, & Shapiro 1984).[18] The only way out of this dilemma is to compensate in a lump-sum fashion: As Miceli and Segerson (2000) demonstrate, the amount of compensation is efficient if it depends directly on the efficient level of private investment on the land parcel in question: "[A] compensation rule that pays landowners the full value of their land at the efficient level of investment results in both efficient investment in land and efficient takings decisions when the government has fiscal illusion" (335).[19] Here again, as in the case of the normative Hobbes Theorem, discussed earlier, the policy maker or judge has to determine which level of investment is efficient under the given circumstances – a task that is, of course, subject to the well-known information and motivation issues any state action is subject to.

Setting aside these obstacles, we can identify a common thread within law and economics' treatment of both bilateral land use conflicts and compensation decisions. In both cases, the instrumental rule guiding policy makers and judges centers around the welfare-maximizing way to use the parcels of land in question. Coase's ideal friction-free bargaining results in exactly that property rights allocation or land use constellation which a rational, integrated "single owner" of all land affected would have chosen. Efficient compensation is a function of efficient investment, that is, welfare-maximizing land uses by all parties involved. It's then straightforward to examine the question whether this single-owner rule indeed offers a satisfying answer to the legal policy issues involved. Hence, after having sketched the main instrumental implications of the CT, let's examine the theoretical and practical gaps in this argument.

Theoretical and Practical Gaps in the Coasean Perspective

As outlined in the introduction, the present chapter is concerned with two gaps that weaken both the theoretical consistency and the practical relevance of the Coasean perspective on land use conflicts and takings decisions. Whereas the former concerns the distributional zero-sum conflict that is inherent in any bilateral Coasean bargaining, the latter concerns the economic interpretation of key concepts in the

---

[18] A similar problem arises, obviously, in the somewhat less likely case that the probability of a taking depends on the parcel's value (Miceli 1991).
[19] See also Fischel and Shapiro (1989).

legal resolution of land use conflicts and takings issues (such as "reasonable," "legitimate," "just," etc.). Before we discuss those "internal" issues afflicting the application of the CT in general, let's briefly point out a much more specific problem with the CT and the focus on static efficiency in the context of land use conflicts, particularly those within densely populated urban areas.

One might argue that the focus of standard law and economics on isolated land use conflicts, abstracting from the context in which those conflicts are situated, is fundamentally at odds with the reality of urban land use conflicts. For urban agglomerations should be seen as continuously evolving systems of highly interdependent elements – that's why they tend to be studied by means of nonlinear modeling techniques (e.g., Krugman 1996). In our context, what matters is the fact that within a densely populated urban area, there's hardly anything like a purely private exchange of land use rights. Most modifications of land use cause repercussions, however slight at first, throughout the whole urban system. To illustrate, Thomas Schelling has given an example of such indirect but powerful effects in his *racial segregation model* (Schelling 1978). These considerations may serve as an additional argument for overcoming the narrow focus on static efficiency – so fitting for closed economic systems – that characterizes standard law and economics. Incorporating fairness criteria may be a first step towards a fully adequate normative assessment of land use conflicts in settings such as these.

Limits of Coasean Bargaining

Back, then, to the internal problems of applying the CT in general: From a game-theoretic perspective, the CT is tantamount to the hypothesis that a one-shot, cooperative, two-person game on the distribution of a given surplus has a solution. This hypothesis is, however, rather optimistic, because the parties are typically involved in a bilateral conflict over the use of property rights (Cooter 1982; Demsetz 1972). There is typically exactly one party on the demand side and one party on the supply side regarding the property right in question (i.e., we are facing a bilateral monopoly situation).[20]

---

[20] Compare this to Stigler's influential interpretation of the CT, according to which "under *perfect competition* any assignment of rights leads to the optimal resource allocation" (Stigler 1966: 113, my italics).

Thus, rational agents have an incentive to strategically hide their true preferences in order to maximize their own share of the cooperative surplus. As a consequence, the surplus dissipates, since both parties spend all their available resources with the aim to maximize their share of the cake (Mumey 1971).[21] Interestingly, this incentive even increases with decreasing transaction costs, because decreasing transaction costs, in turn, negatively affect the costs of any delay in the bargaining process (Cooter 1982). This whole issue may be illustrated by three problems that may prevent successful bargaining and therefore the joint production of the surplus in the first place.

Consider first the incentive to "extort" the other party. Given two neighboring landowners, A and B, it may be rational for party A, say, to propose an actually inefficient project that has the potential to harm party B, just with the aim to sell the nonrealization of the project (Schlicht 1996). Party B may then rationally offer a price to obtain the property right in question. Second, consider the situation, already described in Coase (1960), of a liability rule regime where the value of a farmer's corn fields is negatively affected by a railroad's sparks. Let's assume that land is traded on a competitive real estate market, that the property right is initially with the farmer, and that due to the reciprocal nature of the problem, efficiency requires *both* parties to invest in avoidance technology: the farmer, for instance, should ideally face incentives that lead him not to grow corn just beside the railways. A rule that compensates him for all the harm caused by the sparks would not establish such incentives, because it would make damages a function of action parameters under the control of the farmer! He would invest excessively in his fields. A superior rule would link the damages payable to the farmer to the loss in market value caused by the sparks – that rule would be superior because the farmer cannot – by hypothesis – directly influence market prices.[22] The bilateral monopoly problem can thus be overcome by cutting the link between the parties' action parameters and the price of the relevant property right (i.e., the amount of damages to be paid). Third and finally, consider the hold-out problem, already

---

[21] See also Witt (1996: 121–124). Notice that Coase (1960: 8; 1988: 162) tried to downplay this argument's relevance.

[22] Due to nonconvexities in real estate, market values will probably fail to reflect true social costs, but we will abstract from that particular problem here; see, however, Baumol and Bradford (1972) and Papandreou (2003).

mentioned earlier: Again, on one side of the bargaining table, several parties will have the incentive to hide their true valuations of the property right in question in order to maximize their individual shares of the surplus. This behavior can be expected if the other party (the one on the demand side) needs the approval of every single property right holder, making every one of them effectively a monopolistic supplier. Again, strategic behavior may eventually block the bargaining process – a solution would need to provide for the exogenous determination of the property rights' implicit price.

Given these theoretical intricacies, it is straightforward that most of the practical issues involved in land use and takings decisions refer to the problem of how to provide for an exogenously set price for the property rights in question. Moreover, given that many real-world bargaining processes do indeed suffer from obstacles that can be traced back to the bilateral monopoly nature of the interaction – although such obstacles have obviously been successfully overcome in many real-world settings – we have to probe under which conditions we can expect bargaining to be successful. Real-world individuals are apparently often better at solving the issues identified than *Hominess economici*.[23]

Before we do that, however, we have to discuss a set of practical problems where the solution to the "price problem" presumably plays a symmetrical role. Because we are concerned with both land use conflicts and takings decisions, we have to investigate these two realms in turn. Let's start with the former. According to the Calabresi/Melamed rule described earlier, liability and property rules should be allocated in such a way as to either induce or reconstruct the outcome of a friction-free bargaining process. As a heuristic to achieve this, the "single owner" thought experiment plays a decisive role (see the earlier section).

Practical problems emerge when it comes to "selling" the concrete policy implications of this heuristic to (i) the legal community and (ii) the public at large. The sharp criticism by Canaris (1993) against the "single owner" approach is a case in point: According to him, the Calabresi/Melamed approach systematically neglects the intrinsic value of people's *rights*. For in a Coasean bargaining, the parties'

---

[23] For some experimental and field evidence see, e.g., Hoffman and Spitzer (1986) and Ellickson (1995).

initial endowment of rights has a highly limited function only: it defines initial threat points in a bargaining game. This, however, runs counter to the actual meaning, rationale, and social function of rights, which mainly consists in guaranteeing and securing a minimum sphere of privacy, where the agent can act as she sees fit, whatever the effects on efficiency.[24] The social function of rights is also reflected in the informal social norms people adhere to and that also express widely held perceptions of "fair" patterns of outcomes (Ellickson 1995; Frey, Oberholzer-Gee, & Eichenberger 1996). This observation is highly relevant for the economic assessment of law, as informal social norms seem to be extremely significant for the perceived legitimacy of legal rules (Tyler 1990).

An analogous problem arises with respect to the efficiency calculus that underlies the orthodox answer to the twofold question: (i) Under which conditions (ii) how much compensation should be paid to the agent whose land has been taken? As to the first question, we have seen that the law proposes essentially four ways to determine the boundary between ordinary land use regulation and takings (discussed earlier). We can now see that all four alternative solutions require additional information in order to be made operational: The first option ("harmful" vs. "reasonable") needs some "benchmark of neutral conduct" (Miceli & Segerson 2000: 340) which arguably depends on local circumstances and can be found by relying on the epistemic resources of local "community standards for normal land use" (Fischel 1985: ch. 8; Fischel 1995). This would not only raise the perceived legitimacy of the adjudication in question but also stabilize expectations.

The second option ("excessive value loss") refers to some notion of "investment-backed expectations" – and again, there's an obvious relationship to widely held social norms concerning issues of distributive and procedural fairness. To judge some value loss "excessive" presupposes some agreed-upon standard of "fairness." On the other hand, the aim to respect "investment-backed expectations" refers directly to procedural fairness and to the general social function of rights, which is to allow agents to build stable expectations.

By referring to "discrimination," the third option is even more strongly tied to concerns of procedural fairness. As shown earlier, the discrimination test can be linked to a contractarian thought experiment

---

[24] See also Coleman and Murphy (1990: 71–82).

(Epstein 1985: 196), which in turn is based on an "original position" model that ideally reflects deeply held intuitions about the nature of "fair" behavior (Binmore 2005; Cordes & Schubert 2007).

Finally, the fourth option refers to the existence of a "reasonable" nexus between the *quid* and the *quo* involved in bargaining on land use rights. As this rule concerns the terms of bargaining, it is again closely linked to the question: Which way to distribute the cooperative surplus generated by successful bargaining is considered "fair"?

Hence, the orthodox "single owner" approach should be complemented by taking into account the way real-world individuals think about rights, their social function, allocation, and distribution. It seems that the simple model of *Homo economicus* does not adequately capture these aspects. Note that it is not simply incomplete in a positive sense but also from an instrumental angle. Practical legal policy issues cannot be adequately resolved without taking into consideration aspects such as the agents' informal social norms regarding the "fairness" of the way cooperative surpluses are shared among the participants. Given the interdependence between the generation and the distribution of a surplus, it's hardly surprising that the law needs to rely on external standards of fairness that cannot be reduced to the simple maximization of static efficiency. Rather, the epistemic resources needed to define the content of those standards have to be found within the given informal institutional background of society (i.e., the relevant social norms).

Note that these considerations can be argued to follow Coase's own methodological suggestion that "a situation in which transaction costs ... are assumed to be zero ... is in any case but a preliminary to the development of an analytical system capable of tackling the problems posed by the real world of positive transaction costs." The real world is one in which, among other things, agents hold specific beliefs about what constitutes a fair division of a jointly created surplus and a fair treatment of individual rights. The next subsection will enquire into what an evolutionary account can tell us about the nature and dynamics of the informal fairness norms in question.

A Brief Evolutionary Account of "Fairness" Norms

Although it's easy to make the case for the theoretical desideratum to incorporate fairness considerations into the law and economics analysis of land use conflicts, we still need to establish the point that real-world human beings do, in fact, care about fairness, in both a procedural and distributive sense, when placed in situations of anonymous market exchange. Are preferences for fairness really sufficiently widespread to allow us to argue that introducing such considerations can command general assent?

Probably the best way to probe this point is to consult evolutionary-anthropological theories about the origin and emergence of fairness norms.[25] Consider Henrich et al. (2010a) who argue that the evolution of large-scale societies, characterized by frequent "ephemeral," yet mutually beneficial, transactions among strangers, in fact required the co-evolution of social norms that sustain fairness far beyond local kin. That implies that in modern societies, prosocial behavior does not merely reflect innate psychological dispositions but also social norms that have evolved over millennia in the course of human history.

It's obvious that market exchange – involving both one-shot and repeated interactions among strangers – gets more efficient to the degree that market participants share common trust-promoting social norms related to fairness (Henrich et al. 2010a: 1480). During most of man's evolutionary history, though, mutually beneficial transactions were strictly confined to small networks of related kin; going beyond that into situations that, due to their anonymity, lacked relationship information was typically fraught with mistrust and exploitation. What's puzzling, then, is the fact that "market norms" – crucially involving fairness-sustaining norms – seem to have evolved in the course of societal evolution in contexts where established social relationships (such as kin or status) turned out to be insufficient. If that's the case, then measures of fairness should display a positive covariation with the degree of a society's market integration (and, incidentally, also with adherence to a world religion such as Christianity or Islam). Henrich et al. report cross-cultural experimental evidence that confirms this hypothesis. Observing the strategy choices of participants from 15 societies around the globe (ranging from hunter-gatherer to wage laborers) in dictator games (DG), ultimatum games (UG), and

---

[25] See, e.g., Witt (1989) for an account and an illustration of the evolutionary mechanisms involved.

third-party punishment games (TPG),[26] the authors conclude that "going from a fully subsistence-based society (market integration at zero) with a local religion to a fully market-incorporated society (market integration at 100 percent) with a world religion predicts an increase in percentage offered of roughly 23, 20, and 11 in the DG, UG, and TPG, respectively" (Henrich et al. 2010a: 1482). Also, the largest societies and those displaying the most advanced degree of market integration engage in substantially greater punishment of choices deemed unfair than the smallest-scale societies studied (Henrich et al. 2010a).

Hence, evolutionary-anthropological accounts support the case that the emergence of modern mass-market societies is closely linked to social norms that, by fostering fairness considerations, are able to sustain cooperation in anonymous interactions. Note that the findings of Henrich et al. contradict the hypothesis, associated with Hayek and popular among Austrian economists, that successful interaction in large-scale societies arises from a psychological disposition that mistakenly applies ancient kin- and reciprocity-based heuristics to anonymous strangers. Finally, the findings by Henrich et al. also challenge much work in experimental economics that is confined to studying fairness norms in industrialized and democratic market societies.[27] In that case, findings may reflect social norms that have evolved to facilitate interactions among anonymous strangers, that is, the interplay between a particular set of norms and our evolved psychology, rather than the "nature" of human psychology per se.

Binmore on the Evolution of Fairness Norms

In a series of much-cited contributions, Kenneth Binmore has tried to specify, in a thoroughly naturalistic fashion, the background of the

---

[26] A third-party punishment game is basically a dictator game (with players 1 and 2) with an added third player who has the option to punish player 1 for amounts deemed unfair. Player 3 starts with the equivalent of half of player 1's stake. Punishment is costly for both 1 and 3: If punished, 1 loses triple the amount invested by 3 in punishment. To illustrate, if player 1 starts with an 100 € endowment and decides to give away 10 € to player 2, then player 3 may decide to punish this choice by investing 10 €: Player 1 then ends up with 60 € (90 – 30 €), player 2 with 10 €, and player 2 with 40 € (50 – 10 €), see (Henrich et al. 2010a: 1481).

[27] See the acronym WEIRD (Western educated, industrialized, rich, democratic), referred to in Henrich, Heine, and Norenzayan (2010b).

evolutionary origins of fairness norms (e.g., Binmore 2005, 2006). He argues, in a nutshell, that "fairness evolved as Nature's answer to the equilibrium selection problem in the human game of life" (Binmore 2006: 11). According to Binmore, equilibrium selection is a key problem human agents have to cope with as they go about their daily lives. Game theory can best illustrate this kind of problem. Consider the Battle of the Sexes or the Stag Hunt game. These games contain (at least) two possible Nash equilibria, forcing the players to find ways to somehow coordinate on one of them. Insofar as people (explicitly or, most often, implicitly) manage to agree to coordinate their individual strategy choices on one among many conceivable equilibria, high levels of cooperation can be sustained even among pure egoists. Unsurprisingly, reciprocity is essential here, as is people's willingness to punish anyone who fails to carry out their side of the agreement. Reciprocity can, then, appropriately be described as the "mainspring of human sociality" (Binmore 2006: 14). The device that ultimately does the job of selecting a specific equilibrium in what Binmore refers to as the "game of life," though, is *fairness*.

Nonhuman animals can be observed to enter implicit agreements to share food on a reciprocal basis, which is their way to ensure themselves against periods of bad luck (in hunting, say). Binmore argues that the same logic applies to human beings when they negotiate an insurance contract. Assume two players: Given that they are about to play a repeated game, both are uncertain as to whether they will be lucky in the respective next round. Hence, they find themselves in what social contract theorists refer to as the *original position* behind a *veil of uncertainty*: "If Nature wired us up to solve the simple insurance problems that arise in food-sharing, she ... also simultaneously provided much of the wiring necessary to operate the original position" (Binmore 2006: 18). To illustrate, part of the necessary "wiring" is the ability to *empathize* with others. According to Binmore, this wiring makes the contractarian notion of the original position so intuitive for most people.

The details of the evolutionary tinkering process Binmore suggests need not interest us here (but see Binmore 2006: sect. 12). Suffice it to say that he draws a close analogy between fairness norms and language (Binmore 2006: 23) – both products of cultural evolution share a universal "deep structure," beyond which they tend to differ. In the case of fairness norms, the deep structure, or so Binmore argues, is the original position, while the practical standards of interpersonal comparisons (which tell us who gets how much of a fairly divided surplus) needed to operate the original position differ across contexts and cultures.

Hence, Binmore's approach may serve as a bridge between the hypothesis of Henrich et al. – about the co-evolution of market society and cooperation-enabling fairness norms – and a contractarian (specifically, Rawlsian) account that will ultimately allow us to engage in normative reasoning about fairness.

Some Normative Implications

Given both the *need* to incorporate informal social norms on fairness in the law and economics calculus as applied to land use conflicts and the widespread existence (and acceptance) of such norms, the question arises *how* to incorporate them in practical policy making. We will tackle this issue from three different angles. For the sake of simplicity, we proceed backwards, as it were, and start with (i) a brief remark on the way courts integrate social norms in their adjudication; we continue (ii) with a proposal concerning the incorporation of fairness aspects into the legal decision calculus and then proceed (iii) to the most important problem, viz., the generation of well-founded (legitimate) fairness norms by means of normative theorizing.

The Incorporation of Fairness Criteria

First, the instrumental advice that courts faced with land use conflicts should – at least partly – rely on the informal fairness norms of a given society runs counter to the standard approach to law and economics. According to the latter, even imperfectly informed judges should attempt to gather all knowledge necessary to engage in the sort of efficiency calculus required to identify the welfare-maximizing allocation of rights. If this task proves prohibitively costly, judges should resort to precedent that (hopefully) guides them toward the efficient solution (e.g., Cooter & Ulen 2011).[28]

---

[28] See Aranson (1986) for the assumptions and hypotheses underlying the efficiency of the common law theory that is pertinent here.

However, as Ott and Schäfer (1994) show, adjudication cannot be reduced to the mechanical application of a pure efficiency calculus. It is rather typically based on the epistemic resources inherent in relevant social norms. On the one hand, in order to maintain his reputation among his peers, the single judge cannot afford to depart too much from established precedent; on the other hand, he cannot afford to depart too much from widely held social norms, as that would jeopardize the perceived legitimacy of his (and his peers') rulings. To be sure, in order to serve as a basis for any adjudication, social rules are made subject to a multilayered normative test. First, their consistency with supreme normative legal principles has to be checked; since efficiency obviously does not figure prominently among those principles, the "efficiency check" (Cooter 2000) will probably be only one among several tests. It seems, then, that the court requires a plausible and economically rational set of criteria of distributive and procedural fairness. What could such a set of criteria possibly look like though?

This question brings us to the second issue raised earlier, viz., a proposal as to how to incorporate fairness aspects into the court's decision calculus. Among the very few substantial contributions to this problem, Michelman's (1967) stands out: In the context of the compensation problem, he demonstrates that besides the pure efficiency criterion, fairness criteria can play a limited role in the calculus determining takings decisions. Inspired by Rawls (1958), he operationalizes fairness as an extra cost category, namely "demoralization costs," and integrates them into the quasi-utilitarian consequentialist calculus of law and economics by assuming that in the case of noncompensation it's not only the landowners directly affected that suffer but all other observers (being, as they are, potentially affected by the precedent created) as well. For in that case, these agents will infer that what they are witnessing is a case of "majoritarian exploitation" (see Rawls 1958: 1214, 1217). Michelman devises a rule that prescribes to compensate the landowner if it is the case that demoralization costs (D) exceed the administrative costs of compensation (S) *and* the welfare gains generated by the taking (W) exceed the minimum value of D and S. As to its practical impact, this rule stands right between the Kaldor Hicks criterion and the original Pareto criterion: It allows individual losses, but accords them a relatively high weight in the social decision calculus (Miceli & Segerson 2000: 335f.).

While this middle range position indicates a certain superiority of Michelman's rule in terms of its consistency with widely held fairness intuitions, the proposed calculus is, however, seriously deficient. It neglects the partly nonconsequentialist nature of any plausible conception of rights. Their value cannot plausibly be reflected by a calculus that makes any individual right a perfect substitute to any other. Consequently, such a calculus misses a key (namely, procedural) aspect of fairness. Rights have rather an intrinsic value as well, and this should be taken into account by any normative theory that is to guide the instrumental applications discussed so far.

Two Rawlsian Fairness Criteria ...

Having discussed one deficient way to conceptualize and incorporate fairness criteria, we now turn to the third issue raised at the beginning of this section, to wit, the generation of well-founded (legitimate) fairness norms by means of normative theorizing. As to the issue of legitimacy, we can safely ignore most of the polemics against fairness criteria brought forward by law and economics scholars such as Posner (2010) by simply noting (i) the empirical fact that real-world individuals do care about matters of distributive and procedural fairness (as elements entering their utility functions)[29] and (ii) the weak normative statement that any utilitarian calculus should include all variables influencing the individuals' well-being.

In what follows, we will introduce a contractarian approach that can provide us with the set of plausible fairness criteria we need, including, as it does, a distributive and a procedural fairness criterion. This approach satisfies two basic conditions that have been identified in earlier sections: First, it links the criteria to widely held informal norms of fairness that arguably shape people's beliefs about the legitimacy of legal rules in general and court rulings in particular. It does so by embedding the contractarian model of an "original position" within the informal institutional context of a given society. Second, it can be used to deliver appropriate clarification and definition of "tricky" yet important legal terms such as "reasonable" and "just" that, as we have seen, play such a key role in land use adjudication. There is a third advantage, though: If properly interpreted, the

---

[29] See, e.g., Güth (1995) and Fehr and Fischbacher (2002).

Rawlsian approach can serve as a model for a deliberative concept of the legal process, that is, one that takes into account the function of court rulings to not only attach implicit prices to alternative land use strategies (as orthodox law and economics has it) but also to signal normative expectations. By performing the latter function, adjudication attempts to shape the preferences of the agents involved. Thus, we are now facing the theoretical challenge to depart from the neoclassical pet assumption of given and stable preferences.

Let's have a closer look at Rawls's basic approach. Rawls is widely referred to as the initiator of the renaissance of contractarian thought in the late 20th century (O'Neill 1998). By means of his notion of "justice as fairness," developed in his *Theory of Justice* (Rawls 1971), he aims at deriving a set of fundamental principles of justice that are supposed to govern the design of society's "basic structure." The latter term encompasses all rules and procedures that regulate the distribution of basic resources. In other words, the principles of justice serve "to assign basic rights and duties and to determine the division of social benefits" (Rawls 1971: 11). Hence it's not the detailed distribution of dollars or euros that is to be regulated, but rather the distribution of multipurpose goods such as rights and entitlements. It's also worth remembering that Rawls's approach starts from the explicit assumption of a plurality of values. This makes it necessary to qualify the status of the contractarian results – they are meant to be derived from a political agreement, rather than from some metaphysical insights.

Rawls applies the basic contractarian logic in arguing that the way the costs and benefits issuing from processes of social cooperation are distributed is "just" to the extent that it corresponds to principles that rational agents would plausibly have agreed upon behind a veil of ignorance, which in turn is supposed to represent a condition of neutrality or "fairness." This "fairness" proviso refers to the specific way the original position is modeled. It includes assumptions about the kind of information available to the individuals (the "thickness" of the veil of ignorance), the individuals' preferences (notably, those for risk), and a normative rule concerning the relative weight of the individuals' preferences in the derivation of social welfare judgments. The whole methodology is centered around the concrete specification of the original position.

Assuming that at the constitutional stage, individuals are ignorant about the position they will assume in future subconstitutional market games, Rawls develops two positive hypotheses about the agents' choices under those conditions. First, he conjectures them to behave in a quite risk-averse fashion (i.e., to choose according to the *maximin* rule). When choosing among the available sets of constitutional rules, agents will focus exclusively on their respective worst consequences; then they choose the set that displays the (for them) most advantageous "worst" consequences. On the grounds of this decision-theoretic assumption, Rawls concludes that behind the veil of ignorance, rational agents will agree upon the following notion – which he refers to as the principle of "justice as fairness," which actually contains two subprinciples and one priority rule:

1. Each person is to have an equal right to the most extensive total system of equal basic liberties compatible with a similar system of liberty for all.

   2. Social and economic inequalities are to satisfy two conditions. First, they must be attached to offices and positions open to all under conditions of fair equality and opportunity; and second, *they must be to the greatest benefit of the least advantaged members of society* (Rawls 1971: 302, italics added).

Rawls explains the second part of the second principle (his famous *Difference Principle*) as follows:

[T]he higher expectations of those better situated are just if and only if they *work as part of a scheme* which improves the expectations of the least advantaged. (Rawls 1971: 75, italics added)[30]

The principles are complemented by the following priority rule:

The principles of justice are to be ranked in lexical order and therefore liberty can be restricted only for the sake of liberty. (Rawls 1971: 302)

Notice that these principles offer preliminary answers to the two main desiderata of our law and economics endeavor: First, they determine a noninstrumental value for individual rights. Second, they formulate a criterion for evaluating alternative distributional patterns.

Hence, according to Rawls, every member of society should be granted a minimum endowment of basic multipurpose resources ("primary goods"); at the same time, no individual should be systematically excluded from sharing in the cooperative surplus generated

---

[30] On the normative intuition underlying the Difference Principle, see, e.g., Heider and Mukerji (2015).

by the very mutual behavioral constraints that will be agreed upon at the constitutional stage. According to Rawls, a contractual agreement is legitimate only to the extent that it is made sure that no individual member of society will be systematically discriminated ex post. In the end, the well-known maximin principle appears to reflect only one highly specific facet of an overarching, much more plausible normative idea – which itself will have to be further specified, to be sure. In the following subsection, it is however not the content of the Rawlsian principle of "justice as fairness," but rather the procedure through which it is supposed to be generated that will be center stage. First and foremost, what Rawls offers us is a *procedural* theory of justice.[31]

... And Their Deliberative Generation

For the purposes of this chapter, the most important feature of Rawls's approach is the fact that he combines two different legitimization procedures in order to derive widely acceptable principles of justice. Beyond the classical contractual method sketched earlier, he employs a "coherentist" method (Daniels 1979; O'Neill 1998; Hahn 2000). This will be discussed in this subsection.

As has been shown, the specification of the original position and its informational structure plays a crucial role in any contractarian theory. The informational constraints serve as a model of the "moral viewpoint" a hypothetical impartial observer would adopt. What underlies this model is a set of normative statements about what kind of arguments are considered acceptable in a normative discourse. In order to specify such a model, one has to choose one of two possible

---

[31] To be sure, Rawls's argument has been extensively criticized: See, e.g., Harsanyi (1975) and Binmore (2005). Note, however, that Rawls, Harsanyi, and Binmore accept the notion that the choice problem individuals face behind a veil of ignorance can be reduced to the choice situation of an isolated single ("representative") agent. Thus, under these highly idealized circumstances, social and individual choice become identical. It is, however, generally a *non sequitur*, to reduce social to individual choice in such a manner, for the following reason: Under uncertainty, there is a categorical difference between the two kinds of choices. While it may be perfectly rational for a single agent to choose a strategy (say, driving his car) that involves a small risk of yielding a negative payoff (an accident, say), things look quite differently at the social level. In that latter case, "rational" should be replaced by "subject to general consent."

procedures. On the one hand, the model can be set axiomatically (e.g., Harsanyi 1982). This is the approach that, for instance, Kant took when proposing the original position cum social contract metaphor as a model for the categorical imperative – which, in turn, was based on purely theoretical, rationalistic (i.e., nonempirical) reasoning.

On the other hand, a conventionalist perspective can be taken: then, normative reasoning starts not from the philosopher's armchair, but rather from an empirical inquiry into the moral intuitions and social norms that actually prevail in the historical-cultural setting under consideration. Hence, the individuals' moral common sense is set at center stage in the contractarian argument. Rawls suggests that the empirically prevailing set of informal social norms should guide the specification of the contractarian original position. Instead of setting an axiomatic definition, he proposes to explicitly develop the contents of the original position (i.e., he proposes to *endogenize* it). Within the contractarian literature, that's a highly original endeavor indeed.

However, in order to avoid the notorious "naturalistic fallacy," Rawls needs to construct a methodological bridge to overcome the logical gulf between the is-world of empirically valid social norms and the ought-world of evaluative and prescriptive statements. To this end, he constructs the model of a public deliberation procedure that takes both the individual moral intuitions and the collectively shared social norms as a ("crude") input and transforms them into a set of abstract principles of justice. These principles shall be gained in the course of a rule-guided multistep procedure. In a nutshell, the individual participants at a given constitutional discourse move first by expressing their moral intuitions, social preferences, and social norms. As this will likely result in a vast amount of "normative knowledge" that is both nonoperational and highly contradictory (and partly nonsensical, too), social philosophy enters the stage and assumes the task of summarizing these utterances, in the sense of distilling their common ground. The few abstract principles that will come out of this philosophical scrutiny will then again be suggested to the individuals, who will probably reject some of them, but who may also critically revise and adjust some of their own original "inputs." Eventually, this interactive learning process will (hopefully) result in a coherent set of abstract normative statements that properly reflect the generalizable core of the agents' preferences. Those statements constitute what Rawls calls the "reflective equilibrium" of a given society.[32] This equilibrium is supposed to guide the way the original position is specified. It represents Rawls's idea of a genuinely political (compromise-based) agreement on normative issues (i.e., one that dismisses any metaphysical pretensions). Moreover, despite its misleading "equilibrium" notion, the resulting set of principles is not meant to be developed once and be statically valid thereafter. Rather, it serves as a device to solve normative problems, as long as it yields generally acceptable results. If that's no longer the case, it will be adjusted and modified accordingly.

Concluding Remarks

In the present chapter, we have shown that law and economics is in need of an enrichment by an institutional-evolutionary account of fairness norms. This has been illustrated for the case of bilateral land use conflicts and takings decisions in densely populated (urban) areas. From the viewpoint of the orthodox, supposedly "Coasean" approach, these regulatory problems can best be solved by applying the "single owner" heuristic and calculating both the welfare-maximizing way to reallocate the relevant property rights and the incentive-compatible amount of compensation for the taking of private land.

This approach suffers from two shortcomings, though. First, it cannot provide a solution to the distributional conflict underlying any bilateral bargaining game. Second, it cannot supply a plausible economic interpretation of key legal terms such as "reasonable" and "fair" that are essential when it comes to identifying solutions to bilateral land use conflicts. We have argued that the way out of this impasse leads to the incorporation of informal social norms into the law and economics calculus. Although it can be empirically shown that courts do indeed take account of the institutional context of the agents involved in litigation, there is unfortunately no straightforward way to generate the required fairness criteria. Whereas Michelman's approach neglects the nonconsequentialist value of individual rights, Rawls's conventionalist approach can indeed be used as a deliberative

---

[32] See Rawls (1971: 20) and the critical analysis by Hahn (2000).

model of the process that delivers acceptable criteria of distributive and procedural fairness.

Notice finally that this fairness-oriented perspective on two classic law and economics issues (land use conflicts and takings) not only follows Coase's methodological suggestion to explore the characteristics of a world of positive transaction costs but can also be seen as starting from an evolutionary view on the economic nature of land use conflicts that is much more realistic than the view implicitly informing the orthodox approach. For if we conceptualize land use patterns as temporary results of ongoing nonlinear processes of endogenous urban change, then we can interpret land use conflicts as reflecting the costs of adapting to these ever-changing patterns and the novelty they bring about.[33] Put differently, while land use patterns change continuously, a subset of the configurations produced in the process will be undesirable from the point of view of (some) agents affected: They bring about all kinds of adaptation costs. These costs, though, have to be shared in some way by the individual users of the urban agglomeration – and it is a plausible answer to this fundamental distributional problem that law is supposed to give. Law and economics should finally start accepting this challenge.

References

Aranson, P. H. 1986. Economic Efficiency and the Common Law: A Critical Survey. In: Schulenburg, J. M. v. d. and Skogh, G. (eds.) *Law and Economics and the Economics of Legal Regulation*. Dordrecht: Kluwer.

Babcock, L. and Loewenstein, G. 1997. Explaining Bargaining Impasse: The Role of Self-Serving Biases. *The Journal of Economic Perspectives*, 11, 109–126.

Baumol, W. J. and Bradford, D. F. 1972. Detrimental Externalities and Non-Convexity of the Production Set. *Economica*, 39, 160–176.

Binmore, K. 2005. *Natural Justice*. New York: Oxford University Press.
     2006. *The Origins of Fair Play*. Jena, Germany: Max Planck Inst. of Economics, Evolutionary Economics Group.

---

[33] On the intricate normative issues raised by economic novelty, see Schubert (2012).

Blume, L., Rubinfeld, D. L., and Shapiro, P. 1984. The Taking of Land: When Should Compensation Be Paid? *The Quarterly Journal of Economics*, 98, 71–92.

Bromley, D. W. 1997. Constitutional Political Economy: Property Claims in a Dynamic World. *Contemporary Economic Policy*, 15, 43–54.

Calabresi, G. and Melamed, A. D. 1972. Property Rules, Liability Rules, and Inalienability: One View of the Cathedral. *Harvard Law Review*, 85, 1089–1128.

Canaris, C.-W. 1993. Funktion, Struktur und Falsifikation juristischer Theorien. *Juristenzeitung* 48, 377–391.

Coase, R. H. 1960. The Problem of Social Cost. *The Journal of Law & Economics*, 3, 1–44.

1988. *The Firm, the Market, and the Law.* Chicago: University of Chicago Press.

Coleman, J. L. and Murphy, J. G. 1990. *Philosophy of Law.* Boulder, CO: Westview Press.

Cooter, R. 1982. The Cost of Coase. *The Journal of Legal Studies*, 11, 1–33.

Cooter, R. D. 2000. Law from Order: Economic Development and the Jurisprudence of Social Norms. In: Olson, M. and Kähkönen, S. (eds.) *A Not-So-Dismal Science.* New York: Oxford University Press.

Cooter, R. and Ulen, T. 2011. *Law and Economics.* Reading, MA: Prentice-Hall.

Cordes, C. and Schubert, C. 2007. Toward a Naturalistic Foundation of the Social Contract. *Constitutional Political Economy*, 18, 35–62.

Daniels, N. 1979. Wide Reflective Equilibrium and Theory Acceptance in Ethics. *The Journal of Philosophy*, 76, 256–282.

Demsetz, H. 1972. When Does the Rule of Liability Matter? *The Journal of Legal Studies*, 1, 13–28.

Ehrlich, I. and Posner, R. A. 1974. An Economic Analysis of Legal Rulemaking. *The Journal of Legal Studies*, 3, 257–286.

Ellickson, R. C. 1995. *Order without Law: How Neighbors Settle Disputes.* Cambridge, MA: Harvard University Press.

Epstein, R. A. 1985. *Takings: Private Property and the Power of Eminent Domain.* Cambridge, MA: Harvard University Press.

Fehr, E. and Fischbacher, U. 2002. Why Social Preferences Matter – The Impact of Non-Selfish Motives on Competition, Cooperation and Incentives. *The Economic Journal*, 112, C1–C33.

Fischel, W. A. 1985. *The Economics of Zoning Laws.* Baltimore: Johns Hopkins University Press.

1995. *Regulatory Takings.* Cambridge, MA: Harvard University Press.

Fischel, W. A. and Shapiro, P. 1989. A Constitutional Choice Model of Compensation for Takings. *International Review of Law and Economics*, 9, 115–128.

Frey, B. S., Oberholzer-Gee, F., and Eichenberger, R. 1996. The Old Lady Visits Your Backyard: A Tale of Morals and Markets. *Journal of Political Economy,* 104, 1297–1313.

Grigoleit, K. J. 2000. Normative Steuerung und kooperative Planung. *Die Verwaltung,* 33, 79–109.

Güth, W. 1995. On Ultimatum Bargaining Experiments – A Personal Review. *Journal of Economic Behavior and Organization,* 27, 329–344.

Hahn, S. 2000. *Überlegungsgleichgewicht(e) – Prüfung einer Rechtfertigungsmetapher.* Alber: Freiburg.

Harsanyi, J. C. 1975. Can the Maximin Principle Serve as a Basis for Morality? A Critique of John Rawls' Theory. *American Political Science Review,* 69, 594–606.

  1982. Morality and the Theory of Rational Behavior. In: Sen, A. K. and Williams, B. (eds.) *Utilitarianism and Beyond.* Cambridge: Cambridge University Press.

Hayden, G. M. and Ellis, S. E. 2007. Law and Economics after Behavioral Economics. *University of Kansas Law Review,* 55, 629–675.

Healey, P., Purdue, M., and Ennis, F. 1995. *Negotiating Development: Rationales and Practice for Development Obligations and Planning Gain.* London: E & FN Spon.

Heider, L. and Mukerji, N. 2015. Rawls, Order Ethics, and Rawlsian Order Ethics. In: Lütge, C. and Mukerji, N. (eds.) *Order Ethics – A Compendium.* Berlin: Springer.

Henrich, J., Ensminger, J., Mcelreath, R., et al. 2010a. Markets, Religion, Community Size, and the Evolution of Fairness and Punishment. *Science,* 327, 1480–1484.

Henrich, J., Heine, S. J., and Norenzayan, A. 2010b. The Weirdest People in the World? *Behavioral and Brain Sciences,* 33, 61–83.

Hoffman, E. and Spitzer, M. L. 1986. Experimental Tests of the Coase Theorem with Large Bargaining Groups. *Journal of Legal Studies,* 15, 149–171.

Jolls, C., Sunstein, C. R., and Thaler, R. 1998. A Behavioral Approach to Law and Economics. *Stanford Law Review,* 50, 1471–1450.

Kaplow, L. and Shavell, S. 1996. Property Rules versus Liability Rules: An Economic Analysis. *Harvard Law Review,* 109, 713–790.

  2002. *Fairness versus Welfare.* Cambridge, MA; London: Harvard University Press.

Kim, I. and Kim, J. 2004. Efficiency of Posner's Nuisance Rule: A Reconsideration. *Journal of Institutional and Theoretical Economics (JITE) / Zeitschrift für die gesamte Staatswissenschaft,* 160, 327–333.

Krugman, P. 1996. *The Self-organizing Economy.* Cambridge: Blackwell.

Medema, S. G. 1999. Symposium on the Coase Theorem: Legal Fiction: The Place of the Coase Theorem in Law and Economics. *Economics and Philosophy*, 15, 209–233.

Miceli, T. J. 1991. Compensation for the Taking of Land under Eminent Domain. *Journal of Institutional and Theoretical Economics*, 147, 354–363.

Miceli, T. J. and Segerson, K. 2000. Takings. In: Bouckaert, B. and Geest, G. D. (eds.) *Encyclopedia of Law & Economics*. Aldershot: Edward Elgar.

Michelman, F. I. 1967. Property, Utility, and Fairness: Comments on the Ethical Foundations of "Just Compensation" Law. *Harvard Law Review*, 80, 1165–1258.

Mishan, E. J. 1971. The Postwar Literature on Externalities: An Interpretative Essay. *Journal of Economic Literature*, 9, 1–28.

Mumey, G. A. 1971. The "Coase Theorem": A Reexamination. *The Quarterly Journal of Economics*, 85, 718–723.

O'Neill, O. 1998. The Method of A Theory of Justice. In: Höffe, O. (ed.) *John Rawls. Eine Theorie der Gerechtigkeit*. Berlin: Akademie-Verlag.

Ott, C. and Schäfer, H. B. 1994. Entwicklung und Konstruktion effizienter Normen im Rechtssystem des deutschen Zivilrechts. *Homo Oeconomicus*, 11, 293–329.

Papandreou, A. A. 2003. Externality, Convexity and Institutions. *Economics and Philosophy*, 19, 281–309.

Papier, H. J. 1994. Art. In: Maunz, T. and Dürig, G. (eds.) *Grundgesetz-Kommentar*. München: C. H. Beck.

Posner, R. A. 1979. Utilitarianism, Economics, and Legal Theory. *The Journal of Legal Studies*, 8, 103–140.

2010. *Economic Analysis of Law*. New York: Aspen Publishers.

Rawls, J. 1958. Justice as Fairness. *Philosophical Review*, 67, 164–194.

1971. *A Theory of Justice*. Cambridge, MA: Belknap Press of Harvard University Press.

Schelling, T. C. 1978. *Micromotives and Macrobehavior*. New York: Norton.

Schlicht, E. 1996. Exploiting the Coase Mechanism: The Extortion Problem. *Kyklos*, 49, 319–330.

Schubert, C. 2006. *Die rechtliche Steuerung urbanen Wandels: eine konstitutionenökonomische Untersuchung*. Tübingen: Mohr Siebeck.

2012. Is Novelty Always a Good Thing? Towards an Evolutionary Welfare Economics. *Journal of Evolutionary Economics*, 22, 585–619.

Stigler, G. J. 1966. *The Theory of Price*. New York: Macmillan.

Swanson, T. and Kontoleon, A. 2000. Nuisance. In: Bouckaert, B. and Geest, G. D. (eds.) *Encyclopedia of Law and Economics*. Aldershot: Edward Elgar.

Tyler, T. R. 1990. *Why People Obey the Law*. New Haven, CT: Yale University Press.

von Wangenheim, G. V. 2011. Evolutionary Theories in Law and Economics and Their Use for Comparative Legal Theory. *Review of Law & Economics*, 7, 737–765.

Witt, U. 1989. The Evolution of Economic Institutions as a Propagation Process. *Public Choice*, 62, 155–172.

——— 1996. Innovations, Externalities and the Problem of Economic Progress. *Public Choice*, 89, 113–130.

Wolf, M. 2005. *Sachenrecht*. München: C. H. Beck.

PART V

Evolutionary Perspectives on Welfare and Sustainability

11 As Innovations Drive Economic Change, Do They Also Improve Our Welfare?

MARTIN BINDER AND ULRICH WITT

Introduction

The huge increase in innovative economic activities over the past two centuries has been a main driver of technological progress, increasing resource productivity, and the growth of per capita income and consumption in the developed economies (Schumpeter 1942; Rosenberg & Birdzell 1986; Dosi 1988; Mokyr 1990; Nelson 1996; Aghion & Howitt 1998; Metcalfe 1998). Relatedly, the business world perceives of innovative activities as a prime strategy for gaining competitive advantages and economic profits. Not surprisingly, a generally positive attitude towards innovative activities prevails in public and supports policies that foster innovations (Flanagan, Uyarra, & Laranja 2011). Economists have long since endorsed such policies with the argument that (new) knowledge required for generating innovative opportunities can have the character of a public good. It may therefore not be provided to a desirable extent on a private basis (Gustafsson & Autio 2011).

However, on closer scrutiny several questions arise. If innovations are not an end in their own, what precisely are the ends they serve? What normative justification can be given for these ends? Is the fact that, in the past, innovations played a decisive role in overcoming poverty, drudgery, and malady sufficient justification for their pursuit? What to do about conflicts between ends which innovations can cause and have caused? History shows that innovations were not always unanimously welcomed (not to speak of the fact that not all innovations developed beneficial effects). Moreover, times of starvation have been left behind at least in the developed economies. On what account can the now even broader call for innovations particularly in the developed economies, then be justified?

From the point of view of economic theory, a way to answer these questions is to judge innovations by the welfare effects they entail. The notion of welfare commonly refers to how well an individual or

343

a society fares. The problem thus is to determine whether innovations make the members of society better off – as is usually implicitly or explicitly presumed in the innovation policy literature. The criteria by which this can be assessed differ. Yet even on the basis of specific criteria, it is often difficult to derive definite conclusions about the welfare effects of innovations. The present chapter is devoted to a discussion of the problems a normative assessment of innovations faces.

Our discussion proceeds as follows. Because there is not much consensus in the literature on what welfare measure to choose (McQuillin & Sugden 2012, see also the discussion in Binder 2010), we first take stock in the next section of the major concepts that can be used. Following Parfit's (1984: 493–503) classification of welfare theories, the criterion for assessing welfare effects of innovations can be (i) individual preference satisfaction, (ii) a hedonistic mental state account, or (iii) a list of objective measures. After introducing these welfare measures we elaborate in the third section on obstacles arising for assessing the welfare effects of innovations from the externalities they cause. First, innovations always have so-called "pecuniary" externalities. This means that – as Schumpeter (1942: 84) already recognized – the benefits and costs of innovations are unevenly distributed within the economy and over time. As we will show, this condition hampers welfare assessments in the case of all three measures. Second, innovations can have negative technological externalities which, due to the very nature of innovations, cannot fully be anticipated at the time when they are implemented (Witt 1996, 2009). They can "bite back" and do so surprisingly often (see Tenner 1997). Because of potentially very severe, nonanticipatable social costs, it cannot be excluded that innovations can even cause negative welfare effects.

For expository convenience, the discussion in the third section assumes that the respective criteria for assessing the welfare effects of innovations are not changing under the influence of innovations. However, as already pointed out by Elster (1983) and recently acknowledged in the emerging behavioral welfare theory in economics (von Weizsäcker 2005; Bernheim & Rangel 2009), this assumption is often violated, particularly by new-consumption goods and services. The fourth section therefore turns to the difficulties arising when innovations influence the measuring rod by which their welfare effects are supposed to be assessed. We explore the implications for each of the three theories of welfare in turn. As it will turn out, under these conditions, an unambiguous assessment of the welfare effects of innovations is difficult, if not impossible, to derive in all three cases. The fifth section presents the conclusions, among them a few remarks regarding the role of our analysis for policy making.

How to Measure Welfare Effects of Innovations

What do we understand by "welfare"? As can be seen from the etymological roots of the term, the notion refers to – broadly speaking – how well an individual or society fares. Hence, it implies an assessment of well-being or the quality of life of the members of society according to a certain measuring rod. Theories of welfare differ with respect to the measuring rod they use.[1] Following Parfit's (1984: 493–503) taxonomy, we will consider here three types of theories (implying different notions or criteria) of welfare. The first one is preference satisfaction theory. Its criterion for welfare is the outcome which, according to one's own preferences, is the best one that is feasible under the given constraints.[2] Second, we consider mental state accounts of welfare. These hedonistic theories have seen a revival under the recent label of "subjective well-being" (or "happiness") accounts (e.g., Helliwell, Layard, & Sachs 2015). They come mainly in two versions, as either evaluative or experiential accounts. The former refer to measures of self-assessed life satisfaction (a cognitive measure or attitude about how well one's life is judged to go overall), whereas the latter refers to a more narrowly hedonistic assessment of one's emotions and affect (sometimes also called "happiness" in a narrower sense). Finally, we have a look at objective list theories of welfare. They refer to a list of

[1] Theories of welfare also differ with respect to their approach to the legitimization/justification of their concept of welfare: constitutional-economic (contractarian) approaches see the individual as the addressee who confers legitimacy to such notion, and traditional welfare-economic approaches address the social planner who attempts to maximize a certain social welfare function (Sugden 2013; Vanberg 2014). In this chapter, we abstract from the issue of justification and deal with a descriptive analysis of notions of welfare.

[2] Preference satisfaction theories are sometimes also called desire theories. However, desires are directed at objects or sets of objects, while a preference in the economic context is always a binary relation: one of two objects (e.g., a bundle of goods and services) is either preferred over or equivalent to the other. We stick to the narrower interpretation of preference satisfaction in the following.

criteria that are measurable independently of the individuals' experience and assessment of their condition and are in this sense objective.[3]

The preference satisfaction approach is the standard theory of welfare in economics. Unlike in the two other theories, in this framework it is not specified more concretely on what individual welfare depends. It is just the individuals' feasible alternative most highly valued according to *their* preferences that determines welfare, whatever their preferences (or the arguments of their corresponding utility function) are. This is an outcome-oriented approach. Accordingly, welfare is improved, if individuals can reach an outcome that better satisfies their preferences (indicated by a higher utility index). In textbook form, the theory is usually presented in the framework of a consumer choice problem. Let the optimal consumption bundle that is feasible for an individual i with income I be given by the vector $x^* = (x_1, ..., x_n)$ of n goods and services. Assume the income constraint is relaxed by the amount ΔI (or by a change of prices with equivalent effect). If such an event makes an optimal bundle $x^{*\prime} = (x_1', ..., x_n')$ feasible which is preferred to x^* – that is, if the individual's utility index $u_i(x^{*\prime}) > u_i(x^*)$ – this amounts to a welfare increase. More generally speaking, a relaxation of the constraints on an individual's preferred opportunities usually results in an improved preference satisfaction (i.e., a welfare increase). In this approach, rising incomes can therefore be considered ordinally equivalent to rising welfare compatible with the strong focus on per capita income measures in economic policy making.

The preference satisfaction theory of welfare cannot, and does not, claim to explain why particular choices cause satisfaction as, for example, theories of needs or wants try to do (Broome 2008). Preference satisfaction (the generation of utility) is stripped of any material content, except the tacit psychological assumptions implied by the usual formal axioms, such as the convexity axiom implying a preference for variety. Observing the individual to choose $x^{*\prime}$ over x^* is not assumed to reflect any increased enjoyment, satisfaction, or happiness but only that the individual prefers one over the other (and without any actual judgment on the intensity of preference, since the

---

[3] For space reasons a discussion of whether Parfit's three ideal types of welfare theories can be extended in a useful way by combined types as, e.g., in Schubert (2015), has to be left out here.

whole theory operates on an ordinal level). The arguments in the individual utility functions are placeholders for unspecified objects of choice (Broome 2008, compare also Hausman & McPherson 2006). In this theory, the explanation of how innovations affect preference satisfaction (welfare) must therefore be confined to the income or price effects that they can cause. Whether and when innovations are valued and trigger a recomposition of the feasible choice set has to be left open. Consequently, preference satisfaction theory can offer no explanation for why some innovations succeed and other ones fail. At the same time, the formal assumptions about the individual preferences that are made rest on a strong concept of rationality, including the well-known transitivity, completeness, and invariability axioms (see, e.g., Mas-Colell, Whinston, & Green 1995). The empirical relevance of many of these axioms is increasingly challenged in the emerging field of behavioral economics for their poor experimental support (for surveys see DellaVigna 2009 and more comprehensively, Angner 2016).

The second class of welfare theories to be considered here – the hedonistic theories or mental state accounts of welfare – do not require the incriminated rationality assumptions and rather focus on the individuals' subjective evaluation of their lives (measures of life satisfaction) or their experiential account of their affective states and emotions (measures of positive/negative affect). Most of the empirical literature on subjective well-being refers to cognitive (rather than affective) layers of well-being (Helliwell, Layard, & Sachs 2015), that is, the cognitive self-assessment of one's subjective well-being. In this interpretation, life satisfaction, a cognitive judgment-cum-endorsement, is seen as constitutive of welfare.[4]

Despite the subjective nature of the construct and contrary to criticisms regarding what it actually measures,[5] subjective well-being

---

[4] See, e.g., Frey and Stutzer (2002). In happiness surveys both the scale, normalized to a range 0 to 10, say, on which subjective well-being is measured and the choice of a particular value on that scale are subjectively determined by the respondents themselves.

[5] Subjective concepts of well-being run the risk of resulting in a solipsistic measure, if well-being is taken to be solely a mental state, independent of the actual states of world, see, e.g., Nozick (1974: 42–45). Having a pleasurable state of mind is obviously not necessarily contingent on living a life that causes pleasurable feelings.

assessments have been claimed to have a high level of validity and reliability (see Diener et al. 1999).[6] Supporting this view, psychological research has shown that self-reported well-being is partly a stable condition that seems to be influenced by personality traits (Diener et al. 1999) and/or genetic endowment (Lykken & Tellegen 1996). It has further been shown that self-reported well-being scores are strongly correlated with objectively measurable emotional expressions like smiling (Fernández-Dols & Ruiz-Belda 1995) and affective brain activity (Shizgal 1999). Self-reported happiness scores have also been found to be affected by objective changes of life conditions such as repeated unemployment, marriage, or childbirth (Headey 2010). Moreover, where this is possible, subjects seem to respond to negative influences on their subjective well-being by discontinuing behavior to which they attribute the negative influence (Shiv & Huber 2000).[7]

It is important to note that, unlike preference satisfaction theory, subjective well-being accounts can be based on a cardinal measure. This means that they allow one to conceive of welfare in terms of the individuals' time profiles of well-being (e.g., in terms of pleasures and pains; see Broome 2008; Binder 2010 for a discussion), Accordingly, they can provide a welfare measure that ranks actions in terms of their intensity (Redelmeier & Kahneman 1996; Kahneman, Wakker, & Sarin 1997).

Finally, there are objective list theories of welfare. An example is Amartya Sen's (1985a, b) capabilities and functionings approach that has gained some prominence in economics. In order to assess the welfare of particular individuals or groups of individuals he suggests focusing on the objective conditions under which they live and evaluating them according to prudential and ethical considerations. The objective conditions are captured more specifically by the dual conception of "functionings" and "capability to function."

---

[6] However, over a period of two weeks, the test-retest reliability of subjective well-being constructs has observed to only be 0.5 to 0.7 in experiments with both cognitive and affective measures; see Krueger and Schkade (2008).

[7] Support for the conjecture that self-reported well-being reflects objective conditions of life is also provided by interpersonal well-being assessments. By observing the situation of other individuals, subjects seem to a certain extent able to predict happiness scores and life satisfaction of other individuals (Sandvik, Diener, & Seidlitz 1993; Diener & Lucas 1999).

The functionings refer to what a person does and is, for example, "being nourished," "avoiding premature mortality" (Sen 1992: 39) or "being in good health," "being well-sheltered," "being educated," or being able to "move about freely" (Kuklys 2005: 10). In Sen's view, such functionings have intrinsic value and cannot be reduced to other, more basic values. The list of values is seen as open-ended and supposed to contain "the plurality of our concerns" (Sen 1992: 70).

For assessing an individual's welfare, Sen proposes to measure the extent to which the individual has the substantive freedom to choose among these valuable functionings. This means to measure welfare in terms of opportunities rather than outcomes, implying a radical break with the traditional approach in welfare economics. Put slightly more formally, the welfare of an individual i is characterized in Sen's theory by a vector b_i of functionings (Sen 1985a; Kuklys 2005). b_i is assumed to depend on a vector of commodities, including nonmarket goods and services x_i that is feasible for i. x_i is mapped into a vector c_i in the characteristics space (Lancaster 1966) via a conversion function $\varphi(x_i)$ denoting the characteristics associated with the commodity vector x_i. A function f_i maps the characteristics feasible to individual i into a vector of functionings

$$b_i = f_i(c_i = \varphi(x_i) \,|\, z_i, z_s, z_e)$$

The mapping is contingent on specific individual, social, and environmental factors $z_i, z_s,$ and z_e, respectively.[8] These factors can be seen as additional nonmonetary constraints which i faces in her functionings.[9] The union of all functioning vectors that are feasible to an individual i is called the capability set Q_i. It represents the opportunities an individual has. These opportunities, rather than the actually chosen b_i (which represents just one specific, idiosyncratically chosen

---

[8] See Kuklys (2005: 11). Individual factors could be gender, intelligence, or the mentioned physical (dis)abilities, etc. Social influences could comprise, for example, legal regulations. An example for an environmental factor would be climate or the level of pollution of one's surroundings.

[9] Sen assumes that the characteristics of a commodity are the same for all individuals. But not every individual can benefit equally from the characteristics. For example, having a disease or disability might entail that one can benefit less from the same set of characteristics than someone healthy (Sen 1985b: 9).

outcome for that individual) are taken as the measure for assessing the individual's welfare.[10]

The question to be explored in the remainder of this chapter is what assessment of the welfare effects of innovations can be derived from the just outlined approaches to measuring welfare. Innovations are commonly perceived to contribute to technological progress and to increasing resource productivity. This may generate competitive advantages to firms and entire countries. The welfare implications of these supply-side effects of innovations are determined, however, by the fact that more efficient production leads to falling costs allowing, in turn, for greater profits and/or higher per capita real income and consumption.[11] It seems straightforward therefore to assume that the welfare effects of innovations should be positive, whichever of the alternative measures is applied. However, there are obstacles to actually deriving such a positive assessment. The discussion of these obstacles is the topic of the next two sections.

Whose Welfare Will Be Affected by Innovations and How?

In this section we will focus on the obstacles to measuring welfare that arise when innovations cause externalities. (The discussion of the problems arising from the possibility that innovations influence the measurement of their welfare effects will, for expository convenience, be postponed to the next section.) There is no doubt that, for the developed economies, innovations have been the major driver of economic growth and the rising "standard of living of the masses," as Schumpeter (1942: 84) put it. If the standard of living were defined in terms of a list of objective criteria as in Sen's capabilities approach,

---

[10] It is not entirely clear how Q_i is evaluated. One possibility is to postulate a valuation function that assigns a numerical value to each $b_i \in Q_i$ according to the best element in the vector. Sen calls such a rule "elementary evaluation" (Sen 1985b: 61). The value of Q_i would then be the value of the best element in Q_i. Another possibility is to evaluate Q_i according to the number of elements in Q_i (a "cardinality valuation", Sen 1985b).

[11] By technological innovations it is often possible to reduce negative external effects of existing production activities and thus to improve welfare; see the next section. Furthermore, the historical record shows that innovations in production technology have helped make working conditions healthier and safer, thus reducing the dis-utility of working. In the standard microeconomic analysis a reduction of dis-utility is tantamount to an increase in individual welfare.

one could say that the capability set and, hence, the welfare of an *average* individual in the developed economies have been strongly improved by the continued innovative activities.

However, as also already recognized by Schumpeter, the immediate benefits and costs of innovations, and often also their longer run effects, are very unequally distributed in the economy. It is by no means clear therefore that the capabilities and welfare of *all* individuals have been improved. On the supply side of the markets many innovating agents certainly benefited from realizing innovation rents which may have boosted their capability sets tremendously. Also for the agents on the demand side who adopted innovations, it can be inferred that they did so because they had experienced that their capability sets, too, were improved that way.[12] Furthermore, the indirect positive effects through innovation-induced expansion of demand, and the thus induced multiplier effects, have contributed to improving the capability to function of many agents, whether directly in touch with innovations or not.

Nonetheless, the capability sets of many agents – in extreme cases of the majority in an economy – did not benefit from the innovations, or at least not in the short or medium run. To the contrary, due to losses in income, wealth, or status, these agents may have experienced a deterioration of their situation. The reason is that innovations selectively improve the competitive position of single firms or single industries and induce substitution processes at the expense of other firms or industries competing for the same customers' spending. As a consequence of such "pecuniary" externalities, specific investments – made before an innovation was introduced – may be devalued or even lost. Capital owners may face losses of expected returns. Labor may face being laid off and forego expected returns on human capital investments when forced to accept employment elsewhere. In short, innovations often cause massive interpersonal redistribution of welfare. How do objective list theories of welfare such as Sen's capabilities

---

[12] An inference of this kind implicitly presumes that the problem of evaluating the high-dimensional capability set Q_i is spontaneously solved by the adopters of an innovation. Thus, if an innovation affects different functionings in the conflicting way of a trade-off, the decision maker is assumed to be able to weigh innovation-induced benefits in one dimension against innovation-induced sacrifices in a different dimension. Sen's capabilities approach neither explains, however, how decision makers accomplish this task, nor does it offer normative advice as to how the task should be accomplished.

approach account for this fact? To lend support to the widespread public approval of innovations, a value judgment would be necessary that rectifies trading off the at least temporarily negative welfare effects for some individuals for the positive welfare effect for the *average* individual. Yet objective list theories of welfare offer no normative foundation for such a value judgment.

In contrast, the preference satisfaction theory of welfare has a normative foundation expressed in a nutshell by the Pareto criterion. As is well known, this criterion attributes welfare improvements to events if, and only if, they make at least one individual better off in terms of her preference satisfaction without making any other individual worse off. Yet this implicit value judgment delimits the possibilities for assessing welfare effects whenever redistributions occur. Constitutive for the preference satisfaction theory of welfare is the utility calculus of *every* affected individual and not that of an average or representative individual. This means that, in the case of the innovation-induced pecuniary externalities, an assessment of welfare effects is ruled out, because the Pareto criterion is not satisfied. In its strict form, the preference satisfaction theory of welfare can therefore not be used to back the positive perception of innovations in the public – except a strong assumption is added.

To explain which assumption this is, a short digression is necessary. Under competitive conditions, the gains from an innovation are usually larger for the economy as a whole than the sum of the losses caused by pecuniary externalities. This is the very reason for why innovations *do* lead to a growth of per capita income (and a different way of saying that sometimes heavy damages to the welfare of some individuals do not exclude a positive average welfare effect of innovations). Because of this very fact it would, in principle, be possible to compensate all who lose out of the gains of the winners. Yet such compensations hardly ever take place. Nonetheless, when the mere possibility exists – when the so-called Kaldor-Hicks compensation criterion is fulfilled (Kaldor 1939; Hicks 1939) – this is often considered sufficient for claiming that society as a whole can realize a welfare gain through innovations (ignoring the distributional contingencies of welfare assessments, see Gowdy 2005).

Many researchers and policy makers advocating proactive strategies of fostering innovations seem to hold such a view. Strictly speaking it can only be defended, however, if one is willing to accept strong assumptions that were commonly made in the early days of utilitarianism: (i) that an interpersonal comparison of utility is feasible by which innovation-induced utility gains and losses can be set off against each other and (ii) that in case of a positive balance the innovation is warranted even in the absence of a compensation (because it implies "the greatest happiness of the greatest number" as Bentham put it). However, subjective well-being theories (mental states accounts) often tend to accept the evidence that (i) interpersonal comparisons of utility (read: well-being) are feasible, they similarly need to accept the utilitarian value judgement (ii) and hence require the same type of value judgement that preference satisfaction theories do.

Apart from the problem of pecuniary externalities, the balance of gains and losses, and with it the intuitively approving view of innovations, changes when innovations develop negative "technological" externalities, that is, if the economic activities of some agent(s) harm the condition (property, health, etc.) of other agents without (fully) compensating the harm. Because of the nature of innovations, all their properties cannot yet be completely known when their implementation starts. Although many innovations develop highly welcome effects as expected (often even reducing existing negative externalities) it can never be excluded *ex ante* that an innovation triggers negative externalities. Often it turns out only with considerable time delay after an innovation has been implemented that such externalities occur. Examples are not difficult to find: think of the damages that new material such as asbestos or chlorofluorocarbon gas caused, or of new pesticides such as DDT, new drugs such as thalidomide (Contergan) and rofecoxib (Vioxx), new techniques such as nuclear power generation and deep sea drilling, and so on.[13]

In cases like these, the social costs that have been caused by the innovation are already substantial when their damaging potential is recognized. In terms of Coase's (1960) classical formulation of the problem of social costs, the inevitable risk of yet unknown negative technological externalities of innovations means that there are inherent, irreducible transaction costs. They exclude the possibility of *ex ante* negotiations as a way of efficiently internalizing the social costs either by the innovator who causes the externality or by those who are affected. From the perspective of all three theories, the

---

[13] See, e.g., Tenner (1997) on many examples of how innovations "bite back" and have unintended negative consequences that are hard to cope with.

consequence is a substantial uncertainty. At the time of its implementation, an innovation may appear unambiguously favorable in terms of increasing capability sets, preference satisfaction, or subjective well-being. But it can never be excluded that, due to negative technological externalities, the very same innovation causes deteriorations in the capability sets, in preference satisfaction, or in subjective well-being in the future. Indeed, these deteriorations can be so substantial that in the future the losses for society as a whole exceed society's initial innovation gains. If these losses are not fully born by the generation that introduced the innovation, an intergenerational distribution problem arises in addition to the already discussed interpersonal distribution problem. And with respect to this problem, too, no advice is offered by the three theories of welfare as to solve it – except more or less arbitrarily chosen value judgments are added.

Endogenous Change of Welfare Assessments of Innovations

When innovations cause negative technological externalities, this has welfare-reducing effects. When they cause pecuniary externalities, it is difficult to assess their welfare effects unless strong assumptions and value judgments are added. But even if this were different, welfare judgments would for yet another reason rest on shaky foundations. The reason is a simplifying assumption that has so far been made: The measuring rod for assessing welfare – be it a list of objective criteria, a mental state account, or preference satisfaction – has been assumed not to change under the influence of innovations. However, in the light of how humans adapt to new action possibilities, this is a counterfactual assumption. Behavior is not only adapted to newly acquired information. It also changes as a result of an emerging appreciation of new options and a fading appreciation of older ones. Both know-how and liking (i.e., practical and evaluative knowledge) are malleable over time in a way that depends on the innovations that are experienced. In this section we turn to the implications of this phenomenon for judging the welfare effects of innovations, particularly innovations in consumer goods and services, leaving aside the complications arising from the externality problem.

In the preference satisfaction theory of welfare, the malleability problem occurs in the context of preference learning (see Witt, 2017). Learning new preferences in response to the experience of new choice options made available by innovations can be represented as an extension of the preference order an individual holds. (Due to a constrained preference memory, such extensions may result in other parts of the preference order falling into oblivion.) The extension may or may not be compatible with the preexisting preference order in the following sense: All preference relations revealed over alternatives that are feasible before and after an innovation is introduced remain the same (see von Weizsäcker 2005; Bernheim & Rangel 2009). This condition ensures an intertemporal transitivity of preferences over those elements of the feasible set not changed by an innovation (no "menu dependence of preferences," see Kőszegi & Rabin 2008). It is *not* sufficient, however, to ensure consistent intertemporal preference relations and, hence, welfare judgments between pre-innovation options and the newly emerging post-innovation options.

In order to prove this claim, recall the notation in the earlier section and assume that at time t_1 there exist n goods and services from which an individual chooses a bundle $x^* = (x_1, ..., x_n)$ that maximizes her utility under the given income constraint. Let the individual choose a bundle $x^{*\prime} \neq x^*$ as the optimal solution, if income increased by the amount ΔI (or prices were changed with similar effect). Hence the relation

$$u_{t_1}(x^{*\prime}) > u_{t_1}(x^*) \tag{11.1}$$

holds. Now suppose an innovation is introduced in t_2 such that there are n + 1 goods and services. Furthermore, let the individual's income in t_2 be increased exactly by the amount ΔI. Assuming that the individual has learned to appreciate the new good or service, that is, her preferences have been extended in t_2, let the new optimal bundle be $x^+ = (x_1^+, ..., x_{n+1}^+)$. The individual's post-innovation preferences thus yield the order relation

$$u_{t_2}(x^+) > u_{t_2}(x^{*\prime}) > u_{t_2}(x^*). \tag{11.2}$$

As inequality (11.2) shows, the pre-innovation order relation between $x^{*\prime}$ and x^* corresponding to inequality (11.1) is still valid in t_2, that is, the intertemporal transitivity condition is satisfied for the still feasible bundles. But the innovation has made a bundle x^+ feasible, which makes the individual better off. This means conversely that the welfare of the individual would be reduced if the innovation would be removed from her choice set at a later time point. However, had the new preferences not been learned, nothing would have been missed if the new option had been removed.

Indeed, if judged by the pre-innovation preferences at time t_1, the order relation would be

$$u_{t_1}(x^{*\prime}) \geq u_{t_1}(x^+),$$ (11.3)

because the individual would, at best, be indifferent with respect to the new good or service it has not yet learned to appreciate.[14] If the individual rejects what is still alien to her, the inequality sign in Eq. (11.3) holds. By comparison of the inequalities in Eqs. (11.2) and (11.3) it follows that no consistent intertemporal preference relations exist. Pre-innovation and post-innovation welfare judgments contradict each other. Put differently, whether or not an innovation is welfare increasing hinges on whether the pre-innovation or the post-innovation preferences are taken as the relevant measuring rod. A value judgment is necessary regarding which of the two to take as the reference basis (see the exemplary discussion of Sugden's (2004) approach later). This result points to a peculiar preference relativism. Taken by itself preference satisfaction theory is not sufficient to decide whether or not innovations result in positive welfare effects.

Within the framework of the preference satisfaction theory of welfare, innovations induce adaptations in the form of preference learning. In hedonistic theories of welfare, the analogue innovation-induced adaptation occurs at the level of learning of new, not previously experienced, pleasures. After they have been learned, removing them from the choice set would also lead to decreased well-being. Hence, the asymmetry in assessing the welfare effects of innovations results in the hedonistic theories of welfare too.[15] However, if we make the enjoyment of pleasurable feelings the criterion for welfare (i.e., focus on pleasure or happiness profiles over time), we have

---

[14] Note that when the set of feasible choices is extended by a relaxation of the income constraint to elements previously known to the decision maker [the case of inequality Eq. (11.1)], pre-relaxation and post-relaxation preferences cannot fall apart.

[15] This was already expressed by Elster (1983: 135) as follows: "We were happier before we got these fancy new things, but now we would be miserable without them". Had the new pleasure not been learned they would, of course, not be missed when withdrawn. In fact, spending on the innovation would not generate pleasure, but would require sacrificing spending on other pleasures and, hence, cause a welfare loss – the analogue to the just analyzed preference relativism.

to account for the particular adaptation dynamics they are subject to. The framework for the adaptation dynamics is set by the fact that our inbuilt sensory capacities for enjoying pleasures per period – 24 hours, say – has an upper bound.[16] It cannot be exceeded by pleasurable stimuli triggered by ever more innovations.

At the same time, there is a sensory mechanism called hedonic adaptation (Frederick & Loewenstein 1999). We get used to continuously experienced pleasurable stimuli and in this process the intensity of their enjoyment decreases over time.[17] Even if the pleasures experienced by enjoying some innovation(s) would temporarily reach the upper bound of our capacities, getting used to the innovation(s) would sooner or later result in hedonic adaptation, and the enjoyment caused by the very same innovation(s) would decline. To uphold or again raise the level of enjoyment, new forms of triggering pleasurable feelings are required. They may arise from the newly learned pleasures of consuming yet other innovations – again without lasting for long. Because a continued consumption of such new pleasurable stimuli is rarely feasible without extra effort or extra spending, one may associate this phenomenon with what is called in the literature the hedonic treadmill effect (see, e.g., Binswanger 2006).[18]

The phenomenon is not dependent on income, status, or health conditions. Very rich, highly adored, or very healthy individuals are

---

[16] This bound finds its correspondence in subjective well-being questions being anchored by the extreme values representing the "best possible world" (Gallup) or being "completely" satisfied/dissatisfied. Similar anchors also exist for other pleasure and pain ratings (e.g., Redelmeier & Kahneman 1996; Kahneman, Wakker, & Sarin 1997).

[17] An analogue adaptation can also be observed over the historical time dimension. While, for instance, relief from suffering hunger, drudgery, and early death was a source of newly gained pleasure that meant a huge innovation-induced welfare gain to our grandparents, in today's developed world these pleasures are normally a matter of course hardly noticed anymore.

[18] Pleasure and pain have a clear biological basis and role in homeostasis, acting as cues that facilitate survival of the organism (Cabanac 1992; Camerer, Loewenstein, & Prelec 2005: 27): While humans might consider attainment of pleasures and avoidance of pain to be goals in themselves, from a biological point of view they are instrumental for survival, and humans can be conjectured to be adapted with a view to survival, but not necessarily adapted to the experience of pleasures. These discrepancies between "nature's demands" and what humans consider valuable would warrant further discussion (see also more extensively Binder 2010: 99–107, on the relation between pleasure and pain, their role in homeostasis, and a hedonic notion of welfare).

not excepted from developing nonexcited feelings about their condition, which they may once may have felt as great pleasure (and still may be great pleasures for all who have to forego such conditions). On the other hand, hedonic adaptation works also in the opposite way, thus also diminishing over time the negative feelings of pain arising from disappointment, frustration, and other forms of mental suffering, for example, through the loss of wealth, status, or freedom from bodily harm. The occasionally absurd consequence has been highlighted by the "Paradox of the Miserable Millionaire and the Happy Beggar" (who has learned to adapt to his condition and enjoys the small pleasures left to him in his misery; see Graham 2010).

Hedonic adaptation poses serious problems when it comes to assessing welfare effects of innovations in an intertemporally consistent way (see Binder, 2010: 174–191). If individuals get used to negative circumstances, their welfare assessment will be high despite objectively miserable conditions, something that will be (ethically) problematic in the case of judgements of distributive justice (Sen 1987). But even in the case of diminishing pleasures, hedonic adaptation will give rise to an "innovation treadmill" on which societies might be on: Imagine a situation of bliss in society, where everyone faces a high level of well-being due to its momentary bundle of goods and services. Over time, enjoyment of these will fade and welfare decrease, necessitating innovativeness to find different ways to keep people satisfied (or even increase welfare, albeit temporarily).

In the case of preference satisfaction theory, the criteria by which the effects of innovations are measured tend to become endogenous to the innovative process they are supposed to evaluate. As a consequence, pre-innovation and post-innovation welfare assessments can fall apart and give room to preference relativism implying an arbitrary element in any judgment about the welfare effects of innovations. The conclusion to be drawn for the hedonistic theory of welfare may be even more disenchanting. From the point of view of hedonistic theories, "quick innovation fixes" become necessary to sustain given levels of well-being. The question arises whether there can be any lasting (cumulative) welfare-increasing effect of continued innovativeness at all.

In view of these complications it may seem straightforward to consider measuring the welfare effects of innovations on the basis of a list of objective criteria rather than in terms of the inherently malleable subjective preferences or mental states. Indeed, the phenomenon of hedonic adaptation and the resulting paradox of happy beggars has motivated Sen (e.g., Sen 1987: 45) to propose his capabilities approach.[19] Such paradoxical effects are simply not relevant when welfare is measured in terms of the capability set Q_i.

However, objective list theories of welfare like Sen's capabilities approach face other difficulties. They invite us to ask on whose value judgment the choice of the particular criteria and the omission of other criteria rests (see Sugden, 1993). Whose judgment is it to attach equal rather than a differentiated weight to the chosen criteria? What is the legitimation for invoking particular criteria, or is this simply a case of paternalism (Sugden 2006: 50)? It is conceivable that a list of functionings that is chosen as an allegedly objective reflection of individual welfare differs from what the affected individuals actually value or experience as determining their welfare.[20]

Moreover, a list of relevant functionings that may find broad consent today may not have found equal consent in the past, or will do so in the future. The "objective" list of prudentially and ethically valued functionings nominated today reflects not least the innovations of the past. A corresponding list put together at some future date is likely to reflect the influence of the innovations of the future. As a consequence of continued innovativeness, different functionings gain relevance and others may lose relevance. If so, the capabilities approach faces no less a problem of an intertemporally changing measuring rod for welfare than the preference satisfaction approach. The assessment may vary as a consequence of whether the pre-innovation list of functionings is chosen as a basis or the post-innovation list. The choice between the two alternatives involves a value judgment. Hence, the relativism and arbitrariness inherent in assessing the welfare effects of innovations on the basis of the preference satisfaction theory of welfare is not really overcome by objective list theories

---

[19] In his account, the paradox is denoted as the "hopeless beggar" problem, where a person in objectively miserable conditions would judge her welfare unrealistically high in the metric of preferences or hedonistic utility.

[20] Sugden (1993) and Nussbaum (2003) ask who decides on what functionings are to be included in the list. Even if, as Sen (1993: 31–32; 46–49) stresses, it is a question of the concrete purpose of the examination of which functionings are to be included, the question remains who decides on this. Nussbaum (2003: 41–42) tries to derive a list from Aristotle's concept of a commonly shared eudaimonia ("human flourishing"). Yet this is a notion from Aristotelian ethics, which, as a normative claim, is not "objective" in the sense of necessarily being universally shared.

of welfare, unless they can defend a universally valid list of things individuals have reason to value, something that is itself a matter of ethical valuation.

In reaction to the dilemma, some economists have proposed to replace a detailed list of objective criteria with a kind of degenerate, "objective" list approach. In this approach only one criterion makes it onto the list, a criterion that is supposed to reflect what the individuals themselves value: the set of opportunities an individual is able to command. If an event – an innovation – enlarges the opportunities of an individual, this amounts to welfare improvements (Hayek 1960; North 1999; Sartorius 2003). A more formal version of this approach has been devised by Sugden (2004). His contribution connects to the recent debate on welfare theory in behavioral economics. A key premise there is that individual preferences are often distorted and context dependent. Assuming full rationality as in preference satisfaction theory therefore sets an unrealistic framework for welfare assessments.

In line with this critique Sugden (2004) reiterates a value judgment to which preference satisfaction theory subscribes too, namely the "apparently simple normative intuition: it is good that each person is free to get what she wants" (Sugden 2004: 1016). However, he focuses on opportunities for, instead of the outcomes of, preference satisfaction, more specifically on the size of the individuals' opportunities set as the relevant welfare criterion.[21] He submits that, with

---

[21] Let the vector $x = (x_1, ..., x_n)$ denote a bundle of n goods and services and e_i the bundle of individual i's initial endowment with these goods and services. The opportunity set Ω_i is then defined as the set of all x which i can obtain by engaging in a series of trades starting from $e_i \in \Omega_i$. Assume that i gets from e_i to $x_i' \in \Omega_i$ through trade. Let $x_i^* \neq x_i'$ be a bundle that i would prefer over x_i'. According to Sugden a bigger opportunity set is a reliable indicator of an increasing welfare under the following condition. When an innovation induces a bigger Ω_i' but i still sticks to x_i', then either $x_i^* \notin \Omega_i'$ – meaning that x_i^* is not (yet) feasible – or $x_i^* \in \Omega_i$, yet it is i's responsibility that she fails to choose it. The rationale behind the responsibility argument is the following. If individuals falling short of the full rationality standard fail to realize the potential offered by an innovation-induced enlargement of their opportunities set, then outcomes do not follow the opportunities. A gap opens up here that may be argued to invalidate the size of the opportunities set as an adequate welfare measure. To defend his approach, Sugden claims that the gap has no normative relevance. He holds that the prerogative of freedom of choice also implies a responsibility for one's choices. Any failure to translate an enlarged opportunities set into a superior outcome lies in the individuals' responsibility and does not impair objective welfare conditions the individuals face.

this criterion, difficulties can be circumvented that arise from inconsistent preferences and preference changes. The reason is that the size of the opportunities set is an exogenously determined constraint, not dependent on the individual's preferences and, hence, on whether and how they err or what they learn concerning their preferences. Since it is left open what precisely the individuals make of their opportunities, suggesting the size of the opportunities set as a welfare measure avoids in addition the paternalism reproach that has been raised against the objective list theories.

Yet the core of Sugden's approach – that a greater opportunity set is to be preferred to a smaller one – is a value judgment. As with all value judgments, one may reason (in a deliberative manner) about why it may, or may not, be desirable to adopt them. In the case of the pros and cons for subscribing to Sugden's normative judgment, the devil is in the detail. Empirical research has shown that the value which individuals attribute to their opportunity set does not necessarily vary monotonously with the size of the set as the simple "bigger is better" rule suggests. There are upper limits to the welfare that individuals derive from a growing opportunity set (e.g., Loewenstein 1999; Schwartz 2000). With an increasing number of choices, humans tend to develop increased regret aversion to the number of alternatives not chosen. This has been called the "multioption treadmill": despite the fact that we face ever more options, welfare does not necessarily increase significantly (Binswanger 2006). Positing thus that an unbounded increase of opportunities should result in an equally unbounded welfare increase seems at odds with the actual experience of having ever more options. The theory is therefore either descriptively inaccurate as an account of individual welfare or paternalistic in prescribing that individuals should always value opportunity sets higher if they are bigger.

Moreover, even if not fully consistent in their ordering of alternatives, individual decision makers are likely to see a trade-off between the size of the opportunity set and the quality of its elements. If so, the "bigger is better" rule is not necessarily valid, if the enlarged (post-innovation) set does not contain the smaller (pre-innovation) set as a subset. This can happen if previously existing opportunities disappear from the growing set, for example, handcrafted products that are driven out of the market by substitutes of increasingly differentiated, cheap mass products. The point then is that, in order to decide whether the enlarged opportunity set is better than the smaller one, it is necessary to evaluate the opportunities themselves. In that case, one would again be confronted with pre-innovation vs. post-innovation preference inconsistencies and all their implications.

These complications and the doubts regarding what a growing size of the opportunities set actually measures raise questions about the adequacy of the approach for assessing welfare changes. A degenerate, "objective" list focusing on that size may not appear more convincing as a welfare measure than the full-fledged objective list approaches. The problem that the assessment of welfare effects of innovations can change endogenously as a result of the innovations that plagued the other approaches enters through the backdoor here too. It seems, thus, that choosing pre-innovation or post-innovation measuring rods for welfare crucially influences the resulting assessment of the welfare effects of innovations in all cases and involves more or less arbitrary value judgments. As always, when very different value judgments are advocated, a certain relativism can be argued to be inherent to assessing the benefits of innovations for individual welfare and, perhaps, a skeptic view on the calls for ever more innovations. From the perspective of the discussed theories of welfare this seems to follow at least once utter poverty, drudgery, and malady have been overcome in an economy.

Conclusion

In this chapter we set out to discuss what the welfare effects of innovations are. In order to answer the question, it is necessary to choose a criterion or criteria by which the effects should be measured. The choice can be expected to influence the result of the exercise. For that reason we considered three alternative theories of measuring welfare. Characterized by the criteria they use, these were the theory of preference satisfaction, hedonistic theories of mental state accounts, and theories that use lists of objective criteria. In the discussion many problems turned up that make it difficult, if not impossible, to unambiguously determine the effects in a general way. In particular, we have identified two major complications that make an assessment difficult. The first results from the fact that innovations inevitably cause externalities that cannot be predicted. In the case of pecuniary externalities, the consequence is an interpersonal redistribution of income and wealth. None of the three theories is able to account for it in its welfare assessment without adding more or less arbitrary value judgments regarding the distribution effects. In the case of technological externalities, social costs arise that can develop a welfare-reducing effect for society as a whole.

The second complication results from the fact that innovations can influence the very measuring rod by which their welfare effects are supposed to be evaluated. In the case of the preference satisfaction theory and the hedonistic theory of welfare, the influence is exerted via endogenous processes of preference learning and hedonic adaptation. Hedonic adaptation tends to erode welfare gains accruing from innovations. In the case of objective list theories of welfare, the influence of innovations on the measuring rod is mediated by the researchers' (exogenous) choice of the objective criteria by which to measure welfare. This choice is likely to adapt to the new facts that innovations create. In any case, the influence undermines the construction of intertemporally consistent welfare measures that would be required for comparing pre-innovation to post-innovation states of welfare.

The question thus arises whether and when it can be concluded that innovations definitely improve individual welfare and do so in an enduring fashion. If there are no induced preference changes that impede clear welfare assessments, the answer depends on whether and to what extent innovations cause unforeseen negative technological externalities. With respect to the pecuniary externalities of innovations, the answer depends on whether and how one accounts for the resulting wealth and income redistribution. For innovations that do cause preference changes, any welfare assessment is contingent on how the loss of an intertemporally consistent measuring rod is compensated. As has been shown, a value judgment is required in any case and leads to diametrically opposed welfare assessments. We have concluded that this fact renders the assessment of the welfare effects of innovations rather arbitrary.

Thus, whichever of the three welfare theories is used, innovations cannot in a wholesale manner be attributed to positive welfare effects as is usually done in both the academic debate and in politics. The wisdom of calling for ever more innovative activities may therefore be challenged – particularly in the already highly prospering economies in which a substantial share of innovativeness goes into the creation of differentiated and new consumer goods that fuel preference change. For reasons of space, a discussion of the policy implications of our analysis is not possible here and merits a paper of its own. It is clear, though, that the policy conclusions to be drawn hinge on basic value judgments in quite complex ways. Is the innovation-induced redistribution of income and wealth to be compensated before the welfare effects can be assessed? Is the pre-innovation state of preferences the relevant reference base or the post-innovation state of preferences? In the case of potential technological externalities of innovations such value contingencies would not matter for giving policy advice. However, in this case the inherent unpredictability of the effects constrains the room for policy making. A major task may be the design and implementation of institutional arrangements that stop innovations with damaging effects as early as possible. In this way, the risk of innovation-induced welfare losses can be reduced, but not eliminated. As argued in Witt and Schubert (2008), society will ultimately settle on the basis of the risk attitudes of its decision makers whether the risks or the prospects of running a more or less innovative economy are weighed higher.

References

Aghion, P. and Howitt, P. 1998. *Endogenous Growth Theory*. Cambridge, MA: MIT Press.

Angner, E. 2016. *A Course in Behavioral Economics*. London: Palgrave/MacMillan.

Bernheim, B. D. and Rangel, A. 2009. Beyond Revealed Preference: Choice-theoretic Foundations for Behavioral Welfare Economics. *The Quarterly Journal of Economics*, 124, 51–104.

Binder, M. 2010. *Elements of an Evolutionary Theory of Welfare*. London: Routledge.

Binswanger, M. 2006. Why Does Income Growth Fail to Make Us Happier? Searching for the Treadmills behind the Paradox of Happiness. *Journal of Socio-Economics*, 35, 366–381.

Broome, J. 2008. Can There Be a Preference-based Utilitarianism. In: Fleurbaey, M., Salles, M., and Weymark, J. (eds.) *Justice, Political Liberalism and Utilitarianism: Themes from Harsanyi and Rawls*. Cambridge: Cambridge University Press.

Cabanac, M. 1992. Pleasure: The Common Currency. *Journal of Theoretical Biology*, 155, 173–200.

Camerer, C., Loewenstein, G., and Prelec, D. 2005. Neuroeconomics: How Neuroscience Can Inform Economics. *Journal of Economic Literature*, 43, 9–64.

Coase, R. H. 1960. The Problem of Social Cost. *The Journal of Law and Economics*, 3, 1–44.

DellaVigna, S. 2009. Psychology and Economics: Evidence from the Field. *Journal of Economic Literature*, 47, 315–372.

Diener, E. and Lucas, R. E. 1999. Personality and Subjective Well-Being. In: Diener, E. (ed.) *The Science of Well-Being: The Collected Works of Ed Diener*. Dordrecht: Springer Netherlands.

Diener, E., Suh, E. M., Lucas, R. E., and Smith, H. L. 1999. Subjective Well-Being: Three Decades of Progress. *Psychological Bulletin*, 125, 276–302.

Dosi, G. 1988. Sources, Procedures, and Microeconomic Effects of Innovation. *Journal of Economic Literature*, 26, 1120–1171.

Elster, J. 1983. *Sour Grapes*. Cambridge: Cambridge University Press.

Fernández-Dols, J.-M. and Ruiz-Belda, M.-A. 1995. Are Smiles a Sign of Happiness? Gold Medal Winners at the Olympic Games. *Journal of Personality and Social Psychology*, 69, 1113–1119.

Flanagan, K., Uyarra, E., and Laranja, M. 2011. Reconceptualising the "Policy Mix" for Innovation. *Research Policy*, 40, 702–713.

Frederick, S. and Loewenstein, G. F. 1999. Hedonic Adaptation. In: Kahneman, D., Diener, E., and Schwarz, N. (eds.) *Well-Being: The Foundations of Hedonic Psychology*. New York: Russell Sage Foundation.

Frey, B. S. and Stutzer, A. 2002. *Happiness and Economics*. Princeton, NJ: Princeton University Press.

Gowdy, J. 2005. Toward a New Welfare Economics for Sustainability. *Ecological Economics*, 53, 211–222.

Graham, C. 2010. *Happiness around the World: The Paradox of Happy Peasants and Miserable Millionaires*. New York/Oxford: Oxford University Press.

Gustafsson, R. and Autio, E. 2011. A Failure Trichotomy in Knowledge Exploration and Exploitation. *Research Policy*, 40, 819–831.

Hausman, D. M. and Mcpherson, M. S. 2006. *Economic Analysis, Moral Philosophy and Public Policy*. Cambridge: Cambridge University Press.

Hayek, F. A. 1960. *The Constitution of Liberty*. Chicago: The University of Chicago Press.

Headey, B. 2010. The Set Point Theory of Well-being Has Serious Flaws: On the Eve of a Scientific Revolution? *Social Indicators Research*, 97, 7–21.

Helliwell, J., Layard, R., and Sachs, J. 2015. *World Happiness Report*. New York: Sustainable Development Solutions Network.

Hicks, J. R. 1939. The Foundations of Welfare Economics. *Economic Journal*, 49, 696–712.

Kahneman, D., Wakker, P. P., and Sarin, R. 1997. Back to Bentham? Explorations of Experienced Utility. *The Quarterly Journal of Economics*, 112, 375–405.

Kaldor, N. 1939. Welfare Propositions of Economics and Interpersonal Comparisons of Utility. *The Economic Journal*, 49, 549–552.

Kőszegi, B. and Rabin, M. 2008. Choices, Situations, and Happiness. *Journal of Public Economics*, 92, 1821–1832.

Krueger, A. B. and Schkade, D. A. 2008. The Reliability of Subjective Well-Being Measures. *Journal of Public Economics*, 92, 1833–1845.

Kuklys, W. 2005. *Amartya Sen's Capability Approach – Theoretical Insights and Empirical Applications*. Berlin: Springer.

Lancaster, K. J. 1966. A New Approach to Consumer Theory. *Journal of Political Economy*, 74, 132–157.

Loewenstein, G. F. 1999. Is More Choice Always Better? *Social Security Brief*, 7, 1–8.

Lykken, D. and Tellegen, A. 1996. Happiness Is a Stochastic Phenomenon. *Psychological Science*, 7, 186–189.

Mas-Colell, A., Whinston, M. D., and Green, J. R. 1995. *Microeconomic Theory*. New York; Oxford: Oxford University Press.

McQuillin, B. and Sugden, R. 2012. Reconciling Normative and Behavioural Economics: The Problems to Be Solved. *Social Choice and Welfare*, 38, 553–567.

Metcalfe, J. S. 1998. *Evolutionary Economics and Creative Destruction*. New York; London: Routledge.

Mokyr, J. 1990. *The Lever of Riches: Technological Creativity and Economic Progress*. New York: Oxford University Press.

Nelson, R. R. 1996. *The Sources of Economic Growth*. Cambridge, MA, Harvard University Press.

North, D. C. 1999. Hayek's Contribution to Understanding the Process of Economic Change. In: Vanberg, V. J. (ed.) *Freiheit, Wettbewerb und Wirtschaftsordnung*. Freiburg: Haufe.

Nozick, R. 1974. *Anarchy, State and Utopia*. New York: Basic Books.

Nussbaum, M. 2003. Capabilities as Fundamental Entitlements: Sen and Social Justice. *Feminist Economics*, 9, 33–59.

Parfit, D. 1984. *Reasons and Persons*. Oxford: Oxford University Press.

Redelmeier, D. A. and Kahneman, D. 1996. Patients' Memories of Painful Medical Treatments: Real-time and Retrospective Evaluations of Two Minimally Invasive Procedures. *Pain*, 66, 3–8.

Rosenberg, N. and Birdzell, L. E. 1986. *How the West Grew Rich – The Economic Transformation of the Industrial World.* New York: Basic Books.

Sandvik, E., Diener, E., and Seidlitz, L. 1993. Subjective Well-Being: The Convergence and Stability of Self-report and Non-Self-report Measures. *Journal of Personality,* 61, 317–342.

Sartorius, C. 2003. *An Evolutionary Approach to Social Welfare.* London: Routledge.

Schubert, C. 2015. What Do We Mean When We Say That Innovation and Entrepreneurship (Policy) Increase "Welfare"? *Journal of Economic Issues,* 49, 1–22.

Schumpeter, J. A. 1942. *Capitalism, Socialism, and Democracy.* New York: Harper.

Schwartz, B. 2000. Self-determination: The Tyranny of Freedom. *American Psychologist,* 55, 79–88.

Sen, A. 1985a. *Commodities and Capabilities.* Amsterdam: North-Holland.

1985b. Well-Being, Agency and Freedom: The Dewey Lectures 1984. *The Journal of Philosophy,* 82, 169–221.

1987. *On Ethics and Economics.* New York: B. Blackwell.

1992. *Inequality Reexamined.* Oxford: Clarendon Press.

1993. Internal Consistency of Choice. *Econometrica,* 61, 495–521.

Shiv, B. and Huber, J. 2000. The Impact of Anticipating Satisfaction on Consumer Choice. *Journal of Consumer Research,* 27, 202–216.

Shizgal, P. 1999. On the Neural Computation of Utility: Implications from Studies of Brain Stimulation Reward. In: Kahneman, D., Diener, E., and Schwarz, N. (eds.) *Well-Being: The Foundations of Hedonic Psychology.* New York: Russell Sage Foundation.

Sugden, R. 1993. *Welfare, Resources, and Capabilities: A Review of Inequality Reexamined by Amartya Sen.* Nashville, TN: American Economic Association.

2004. The Opportunity Criterion: Consumer Sovereignty without the Assumption of Coherent Preferences. *The American Economic Review,* 94, 1014–1033.

2006. What We Desire, What We Have Reason to Desire, Whatever We Might Desire: Mill and Sen on the Value of Opportunity. *Utilitas,* 18, 33–51.

2013. The Behavioural Economist and the Social Planner: To Whom Should Behavioural Welfare Economics Be Addressed? *Inquiry,* 56, 519–538.

Tenner, E. 1997. *Why Things Bite Back: Technology and the Revenge of Unintended Consequences.* New York: Vintage.

Vanberg, V. J. 2014. Evolving Preferences and Welfare Economics: The Perspective of Constitutional Political Economy. *Jahrbücher für Nationalökonomie und Statistik*, 234, 328–349.

von Weizsäcker, C. C. 2005. The Welfare Economics of Adaptive Preferences. In: Institute, M. P. (ed.) *Preprints of the Max Planck Institute for Research on Collective Goods*. Bonn: Max Planck Institute.

Witt, U. 1996. Innovations, Externalities and the Problem of Economic Progress. *Public Choice*, 89, 113–130.

2009. Novelty and the Bounds of Unknowledge in Economics. *Journal of Economic Methodology*, 16, 361–375.

2017. The Evolution of Consumption and Its Welfare Effects. *Journal of Evolutionary Economics, Journal of Evolutionary Economics*, 27, 273–293.

Witt, U. and Schubert, C. 2008. Constitutional Interests in the Face of Innovations: How Much Do We Need to Know about Risk Preferences? *Constitutional Political Economy*, 19, 203–225.

12

Sustainable Consumption Patterns and the Malleability of Consumer Preferences

An Evolutionary Perspective

ANDREAS CHAI

Introduction

A predominant view in ecological economics is that current levels and paths of consumption are unsustainable and should be corrected accordingly. This position often builds upon the background assumption that consumer preferences are not exogenously "given" but rather endogenously influenced by socioeconomic and institutional factors (Røpke 1999, 2009; O'Hara & Stagl 2002). Hence, it may be necessary to promote sustainability by – among other things – influencing people's current preferences, ideally towards "less material consumption-oriented forms of satisfaction" (Norton, Costanza, & Bishop 1998) or "nonrival goods" (Wagner 2006). Information campaigns, advertisements, "nudges" (Thaler & Sunstein 2008) or some functionally equivalent device may be needed in order to overcome such locked-in consumption patterns. Influencing the demand side of the economy in this way may be a particularly powerful tool to promote sustainable behaviour (Brennan 2006).

However, although many of these scholars reject the orthodox assumption that consumer preferences are fixed and exogenous (Stigler & Becker 1977), they do not provide an alternative view of how consumer preferences may evolve and of the process through which they are shaped. As a result, a drawback of this criticism is that it does not consider the possibility that pro-environmental preferences may emerge among consumers on their own accord. A better understanding is needed of how exactly consumer preferences are endogenous and why they lack the capacity to change in the future (Bisin & Verdier 2001). Under what specific conditions can preferences really be considered permanently "locked in" so that there is no possibility for consumers to fundamentally change what they choose to consume (Sanne 2002; Chai et al. 2015)? Adopting Witt's detailed

369

account of preference evolution (Witt 2001), we argue that new preferences are acquired either "actively" via insightful learning involving mental deliberation or "passively" via associative learning, which does not involve mental deliberation on the part of consumers. Therefore, depending on the underlying mechanism of learning through which consumers acquire preferences and the degree to which the consumer is actively engaged in the accumulation of specialised knowledge, preferences may be considered to be more or less malleable. In particular, we argue that preferences are more malleable and subject to pro-environmental change on their own accord in situations where consumers possess specialised knowledge about consumption activities and awareness of how their activities affect long-run environmental conditions.

This working hypothesis raises the deeper question of what kind of market conditions help foster the degree to which consumers are specialised and are thus more likely to exhibit preference malleability and enable the emergence of pro-environmental preferences. In this regard, adopting Menger's (1950) view that markets are higher-order tools that emerged in the process of economic evolution to serve the needs of consumers, we argue that it is not clear that markets inhibit the accumulation of specialised knowledge among consumers. Indeed, there are many cases where market evolution can stimulate the accumulation of knowledge and thereby help create the conditions in which preferences become more malleable. Thus, by better understanding the co-evolutionary relationship between market conditions and consumer knowledge, policy makers wishing to promote more sustainable consumption patterns could adopt a more indirect approach that seeks to promote the appropriate market conditions that promote consumer specialisation and help bring about the emergence of pro-environmental preferences in a more autonomous manner.

The argument proceeds as follows. The next section discusses the position found in ecological economics about the locked-in and endogenous nature of preferences. The third section presents an account of the consumer specialisation process which occurs via the dynamic interplay between insightful and associative learning that induces consumers to develop ever more specialised preferences. This affects the extent to which these preferences are malleable and tend to change on their own accord, as outlined in the fourth section. The fifth section discusses the role that markets play in fostering the specialisation process. The sixth section concludes the chapter.

Endogenous Preferences and Ecological Economics

There is a general consensus in ecological economics that contemporary consumption patterns are not sustainable. Studies have shown that this applies in a wide range of consumption activities such as energy and food consumption (Myers & Kent 2003). The problem is exacerbated by the fact that a large part of consumption is driven by potentially self-defeating and wasteful status concerns (Frank 1999), that consumers are generally ignorant about the effect that their consumption choices have on the environment (Brown & Cameron 2000) and that many of the relevant consumption acts give rise to "tragedy of the commons" scenarios.

Consequently there have been calls for policies that promote sustainable consumption by fostering pro-environmental or "green" preferences among consumers. While the approach of traditional textbook economics would be to recommend appropriate tax and subsidy schemes (i.e., incentive management) to promote sustainable consumption (e.g., Wagner 2006), there is a growing tendency to reject the underlying assumption that consumer preferences are "fixed and given" and to explore policy implications that are grounded in a more realistic view of preferences. For example, Norton, Costanza, and Bishop (1998) have called on policy makers to "encourage" the adoption of a less materialistic lifestyle and have further argued that society should establish democratic processes of public deliberation to discuss and re-evaluate consumer preferences.

The fundamental starting point for this position is the rejection of the widely accepted notion that consumer preferences should be treated as fixed and given (Stigler & Becker 1977). Rather, preferences may be affected by a number of economic, sociocultural and institutional factors (Lintott 1998; Røpke 1999). Different stages and forms of economic development may yield important systematic differences in the nature of preferences (Bowles 1998). Accordingly, certain factors may have grown in importance with the emergence of the affluent society and may contribute to the "lock-in" of consumption patterns (Sanne 2002; Chai et al. 2015). The unsustainable nature of current consumption is particularly attributed to deeply embedded cultural changes that are beyond the individual's control, such as the secular rise of individualism (Røpke 1999). It has also been attributed to the tendency of consumers to form habits which are rarely revised (Maréchal 2010).

In this context, a key issue here is the need to better understand the manner in which consumer preferences are shaped and whether "green" preferences can emerge on their own accord. If this is possible under certain (institutional) conditions, then this would be significant information for policy makers who could work towards indirectly promoting sustainable consumption patterns by creating the institutional conditions for green preferences to emerge, rather than explicitly attempting to indoctrinate consumer preferences. There is indeed growing evidence that at least in certain areas, consumption patterns appear to be shifting in a "green" direction on their own accord, without any change in external incentive structures (e.g., Pedersen 2000). To illustrate, a 1999 survey of US households suggest that 70% of households are willing to pay at least $5 per month more for electricity from renewable sources, with 38% willing to pay at least $10 per month more, and 21% even willing to pay at least $15 per month more (Farhar 1999).

Indeed much work has been done since the 1980s on how pro-environmental changes in the individual's consumer preferences and activities can be stimulated through nonprice factors, including how the consumer's social environment may influence their attitudes (Ölander & Kahneman 1995; van den Bergh 2008). It is notable that many studies highlight a link between how much knowledge consumers possess about a particular consumption activity and their receptiveness to public information campaigns that promote pro-environmental behaviour in relation to that consumption activity. For example, the likelihood of some action being motivated by intrinsic motivations depends on such factors as "how interesting the act is to the consumer" and "how much individuals may influence the nature of the act" (Frey 1993: 645). Elsewhere, in a study of consumers who chose to purchase green electricity, Arkesteijn and Oerlemans (2005) found that early adopters were particularly knowledgeable of sustainable energy features and had a positive attitude towards the environment. Hence the accumulation of specialised knowledge by consumers represents an important factor that can account for whether or not green preferences may emerge on their own accord.

Apart from the role of knowledge, the other fundamental issue in understanding the preference formation process is the underlying motivation that drives consumers and the relationship between its genetically hard-wired foundations, on the one hand, and cultural learned influences, on the other hand (Norton, Costanza, & Bishop 1998; Robson 2001). In order to understand the role of biological evolution, scholars in ecological economics have sought to identify a set of objective human needs. This may help to ascertain to what extent current consumption goes beyond these needs and may therefore be seen as potentially "wasteful" (Jackson, Jager, & Stagl 2004). Needs schemas that shed light on the functional nature of consumption, such as those developed by Galtung (1980) and Max-Neef, Elizalde, and Hopenhayn (1991), have attempted to explain how the long-run growth of consumption expenditure has not only involved the emergence of new goods and services to satisfy existing needs but also an expansion of the number of underlying needs that consumers seek to satisfy.

While the role of needs should be taken seriously, these approaches suffer from two shortcomings. First, psychological schemas are difficult to apply as they tend to include relatively hard-to-observe needs, such as the need for self-determination (Jackson & Marks 1999). This poses a challenge to researchers, as it is difficult to discern what types of goods and services are used in the satisfaction of such a need. In contrast, earlier drive theories of motivation attempted to explain human behaviour as being related to a limited number of objectively identifiable primary reinforcers whose effects can be observed in the laboratory. For example, Hull (1943) argued that all behaviour is ultimately based on four primary drives: hunger, thirst, sex and the avoidance of pain. This relatively short list, though oversimplified, is much easier to manage in terms of uncovering what types of goods and services are used to satisfy these needs.[1]

A second drawback of these psychological schemas is that they presume the set of needs that drive the long-run growth of consumption to be pre-existing, constant and independent of the socioeconomic context of consumption. In that sense, the notion of fixed preferences re-enters through the back door. This is because the broad pattern of change in consumption behaviour that takes place as consumers

---

[1] See also Rolls (2005:19).

become more affluent is predetermined by the hypothesised hierarchy of needs. In other words, the consumer's preferences may be nonhomothetic in the sense that as income rises, the type of needs she seeks to satisfy will change, though the manner in which these needs will change is essentially fixed. So these approaches not only assume that all consumers possess the same set of needs but also that the income effects on consumption expenditure are identical across the population of consumers. Put differently, the preferences of any two consumers with the same initial income level will alter in an identical fashion in light of some increase in income, irrespective of the individuals' own experiences. Importantly, the interaction of the consumer with her socioeconomic environment is assumed not to have any effect on her set of needs.

An Evolutionary Theory of Consumer Specialisation

This section discusses how the theory of learning consumers (Witt 2001, 2016) may be useful to understanding some of these open questions about the malleability of consumption patterns. Among other things, this theory provides a more comprehensive picture of how preferences are shaped and describes the dynamic interaction between, on the one hand, the way consumers acquire needs and, on the other hand, the way they accumulate knowledge, through what is known as the consumer specialisation process (Witt 2001). We argue that this specialisation process can help shed light on the circumstances in which preferences are either likely to be "locked in" due to socioeconomic factors or are subject to change due to the more "active" role played by knowledgeable consumers. This account begins with the notion that consumer preferences are the product of the interplay of biological and cultural evolution – a view shared by scholars in ecological economics (as noted in the previous section).

A chief question in evolutionary economics is to understand the forces governing the distribution of knowledge in the economy and the rate at which it accumulates and is used by agents (Dopfer & Potts 2007). In terms of understanding consumer learning patterns, two very distinct views of consumer learning are popular (Brenner 1999). Some argue that due to her cognitive constraints, a consumer is guided by habits and rules, and that social institutions, peers and experts help her form appropriate rules (Earl & Potts 2004;

Nelson & Consoli 2010), whereas, in strong contrast, other studies have tried to account for the role of highly specialised, creative consumers in co-developing commercial innovations. Many scholars have noted that it is not uncommon for inventors and entrepreneurs responsible for introducing novel goods to also be users of the goods, and their interest in developing innovation may be personal as well as pecuniary (Bianchi 2002; Buenstorf 2003; Jeppsen & Molin 2003; van den Ende & Dolfsma 2005; von Hippel 2005).

How can these strongly contrasting views be reconciled? Human learning is the evolved capability of a species to adapt to change by modifying its behaviour in response to environmental stimuli (McFarland 1987). The capability to learn evolved in humans over a very long time span in a relatively piecemeal fashion, such that there was *no* smooth substitution of more advanced learning mechanisms for more primitive ones (Flinn 1997: 33, Sartorius 2003: 30). Rather, development was sticky, with more advanced mechanisms emerging to complement older mechanisms. Thus it is fundamentally important to consider the existence of multiple modes of learning, and how these modes may interact, to understand why preferences may change relatively quickly in some areas of consumption but not change at all in other areas. So we can recast the question of why consumer preferences are "locked in" as the question of why consumer behaviour is not adapting or is adapting at a relatively slow rate.

An important fact that may help explain why some of the needs that drive consumption are neither constant nor fixed is that the set of stimuli which deliver reinforcement is altered by experience via associative learning (Witt 2001). In particular, secondary reinforcers are formerly neutral stimuli whose repeated pairing with primary reinforcers results in them exerting a reinforcing effect in their own right (Anderson 2000: 39). For example, aesthetic tableware may become associated with the attainment of food, which may lead consumers to develop a "liking" for tableware (Witt 2001: 35). Thus, in addition to basic needs, the consumer may acquire other needs that are unique to her particular learning history, and different consumers with different learning histories will turn out to have different sets of such acquired needs. These acquired needs are reversible in that they may become extinct if the neutral stimuli become disassociated with primary reinforcers (Myers & Davis 2007). Hence by allowing a component of the consumers' needs to evolve in accordance with the types of reinforcers that they are exposed to, a more dynamic approach to studying consumer preferences emerges.

In contrast to associative learning, *insightful* learning describes a situation in which the consumer is in a highly alert state and predisposed to engage in mental deliberation (Posner & Petersen 1990). Outcomes of this process depend on the creative capacity of agents to analyse situations in order to find appropriate solutions (Hergenhahn & Olson 1997: 263). Relative to associative learning, behaviour here tends to adapt at a much faster pace and also displays greater variability. Thus consumer choice is understood as a problem-solving exercise involving a sequence of activities, the outcome of which is principally determined by the agents' cognitive functioning and the way they process information (Earl 1986). An essential determinant of learning in these circumstances is the information that consumers possess, which derives from the peers and experts with whom they interact and their access to knowledge embodied in (informal and formal) social institutions (Bandura 1986; Earl & Potts 2004).

A potential outcome of the dynamic interaction between insightful and associative learning is a specialisation process through which consumers accumulate an increasingly refined set of knowledge and likings about a particular consumption activity (Witt 2001). The consumer's set of likes and dislikes can guide what she tends to insightfully learn about, in that the hedonic value of reinforcement acts as a marker that helps guide which information is worth paying attention to (Goodson 2003: 115). At the same time, insightful learning can influence associative learning because it can facilitate the formation of new associations between sources of reinforcement and neutral stimuli (Witt 2001: 36). Together, the two effects may be mutually reinforcing and lead to the refinement of both what consumers know and what they like or dislike.

Via this specialisation process, consumers not only attain greater knowledge about a particular consumption activity but also get a more specific set of acquired (dis)likes in relation to a consumption activity. It is a well-established fact in consumer research that more experienced consumers have more differentiated preferences. For example, expert bird watchers have greater interest in "lower-profile" wildlife species than unspecialised bird watchers (Martin 1997) and specialised tourists tend to derive more satisfaction from visiting historic sites than unspecialised tourists (Kerstetter, Confer, & Graefe

2001).[2] In this way, Witt's theory of specialisation emphasises the role of associative learning in shaping what comes to the attention of consumers in the first place. What the consumer tends to specialise in is not so much a consequence of forward-looking investment decisions in which consumers take into account future payoffs, but rather a result of the consumer's previously acquired needs and existing knowledge, which have both emerged from the consumer's learning history.

Specialisation and the Malleability of Preferences

At the individual level, an important outcome of specialisation is that it leads to consumers possessing a relatively greater propensity to vary the details of the consumption activity (Chai 2011). Through their knowledge and their tendency to modify, specialised consumers are more likely to reflect on and modify their preferences. Essentially, gaining more detailed knowledge and a more refined set of acquired needs tends to change the way consumers assess the performance of goods and services. Due to specialisation, goods used in the past that were once deemed adequate may be regarded as no longer suitable. Specialised consumers turn to new types of goods and services that enable them a greater degree of flexibility and control in changing aspects of the consumption activity or are better adapted to the more refined state of the consumer's knowledge and likings, such as high-performance sports cars (discussed in the next section).[3] Indeed, specialised consumers tend to be among the first to adopt new goods

[2] This account of specialisation from the evolutionary perspective is quite different from the theory of rational addiction where consumers may accumulate "personal capital" which can influence the marginal productivity of their future consumption activities (Becker & Murphy 1988). In the earlier account, specialisation leads to *qualitative* changes in the nature of the consumption activity, whereas in Becker and Murphy's account, the accumulation of capital only leads to changes in the marginal productivity of doing exactly the same consumption activity as before.

[3] In some cases, consumer specialisation can lead to greater path dependence in consumption patterns and the prolonged use of goods and services if consumers have developed specific skills and tastes related to a particular good (Moreau, Lehmann, & Markman 2001). One such example is the analogue (shutter-operated) camera, which is still used by many experienced camera enthusiasts, despite the fact that it has been superseded by the digital camera (Moreau, Lehmann, & Markman 2001).

and services (Rogers 1962), and can even play a role in the development of new products (as discussed in the previous section).

The notion that specialised consumers have a greater propensity to vary their consumption activities does not rule out the possibility that the consumption patterns of unspecialised consumers may also frequently change. Rather, what is unique about the consumption patterns of specialised consumers is that they are more likely to change in a self-directed, autonomous manner (Khalil 2003; Binder & Lades 2015). Changes in the consumption patterns of unspecialised consumers may still take place due to external influences, such as social influences (Bikhchandani, Hirshleifer, & Welch 1992; Earl & Potts 2004; Dulleck & Kerschbamer 2006; Chai, Earl, & Potts 2007).

To this end, we may define "genuine lock-in" as a situation where consumption patterns are path dependent not because of external conditions but rather because consumers do not possess the required behavioural propensity to adapt their behaviour. For example, habit formation tends to be very strong in consumption domains that are routine (Foxall 1989; Maréchal 2010). Depending on the individual, this could include anything from the weekly shopping to the annual package holiday. In consumption areas where consumers do not possess knowledge and do not pay attention to consumption activity and the general context in which goods and services are consumed, there is little reason to expect self-directed change in consumer preferences to occur. In contrast, there are other cases where consumption patterns are locked in due to institutional or technological conditions (Sanne 2002; Jackson & Papathanasopoulou 2008). In those circumstances, consumers may wish to adapt but lack the opportunity to do so for various reasons.

In terms of "genuine lock-in" this can occur for various reasons: increasing income may lead to stronger time constraints that inhibit consumer specialisation (Lindner 1970; Schor 1991), consumers may be "slack" or inattentive (Witt 2001: 39; Cordes 2003; Maréchal 2010) or there may be an epistemic barrier to specialisation as knowledge in certain consumption domains is abstract and difficult to relate to the consumption act (Earl & Potts 2004). This latter case is especially prominent in advanced economies where the accumulated knowledge grows relatively quickly and becomes qualitatively more abstract (Hayak 1937; Shackle 1972; Dulleck & Kerschbamer 2006).

The possibility that green preferences will emerge on their own accord among specialised consumers has ramifications for the ongoing debate about whether green preferences may emerge on their own accord. As argued by Buenstorf and Cordes (2008), pro-environmental behaviour can emerge if there is sufficient information about the effects of excessive consumption on the environment and the consumer has a sufficient level of specialisation in a particular consumption activity to be receptive to such information. At the same time, these authors are pessimistic about the likelihood that green preferences will emerge among unspecialised consumers. This is due to a "hedonic bias" which makes unspecialised consumers prefer alternatives that offer more rewarding sensory experiences (Buenstorf & Cordes 2008: 649).

However, Buenstorf and Cordes are unclear about why green products may not be closely associated with rewarding sensory experiences. They also neglect the fact that typically there is an interactive effect between the consumption patterns of specialised and unspecialised consumers, in that unspecialised consumers tend to imitate the consumption patterns of expert consumers in many instances (mentioned earlier). Because social recognition is generally accepted as a primary reinforcer (Bandura 1986), it seems far from obvious that a "hedonic bias" will always inhibit the emergence of green preferences amongst unspecialised consumers, which weakens the argument that green preferences are not "self-reinforcing," as Buenstorf and Cordes put it (2008: 649).

Rather, under the correct institutional settings, unspecialised consumers could satisfy their basic need for social recognition through imitating green preferences of specialised consumers. A good example of such status-driven dispersion of green behaviour is the Prius Halo: US consumers appear to have a higher willingness to pay for the Toyota Prius over other, less conspicuous hybrid cars such as the Honda Civic hybrid because it is a relatively clear and unique signal of the consumer's environmental attitudes (Sexton & Sexton 2014). Consumers may therefore undertake costly actions in order to signal their "green" credentials.[4]

Of course, not all specialised consumers will necessarily develop green preferences. Indeed there may be many cases where specialised knowledge in consumption domains can foster more environmentally damaging forms of consumption. For example, developing a

---

[4] The notion that consumers imitate role models does not refute the model in Buenstorf and Cordes (2008).

specialised interest in travelling to exotic distant locations (Higham & Cohen 2011) or in undertaking off-road four-wheel-drive recreational drives (Bishop 1996) probably results in more carbon-intensive consumption patterns. Rather, an important precondition for green preferences to emerge in the specialisation process is that consumers possess an underlying concern about how their consumption lifestyle is affecting the environment and the ability for society to adapt to climate change. Here, we argue that the greater propensity for specialised consumers reflect on and modify aspects of their consumption activity should enable them to act on these pre-existing concerns so that these concerns are better reflected in the consumer's actions and actual preferences orderings. Many studies suggest that although the majority of consumers are concerned about the environment and climate change, there is a yawning gap between these expressed concerns and the consumer's propensity to *act* on these concerns by adopting sustainable consumption practices (e.g., Gifford, Kormos, & Mcintyre 2011; Chai et al. 2015).

Markets as Tools

Markets play a central role in economic analysis, although Coase notes that what orthodox microeconomics offers us are models of "exchange without markets": what is called a market is simply a label for an intersection of supply and demand correspondences, from which equilibrium allocations may be deduced (Coase 1988: 3). Indeed Loasby maintains that it is a categorical mistake to confuse markets with exchange because the latter represents an event within a sequential process, whilst a market is a setting within which this process may take place (Loasby 1999: 107). He cites Marshall in describing this setting as "a group or groups of people, some of whom desire to obtain certain things, and some of whom are in a position to supply what others want" (Marshall 1919: 182). By this definition, it is easy to see how consumer learning processes directly impact markets by affecting both the consumer's wants and the acts by which they are serviced. Suppliers, generally interested in sustaining an ongoing relationship with consumers, need to take heed of changes caused by learning and even, if possible, interact with learning processes in order to ensure that the set of goods and services they offer remain in the favour of consumers.

Simultaneously, markets also fundamentally enable consumer learning to occur. They do this by coordinating and informing consumers where information and tools are available to satisfy their particular wants. From the Mengerian perspective, given their useful nature, one can conceive of markets as a higher-order tool that is causally connected to the satisfaction of wants (Menger 1950: 57). Whether or not consumers use markets depends on the consumers' knowledge of these tools, their past experience in using them and how their use fits with the other sequences of the consumption act. Such higher-order goods emerged in the process of economic development as societies developed increasingly more sophisticated ways of satisfying their wants (Menger 1950). They represent the chief way in which the production of knowledge is coordinated (Hayek 1937) and are an endogenous product of economic development. In short, markets are both influenced by consumer learning processes and play a role in shaping how such learning occurs.

This co-evolutionary process takes place in a number of different dimensions. First, markets may foster specialisation by increasing the amount of information available to consumers about goods and services available. Marketing research shows that consumers with relatively little knowledge tend to choose products according to the service attributes they possess, whereas expert consumers judge a new product according to how it relates to their entrenched knowledge (Moreau, Lehmann, & Markman 2001). Consequently, producers appealing to specialised consumers offer more specific information about the performance capabilities of goods and services, information which would be relatively less effective on generalised consumers (Mueller 1991). Subsequently, the advertisements media firms use to reach specialised consumers would also be more specific. Rather than purchasing relatively expensive and short advertising space in the mass media, firms would tend to use channels that may be unique to specialist communities and whose relatively lower popularity would enable longer or larger advertisements that carry more information appealing to specialists (Foxall 1990: 135). Examples include specialised magazines and radio shows.

In contrast, firms appealing to nonspecialised consumers tend to use advertisements that focus on emphasising the causal connection between the good or service and consumer wants in an easily understood manner. This may come down to a demonstration of the

effectiveness of goods or by simply associating it with positively reinforcing stimuli (e.g., smiling, beautiful people) (Foxall 1990: 133).
Such short, appealing commercials can be communicated to a relatively large audience via the mass media (DeFleur & Ball-Rokeach
1989). Furthermore, when consumers possess relatively little knowledge, there is a tendency to follow the guidance of experts (Earl &
Potts 2004) or fellow consumers (Bikhchandani, Hirshleifer, &
Welch 1992). Hence the diffusion of new products in such cases can
be highly dependent on the nature of the social network (Rogers
1962; Granovetter & Soong 1986; Cowan, Cowan, & Swann 1997;
Janssen & Jager 2001). Second, the institutions through which suppliers and consumers coordinate with one another may also foster or
inhibit consumer specialisation. Langlois notes how the distribution
of knowledge across consumers and producers can influence the
specific institutions by which consumers and suppliers interact
(Langlois & Cosgel 1998; Langlois 2001). In the case of specialised
consumers, who have a greater willingness to self-produce and
demand more differentiated goods, coordination mechanisms tend to
be more modular, which allows consumers a greater degree of custo-
misation. Cosgel and Langlois give the example of the Land's End
catalogue which, by offering a varied assortment of mix-and-match
clothing elements within a coordinated design paradigm, allows consumers to better fine-tune a wardrobe to their personal tastes
(Langlois & Cosgel 1998: 116). Nonspecialised consumers, on the
other hand, may coordinate with suppliers through more standardised goods and services, such as packaged holidays where all aspects
of the holiday are catered for but the consumer has less choice in
terms of the food, accommodation and departure dates (Aguiló,
Alegre, & Sard 2003). More generally, standards can relate to the
technical, durable and performance characteristics of a good
(Farrell & Saloner 1985). Although inflexible, such standards provide
a universal and convenient institution which helps consumers to find
out which goods and services properly satisfy their wants.

Third, the type of product innovations featured in markets can
help to foster consumer specialisation. Hence functional change is
"performance-orientated" as it works towards producing ever more
highly refined goods and services. Scitvosky gives the example of
sports cars that have acquired more gears, more gauges, more lights,
differential locks and other attributes that are designed to give the

driver more control over the vehicle, but at the same time may require more skill that may prove aversive to nonspecialised consumers (Scitovsky 1976: 273). Another example is in using cameras to take pictures (Windrum 2005). Windrum observes how the expert consumer "values the quality of image reproduction and seeks to control the picture taking process and ... has grasped the technicalities of composition and the different creative opportunities afforded by different shutter speeds, lens focal lengths and flash photography" (Windrum 2005: 1050). On the other hand more casual "snapshooters" use the camera relatively infrequently to record important occasions such as birthdays and weddings, and look for cheap, relatively easy-to-operate and reliable cameras. Not surprisingly, von Hippel also finds that specialised users who demand customised products tend to have a higher willingness to pay for these modifications (von Hippel 2005: 40). From a historical perspective, Scranton argues that while modern consumer markets tend to be equated to "mass markets" characterised by homogenous goods and large-scale production, a large array of specialised markets also emerged relatively early in the industrial era which grew in parallel to mass markets, although here production was very far from being standardised. Instead, in markets such as fashion textiles, apparel, jewellery, furniture, carpets, lamps and printing, batch and custom manufacturing techniques grew and remained prevalent into the 20th century (Scranton 1994: 476).

In the case of generalisation, functional change may be of a very different nature. Many have also noted that novel goods and services tend to be periodically redesigned to help the unspecialised consumers learn about their performance and functionality (Bianchi 2002; Saviotti 2002: 122). Furthermore, the effort to make goods and services more convenient and easier to use may involve addressing more aspects of the consumption act and other wants whose satisfaction was previously not addressed. An example is pre-cooked frozen meals available in supermarkets. Although these have always saved the consumer's time and effort by obviating the need to cook, a new generation of such meals emerged in the 1990s which are designed to be more "healthy" in that they have reduced the amount of calories and fat contained in such meals. Hence, not only is the consumer's hunger satisfied but their concern for being healthy is also addressed. Witt notes how such product innovations which appeal to several needs at the same time help drive the long-run growth of demand (Witt 2001: 32).

Thus relative to performance-orientated functional change in the case of specialisation, here functional change is more geared toward improving the convenience of goods and how they may efficaciously fit into the consumer's general lifestyle (total set of wants).

Taken together, these examples show that there are various ways in which the market environment can either foster or inhibit the consumer specialisation process. The accumulation of knowledge by consumers could be stifled if producers do not provide enough information about products, markets are governed by rigid institutions that inhibit coordination and consumer learning or suppliers focus on developing new products that are convenience-orientated in nature. On the other hand, the consumer specialisation process is fostered by widely available information about goods and their performance, modular institutions that promote consumer learning and performance-orientated product innovations.

In terms of policy, some fresh ideas about how to better promote sustainable consumption patterns can be derived from the notion that markets are tools that facilitate (or hinder) the consumers' specialisation process. To date, policy designed to promote sustainable consumption has mainly revolved around information provision to consumers, either through public information campaigns or through labelling initiatives that inform consumers about the environmental quality of goods and services (OECD 2008). However, the theory of learning consumers (Witt 2001) suggests that information provision per se will only be useful to those consumers who are already specialised in a particular consumption domain. Consumers are much less likely to pay attention to information that is unrelated to their particular consumption lifestyle. Instead, policy makers could consider initiatives that promote consumer specialisation within a particular domain they are concerned about. In particular, this can be done by:

(a) discouraging passive, unspecialised forms of consumer learning
(b) encouraging active, specialised forms of consumer learning.

In terms of (a), policy makers could restrict the presence of "convenience goods" (discussed earlier) that appeal to multiple consumer needs. The aim would be to ensure that consumers have to invest substantial time and effort in the consumption process in a way that will encourage them to accumulate more knowledge about that particular consumption activity. In the case of "healthy" frozen, precooked meals (discussed earlier), policy makers could regulate the market in a way that such meals are no longer available. This could encourage consumers wishing to eat healthy meals into substitutes like fresh food that may require more preparation effort and thereby encourage them to learn which types of food are healthy and how to prepare them.[5] Moreover, policy makers can also take steps to restrict the prevalence of associative learning (also discussed earlier) by restricting the use of image advertising that contains low informational value about the product characteristics. It is possible to empirically distinguish between "informative advertising" that provides information to consumers and reduces their search costs and "image" advertising that merely seeks to enhance the "prestige" value of goods (Ackerberg 2003).

Concerning (b), licensing regimes could be used to make consumer access to certain goods conditional on tests that ensure consumers are indeed "eligible" in that they possess certain levels of knowledge about the good's characteristics and their environmental impacts. Much like the use of automobiles is only granted in most countries on the condition that consumers can demonstrate their knowledge of how to operate the vehicle in a way that minimises the potential for negative externalities and injury to others, a similar logic could be applied to providing conditional access to carbon-emitting durables (such as air conditioners or fridges) whose proper operation may lead to substantial reduction in carbon emissions (Dietz et al. 2009). Such a measure would seek to encourage all consumers to cognitively learn about the environmental impact of consuming such goods. A more relaxed version of such a licensing regime is where the good is made available to any consumers who have *not* forfeited their right to consume a good by violating conditions of eligibility (Kleiman 1992; MacCoun, Reuter, & Schelling 1996). In the case of fridges and air conditioners, information about the consumer's current energy use patterns and how this compares to average household energy use could be one way in which policy makers can set conditions of eligibility. This helps ensure that consumers learn about the environmental impact of such goods and operate them in a more environmentally

---

[5] Of course, such restrictions may also encourage the presence of a "black market" for convenience goods, as well as encourage entrepreneurs to devise new goods that will circumvent such restrictions.

friendly manner. Of course, such regulatory regimes do impose greater transaction costs and cognitive burdens on consumers. These must be taken into account when estimating the overall net benefits of such regimes.

Conclusion

There is little doubt that existing consumption patterns among Western developed economies are unsustainable. However, in order to evaluate the best possible ways through which to achieve more sustainable consumption patterns, a better understanding is needed of why exactly existing consumption patterns are "locked in" and the role that markets play in this process. Some of this path dependency may be due to social norms, but in other cases it could be due to the lack of learning and specialisation opportunities available to consumers. Although there is little dispute that preferences are endogenously influenced by economic conditions and social influences, it is not clear the extent to which this really prevents the emergence of green preferences. Preference endogeneity does not by itself imply that the policy makers must directly "target" consumer preferences. Rather, a better understanding of the manner in which markets co-evolve with consumer knowledge can help shed light on less interventionist approaches to promoting the emergence of pro-environmental preferences.

References

Ackerberg, D. A. 2003. Advertising, Learning, and Consumer Choice in Experience Good Markets: An Empirical Examination. *International Economic Review*, 44, 1007–1040.

Aguiló, E., Alegre, J., and Sard, M. 2003. Examining the Market Structure of the German and UK Tour Operating Industries through an Analysis of Package Holiday Prices. *Tourism Economics*, 9, 255–278.

Anderson, J. 2000. *Learning and Memory*. New York: John Wiley & Sons.

Arkesteijn, K. K. and Oerlemans, L. L. a. G. 2005. The Early Adoption of Green Power by Dutch Households: An Empirical Exploration of Factors Influencing the Early Adoption of Green Electricity for Domestic Purposes. *Energy Policy*, 33, 183–196.

Bandura, A. 1986. *Social Foundations of Thought and Action: A Social Cognitive Theory*. Englewood Cliffs, NJ: Prentice-Hall.

Becker, G. S. and Murphy, K. M. 1988. A Theory of Rational Addiction. *Journal of Political Economy*, 96, 675–700.

Bianchi, M. 2002. Novelty, Preferences, and Fashion: When Goods are Unsettling. *Journal of Economic Behavior and Organization*, 47, 1–18.

Bikhchandani, S., Hirshleifer, D., and Welch, I. 1992. A Theory of Fads, Fashion, Custom, and Cultural Change as Informational Cascades. *Journal of Political Economy*, 100, 992–1026.

Binder, M. and Lades, L. K. 2015. Autonomy-Enhancing Paternalism. *Kyklos*, 68, 3–27.

Bishop, P. 1996. Off Road: Four-wheel Drive and the Sense of Place. *Environment and Planning D: Society and Space*, 14, 257–271.

Bisin, A. and Verdier, T. 2001. The Economics of Cultural Transmission and the Dynamics of Preferences. *Journal of Economic Theory*, 97, 298–319.

Bowles, S. 1998. Endogenous Preferences: The Cultural Consequences of Markets and other Economic Institutions. *Journal of Economic Literature*, 36, 75–111.

Brennan, T. J. 2006. "Green" Preferences as Regulatory Policy Instrument. *Ecological Economics*, 56, 144–154.

Brenner, T. 1999. *Modeling Learning in Economics*. Cheltenham: Edward Elgar.

Brown, P. M. and Cameron, L. D. 2000. What Can Be Done to Reduce Overconsumption? *Ecological Economics*, 32, 27–41.

Buenstorf, G. 2003. Designing Clunkers: Demand-side Innovation and the Early History of the Mountain Bike. In: Metcalfe, S. and Cantner, U. (eds.) *Change, Transformation and Development*. Heidelberg: Physica-Verlag HD.

Buenstorf, G. and Cordes, C. 2008. Can Sustainable Consumption Be Learned? A Model of Cultural Evolution. *Ecological Economics*, 67, 646–657.

Chai, A. 2011. Consumer Specialization and the Romantic Transformation of the British Grand Tour of Europe. *Journal of Bioeconomics*, 13, 181–203.

Chai, A., Bradley, G., Lo, A., and Reser, J. 2015. What Time to Adapt? The Role of Discretionary Time in Sustaining the Climate Change Value-Action Gap. *Ecological Economics*, 116, 95–107.

Chai, A., Earl, P. E., and Potts, J. 2007. Fashion, Growth and Welfare: An Evolutionary Approach. *Advances in Austrian Economics*, 10, 187–207.

Coase, R. H. 1988. *The Firm, the Market, and the Law*. Chicago: University of Chicago Press.

Cordes, C. 2003. *An Evolutionary Analysis of Long-Term Qualitative Change in Human Labor*. Jena, Germany: Friedrich Schiller University Jena.

Cowan, R., Cowan, W., and Swann, P. 1997. A Model of Demand with Interactions among Consumers. *International Journal of Industrial Organization*, 15, 711–732.

DeFleur, M. L. and Ball-Rokeach, S. J. 1989. *Theories of Mass Communication*. New York: Longman.

Dietz, T., Gardner, G. T., Gilligan, J., Stern, P. C., and Vandenbergh, M. P. 2009. Household Actions Can Provide a Behavioral Wedge to Rapidly Reduce US Carbon Emissions. *Proceedings of the National Academy of Sciences of the United States of America*, 106, 18452–18456.

Dopfer, K. and Potts, J. 2007. *The General Theory of Economic Evolution*. New York; London: Routledge.

Dulleck, U. and Kerschbamer, R. 2006. On Doctors, Mechanics, and Computer Specialists: The Economics of Credence Goods. *Journal of Economic Literature*, 44, 5–42.

Earl, P. 1986. *Lifestyle Economics: Consumer Behaviour in a Turbulent World*. Sussex: Wheatsheaf Books.

Earl, P. E. and Potts, J. 2004. The Market for Preferences. *Cambridge Journal of Economics*, 28, 619–633.

Farhar, B. C. 1999. *Willingness to Pay for Electricity from Renewable Resources: A Review of Utility Market Research*. National Renewable Energy Laboratory.

Farrell, J. and Saloner, G. 1985. Standardization, Compatibility, and Innovation. *The Rand Journal of Economics*, 16, 70–83.

Flinn, M. V. 1997. Culture and the Evolution of Social Learning. *Evolution and Human Behavior*, 18, 23–67.

Foxall, G. R. 1989. *Consumer Psychology in Behavioural Perspective*. New York; London: Routledge.

Frank, R. H. 1999. *Luxury Fever: Weighing the Cost of Excess*. Princeton, NJ: Princeton University Press.

Frey, B. S. 1993. Motivation as a Limit to Pricing. *Journal of Economic Psychology*, 14, 635–664.

Galtung, J. 1980. The Basic Needs Approach. In: Lederer, K. (ed.) *Human Needs: A Contribution to the Current Debate*. Cambridge: Oelgeschlager, Gunn & Hain.

Gifford, R., Kormos, C., and Mcintyre, A. 2011. Behavioral Dimensions of Climate Change: Drivers, Responses, Barriers, and Interventions. *Wiley Interdisciplinary Reviews: Climate Change*, 2, 801–827.

Goodson, F. E. 2003. *The Evolution and Function of Cognition*. Mahwah, NJ: Lawrence Erlbaum Associates Publishers.

Granovetter, M. and Soong, R. 1986. Threshold Models of Interpersonal Effects in Consumer Demand. *Journal of Economic Behavior and Organization*, 7, 83–99.

Hayak, F. A. 1937. Economics and Knowledge. *Economica,* 4, 33–54.

Hergenhahn, B. R. and Olson, M. H. 1997. *An Introduction to Theories of Learning.* Upper Saddle River, NJPrentice Hall.

Higham, J. E. S. and Cohen, S. A. 2011. Canary in the Coalmine: Norwegian Attitudes towards Climate Change and Extreme Long-haul Air Travel to Aotearoa/New Zealand. *Tourism Management,* 32, 98–105.

Hull, C. L. 1943. *Principles of Behavior: An Introduction to Behavior Theory.* Oxford: Appleton-Century.

Jackson, T., Jager, W., and Stagl, S. 2004. Beyond Insatiability – Needs Theory, Consumption and Sustainability. In: Reisch, L. A. and Røpke, I. (eds.) *The Ecological Economics of Consumption.* Cheltenham: Edward Elgar Publishing.

Jackson, T. and Marks, N. 1999. Consumption, Sustainable Welfare and Human Needs – With Reference to UK Expenditure Patterns between 1954 and 1994. *Ecological Economics,* 28, 421–441.

Jackson, T. and Papathanasopoulou, E. 2008. Luxury or "Lock-in"? An Exploration of Unsustainable Consumption in the UK: 1968 to 2000. *Ecological Economics,* 68, 80–95.

Janssen, M. A. and Jager, W. 2001. Fashions, Habits and Changing Preferences: Simulation of Psychological Factors Affecting Market Dynamics. *Journal of Economic Psychology,* 22, 745–772.

Jeppsen, L. and Molin, M. 2003. Consumers as Co-Developers: Learning and Innovation Outside the Firm. Working Paper Series. Copenhagen: Copenhagen Department of Industrial Economics & Strategy, Copenhagen Business School.

Kerstetter, D. L., Confer, J. J., and Graefe, A. R. 2001. An Exploration of the Specialization Concept within the Context of Heritage Tourism. *Journal of Travel Research,* 39, 267–274.

Khalil, E. L. 2003. The Context Problematic, Behavioral Economics and the Transactional View: An Introduction to "John Dewey and Economic Theory". *Journal of Economic Methodology,* 10, 107–130.

Kleiman, M. 1992. *Against Excess: Drug Policy for Results.* New York: Basic Books.

Langlois, R. 2001. Knowledge, Consumption and Endogenous Growth. In: Witt, U. (ed.) *Escaping Satiation.* Berlin: Springer.

Langlois, R. and Cosgel, M. 1998. The Organization of Consumption. In: Bianchi, M. (ed.) *The Active Consumer.* London: Routledge.

Lindner, S. B. 1970. *The Harried Leisure Class.* New York: Columbia University Press.

Lintott, J. 1998. Beyond the Economics of More: The Place of Consumption in Ecological Economics. *Ecological Economics,* 25, 239–248.

Loasby, B. J. 1999. *Knowledge, Institutions, and Evolution in Economics.* London: Routledge.

MacCoun, R., Reuter, P., and Schelling, T. 1996. Assessing Alternative Drug Control Regimes. *Journal of Policy Analysis and Management,* 15, 330–352.

Maréchal, K. 2010. Not Irrational but Habitual: The Importance of "Behavioural Lock-in" in Energy Consumption. *Ecological Economics,* 69, 1104–1114.

Marshall, A. 1919. *Industry and Trade.* London: MacMillan.

Martin, S. R. 1997. Specialization and Differences in Setting Preferences among Wildlife Viewers. *Human Dimensions of Wildlife,* 2, 1–18.

Max-Neef, M. A., Elizalde, A., and Hopenhayn, M. 1991. *Human Scale Development: Conception, Application and Further Reflections.* New York: The Apex Press.

McFarland, D. 1987. *The Oxford Companion to Animal Behavior.* Oxford, UK: Oxford University Press.

Menger, C. 1950. *Principles of Economics.* Glencoe, IL: The Free Press.

Moreau, C. P., Lehmann, D. R., and Markman, A. B. 2001. Entrenched Knowledge Structures and Consumer Response to New Products. *Journal of Marketing Research,* 38, 14–29.

Mueller, B. 1991. An Analysis of Information Content in Standardized vs. Specialized Multinational Advertisements. *Journal of International Business Studies,* 22, 23–39.

Myers, K. M. and Davis, M. 2007. Mechanisms of Fear Extinction. *Molecular Psychiatry,* 12, 120–150.

Myers, N. and Kent, J. 2003. *The New Consumers: The Influence of Affluence on the Environment.* London; Washington, DC: Island Press.

Nelson, R. R. and Consoli, D. 2010. An Evolutionary Theory of Household Consumption Behavior. *Journal of Evolutionary Economics,* 20, 665–687.

Norton, B., Costanza, R., and Bishop, R. C. 1998. The Evolution of Preferences Why "Sovereign" Preferences May Not Lead to Sustainable Policies and What to Do about It. *Ecological Economics,* 24, 193–211.

O'Hara, S. U. and Stagl, S. 2002. Endogenous Preferences and Sustainable Development. *Journal of Socio-Economics,* 31, 511–527.

OECD. 2008. *Promoting Sustainable Consumption: Good Practices in OECD Countries.* Paris: OECD.

Ölander, F. and Kahneman, D. 1995. Understanding of Consumer Behaviour as a Prerequisite for Environmental Protection. *Journal of Consumer Policy,* 18, 345–385.

Pedersen, L. H. 2000. The Dynamics of Green Consumption: A Matter of Visibility? *Journal of Environmental Policy & Planning*, 2, 193–210.

Posner, M. I. and Petersen, S. E. 1990. The Attention System of the Human Brain: 20 Years After. *Annual Review of Neuroscience*, 35, 73–89.

Robson, A. J. 2001. The Biological Basis of Economic Behavior. *Journal of Economic Literature*, 39, 11–33.

Rogers, E. M. 1962. *Diffusion of New Innovations*. New York: The Free Press.

Rolls, E. T. 2005. *Emotion Explained*. Oxford, UK: Oxford University Press.

Røpke, I. 1999. The Dynamics of Willingness to Consume. *Ecological Economics*, 28, 399–420.

  2009. Theories of Practice – New Inspiration for Ecological Economic Studies on Consumption. *Ecological Economics*, 68, 2490–2497.

Sanne, C. 2002. Willing Consumers – or Locked-in? Policies for a Sustainable Consumption. *Ecological Economics*, 42, 273–287.

Sartorius, C. 2003. *An Evolutionary Approach to Social Welfare*. New York: Routledge.

Saviotti, P. 2002. Variety, Growth and Demand. In: McMeekin, A., Green, K., Tomlinson, M., and Walsh, V. (eds.) *Innovation by Demand*. Manchester, UK: Manchester University Press.

Schor, J. B. 1991. *The Overworked American: The Unexpected Decline of Leisure*. New York: Basic Books.

Scitovsky, T. 1976. *The Joyless Economy: An Inquiry into Human Satisfaction and Consumer Dissatisfaction*. New York: Oxford University Press.

Sexton, S. E. and Sexton, A. L. 2014. Conspicuous Conservation: The Prius Halo and Willingness to Pay for Environmental Bona Fides. *Journal of Environmental Economics and Management*, 67, 303–317.

Shackle, G. L. S. 1972. *Epistemics and Economics*. Cambridge, UK: Cambridge University Press.

Stigler, G. J. and Becker, G. S. 1977. De Gustibus Non Est Disputandum. *The American Economic Review*, 67, 76–90.

Thaler, R. H. and Sunstein, C. R. 2008. *Nudge: Improving Decisions about Health, Wealth and Happiness*. New Haven, CT: Yale University Press.

van den Bergh, J. C. J. M. 2008. Environmental Regulation of Households: An Empirical Review of Economic and Psychological Factors. *Ecological Economics*, 66, 559–574.

van den Ende, J. and Dolfsma, W. 2005. Technology-push, Demand-pull and the Shaping of Technological Paradigms – Patterns in the Development of Computing Technology. *Journal of Evolutionary Economics*, 15, 83–99.

von Hippel, E. 2005. *Democratizing Innovation*. London: MIT Press.

Wagner, J. 2006. On the Economics of Sustainability. *Ecological Economics, 57*, 659–664.

Windrum, P. 2005. Heterogeneous Preferences and New Innovation Cycles in Mature Industries: The Amateur Camera Industry 1955–1974. *Industrial and Corporate Change*, 14, 1043–1074.

Witt, U. 2001. Learning to Consume – A Theory of Wants and the Growth of Demand. *Journal of Evolutionary Economics*, 11, 23–36.

  2016. The Evolution of Consumption and Its Welfare Effects. *Journal of Evolutionary Economics*, 27(2), 1–21.

Index

393